English Literature

in the

Age of Disguise

PUBLISHED UNDER THE AUSPICES OF THE
WILLIAM ANDREWS CLARK MEMORIAL LIBRARY
UNIVERSITY OF CALIFORNIA, LOS ANGELES

English Literature
in the
Age of Disguise

Edited by
MAXIMILLIAN E. NOVAK

Clark Library Professor, 1973—1974

1977
UNIVERSITY OF CALIFORNIA PRESS
BERKELEY • LOS ANGELES • LONDON

University of California Press
Berkeley and Los Angeles, California

University of California Press, Ltd.
London, England

CONTENTS

INTRODUCTION

Maximillian E. Novak

Professor of English, University of California, Los Angeles

> Thus while the crafty and designing part of mankind, consulting only their own separate advantage, endeavour to maintain one constant imposition on others, the whole world becomes a vast masquerade, where the greatest part appear disguised under false vizors and habits; a very few only showing their own faces, who become, by so doing, the astonishment and ridicule of all the rest.
>
> Henry Fielding, "An Essay on the Knowledge of the Characters of Men"[1]

Fielding's complaint that the world was "a vast masquerade" was hardly unusual for him or for any writer in England from the Restoration up to his time. In the preface to *The Miscellanies,* he maintained that if he might have some doubts about the truth of

---

[1] *The Complete Works of Henry Fielding,* ed. William Henley (New York: Barnes and Noble, 1967), XIV, 283.

1

the commonplace notion that Newgate prison was "no other than Human Nature with its Mask off," he was much more willing to entertain the idea that "the splendid Palaces of the Great are often no other than Newgate with the Mask on."² The same kind of complaint came from Daniel Defoe earlier in the eighteenth century. "This Sir," he wrote, "is an Age of Plot and Deceit, of Contradiction and Paradox. . . . It is very hard under all these Masks, to see the true Countenance of any Man."³

When metaphors of disguise and mask are so pervasive in a period, they tend to condition the terms by which people think, and the variations on the theme were endless. Lord Rochester's Alexander Bendo proclaims that the naked face concealed more than a mask.⁴ William Wycherley, in his dedication to *The Plain Dealer*, praised London's most infamous procuress, Mother Bennet, for her honesty, remarking that "by that mask of modesty which women wear promiscuously in public, they are all alike, and you can no more know a kept wench from a woman of honor by her looks than by her dress."⁵ And Congreve's Maskwell rejoices in the power that accompanies a commitment to deception:

Well for Wisdom and Honesty, give me Cunning and Hyprocrisie; oh, 'tis such a Pleasure to angle for fair fac'd Fools! Then that hungry Gudgeon Credulity, will bite at any thing — Why, let me see, I have the same Face, the same Words and Accents, when I speak what I do think; and when I speak what I do not think — the very same — and dear Dissimulation is the only Art, not to be known from nature.⁶

Maskwell may be a villain, but almost all of the relationships between characters in *The Double Dealer* are based on disguise and lies. One need not be a Jeremy Collier to view this as a general comment on contemporary social life. The notion of the necessity of disguise is Tattle's lesson to Prue in Congreve's *Love for Love*, a play in which the hero, Valentine, pretends to be mad and, in

²(London: A. Millar, 1743), p. xx.
³*A Letter to Mr. Bisset* (London: J. Baker, 1709), p. 10.
⁴John Wilmot, Earl of Rochester, *Alexander Bendo's Advertisement*, in *Collected Works*, ed. John Hayward (London(Nonesuch Press, 1926), pp. 155-160.
⁵Leo Hughes, ed. (Lindoln: University of Nebraska Press, 1967), p. 5.
⁶*Comedies*, ed. Bonamy Dobrée (London: Oxford University Press, 1925), 149-150 (II, viii).

the disguise of Truth, satirizes contemporary society. When Valentine attempts to throw off his disguise in order to confess his love to Angelica, that heroine, playing our her own role, refuses to recognize his sanity: "Never let us know one another better; for the Pleasure of a Masquerade is done, when we come to shew our Faces."[7]

Congreve, like so many of his contemporaries, regarded disguise and role playing as parts of the mixed benefits of civilized life. His wits play their parts better than the villains and win both the ladies and their fortunes. His ladies were able to dissimulate while remaining virginal, an idea that many moralists of the eighteenth century thought impossible. The masculine writers, who dominated the literary scene, often depicted the ways in which the excitement of a ball might promote seduction and the use of disguises ensure it. Defoe pictures a young girl stealing out of her parents' house to attend the masquerade:

Now imagine the poor giddy Creature in the midst of an Assembly all dissolved in Luxury; her Spirits put into a Ferment by Dancing and Champagne; her Ears entertained with loose and wanton Discourse; her Mind so captivated and soften'd by the Gaiety of every Thing about her, that she is fit to receive any Impressions; and, lest Shame should be a Restraint to the Business of the Place, (as a reverend Prelate lately well observ'd,) there is an Expedient found to remove that too, by putting on Masques. I say, when all this is considered, where is the Wonder that an unexperienced young Thing should suffer her Thoughts to go astray, especially when she sees such Numbers to keep her in Countenance.[8]

Quoting the maxim, "Fresh Masquerades furnish fresh Mistresses," Defoe then provides a type of "harlot's progress." If, by chance, this appears like an extreme moral position, the same concept appears in Fielding's *Amelia,* where the heroine is saved from seduction at a masquerade only by the intervention of Mrs. Bennett, who had herself been the victim of an earlier masquerade.[9] Tom Jones is carried off by Lady Bellaston after a meeting at a masquerade, and Samuel Richardson has Pamela's Mr.

[7]*Comedies,* p. 311 (IV, xx).
[8]*A Collection of Miscellany Letters Selected out of Mist's Weekly Journal* (London: T. Warner, 1727), III, 174.
[9]*Complete Works,* VII, 9-64 (Bk. 7).

B—— seduced by a Countess at a similar event: "My Spaniard was too amiable, and met with a lady who was no nun, but in habit. Everyone was taken with him in that habit, so suited to the natural dignity of his person. — O these wicked, wicked masquerades."[10]

Although women continue to assume disguises in eighteenth-century fiction, and some of the Restoration's play with the concept of disguise remains current, the disguises of a Moll Flanders or a Roxana have to be read against a negative current of thought where women were concerned. In part, the improved status of women during the eighteenth century was purchased at the price of their assuming a higher moral tone than the men. Yet disguises might be dangerous for men as well as women. In "An Essay on Masquerade," published in the London Magazine in 1774 and almost certainly written by James Boswell, some attempt was made to suggest what the dangers of disguise might be. When a disguise was assumed, "those whom modesty restrained, being by means of it set loose from that check of sensation, which in some degree supplies the place of principle," felt a sudden freedom to follow their passions.[11] Such an idea lay behind the severe attitude of Sir Bertram toward the performance of Lovers' Vows in Jane Austen's Mansfield Park. If a masquerade could unleash hidden passions, so might even the most innocent play. To step out of one's own personality into the role of another character was to endanger not only innocence but the moral integrity of the self.

But if disguises might be dangerous for men as well as women, that danger might be accompanied by considerable fun, and none knew this so well as the writers of the first half of the eighteenth century. Even the great moralist of the period, Dr. Johnson, gave his approval to the freedom permitted to authors using various disguises: "'A mask,' says Castiglione, 'confers a right of acting and speaking with less restraint, even when the wearer happens to be known.' He that is discovered without his own consent, may claim some indulgence, and cannot be rigorously called to justify those sallies or frolicks which is disguise must

[10]The Novels of Samuel Richardson, ed. Ethel McKenna (London: Chapman and Hall, 1902), IV, 83 (Letter 17).
[11]London Magazine, 43 (1774), 80-83.

prove him desirous to conceal."[12] The disguise liberated the writer in a number of ways. He could take more risks. He could even, if he were a journalist like Defoe, write on a single subject from a variety of viewpoints.

The practice of using masks had become so common that in 1690 Adrien Baillet devoted a lengthy treatise to the subject under the title, *Auteurs déguisez sous des noms étrangées*. It was welcomed by the *Journal des scavans* on the grounds of its thoroughness and the crying need for such a work.[13] Of course the classification of motives underlying the use of pseudonyms may seem simple enough to us today; they range from simple prudence to the devilish device of destroying reputations by writing blasphemous works under the names of pious contemporaries. Probably the most interesting classification in Baillet's treatise, at least for us, is one of the briefest entries and the last on the list— "gayeté."[14] By this Baillet means a play of mind by the author. It stands out among the many prudential motives and suggests some of the sense of freedom mentioned by Dr. Johnson.

Writing about the use of masks in this age of disguise achieved a brief popularity during the 1950s, but the concept was used so loosely as to involve a confusion with the notion of the persona and, ultimately, with the personality of the author as it appears in his work. Through a brilliant essay analyzing this confusion, Irvin Ehrenpreis turned the interests of students of the eighteenth century away from the masks of writers to the manifestation of the personalities of the writers in the works.[15] Recently, however, Donald Siebert has rightly suggested the need for another look at the authorial play underlying Swift's use of masks.[16] For at a masquerade as in a literary work, the selection of the outward covering has important significance for any interpretation of the underlying reality. That many writers had recourse to Baillet's

[12] *The Rambler,* ed. W. J. Bate and Albrecht Strauss (New Haven: Yale University Press, 1969), V, 317.

[13] 4 December 1690, 365-368. Baillet's study was reprinted in 1722 in volume sixteen of the *Jugemens des savans.*

[14] (Paris: Dezallier, 1690), p. 218.

[15] "Personae," *Restoration and Eighteenth-Century Literature,* ed. Carroll Camden (Chicago: University of Chicago Press, 1963), pp. 25-37.

[16] "Masks and Masquerades: the Animus of Swift's Satire," *The South Atlantic Quarterly,* 74 (1975), 435-445.

treatise for choosing a given mask is questionable. That work was intended to describe a contemporary phenomenon, not to act as a handbook for authors. But to ignore the concept of disguise in the writings of the Restoration and eighteenth century is to disregard one of the distinguishing aspects of the age.

Disguise entered into the writings of the age not only through the disguises of the writer and as a theme but also as the very texture of literary style itself. Recently Lionel Gossman has argued that irony itself is a form of disguise that identifies the age:

> The predominantly ironical mode of eighteenth-century writing is in itself significant. Irony is preeminently an instrument of inclusion and exclusion, and its playful exterior disguises a certain repressiveness. As the Enlightened critic unmasks the religious enthusiast, the historical hero, the devoted spouse, the metaphysician, as he reveals what is 'behind the back' of the other's noble discouse, he is careful not to expose his own back. It often happens that irony in eighteenth-century French literature does not point to a hidden sense which is the opposite of the manifest one — the traditional meaning of irony. It is infinitely receding, turning the reader back from every formulation of a position, so that the laws by which all others are judged — are never enunciated. It both permits and requires the values through which the initiated come together and recognize each other to remain unspoken.[17]

What Gossman has to say about class in this connection may be questionable, but the function of irony as disguise was as true for English literature as for French. Anthony Collins, following Shaftesbury, maintained that irony was the inevitable product of repression—that through irony the unspeakable might be spoken.[18] In the literature, irony in its various rhetorical forms became the dominant mode, and the surface of the literary work invariably concealed a secret message.

The irony and wit that flourished in the Restoration and in the first two decades of the eighteenth century was gradually to give way to an admiration for what one critic has recently called the

---

[17]*Eighteenth-Century Studies,* 7 (1973/1974), 139.

[18]*A Discourse concerning Ridicule and Irony in Writing* (London: Brotherton, 1729), pp. 24-27. See also Shaftesbury's *Characteristics,* ed. John Robertson (Indianapolis: Bobbs-Merrill, 1964), I, 51.

"sincere ideal."[19] But Fielding remained very much a master of ironic disguise, and, as Professor Traugott demonstrates in the penultimate essay of this volume, Samuel Richardson, for all his moral posturing, revealed in *Clarissa* exactly the kind of pleasure in a play with disguise that would be expected of a writer born in 1689. This essay, like the others in this volume, concerns itself with aspects of concealment and openness in English literature during what I have called, "The Age of Disguise."

The first essay, on Defoe's political thought by Professor Schonhorn, treats a writer who once complained of the Deist, John Toland, that he had hidden under so many names that it might be said that he had "liv'd his Life in a Mask."[20] This was an odd remark coming from a writer who, if he signed his works at all, would indicate that it was "by the Author of *The True Born Englishman*," his most famous political poem, or "By the Author of the *Review*," his notorious journal. He was more likely, however, to write under the guise of a Turk, Quaker, Pope or Devil, though occasionally he would choose more honorable titles, like a Scotch Officer, Countess, or Clergyman.

Professor Schonhorn works his way through Defoe's many pamphlets, their many different masks and angles of vision on politics, to suggest that *Robinson Crusoe* and some of Defoe's other fictions reflect an image of government through a single leader who would be both ruler over a nation's political and military activities. This represents a new and startling reading of Defoe's politics. As Professor Schonhorn indicates, Defoe has often been read off as an abject follower of Locke. But the great pamphleteer of the Age of Queen Anne appears in this essay as even more radical than his contemporaries believed him — radical enough to doubt the efficacy of a parliamentary system which worked through bribery and corruption, and to suggest that, in an ideal world, the best government would be a warrior monarch selected implicitly or by actual election, by the people, and by implication, God. Professor Schonhorn shows how such a concept under-

---

[19]See Leon Guilhamet, *The Sincere Ideal* (Montreal: McGill-Queens University Press, 1974).

[20]*An Argument Proving that the Design of Employing and Enobling Foreigners Is a Treasonable Conspiracy* (London: Booksellers of London, 1717), p. 51.

lies much of the ambiguity of Defoe's numerous political writings and how he worked through these possibilities in his imaginative fiction through a variety of narrators—as "poor Robinson Crusoe" telling us the story of his island or as Captain Charles Johnson, historian of the lives of contemporary pirates, mingling fictions with facts to make his points. Professor Schonhorn suggests that if success is a sign of worth, the practical, exploitive government of Captain Tew may be Defoe's pragmatic mode for government, but we may wonder if there were not enough of the idealist in Defoe to wish that the Communist colony of Libertalia could survive.

Like the other essays in this volume, Professor Schonhorn's grew out of a series of seminars presented at the William Clark Memorial library, during my term as Clark Professor in 1973-74, titled "New Perspectives on English Literature in the Restoration and Eighteenth Century." Where the discussions arising after the presentation of a paper were enlightening, I will mention them briefly. During the question period, Professor Roper asked whether the theories advanced by Defoe were not merely a kind of seventeenth-century republicanism incorporating the *dux bellorum*. Professor Schonhorn agreed that there was some resemblance but pointed out the absence of a senate in Defoe's schemes and his general dislike of the parliament, which he regarded as an institution operating in its own interest rather than those of the nation. The discussion then turned to the question of whether this was not the fantasy of the Left as, what Professor Kramnick has called "the politics of nostalgia," was a fantasy of the Right. Professor Schonhorn agreed that the idea of an incorruptible and efficient leader was probably easier to indluge in after 1688, when the Revolution had finally established the power of Parliament.

The "Nymphs of the City" of Professor Rawson's title may be seen as metaphoric representations of the city itself. Like our cities, the city of Swift's poetry is both the place where garbage accumulates and where the *surface* of civilized life is at its finest. For Swift, nowhere was the presence of the excrescence that accompanies civilization so obscured as in the presence of a beautiful woman. But Swift was intent on revealing the reality that was disguised by cosmetics, which, when used by an ancient whore in an attempt to disguise rotting teeth and a fallen nose, only made her appear more terrifying. And for the most devoted admirer of Chloe to see her through a cranny in the wall of a "house of Ease" would be enough to disillusion him forever. Without allying himself with those critics who would see Swift advocating some golden mean, Professor Rawson suggests, through quoting Swift extensively, that civilization must mask its smells and indecencies as the puppet master conceals the wires and wooden handles that move his figures.

The images of "Nymphs of the City" also function for Professor Rawson as ways of coming to terms with the city as a subject for poetry—the city of ugly realities and occasional triumphs of beauty. Rawson demonstrates that "in the face of life's teeming disorders, the order of art seemed to Swift a falsifying thing." Hence Swift's use of a version of Hudibrastic verse and mock-epic to disguise "the rowdy indecorum of fact." And hence Professor Rawson's discussion of the Stella poems at the end of his essay, for Swift did not try to turn Stella into some primitive Roman matron. She is part of the civilization of life during the eighteenth century that must, finally, be associated with the city. Swift was hardly a poet of country life, country gardens, or the country estate. If Dublin was not the city in which he would have wanted to pass most of his time, it was, nevertheless, very much of a city, and the image of Swift as the patriot and hero of the Irish people is, ironically enough, one of the city and its mobs.

But Professor Rawson's essay is not so much about the city as a theme as about the particular quality of Swift's urban verse. And in order to establish the exact nature of that poetry, he uses T. S. Eliot and Baudelaire as modes of comparison. The results are illuminating. Swift emerges as a poet who was often at his most energetic, exuberant, and yet controlled in passages portraying the ugliness of city life. For all Eliot's vividness in depicting the squalor of the modern city, it is Eliot, not Swift, who will risk personal passages; and for all the accusations against Swift's personal involvement in scatology, it is Baudelaire, more than Swift, who is "given to indulgences of revulsion." Swift's insistence on seeing truly, on refusing to romanticize or indulge himself, may, Professor Rawson argues, support rather than undercut the powerful feeling in his poetry.

An important point was raised during a lengthy discussion period that followed Professor Rawson's lecture—a discussion which focussed entirely on the case to be made for Swift as an important English poet. One member of the audience, agreeing with Professor Rawson's remarks on Baudelaire's self-indulgence in depicting scenes of rotting flesh and pervasive decay, remarked that Baudelaire was able to liberate from such scenes a poetic power that, in spite of all the intelligence, craft and control that Swift had at his command, somehow surpassed anything in the poetry of the Dean of St. Patrick. Professor Rawson was unwilling to concede the point entirely. The ensuing discussion, though it did not resolve the issue, was extremely suggestive.

Professor Cohen's essay concerns the nature of meaning in Pope's poetry and the poetic concept that lay behind that meaning. In a complex series of arguments, Professor Cohen suggests that out of his own anxiety over change, Pope perfects a poetry that works through a pattern of disguises. The real energy of the poem, the force that sustains it, is disguised by the art of the poet, who propounds a theory of established limitations within the flux of life as a theory of art and life:

> He gains all points, who pleasingly confounds
> Surprises, varies and conceals the Bounds.

The key to his skill is to be found in a "readjustment of the relation between mimesis and energy," Professor Cohen argues. Showing how Pope draws analogies from the reflection of a sky or a landscape in a pond or stream, he demonstrates Pope's idea of poetry as a transformation of experience into the milder and more graceful form of art.

Just as Yeats has his poet in "Adam's Curse" remark in conversing about poetry,

> A line will take us hours maybe;
> Yet if it does not seem a moment's thought,
> Our stitching and unstitching has been naught,

so Pope is shown as aiming at "an ease for the reader that disguises the effort of the writer." And as the effort of the poet is disguised, so the poem itself reveals itself reluctantly. Professor Cohen quotes Pope's statement:

> Let not each beauty ev'ry where be spy'd
> Where half the skill is decently to hide.

Writing with an awareness that he was living in an age in which the sublime, as a poetic affect, had been practically lost, Pope, nevertheless, could use it triumphantly in sections of the *Essay on Criticism* and the end of the *Dunciad*. But for the most part, his art and much of the art of his time, was achieved through a process of concealment and sudden appearances of the living nature that informed each work.

"I found it necessary to say only that from the beginning mankind experienced states of boredom but that no one had ever approached the matter front and center as a subject in its own right." So muses Charles Citrine in Saul Bellow's *Humboldt's Gift,* as he contemplates his notes for his major study of this subject. He prefaces this with the remark that he "didn't want to get mixed up with theological questions about *accidia* and *tedium vitae*,"[21] but perhaps Professor Greene's essay would solve many of his problems, if, for a moment, it might be permissible to transfer Citrine from his fictional world to a real character and reader of this volume. At least it would go far toward explaining what the eighteenth century thought of accidie or boredom.

Professor Greene's essay works in a different direction from most of the others in this collection. When we come to Thomson, we encounter the first writer actually born in the eighteenth century. As Professor Leon Guilhamet has suggested recently, Thomson was influenced by Aaron Hill and his group to proclaim that the aim of his popular poem, *The Seasons,* was directness and sincerity.[22] Although it is far from being a poem about the poet himself, Thomson is in *The Seasons,* feeling, seeing and experiencing. Yet as Professor Ralph Cohen demonstrated a number of years ago, *The Seasons* is filled with disguised meanings and must be read as the kind of poem to be expected of a contemporary of

[21](New York: Viking, 1975), p. 199.
[22]*The Sincere Ideal,* pp. 77-101.

Pope, full of word play and wit.[23] But *The Caste of Indolence,*
generally regarded as next to *The Seasons* in excellence among
Thomson's long poems, has always been treated as either a document in the history of ideas—a Whig Panegyric to progress—or
as a Spenserian imitation. Professor Greene reads the poem
against the context of eighteenth-century poetry dealing with psychological depression, boredom, the spleen.

In addition to providing us with a new reading against a previously misunderstood intellectual background, Professor Greene
suggests that *The Castle of Indolence* is an intensely personal
document, the product of a poet whose feelings of listlessness and
anomie were no more comic than those of Samuel Johnson later
in the century. Thomson's praise of work is not a trivial hymn to
progress and industry as the proper direction of the Protestant
work ethic. Rather it is a statement of hope that somehow action
and work can rescue him, and men like him, from hypochondria,
despair, melancholy, sloth, and boredom. Thomson, of course,
in spite of the presence of the narrator in the poem, does not
write what we would think of as a fully confessional poem, but
after reading Professor Greene's essay, few will doubt the poet's
deep, personal involvement in *The Castle of Indolence.*

Like James Thomson, Samuel Richardson was under the influence of that disciple of sincerity, Aaron Hill, and Richardson the
public man, the prosperous printer and admired novelist—what
Professor Traugott calls the "banal Richardson"—would have
ascribed to Hill's belief in a literature of sincerity. And it is the
sincere and honest printer that Richardson's latest and most thorough biographers, Professors Eaves and Kimpel, portray. Professor Traugott attempts in his essay to give us a Richardson that his
biographers confessed eluded them—the Richardson who wrote
Clarissa, one of the world's greatest novels. Proceeding from the
teasing nature of Richardson's correspondence with Lady Bradshaigh and the provocative quality of his correspondence with his
other lady friends, Professor Traugott attempts to show a Richardson capable of staging a conflict between "moral sincerity"
and what he calls Richardson's "comic sense."

[23] *The Art of Discrimination* (Berkeley and Los Angeles: University of California Press, 1964), pp. 315-380; and Cohen, *The Unfolding of the Seasons* (London: Routledge, 1970), pp. 36-39.

The result is a reading of Richardson as "anachronistic" in the sense that he retains an admiration for the disguise of the libertine wit comedy of the Restoration, using Lovelace's plots and comic masks to test is own interior drama. Professor Traugott reminds us that Lovelace's talent for comedy, for playing a part, is also Richardson's. And the very fact that Clarissa too plays her own tragic role inspires him to become the "master of acting, stage managing and disguise." The conflict in *Clarissa* is not merely between two titanic game players; it is a struggle between the world of serious consequences associated with tragedy and that arena of farce and comedy in which no one actually gets hurt for all the blows struck and all the pratfalls. In a wonderful image, Professor Traugott suggests how thoroughly Lovelace misreads the script and ends up playing to an empty house.

The final contribution to this volume is by Professor Maynard Mack and consists of an essay on Alexander Pope's library and a list of the books now extant that Pope owned, along with any annotations he may have made in them, and their location. The value of the checklist as a research tool for the study of Pope needs little elaboration, but the essay on the books that Pope owned is, to a large extent, an exploration of the poet himself. Weak in health from his early childhood, Pope used books as a means of carrying his mind beyond the confines of his study or his grotto "into a world of imagination always to be longed for, never possessed." Professor Mack suggests that, alone with his books, Pope had something of the quality of the very pedants he satirized so powerfully in his *Dunciad* and that his understanding of their concentration on the minutiae of learning came from firsthand experience.

If few writers were so adept at stratagems and disguises in his life and, as Professor Cohen has suggested, in his art, the Pope we see writing marginalia to himself was the poet with his mask off. Professor Mack notes that few of Pope's books are so thoroughly annotated as his copy of Montaigne, the master of self-analysis. At the end of that book, Pope writes, "This Author says nothing but what everyone feels at the Heart. Whoever deny it, are not more wise than Montaigne, but less honest." As Professor Mack demonstrates, Pope identified with Montaigne's confessions of his inner doubts and fears. At one point Montaigne gives an account of his education and his fear that he might, through sloth, prove useless. Next to that passage Pope wrote, *"Alter ego."* It seems appropriate to end with this intimate glimpse into Pope, for the direction of history was toward sincerity and toward the notion of art as personal expression. Not until the twentieth century were the ironies and indirection underlying the surfaces of the literature of the Age of Disguise to be fully appreciated.

I

DEFOE: THE LITERATURE OF POLITICS AND THE POLITICS OF SOME FICTIONS

Manuel Schonhorn

*Professor of English, Southern Illinois University**

> And when will they learn to know,
> that the Absolute Government of a
> Vertuous Prince, who makes the
> Good of his People his Ultimate
> End, and esteems their Prosperity
> his Glory, is the Best, and most
> Godlike, Government in the World.
> Defoe, *And What if the Pre-
> tender should come?* 1713, p. 20.

I

Jure Divino, Defoe's most ambitious attack on the absolutist phi-
losophies of his day and the *locus classicus* for his political
thought, would appear to be the best text with which to begin a
commentary on that political thought. For the moment, though,
I would like to turn back to Defoe's first piece of revolutionary
propaganda, published in 1689, because it reveals the initial political naiveté of a fervent Williamite and points to his later reading and accounting of scriptural and English history from which
evolved his mature political theories.[1]

15

Defoe's *Reflections Upon the Late Great Revolution, Written
by a Lay Hand in the Country,* is an inconsistent, unselective,
and all-embracing presentation of contemporary ideologies circu-
lating in 1689. His purpose is to refute two false arguments:
(1) that monarchy is *jure divino,* that is, absolute and arbitrary;
and (2) "that if the King command any thing contrary to our
laws, we are yet in conscience obliged to obey and yield obedience
active and passive" (pp. 5-6). There is no single element of Defoe's tract which cannot be traced back to one or other of his predecessors debating the validity of the Revolution or the right of
rebellion against a tyrant. His indebtednesses are obvious, and
also the sense that his ideas had not yet run clear on his subject.
He begins his defense of rebellion with arguments from Scripture,
working well within the tradition which still provided a system of
analysis charged with political meaning for his readers; for example, the active disobedience of the Israelites against Pharaoh, the
necessity of the people's consent to Saul's assumption of the monarchy, the history of regicide, and priestly rejection of passive
obedience. But in the very next breath, he can turn around and
insist that no general rule can be derived from biblical injunc-
tions, that "tis from the Statute-Book, not the Bible, that we must
judge of the Power our Kings are invested withal, and also of our
own Obligations, and the Measures of our Subjection" (p. 35).[2]
In fact, in his blunt dismissal of Christian precepts, Defoe argues
that the altered circumstance of Christians in worldly respects
negates the tenets of primitive times, that obedience to Christ's
commands, rather than sustaining and strengthening the Christian religion, would let in confusion and disorder; "so that a lit-
teral Performance of those Duties, would, in our present Circumstances, destroy one of the great Designs of Christianity . . ." (p.
61). Noticeably absent from the tract is any mention of an eternal
Law of Nature or the equally intoned Right Reason, perhaps
because Defoe was aware that neither could be reconciled with
the geographical and meteorological argument for the variations
in societies that we have come to identify with Sir William
Temple, which he cursorily echoes in his introductory sentences.
There Defoe suggests that proper governments are set up by
recognizing those varied circumstances of time and place which
determine the most beneficial and agreeable polities. The truth

is, Defoe says, no universal rule can be given; "...the Magistrate's Power, and the Measures of the Subject's subjection, are only to be judged of by the particular Laws and Constitutions of that Kingdom" (p. 34), and what is lawful in one place may not be in another.[3]

Defoe can be loose with the theory of compact between the prince and his people, calling it the "cornerstone of Monarchy itself" (p. 28), and at the same time prove that the Jews had little scruples, for they unhesitantly obeyed those kings who had possession of the throne, those who proved the strongest (pp. 20, 27). Only two years later, it should be noted, he was to attack the same *de facto* arguments for submission to the reigning authority made by William Sherlock, Dean of St. Paul's, and for the next twenty years he was never to pass up any occasion when he could strike at the *de facto* apologists in the Anglican hierarchy.[4]

Defoe's tract is a composite of prevailing beliefs, perhaps selected for the random consideration of the layman in the country, for whom he is ostensibly writing. The English reader paid his money and took his pick. One finds distributed throughout such themes as: *vox populi, vox dei, salus populi suprema lex,* and the patriarchal theory of social origins. Defoe also asserted that paternal power is antecedent to all civil laws; repeated the historical argument from the much-cited *Mirror of Justices* that the Saxon kings were initially captains, the military heads of neighboring domains established as rulers by the compact of the tribal princes; and affirmed his faith in mixed monarchy with the customary language. The constitution of England shuns the extremes possible in governments. "For here the Populace have liberty without a Democratical Confusion and Fury; the Nobility have all the Priviledges to which Aristocracy it self could intitle them, without the necessity of running into Factions and Cabals for it; and the King's Power so equally ballanced between the Two other, that his Power can hardly ever degenerate into Tyranny..." (p. 36).

What I would like to underscore is Defoe's uncomfortable relationship to what can still be called orthodox Whiggish doctrines of the day, which can be noted in his brief phrases about, or total neglect of the concepts crucial to the principles of the Revolution and proclaimed steadily thereafter. (I use Whiggish with some conscious hesitation, fully aware, as Professor Rosenheim has warned us, that "neither party of the day can be readily distinguished by a characteristic philosophy. Writers for both sides drew freely upon these political thinkers whose works served, in whole or part, to justify the Revolution and its aftermath.")[5] Defoe's attitudes toward the ancient constitution and fundamental law, the Norman Conquest, and the sovereignty of Parliament and its immemorial right, suggest a yet unarticulated rejection of the major premises and arguments which were the standard ingredients of Revolution rhetoric, and which help us to respond to his later scripturalist and royalist positions.

There is absolutely no reference here to "that most important and elusive of seventeenth-century concepts, the fundamental law," that peculiar outgrowth of common law which attempted to prove that the liberties of the people were antecedent to and greater than the rights of the king because "they partook of the nature of immemorial sacred custom."[6] What the constitutionalists and parliamentarians were forced into, Professor Pocock has shown us, was "a kind of historical obscurantism — compelled to attribute their liberties to more and more remote and mythical periods in the effort to prove them independent of the will of the king" (p. 17). These fundamental laws, one Revolutionary document explained, are "written in the very heart of the Republick, ...held forth with more Evidence, and are far firmlier," just because they are not of pen and paper.[7] Defoe does not turn at all to this omnipresent theme of fundamental law, common custom, or common law, this appeal to the past and the antiquity of the English constitution. And except for its stress in the narrowly argued and ahistorically restrictive *Original Power of the Collective Body of the People of England,* his contribution to the paper war of 1701 against an arrogant Tory Commons, I have found only two isolated references to the fundamental constitution in nearly all of Defoe's writings that I have examined prior to 1715.[8] One is not surprised to find John Tutchin, publisher of the most important political organ of the Whigs, supporting a Parliament "antecedent to all Law, *ab mundi Origine...*," that is, founded in immemorial custom.[9] But even Charles Leslie, the most brilliant of the High Church pamphleteers, turns to the tenets of fundamental law and the immutable customs of the realm to defend the English constitution.[10]

This neglect attends Defoe's early refusal to accept the supremacy of Parliament. "And since the Legislative Power is in all Nations esteemed the Supreme, and ours being so divided, it seems to be a little improper to call any One of the Three the Supreme Power."[11] The principle of legislative sovereignty had been clearly grasped by Bacon, and its implications were made explicit by writers throughout the century. For Tutchin, Parliament is the highest power in the Kingdom, and he quotes with zest the judgment of William Cecil, Lord Burleigh, that he knew not what an Act of Parliament might not do, "For their Power is Prescrib'd by no Law, because it is Antecedent to all Law. . . ."[12]

Years before William's reign ended, years before the Kentish Petition controversy again showed inescapably the dangerous obstructionism of a House of Commons, Defoe argued for the magnipotence, not the omnipotence, of Parliament. To him they were those "Wonderful and Unintelligible Assemblies."[13] Parliament's subservience to the will of the people, embodied in a loving and disinterested monarch, was his lifelong conviction. The implications of legislative sovereignty were, it would appear, unacceptable to Defoe. Given the terms of such a view, the legislature could easily alter the incidence of power, institute oligarchy, democracy, or even some kind of acceptable despotism, as long as the original ends for which civil government was created was not subverted.

Professors Hill, Pocock, and Skinner have detailed for us the importance of the Norman Conquest and the status of the Conqueror in the ideological battles of the seventeenth century and the post-Revolutionary period.[14] For obvious reasons, constitutionalists, republicans, and Whigs denied that any conquest had taken place; for once to assert that William *had* ruled as a conqueror was to accept the sovereignty of the monarch and his absolute power in the making and unmaking of law, and to deny the immemorial role of Parliament in the development of English liberty and the safeguarding of English institutions. "To admit a conquest was to admit an indelible stain of sovereignty upon the English constitution," and was to accept the power of the sword as the foundation of all titles of government.[15]

Here, in the *Reflections,* Defoe began indecisively, calling William a conqueror but adding that he later confirmed ". . . the Ancient Rights and Priviledges of the People, [and was] receiv'd

as their Legal, not their Conquerour, or Arbitrary Governour"
(p. 41). But in his later writings and to the end of his life, Defoe
was consistent in his declamations against both Conquest and
Conqueror. William was entered in the rolls of tyrannic history,
beginning as a usurper and continuing as a tyrant, a mere soldier
ruling rebellious people with a rod of iron and great severity.[16] At
one and the same time, then, Defoe accepted the argument
which subverted the whole parliamentary position and yet
revealed William's invasion and rule as an illustration of naked
political power. His problem, it seems, was to find a way to establish monarchy on the basis of some more permanent principle
than antiquity or conquest. His seemingly ahistorical outlook suggests a skepticism which aligns him with the more iconoclastic
minds of the century, for whom history was relevant only to de-
nounce history, and so it seems that Defoe was forced to conduct
his arguments for monarchy in scriptural terms, outside the
sphere of English history.[17]

Thus it seems to me that the persistent identification of Defoe's
political thought as essentially Lockeian, and his relationship
with John, Baron Somers, during and after the pamphlet wars of
William's reign, have obscured the more conservative aspects of
that thought. The point is not that Defoe is Lockeian; it is clear
to anyone who inquires superficially into Defoe that he read
Locke carefully and favorably; the point is that he rejects so
much that is Lockeian.[18] That sense of radical individualism, for
example, which has disturbed many examiners of Locke's *Second
Treatise,* with the implication that the meanest man has a political importance, is totally absent from Defoe's tracts, here, in *The
Original Power of the Collective Body of the People of England,*
and throughout the eclectic *Jure Divino.* Whether or not one
accepts Laslett's doctrine of "natural political virtue" as distinc-
tively Lockeian, I think we can agree that Locke assumes that
rational human beings have the capacity to organize themselves
into societies that are politically democratic.[19] He stresses what
one critic has called a "terrestrial origin for government authority."[20] His free, independent, and rational individuals contract
and consent to make a head.

Defoe's metaphor for the vast undifferentiated citizenry, the people, is the same as that which images the violent king killers of the Commonwealth — a torrent of irresistible force, hurried on by a current nothing can withstand, momentarily carrying all things before it, but inevitably, when the force is spent, returning back again, with the same violence of motion, and with little of enduring value accomplished.[21]

Locke wrote without much clarity or consistency on the issue of a democratic franchise, but Defoe's position is clear. For him as for Locke, property is the prerequisite of political rights, the vital force for establishing a nation. But for Defoe only property holders, those with the obvious stake in government, are considered responsible and economically committed to shape the direction of society. While Defoe knew that an indiscriminate crowd was inevitably involved in revolution, in *Jure Divino* only men of property fight for freedom and emerge as caretakers of the state.

And unlike James Harrington, whom he read and cited to support his positions on property and constitutional development, Defoe could never have insisted upon the central governmental role of the nobility. I am aware that his accolades to titled heads of England pervade a good many of his prefaces — but that, it seems, is where they generally are, in the prefaces, and the bulk of Defoe's seriously argued positions tend to shy somewhat away from a presentation of present nobility in terms of value. His recognition of an enervated aristocracy comes early and was sustained to the end of his life. During William's reign, and in reflections on it afterwards, he never avoided an opportunity to attack the scarcity of English noblemen in the King's armies, and the effeminacy of the young lords is a scandal whenever he touches on Marlborough's victorious campaigns in the essays in the *Review*.[22]

Professor Béranger, with his exhaustive analyses of each Defoe pamphlet and his discrete presentation, could lead the reader to conclude that Defoe's comment endorsing mixed monarchy was an integral part of his political philosophy.[23] This "idea of mixed or balanced government in England was of course not new; one has to think only of the Answer to the Nineteen Propositions, with its doctrine of sovereignty vested in a kind of equipoise between King, Lords, and Commons."[24] Its appearance in what are Defoe's readings, and in Tyrrell, Halifax, Hunton, and Warwick, testify to its prevalence and its acceptance by writers of diverse positions.[25] But the idea disappears completely from Defoe's constitutional writings. Yet the idea of balance, or equilibrium, is a concept Defoe never retreated from to defend England's foreign policy. William's and Anne's wars were rightful because they helped to restore an equilibrium that had been disrupted. For, Defoe wrote, "it is found by Experience, that the only way to Preserve the peace of *Europe* is, so to form the several Powers and Princes, into Parties and Interests, that either Conjunctively or Seperately, no one Party or Power may be able to suppress another; and so *by addition of the Power supprest* to his own, grow too strong for his Neighbours."[26]

An absolute of foreign policy was never translated into domestic political theory. I would guess that it was because Defoe saw that the idea of balance had been used, by Harrington, for example, to justify the power of Parliament against the court, or by Shaftesbury and his followers, to argue that it was the Lord's role to be that fulcrum maintaining this delicate equipoise between crown and people.[27] His rejection of it would appear to be derived from the fact that it tended to lessen the independence of the crown, even subordinate it to parliamentary importance.

Defoe's reading of English history, even allowing for his partisan defenses of Harley to ward off his impeachment after the fall of the Tories, is a consistent, despairing record of Parliament and people easily rushed into disorders, tumults, and feuds; parties and interests had been responsible for the greed, treachery, and subversion characteristic of his times. His natural hostility to parliamentary government no doubt was strengthened when he viewed all around him the electoral corruption of a growing commercial society. Defoe had no illusions about a trading empire, and the prerequisite parliamentary profiteering; and I think he saw clearly that his society of hastening complexity could never be regulated by the fragmented will of innumerable self-seeking individuals.[28] Defoe's political growth seems to have addressed itself to an examination of, even the necessity for, a unitary executive sovereignty, thus moving in a direction contrary to Locke's antimonarchicalism, which was almost ready to make the prince a mere agent or servant to the general will.

II

One of Defoe's contemporary readers has left a marginal note in his copy of the *Reflections,* now in the Newberry Library. A believer in *jure divino* and passive resistance, he will admit to being converted, he writes, if the author "confutes [these two Arguments] according to Scripture and Reason, and the Doctrine of the Church in the Primitive Age" (p. 5). Defoe didn't and I suspect the reader wasn't. By the end of the tract, Defoe's strongest justification for resistance is James's betrayal of England to papal jurisdiction, setting up a false and spurious heir, and his illegal use of the dispensing power. I think it is fair to conclude that this early political essay showed Defoe to be a politician by the books, a phrase he used contemptuously about the Jesuits; and one who had not gotten his *own* chapters in order.[29]

If, as I have suggested, Defoe's *Reflections* can be seen as a disorderly assemblage of commonplaces of political thought, *Jure Divino,* published in 1706, not only presents evidence of wider and more intelligent reading, but seems to cohere many of these earlier concepts into a political theory that is grounded in Scripture. This is not to deny that *Jure Divino* lacks a salutary consistency. The diversity of ideologies continues. But rather than loose assertions of principles, *Jure Divino* has a system of sorts, and to stress its diffuseness would seem to make one overlook the importance it could have for a reading of the fictions.

One senses greater authority in the sustained voice of refutation, partly induced, of course, by the demands of satire in this twelve-book epic of political error. Now strong declarations replace the hesitant suggestions of value and the polite dismissal of false irrelevancies of the earlier tracts. For example, the blind veneration for antiquity preserved in some dim unrecorded past, the argument from custom to support present and obvious falsehoods, is one of the recurring themes in this confutation of Jacobite absolutism. Not unexpectedly, the author of *The True-Born Englishman* takes on the prepossessions and prejudices of a nation and scores the habit by which the unexamined past becomes a basis for the continuation of foolishness and self-deceit. The examples of traditional history, whether modern or remote, do nothing more than naturalize error:

Custom Legitimates a Nation's Shame,
Serves for a Law, and *sometimes Gains the Name.*
(IV, 1)

Unrecorded antiquity, custom's synonym, becomes

the ancient Usage of a Nation,
Handed to Rolling Times for Imitation;
Improv'd by Craft in Error's Publick Schools,
Brought in by Knaves, and then *Maintain'd* by Fools.
(IV, 3)

Defoe's reading of classical mythology parallels his earlier deni-
gration of ancestor worship mired "in latent Records of the Ages
past," the reveling in "deeds of Heroes done in Days of Yore."[30] In
his hands, a euhemeristic reading of the pantheon becomes something more than a comic and salacious recapitulation of travesties
of sexual encounters between royalty. John Cotton's Juno and
Aeolus — that scratching caterwauling puss and the loudest of
farters — and the X-rated activities of Mars and Venus have little
relation to the rapacious and savage tyrants of Defoe's geneal-
ogy.[31] The reader confronts sacrilege and holocaust and world
conflagrations. Homer, Virgil, and Horace are repositories of
euhemerism run amok, of monsters who have caused the blood of
millions to flow, barbarous furies and usurping kings.

Defoe, the apprentice satirist, had begun his attacks a decade
before by proclaiming his independence of scriptural allusion.
"No Parallels from *Hebrew* Times I take, . . . Of modern Fame . . .
I sing" — [32] and *Jure Divino* had opened with an impassioned
dedication to Lady Reason. However, Defoe's pattern for the origin of society, the emergence of government, and the proper
translation of sovereignty are firmly rooted in his explication of
Jewish history. It is likely that this pattern interpreted his subsequent reading of English history and may help to explain aspects
of the Crusoe story and the fable of his Madagascar pirate utopia.

For Defoe, as for Filmer, "human society originated in one
man — Adam," the first created monarch of God:[33]

No Rival *prompted his Ambitious Breast,*
No Dreams of envied Pow'rs disturb'd his Rest;

The Universal Monarch *rul'd alone,*
The only stated Pleasure of a Throne.
While single he, the World his own *survey'd,*
All all his silent *Subjects,* silently *obey'd:*
The Chastity of Government maintain'd,
Not yet with Cruelty and Rapin stain'd;
No Civil Wars *disturb'd his peaceful Throne,*
No Rebels *aim'd at his exalted Crown;*
No Plots *his Person to assassinate,*
Usurp his Right, or discompose the State.
He had no Parliaments, *or* Peers *to please;* . . .
He'd neither Sword nor Scepter to his Crown.
                                        (VII, 11)

Adam thus begins the type of benevolent ruler, who, a mighty landlord, like God, exercised lordship by creation over the whole world. Monarchy is the design of Heaven, and Defoe's king begins as an embodiment of an entity consecrated by Providence. And Adam's rule Defoe accepts as the only continuous pacific one, the proof being the absence in scriptural history of any record of rebellion against him by his sons.

No Sword was drawn to make his Power known,
Age was his *Scepter,* and *Grey Hair's* his Crown. . . .
                                        (II, 7)

From the projector of that Academy for Women, for whom "that almighty First Cause . . . the fountain of excellence [has] diffused equal qualities and perfections to all the creatures it has made, as the sun does its light, without the least ebb or diminution to Himself," and from Mr. Review, who always had "a tender regard to the Sex," we get a somewhat hesitant acceptance of the myth of the fall from innocence through the seduction of Eve.[34] Citing the difficulty of accounting for evil by noting Milton's own unsatisfying handling of the problem, Defoe sustains patriarchal concord till the times of Adam's descendants and to the families before the deluge. Perhaps because of the exigencies of his argument, but with the weight of tradition behind him, he makes the full descent into sin coincidental with the despotism introduced by Nimrod and his attempt to impose his rule over man. The first hunter of Scripture and his gangs become Defoe's first tyrants, who "not thinking themselves beholding to God for temporal happiness, but to their owne forces, tyrannized over the weaker, and manie wicked banning together extreamly oppressed the more peaceable...."[35]

This, Defoe says, "is the plain Original of Government; Man found the Patriarchal Power deficient in many things when the World began to multiply, and that it was wholly unqualified for large Communities; and some, encroaching upon others, threatened, and began to grow Formidable to the rest. To preserve therefore the Rights and Properties these Families enjoy'd in the World, they first Confederate several of these Patri[ar]chal Families or Kingdoms together for mutual Defense against Invasion, and finding this their only Safety, they continue thus United, choose one Supreme above the rest, and he obtained the Name of Duke or Captain; and after of King..." (II, 16).

It is not only that Defoe thought, as Temple and Tyrrell and others did, that some kingship originated with a military leader, or that the dominance of such a leader was perhaps the transitional stage between a state of nature and the onset of civil government.[36] The successful evolution of chaotic and subjugated communities into civil governments in this post-Noachic period of human development and throughout scriptural history is always dependent upon a warrior; and a double divinity inheres in him by virtue of his divine right and martial might. The crown of the first legally constituted monarchies in the world was a gift of a willing people to their lord who had exhibited military prowess, and whose military successes are themselves providential signs of his right to rule, a public and secondary recognition of what already is presented as divine election.

Defoe's argument for divine, supreme sovereignty in the monarch can be read in his treatment of the First Book of Samuel. While he obviously realized its antimonarchical tendency, which presented the choosing of a king over all Israel as a mistake and a sin, his most imaginative presentation is drawn from what is generally regarded as the early sources, which saw the establishment of kingship as a divinely ordained blessing and the salvation of the nation. The figure of Saul and his election to the throne of Israel adds to Defoe's archetype of political development.

You will recall the narrative of the First Book of Samuel. The elders of Israel, disappointed in the sons of their great judge, demand a king to rule over them. Samuel, commanded by the Lord to hearken to their request, and directed by signs of Providence, found and anointed Saul. But though proclaimed king, Saul was rejected by the people, and not until his victory over the Ammonites was he finally accepted and publicly made their monarch.

Defoe stresses two things in his poetic elaboration of the Old Testament tale: (1) the idea that kingship is a divine thing, a blessing from God, voluntarily bestowed, and not a concession to the people; and (2) the need for the requisite trial of battle, the necessary proof of and support for Saul's right to rule, in spite of the fact that he had been chosen by God.

God's answer to the question the Israelites ask — whether this is "the man shall Judah's Scepter Sway" without the ability to lead the tribes to fight, and their demand that only "personal valour must our Triumphs bring, / Tis such a Man we want, and such a King" (II, 27) — God's answer rendered by Defoe — reveals full acceptance of his people's demurral and skepticism. For monarchs only rule the people they know how to save. Thus God's ordination cannot be ratified by the rulers of the people unless it is secured by victory in the field. Defoe's notes here and elsewhere throughout *Jure Divino* insist that whatever the strength of providential endorsement, kingship is dependent upon efficient military endeavor. The crowns of Nature and Nature's God are first confirmed by the sword; the crowns offered by the community are the outward, visible, and secondary signs of political legitimacy.

Defoe's predecessors had generally accepted and reiterated the position that there had been only two initiating forms of government, conquest and compact.[37] Now, unless I am stretching Defoe's language to argue my position, behind the poetry of *Jure Divino* Defoe assumes a third, inimitable and divine.

> Conquest or Compacts, *form the Rights* of Kings,
> And both are *humane,* both *unsettled* Things,
> Both subject to Contingencies of Fate,
> And so the *Godship of them* proves a Cheat.
>
> (IX, 5)

The later Goths and Saxon kings, while they had been "consecrated by human voice," nevertheless remain for Defoe thieves and villains. Given Defoe's pattern, any advancement to the crown by the sword alone, or even by consent, without any antecedent or recognizable token of providential endorsement, is rendered suspect. Even King Edgar of Saxon fame could not uphold his throne, in spite of his election and honorable management of the kingdom, because his tenure was built upon false and ill-established principles. Obviously, William the Conqueror, beginning as a usurper, in spite of his subsequent election and contractual agreement with his conquered hosts, concluded a tyrant. Providence, in Defoe's model, thus initiates and also supports the needs of the community, and martial merit reaffirms the will of God. In Defoe's construct, the law of reason, human reason, seconds God's exalted choice, making the king "literally Divine." *Vox dei, vox populi.* As far as Defoe could manipulate biblical narrative amenable to multiple interpretations, he shows community initiated by an elect warrior-prince rooted in the patriarchal conventions of Scripture and consented to by a less than discriminate citizenry. This residue left by absolute patriarchal monarchy Defoe never seems to have forgotten.[38]

Attacking the proprietary governors of the Carolinas during the years when *Jure Divino* was being written, Defoe concluded that "they never learnt to be kings;...they have not taken the Hint of *Pater Patriae,* they don't know that a King must be the Father of his People; and that there is a sort of Patriarchal Affection, as well as Obligation, between a King on the Throne, and the People he Governs...."[39] And a decade later, in what was his most sophisticated judgment on the failure of monarchy in his time, he became almost Filmerian about the indivisible and untransferable "Spirit of government, the Paternal Genius of a King," those "incommunicable Attributes of Royal Birth [that] no subject can receive...by Deputation."

If there be any such Thing, as which Religious Men talk much of, viz. *Of Kings being the Lord's Anointed,* it seems to lie here, *Not in the Oyl Sacred at the Coronation of Kings, but in being anointed from Heaven* with the *Spirit of Government* of which *the Sacred Oyl is the Emblem or Type only.*

For Defoe, finally, this sacred authority or spirit of government is "as incommunicable as the Blood Royal, . . . Peculiar to those who are *born Kings*. We will not dispute with any, whether there is such a Spirit of Government, such as Anointing from Heaven, peculiar to all Kings or no; without Doubt to some there has been, and by Consequence may be, and we believe is at this Day."[40]

Defoe's language is more than a concession to patriarchally divine kingship. His defense of monarchy is of course staunchly traditional. The perverters of princely sovereignty are always those who have forgotten its providential origins and introduce a despotism dependent upon the sword of conquest alone; Nimrod's social aggression versus the humble and passive reception of the divine sanction of a Saul. But the divine metaphor for the ruler retains a charged meaning in Defoe's phrases that has been too easily dismissed.

Defoe's *Secret History of State Intrigues in the Management of the Scepter* is his most complete diagnosis of the failures of the English monarchy, one which has led a critic to call him the "earliest of all historians of responsible government."[41] Published in 1715, it sustains the sense that Defoe was unable to think in any but theological terms about royalty and government. But his equal interest in this tract is the devolution of kingship, and the *Secret History* can almost be seen as a secular and historical coda to his scriptural model, though it is admittedly difficult to make a synthesis of somewhat independent parts of his doctrine.

Defoe begins with the traditional regalia of the monarch—the crown, sword and scepter—the order seems important for Defoe—the crown signifying the majesty of the prince, the sword the executive power, and the scepter the ensign of the civil administration. These three are inseparable from the office of the monarchy, and thus ought to be inseparable from the person of the sovereign. Thus to commit either sword or scepter to subordinates is to introduce tumults disruptive of the public good. All monarchs, all reigns, start fresh, with the sword and the scepter conveyed to the wearer of the crown. But while the monarch can project majesty and dignity, the full stability of government can only be maintained by the monarch's delicate balance and secure embrace of all three—crown, sword, and scepter.

It has been the failure to coordinate each and all which has led
to the succession of maladministrations from Charles I's time,
and has eroded the mystique of government. Each successive
monarch, in spite of having the regalia firmly in hand, misunder-
standing the natural tyranny and prejudice of mankind, had
loosened his grasp and had contributed to the loss of integrity due
to the throne. Charles II's indolence, Jesuitical intrigue in James's
reign, King William's ignorance of English affairs — all conduced
to sever the unity of sovereignty and to bring on those national
intrigues destructive of public peace.

As early as 1702, at William's death, Defoe had expressed the
expected anxiety as a woman came to the throne. "For who shall
for us weild the Military? / Who shall the jarring Generals unite; /
First teach them to agree, and then to fight?" Even then he had
concluded that William's death had made the fatal breach so
wide, "that Loss can never, never be-supply'd."[42] And in spite of
the successful — but unnatural — demitting of the sword to Marlborough, the history of Anne's reign had proven Defoe correct,
for her weakness had finally shifted the sword and the scepter to
foreign hands. The inevitable rupture of the administration was a
foregone conclusion, and only the foreseen yet abrupt circumstance of her death and the intransigence of the managers of the
sword and the scepter had prevented the usurpation of the crown
and Jacobite tyranny. The stability of civil administration cannot
be severed from the inviolability and integrity of monarchy, and
thus "almost all the Divisions and Civil Strife, which have happen'd in this Nation, have been the Consequences of separating
the *Sword* and the Scepter from the *Crown*" (p. 6).

*The Secret History of State Intrigues in the Management of the
Scepter,* published three months after the coronation of George I,
enabled Defoe to indulge in the prospect of a fresh dawn. History
was beginning anew, for the days were now come "*when we see
the Sword and the Scepter put again in the same Hands with the
Crown;* and which adds to our Satisfaction, we see Reason to
hope, they shall not be separated again, as they have been. We
see the *Crown* upon the Head of a Prince, equally qualify'd to
hold the Scepter, and of Abilities sufficient to manage the *Sword,*
and both *without Help;* and we doubt not, His Majesty will dis-
charge Himself in all *Three* suitable to the greatest Expectation"
(p. 64).

Less than three years later, Defoe saw clearly that responsible government under a new monarch had again failed, public spirit had been banished from the nation, and self-interest, prompted by greed and power, had led to a fallen kingdom.[43]

III

In the beginning. "In the beginning all the World was America."[44] I would like to begin my comments on *Robinson Crusoe* with this ringing phrase from Locke's *Second Treatise* to argue that Defoe's narrative owes more to Genesis than to the founder of English liberal thought. I also believe that we need not bother any more with judgments that make Crusoe warden of a concentration camp, nor should we be embarrassed about a tinge of "ungracious Hobbesianism" to his activities.[45] Further, despot and tyrant are part of the terminology that I also believe have to be forsaken once the theological base of Crusoe's action becomes clearer.

The structure of the book, which I will develop here, makes Crusoe a recognizable Adamic figure returning anew to the morning of civilization. His displacement enables Defoe to define the most stable or most satisfying of all political units, if, as Crusoe admits, "any such Thing as compleat Happiness can be form'd in a sublunary State."[46] He roams in a planted garden, and the shot fired was from "the first Gun that had been fir'd there since the Creation of the World" (p. 53). No ravenous beasts, no furious wolves or tigers threaten his life, "no venomous Creatures or poisonous, which I might feed on to my Hurt," and despite his later discoveries, "no Savages to murther and devour me" (p. 132).

Natural law theory might appear to support Crusoe's conviction that he was owner of all of the island and thus had a right of possession, but Crusoe, after the earthquake and his conversion, bears a great resemblance to Filmer's patriarch:

By the appointment of God . . . he was monarch of the world, though he had no subjects; for though there could not be actual government until there were subjects, yet by the right of nature it was due to Adam to be governor of his posterity, though not in act, yet at least in habit. Adam was a King from his creation.[47]

To a like extent, so is Crusoe. With some seriousness, he realizes that God's donation to him is the essence of divine monarchy,
if not the substance, and his dormant imperial integrity is vividly
realized in Defoe's picture of him at dinner, prince and lord of
the whole island, a ruler with the lives of all his subjects at his
absolute command, fully exercising the functions of sovereignty,
though with Poll, dog, and cats (p. 148). Much earlier, before
this sense of his recognition of his mock, perfect society, Crusoe is
already thinking in political terminology; the grindstone costing
him as much thought as a statesman would have bestowed upon a
grand point of politics, or a judge upon the life and death of a
man (pp. 82-83); which, like the dinner, anticipates completely
his later positions and activities with the onset of human society.

I believe the marks of Crusoe's kingliness appear very early,
and I have at times thought that Defoe made a conscious attempt
to have his hero take on the mantle of another martial monarch,
who was the deliverer of another island. Crusoe's earthquake, we
know, has been generally interpreted in a privately spiritual way.
But I am reminded of the earthquake in London in 1692, seen as
God's providential intrusion and warning to those questioning
King William's right to reign.[48] And then there is Crusoe's first
seagoing voyage made to take the circumference of his little kingdom. In that month of November, he finds himself caught in a
current he cannot master, with no wind stirring, and being driven
from his beloved island, "for so it appear'd to me now to be," and
in the utmost despair of ever recovering it again. It is only with a
little breeze of wind springing up from the SSE that turns into a
pretty small gentle gale that Crusoe makes land again and safety.
"When I was on Shore, I fell on my Knees and gave God Thanks
for my Deliverance, resolving to lay aside all Thoughts of my
Deliverance by my Boat . . ." (p. 141). The scene should recall the
Protestant wind which brought the restorer of English liberties,
glorious King William, to Torbay's shores. I would contend that
one can very early almost make out a crown on Crusoe's head,
and he can be seen as a putative sovereign of an island commonwealth.[49]

Thus it has been hard for me to understand how scholars clari-
fying the spiritual imagery of Crusoe's story could have overlooked the uses to which that imagery had been put during

William's reign. "The theme of providential delivery, full of biblical and historical precedent and imagery, became the favourite
theme of revolution church oratory, casuistry, and biblical exe-
gisis...."[50] The highest providence of God lay in the ordering of
states. Defoe, who later called providence "the administration of
Heaven's government in the world," was echoing the theme of
many of those sermons preached on the historic 5th of November,
Symon Patrick's, for instance: "If God demonstrates his Providence in anything here in this World, ... he exercises it in the
Governing, Defending, and Protecting of publick Persons and
Societies."[51] God's primary point of concentration was on politics,
and Crusoe's memoirs indicate that his regal authority on the
island is founded in divine providence.

Perhaps the most overlooked support for Crusoe's Adamic in-
heritance introduces the imperial monologue in which Crusoe
talks of being "Lord of the whole Mannor; or if I pleas'd, I might
call my self King, or Emperor over the whole Country which I
had Possession of. There were no Rivals. I had no Competitor,
none to dispute Sovereignty or Command with me." He is, he
realizes then, removed from all the wickedness of the world. "I
had neither the *Lust of the Flesh, the Lust of the Eye, or the
Pride of Life*" (p. 128). Crusoe's freedom from the infernal triad
should remind us of the Church fathers and Protestant theolo-
gians, and their difficulty in reconciling the narratives of Christ's
temptations in Matthew, Luke, and John. By the seventeenth
century, there was no longer any demand to conform point by
point. Compromises were made. The commentators and harmo-
nizers of the gospel accepted the fiction that with Christ's victory
over Satan, all the temptations which Adam had fallen to had
been overcome, since those in the Gospels were variants of the
three basic seductions: Gluttony, Avarice, Vainglory. Flesh,
World, and the Devil. The lust of the flesh, the lust of the eye,
and the pride of life. Thomas Manton, incidentally, called by
Anthony á Wood the prelate of the Protectorate, and often cited
by Defoe as one of the most respected controversialists and theo-
logians among the Dissenting clergy, was one of the many church-
men who saw the absence of these three sins as the condition of
Adam in the garden of God.[52]

Professor Novak has rightly cautioned us about imposing rigid

structural patterns on Defoe's fiction, asking us to be aware
always of Defoe's love of paradox and his changing plan.[53] Defoe,
it seems to me, realized that his political affinities could be called
Hobbesian; that is, that God's initial and his own commonwealth
ideal imposed total sovereignty upon a single magistrate who
directed the society for the general ends of peace and safety.
Complete and absolute power was concentrated in his person.
Thus it appears that the lengthy sequence preceding the rescue of
Friday serves as an emotional reminder of the natural sociability
of mankind and helps to override that damaging, even disloyal
inference. I am aware of the insistent repetitions that Friday's
rescue is an economic act, support for which comes from the
dream in which the cannibal becomes a "servant," and the words
Crusoe first teaches his ward — Master, yes, and no. But critics
have refused to consider the sudden shift in Crusoe's attitude
which makes the rescue of Friday derive from a psychological
need, and they have overlooked the political consequences of the
action.

From the beginning of Crusoe's tenure on the island, three
themes have developed the story, and we can even organize two
hundred years of scholarship around them; they are economic
man isolated on an island, religious man isolated on an island
and adventurous man isolated on an island. Only once it seems
does Defoe focus clearly on isolated man in what can be called the
abstract; that is, in a condition vulnerable to the actualities of
insular solitude. This instance is at the shipwreck preceding Friday's rescue. Remember that this occurred in his twenty-third
year of residence, and I "was so naturaliz'd to the Place, and to
the Manner of Living, that could I have but enjoy'd the Certainty
that no Savages would come to the Place to disturb me, I could
have been content to have capitulated for spending the rest of my
Time there, even to the last Moment, till I had laid me down and
dy'd . . ." (p. 180). Then the shipwreck: "I cannot explain by any
possible Energy of Words, what a strange longing or hankering of
Desires I felt in my Soul upon this Sight; breaking out sometimes
thus; O that there had been but one or two; nay, or but one Soul
sav'd out of this Ship, to have escap'd to me, that I might but
have had one Companion, one Fellow-Creature to have spoken to
me, and to have convers'd with! In all the Time of my solitary
Life, I never felt so earnest, so strong a Desire after the Society of

my Fellow-Creatures, or so deep a Regret at the want of it." After three more paragraphs stressing his anguish at being alone—"*O that it had been but One! O that it had been but One!*"—he sets out for the wreck. It is true that Crusoe realizes "the Comfort, which the Conversation of one of my Fellow-Christians would have been to me" (p. 188), and his examination of the wreck is economic and practical; but it is this unexpected instance of his humanity that precipitates changes in his attitude. His present condition is now "the most miserable that could possibly be, that I was not able to throw my self into any thing but Death, that could be call'd worse..." (p. 197). The dream follows, providence's voice that he get himself "a Servant, and perhaps a Companion, or Assistant" (p. 202). This thus appears to be the one point in the book in which isolation functions to affect vitally the behavior of Crusoe as adventurous, religious, and economic man.

Crusoe's rescue of Friday, by the way, is totally unique. In none of the desert island narratives which have filled a half score of German dissertations, nor in any of the source studies of Defoe's admirers and detractors, does one find the physical and embattled rescue of a companion that continues Crusoe's adventures. In no other Robinsonade does a shipwrecked man build up a new life and a new community through the ordeal of battle.[54] It would seem that the action, the appeal to arms, proves Defoe's theory of societal development; it is that essential sequence in which the latent monarch actualizes the potential necessary for his role as communal leader. Crusoe is here as he is later, the warrior girding his loins for battle. King Crusoe is never distinct from Captain Crusoe, and the introduction of subjects is *ipso facto,* as Defoe would have said, the making of recruits for his army. "In vain," Defoe wrote in *Jure Divino,* "in vain he claims his *primo-genial* Right; / In vain they always claim, that cannot fight" (X, 17). Defoe's vision, as we know, never permits Crusoe to divest himself of either role, as Governor or Generallissimo, for his hero enjoys his title as God's chosen instrument of salvation and also as conqueror in the trial by battle. Like his beloved King William, Defoe's Crusoe never ceases to be a "Praying and Fighting Monarch."[55]

With the introduction of Friday, it is obvious, Defoe has managed to provide Crusoe with the blessings of parenthood without repeating the slavery of Adam to Eve, the burden of copulation, and midnight changes. Crusoe is immediately granted, as Tyrrell, said, "that nobler part of a parent's duty, the trouble and care in educating their children, their highest right and duty to God."[56] Friday's "very Affections were ty'd to me, like those of a Child to a Father," says this fifty-two-year-old mentor of his twenty-six-year-old infant, who was "the aptest Scholler . . ." (pp. 209, 210).[57] And rather than belabor the obvious, I would only remind you of the dialogue between Friday and Crusoe soon after, recapitulating that between the father and the child of *The Family Instructor,* already in its sixth edition in the year of *Robinson Crusoe's* publication. The questions the child asks there which lead him to know both his Creator and his duty to him are: Who made me? What was I made for? What am I? What business have I here? How come I hither? Whither am I? What is my End? What is Good and what is Evil?[58]

In addition, while the absence of a woman does not permit Crusoe to assume the domestic power of a man over his wife, this singular introduction of Friday to Crusoe's garden does enable him to take on those other distinct powers which, since the Creation, have very rarely come together in the same man, that of father over child, master over servant, magistrate over subject, and lord over slave. Locke's purpose, as he began his *Second Treatise,* was to distinguish these powers from one another, "and shew the difference betwixt a Ruler of a Common-wealth, a Father of a Family, and a Captain of a Galley."[59] It is clear that Defoe has no intention of making these distinctions, which would only dilute Crusoe's supremacy.

Let me call your attention to the following action that commentators have been forced to ignore because it cannot be harmonized with the religious or economic motifs they have been stressing. Crusoe does not even try either. I am referring to the massacre of the savages preceding the rescue of Friday's father and the Spaniard. Crusoe's earlier attempts to rationalize the slaughter of savages had been wholly in religious terms, and what tentative conclusions he had reached then actually contradict the principles upon which the later killings take place, in which seventeen natives are destroyed and two prisoners rescued. The fact that Friday's father and the Spaniard are the ones rescued does not modify greatly Crusoe's casuistical confusion. Neither of these men is essential to the religious themes of the book; their rescue does not become an allegorical salvation; it does not reinforce the proselytizing efforts of Crusoe, which have been explicated for us by Professors Starr and Hunter.[60] More important, Crusoe and Friday are not fighting to rescue Friday's father, for they do not know that the victim is Friday's father. The fact that the white Spaniard is not a part of the barbaric culture and therefore should not have to live with the consequences of his unfortunate shipwreck, alters the situation only slightly. He is not essential to the progression of either the economic or religious theme. Perhaps one could argue that the action functions as an adventure for adventure's sake. But it is easier to accept it as a politically motivated sequence, which brings about a further union of king and people and enables Crusoe to establish himself rather legitimately as a benevolent and tolerant monarch.

My Island was now peopled, and I thought my self very rich in Subjects; and it was a merry Reflection which I frequently made, How much like a King I look'd. First of all, the whole Country was my own meer Property; so that I had an undoubted Right of Dominion; 2dly, My People were perfectly subjected: I was absolute Lord and Law-giver; they all owed their Lives to me, and were ready to lay down their Lives, *if there had been Occasion of it,* for me. It was remarkable too, we had but three Subjects, and they were of three different Religions, My Man *Friday* was a Protestant, his Father was a *Pagan* and a *Cannibal,* and the Spaniard was a Papist: However, I allow'd Liberty of Conscience throughout my Dominions. (P. 241)

It could be said that Defoe had neglected to resolve his construct of civil evolution, that the pressures of concluding the narrative forestalled any presentation of Crusoe as a monarch of a more sophisticated society. But a consideration of the generally ignored *Farther Adventures* would suggest that Defoe clearly imagined and consciously accepted the truncated structure of Crusoe's patriarchate in the first island memoir.

IV

I hold, André Gide once wrote, that the best explanation of a work must be its sequel.[61] The astonishing success of the first volume of Crusoe's adventures guaranteed a positive reception to

any further account, and Defoe was thus able to return to his
political story and give full attention to the evolving colonial experience. The sequel more readily permits us to see how he had
been thinking earlier along scriptural lines, and how he wished
now to emphasize that pattern in the dramatization of the genesis
and evolution of civil society.

Immediately upon beginning his tale of his colonists' adventures, Crusoe informed the reader of "a Defect in my former
Relation."[62] His correction is strong evidence for a political reading of his narratives. When he summarized the then unwritten
Farther Adventures at the end of his first volume, three men were
left on the island, Will Atkins and two incorrigible English muti-
neers. With the return of the Spaniards and Friday's father, the
sequel was summarized then as we know it, comprising disagreements, Spanish tolerance, battles with Caribbean Indians, the
capture of five native women, and the population explosion. But
when he begins his story of island dissension and the fragmenta-
tion preliminary to the creation of a complex society in *The Farther Adventures,* Crusoe corrects the earlier relation, and now
tells of a quarrel aboard ship before its departure and the jailing
of the two most refractory seamen. Escaping to the island, these
two found that their compatriots in villainy would have nothing
to do with them. The duo, suddenly reformed, pitched their tents
on the north shore of the island. Thus, when the Spaniards returned, and Atkins and his group were finally expelled because of
their brutish conduct, three settlements had been planted.

Now I am aware that one does not have to think only politically
to find the number three attractive — "the number Three has not
been only admired by the Heathens," Thomas Browne wrote,
"but from adorable grounds, . . . the mystery of the Trinity, admired by many Christians"[63] — but it seems Defoe's choice of this
trinity is more than accidental. It can be said that, given the curious binary form that Defoe's fictions have internally, the pattern
now serves to balance the tripartite division of the community
which Crusoe had initiated earlier. But with *Jure Divino* in mind,
and recalling Defoe's many citations there and elsewhere of
Raleigh's *History of the World,* which reemphasized the tradition, it can be said that this restructuring of the community seems
necessary in order to introduce the post-Adamic, post-Noachic

state of society which followed the comparatively idyllic and ordered one of the earliest patriarchs. Perhaps Defoe is asking the reader to recall the three sons of Adam — rather the three that are named in Genesis, for we are told that Adam had others. It is more likely that Defoe had in mind the three sons of Noah, from whom and their issues new regions were planted and from whence by degrees the rest of the world was also peopled. "The three sons of Noah had the whole world divided amongst them by their Father; for of them was the whole world overspread.... Most of the civilest nations of the world labour to fetch their original from some one of the sons or nephews of Noah...."[64]

Quite simply, in spite of all the movements and accretions of people on and to his island, of servants, wives, slaves, Portuguese, and priest, Crusoe never permits the reader to overlook the fact that his domain has three colonies, three towns, three plantations (pp. 90, 120, 138, 193). This Noachic division and expansion, then, is necessary to initiate the conditions which, according to the Scriptures, are the prerequisite for the creation of civil society. Throughout *Jure Divino,* whenever he considered the origin of government, Defoe declared that the beneficent rule of the early patriarchs was unfit to maintain itself with the multiplication and dispersion of mankind, and that the traditional obedience and respect due the original leaders would inevitably give way to greed and tyrannical rule. And on the island the spread and increase of mankind, following the mythic leader's departure, introduces dissension, cruelty, and oppression.

Now it has been suggested that Crusoe has failed in the duty and office of a king, that he never becomes, as Defoe put it, "...the father, protector, and vigilant defender, as well as the governor and monarch, of his people and kingdom."[65] It seems to me that Crusoe's departures from his island colony do not certify his unfitness as a political leader, that his vision of himself as a patriarch is *not* a delusion, and that his surrender of command over the inhabitants is *not* little more than a histrionic gesture. In fact, Defoe could present the development of his community and the evolution of the island from a quasi-paradisiacal state only by removing his hero from the scene, for *The Farther Adventures* is a continued dramatic rendering of the evolution of society following the record in the Bible.

First among the actors in the villainy is Will Atkins, who plays his part in Defoe's drama with all the eccentricities of a Nimrod. The friendly Spaniards had at first wished to maintain the mutual amity of the three groups, and spoke of the island inhabitants as one family, for their savior had given the land to all to work and share. But like the first *jure divino* tyrants of Genesis, Atkins, speaking for his small army, proclaims that "the Island was theirs, the Governour had given it to them, and no Man had any thing to do there but themselves" (p. 53). So began their bullying of their neighbors, for no one else had a right to the island and no colony was to be planted in their dominions. The insistent plague imagery and destructive burnings of these barbarians remind the reader of the language of *Jure Divino* and the pamphlets, which always equated such with tyrants.[66] Their initial proclamations are familiar; their daily schedule turns out to be a recognizable paraphrase of the activities of that earlier mighty hunter before the lord:

They did nothing but ramble about the Island, shoot Parrots, and catch Tortoises, and when they came home at Night, the *Spaniards* provided their Suppers for them. (Pp. 46-47)

But their tenure is short-lived; for their violences increasing, after civil persuasion fails, they are treated somewhat anachronistically like their modern *jure divino* counterparts, those supporters of Stuart absolutism:

...after a long Debate it was agreed, First, That they should be disarm'd, and not permitted to have either Gun, or Powder, or Shot, or Sword, or any Weapon, and should be turn'd out of the Society, ... that they should be forbid to come within a certain Distance of the Place where the rest dwelt.... (P. 76)

No contemporary would fail to recognize here those acts passed following the Revolution against Catholics — read Jacobites — *jure divino* supporters, maintaining their allegiance to an exiled tyrant; penal statutes "amoving papists and reputed papists" from the environs of London, and prohibiting the possession of "any arms, weapons, gunpowder, ammunition."[67]

According to tradition, great success attended Nimrod's rebellion. But in another beneficial reversal of the pattern, Defoe's copy destroys only beasts; and, true to form, with the turn to the religious theme, Defoe's socially conscious military leader becomes the converted Saint Paul of the island community.

Goethe once remarked that our final impression of a person is derived from the circumstance in which we have last seen him. Since dispute will continue over Crusoe's role in his island's development, it should be said that the colonists, who ought to be able to appraise their situation correctly, greet him as a monarch or a great conqueror, and later, recipients of his care and furnishings, "told me, I was a Father to them, and that having such a Correspondent as I was, in so remote a Part of the World, it would make them forget that they were left in a desolate Place..." (p. 135).[68]

Since I have suggested a relationship, however untidy, in Defoe's dramatic recapitulation of the scriptural legends concerning Adam, Noah, Nimrod, and Saul, let me conclude my observations on the *Crusoe* volumes with another. Joseph. Crusoe's Spanish subject recounts to him his meeting with his shipmates in Friday's nation, and his telling them about his deliverance by Crusoe from the cannibals, and how he was now able to carry them away to safety. "It was like a Dream to them; and their Astonishment, they said, was something like that of Joseph's Brethren, when he told them who he was, and told them the Story of his Exaltation in *Pharaoh's Court*" (p. 45).

Critics explaining the forms of spiritual autobiographies have recently made us aware of the way in which "a number of Biblical people and things...took on well-defined spiritual values. Mere mention of them would suggest the spiritual import of whatever one happened to be describing. Since the process was perhaps too random and informal to be styled iconography, allusive shorthand might be a better term for it."[69] In such a way, casual reference to biblical precedents or analogues makes meaningful and familiar the strange, singular, or exotic. Defoe's allusion to the Joseph situation from Genesis seems to be unique in his writings. But it enables the reader to see the Spaniard, like Joseph, leading his people to safety and beginning the makings of a great nation; and in the Crusoe story the sequence is also more than an event of local significance. Joseph had been sent by God to preserve a posterity in the earth. In the tradition, through a combination of wondrous events and circumstances, he was set over the affairs of Pharaoh's mighty empire to serve the high ends of providence. The miraculous deliverance that followed revealed to a people — or at least a part of it — that it had been called to be a vehicle of divine knowledge to the world and an instrument for the fulfillment of God's redemptive purpose for humanity.[70]

V

Time does not permit any full consideration of Defoe's many writings on piracy and pirate society which reinforce the themes of societal evolution and civil leadership of the pamphlets. During the seventeenth and early eighteenth centuries, pirate narrations and histories revealed the ease with which these so-called outlaws were able to organize and govern themselves in a manner resembling lawful communities. Any reading of their trials also made clear their ability to live under civil articles. In the 1699 preface to Alexander Esquemeling's *Bucaniers of America,* Defoe could have read, and possibly did, the observations of a like-minded journalist, who found it *"very remarkable, that in such a lawless Body as these* Bucaniers *seemed to be, in respect to all others; that yet there should be such an Oeconomy (if I may so say)* kept, *and regularity practised among themselves, so that every one seemed to have his property as much secured, as if he had been a member of the most Civilized Community in the World."*[71]

The subtitle of that superb repository of Defoe's best journalism a quarter of a century later, *The General History of the Pyrates,* is "And Also their Policies, Discipline and Government." In spite of its crude and low content, Defoe felt no need to apologize for his *History.* There was, of course, something more than satire and humor involved when he presented these ruffians defining themselves in contemporary political terminology; when he wrote of secretaries of states and governments by a majority, of the need for strong leadership to quell the continuous malcontentions, of judges and juries, and reigns beginning and ending. And as all constitutions grow old and totter, "so did our [pirate] Commonwealth, in about a Month of its Age feel Commotions and intestine Disturbances, by the Divisions of its Members, which had near hand terminated in its Destruction."[72] In the month of its publication, May 1724, a reviewer in *Mist's Weekly Journal* commended the author, "who has been very curious in inquiring into that policy, which kept them at peace amongst one another, and under the Title of Articles, has produced a system of Government, which I think, (considering what the Persons were who fram'd it) as excellent for Policy as any thing in Plato's commonwealth."[73]

This reviewer of Defoe's *History* might have been Defoe himself; we are not certain. But we do know of the two manuscripts left unpublished at his death, and they have a bearing on Defoe's last important statement on the nature of political society, its origin, development, and degeneration.

Defoe's manuscripts, *Of Royall Educacion* and *The Compleat English Gentleman,* both seem to have been worked on in 1728. Karl Bulbring, who edited them, showed that the former, while it had been begun some time before 1728, was taken up again about that year; *The Compleat English Gentleman's* date of composition is 1728 and the earlier half of 1729. They are complementary texts concerned with the same theme, the contempt for learning that has distinguished the gentry and the aristocracy; and they share common anecdotes, examples, and illustrations. In both, Defoe decries the growing indifference to the need to educate the classes in suitable manners and learning, and seeks to bring blood and merit together. His not too revolutionary ideal becomes a furnished head and a finished mind. Throughout both texts, the examples of merit, worth, honor, and virtue turn out to be the military geniuses, like Gustavus Adolphus and Peter the Great—not surprising coming from the projector of thirty years earlier who considered the art of war the highest perfection of human knowledge, and the campaign the best academy in the world.[74]

In *Of Royall Educacion,* Defoe maintained that there were "souls of differing glory and furnish'd by Nature with infinitely greater capacityes then some others may be, tho' all issuing from the same hand, emitting divine powers and influences to them . . ." (p. 2). These are, Defoe says, the heroes of Scripture, "kings and leaders of armyes, and others, such as were destined to great actions. . . ." He continues: "From these just premises I may most reasonably inferr that the souls of princes, men of nobillity in birth and blood, especially such as the divine prescience has, as above, design'd and determin'd for great employment and glorious accions in life, and as are, *or are to be,* plac'd in high stations, are often times furnish'd thus in an extraordinary manner from a superior hand with powers suitable to, and capable of, the great things they are to do and the great figure they are to make in the world" (p. 3).

Thus education, while it is an advantage to children of meaner birth, is a matter of the highest importance to children of rank. How much, Defoe asks, may be added to the nobility of birth, when it can be said that such a lord or such a young prince is "a man of learning, a man of judgement, a schollar, a man of virtue, he has been so and so educated, and has made a surprising improvement in his studyes; that he is an excellent mathematician; that he has a head turn'd for bussiness, a genius to the war, either to the field or to naval affairs; or that he is known to excell in any particular; that he is well read in history, has studyed the intrest and temper of all the courts and governments in Europe, and the like" (p. 9).

In July 1728 Defoe published the second volume of *The History of the Pyrates.* It contained, in addition to piracy, what Professor Novak has rightly called "one of Defoe's most remarkable and neglected works of fiction."[75] I refer to the account of Captain Misson's utopian pirate commonwealth on Madagascar. It has been read as a dramatization of Locke's *Second Treatise of Government* and proof of the political activity of man in a state of nature;[76] yet it seems to be more a study of a unique and vanishing political ideal, and concludes Defoe's writing career with some sceptical implications on the nature of democratic egalitarianism.

Captain Misson, it is clear, is Defoe's most polished portrait of the consummate gentleman-warrior-prince. Of a distinguished and ancient family, he is given an education equal to his birth; a younger brother—Defoe seems to have always favored younger brothers—he is forced to carve out his future with his sword. Misson, educated early in Humanity and Logic and Mathematics, is sent to the university and then to war, where, as expected, his competence in battle matches his earlier success in academia. Misson's education, incidentally, resembles that of Henry VII's eldest son, who, if he had lived, Defoe wrote, would have become one of the greatest monarchs in Europe.[77] And even though Misson spent a lot of the time with the boatswain and carpenter learning the mechanics of a ship, "yet he behaved himself with such Prudence that they never attempted at a Familiarity, and always paid the Respect due to his family" (p. 384). In a word, his credentials are impeccable and his manner superlative.

Immediately upon taking up the sword in the French naval service in the War of the Spanish Succession, Misson showed his resolute courage and intelligent leadership. He soon took command of the privateer when its superior officers were all killed in an engagement. In short, a martial and learned man has outgrown his apprenticeship and is ready to become the leader of a newly created visionary community on an uncharted Indian Ocean island.

Unmotivated by ambition or any crude egocentric drives, Defoe's prospective monarch is led to reject the established conventions of contemporary society, defy international law, and "...with the Ship he had under Foot, and the brave Fellows under Command, bid Defiance to the Power of *Europe,* enjoy every Thing he wish'd, reign Sovereign of the Southern Seas, and lawfully make War on all the world..." (p. 391). And in the topsy turvy way of revolutionary idealists, Misson's ship will fly, not the black flag of piracy, but the white ensign of free, rational individuals, "*with Liberty painted in the Fly, and...the Motto,* A Deo a Libertate *For God and Liberty, as an Emblem of...Uprightness and Resolution*" (p. 393).

The fact that the platitudes of Locke and the *Second Treatise* justifying rebellion, which lead Misson to withdraw from the present corrupt social and economic scene, are uttered by an ex-Dominican priest of pronounced deistic teachings breeds no ideological alarm. What is obviously Defoe's satire on the basic self-interest of deistic thought — Caraccioli is as ambitious as he is irreligious — remains firmly in the area of rationalistic explication of the Holy Scriptures. Misson's mentor's political ideals stay generally unscathed. Defoe, who does mark that Caraccioli is as

ambitious as Misson, might have felt that his titular hero had to
be taught those rational principles and had to be coerced by a
disciple of Locke to rebel against the prevailing order. But Misson, Defoe makes clear, had earlier lost his Christian faith on a
visit to Rome, where he marked "...the licentious Lives of the
Clergy...the Luxury of the Papal Court, and that nothing but
Hulls of Religion was to be found in the Metropolis of the Christian Church..." (p. 384).

Misson's command of his liberated crew, and his pronouncements that anticipate Liberté, Egalité, and Fraternité, might
seem to usher in a floating democracy, but the pretence of
meaningful participation by his foremast-men is revealed in the
succession of episodes aboard ship, and later when civil society is
established on Madagascar. In nearly every case, in nearly every
decision, his men exclaim, as they exclaimed at his election to
command, *Vive le Capitain Misson,* and unhesitatingly support
his programs. Assent is readily given to the form of representation
he desires aboard ship, a majority votes for his decision to leave
the Caribbean for the coast of Guiney, general applause follows
his impassioned speech against chattel slavery, and on Madagascar, one and all consent to his military plans. Whether they be
French, English, Rochelle Protestants, Dutch, American colo-
nials, or emancipated African slaves—and this does eventually
become the complement of Misson's prototype of the *Pequod* and
the citizenry of Libertalia—their job, foremast-men and officers
alike, is to acquiesce in the decisions of their brave, good Captain. He calls to mind, in fact, Lady Reason, Defoe's dedicatee of
Jure Divino, who reigned with an uncontrolled sovereignty in the
very hearts of her subjects: "And yet your Majesty is far from
being a Tyrant, since at the same time that you Command the
most Absolute Obedience, such is the Demonstration of your
Royal Justice, that You gain upon the very Souls of your Subjects,
and they pay a voluntary Homage to all your Commands" (p. 1).

It is Misson's paternal affection for them, his friends, his com-
panions, finally, his children, that initiates the reformation of
manners aboard ship, and restores the decorum and regularity
necessary for social order. In fact, Misson is that working ideal of
the sovereign, the absence of which had earlier justified the crew's
revolt and mutiny, a governor who had "... Eyes impartial, and

allowed nothing but Merit to distinguish between Man and Man;
and instead of being a Burthen to the People by his luxurious
Life, he was by his Care for, and Protection of them, a real
Father, and in every Thing acted with the equal and impartial
Justice of a Parent" (pp. 392-393).

The stage through which this new community dominated by a
patriarch passes into a sovereign nation is worth a consideration.
I have noted Defoe's habit, in the Crusoe narratives, to reorganize
activity in order to make a transition from the polity of a single
magistrate to a triumvirate. A similarly deliberate and peculiar
break happens here.

Misson's piratical exploits, though fictional, are given the illusion of fact through Defoe's introduction of names, places, and
events rooted in the War of the Spanish Succession, specifically
the naval campaigns of 1707-1708. But before he concludes Misson's utopian venture, he breaks the narrative to write a new
chapter and introduce a new pirate, Captain Thomas Tew. Defoe was aware, it seems certain to me, that Captain Tew had
begun his privateering career in 1691, had traded with the Madagascar pirates, and, on his second voyage to the Red Sea, had
been killed by Moorish gunners in 1696. Tew's injection into the
Misson story is odd, historically inaccurate and seemingly unnecessary. But his joining with Misson and his colony brings on
two actions: (1) it changes the pattern of adventures in that there
are now three leaders who assume control of the colony; and (2) it
increases the number of men, and as we would expect brings on
disagreements and disobedience. A quarrel follows. Tew wishes
the disputants to settle it by the sword. Instead, it proves the
necessity of a new authority, and the next day the three com-
manders meet to propose a form of government to settle difference according to reason and equity. Again, it seems, Defoe has
regulated his genesis of civil development along the lines of Scripture, and property and Locke play less of a role than human
orneriness and God's clear but unstable plan.

It has been said that Libertalia's new order reflects Defoe's
incipient anarchic preferences, or that its form is democratic.
But in spite of its tangential similarity to James Harrington's
Oceana, it is hard to avoid the conclusion that Libertalia's formal
government is something less than a democratic ideal, and that

the republican heritage of the seventeenth century has been seriously attenuated. The supreme power is lodged in the hands of one, "who should have that of rewarding brave and virtuous Actions, and of punishing the vicious, according to the Laws which the State should make; by which, he was to be guided. That such a Power however should not be for Life, nor hereditary, but determinate at the end of three Years, when a new Choice, should be made by the State, or the Old confirm'd for three Years longer.... That such a Chief should have the Title of Lord Conservator, and all the Ensigns of Royalty to attend him" (p. 433).

This too was approved *Nemine contradicente,* "and Misson was chose Conservator, with Power to create great Officers, etc. and with the Title of supream Excellence" (p. 433). With laws made, the constitutional assembly is dissolved by Misson and the state of Libertalia began its short tenure in the family of nations.

Hard generalizations, as you might have gathered, I have tried my best to avoid throughout this paper, but it does seem that Defoe, like a good many of his seventeenth-century contemporaries, is preoccupied with paternal figures, warriors, and great lawgivers, who, like God, seem to be able to create communities in one piece, with little regard to what has gone before, except for Scripture's plan. Not only his fictional heroes but his favorite historical personages, Charles XII of Sweden, Peter Alexowitz, Czar of Moscovy, Gustavus Adolphus, about whom he wrote at length, become in his biographies modern equivalents of Lycurgus and Solon, who, through their own visionary and unaided efforts, lay a foundation of glory and greatness for their blind, ignorant, and obedient subjects.[78] The conception of a community as an organic growth, affected only to a limited extent by the initiating prince, is completely absent from Defoe; absent from the controlling pattern of *Jure Divino* and minimally in evidence in his fictions.

In spite of what I see to be Defoe's similarities to his seventeenth-century contemporaries — Pufendorf, Temple, or Halifax, for example — he seems never to have been able to comprehend the subtle influences of culture, custom, precedents — the unconscious conditioners of political order. Nor could he have responded to Temple's conservative awareness of the power and

beauty of tradition: "...the breaking down an old frame of
Government and erecting a new, seems like cutting down an old
Oak (because the fruit decays, and the branches grow thin), and
planting a young one in the room. Tis true the Son or Grandson
(if it prospers) may enjoy the shade and the maste; but the
Planter, besides the pleasure of Imagination, has no other benefit
to recompense the pains of Setting and Digging, the care of
Watering and Pruning, the fears of every Storm and every
Drought; and it is well, if he escapes a blow from the fall of the
old Tree, or its Boughs, as they are lopt off."[79]

It should not be forgotten that there are two utopias on Madagascar, Misson's and a more communistic and anarchic one, a
rudimentary copy of Libertalia settled by twenty-four sailors
from Captain Tew's colonial privateer. While its ideological base
resembles Misson's—they proclaim their freedom and independence and their hatred of subjection, they have the ballot, and
incessant rotation of the supreme command, which precludes the
creation of parties and divisions—its founder's plan for its future
development drastically redirects it away from Misson's original
humanitarian order. For the blueprint for future colonization is
dependent upon a slave economy, and the inducement to invest-
ments, in mining, milling and commerce, is totally predicated on
the cold, practical fact that Negro slaves on Madagascar can be
purchased for the price of an old coat and that the natural fer-
tility of the soil enables the entrepreneurs to feed their slaves, as
well as themselves, without expense.

Misson's colony is destroyed immediately after its foundation,
wantonly by once friendly natives in the dead of night, and presumably the other withered away. One can't help but ask whether
visionary utopias initiated with the best of intentions, proclaiming goals of humanity and rationality, and responding to the best
natural impulses of man, break down under the burden of and
need for commercial development.

If the ultimate guarantee of order and virtue, the state's originating impulse and the insurer of its sustaining integrity, is the
Warrior Prince, does Defoe suggest that his disappearance, reduction even, constitutionally or otherwise, brings on baleful
change? Is it essential that there should always be but one person
whose mind and methods organized policy for the common good?

Even Crusoe's colony, we recall, in spite of its auspicious directions, disintegrates soon after; Atkins dies, and the remaining colonists write to ask Crusoe that they be permitted to see their home country before they die. But the limitations of Defoe's body of work do not enable us to speculate too easily on the forces that impel the degeneration of governments. Perhaps if asked, he would have replied, like Machiavelli, "the inherent instability of terrestial things."[80] Perhaps Defoe might have pointed to allegiances shifting, from a vision of monarchy, the word and wisdom of which was the mainstay of a moral and creative order, to factions and groupings which inevitably had led to the depression of civil authority. Perhaps his hopes of revolution and government's deliverance from ancient tyranny were undermined by what he knew to be the shameful failure of representational commitment and ministerial rule, and thus were destroyed in the history of his times. But whatever the case, whatever the cause, the foremost pamphleteer of the Revolution age speaks to us today as one who saw the old world and the new through a pair of keen and prescient eyes.[81]

NOTES

*The research for this study was made possible by a fellowship from The Newberry Library and a grant from The American Philosophical Society. To them, their directors and staffs I express my sincere thanks.

The place of publication for texts not fully cited is London.

1. For useful terminological distinctions see Bernard Crick, "Philosophy, Theory and Thought," *Political Studies,* 15 (1967), 49-54.
2. See James Tyrrell, *Patriarcha non Monarcha* (1681), p. 97, for a similar observation. I do not mean to suggest that these and other citations from seventeenth-century writers are Defoe's "sources." They are only meant to show current, prevailing ideas. But when Defoe speaks reverently of "a Kind of *Trinity* in our Government as well as in our Faith," he does seem to echo John Sadler; see *Reflections,* p. 37, and Sadler, *The Rights of the Kingdom; or, Customs of our Ancestours* (1682), p. 86. Sadler's work, first published in 1649, might have been in Defoe's library; see Helmut Heidenreich, *The Libraries of Daniel Defoe and Phillips Farewell* (Berlin: H. Heidenreich, 1970), for what appears to be Defoe's voluminous collection of tracts and books relating to English political and constitutional history.

3. See William Temple, *An Essay upon the Original and Nature of Government,* Augustan Reprint Society, Pub. 109 (1964), p. 47; J. W. Johnson, "Of Differing Ages and Climes," *Journal of the History of Ideas,* 21 (1960), 479-480.

4. See *A New Discovery* (1691), in *A Second Volume of the Writings of the Author of The True-Born Englishman* (1705), p. 11; *A New Test of the Church of England's Loyalty* (1702), in *A True Collection of the Writings of the Author of The True Born English-man* (1703), p. 407. For Sherlock see his *The Case of the Allegiance due to Sovereign Powers* (1691).

5. *Modern Philology,* 66 (1968), 64. For helpful commentary on party in this period see Henry Horwitz, "Parties, Connections and Parliamentary Politics, 1689-1714," *Journal of British Studies,* 6 (1966), 45-69; Geoffrey Holmes, *British Politics in the Age of Anne* (London: Macmillan, 1967), pp. 51-115; Angus McInnes, *Robert Harley* (London: Victor Gollancz, 1970), pp. 28-40.

6. J. G. A. Pocock, *The Ancient Constitution and the Feudal Law* (New York: Norton, 1967), p. 16. For evidence of fundamental law and cultural lag in America see *Documents of American History,* ed. Henry Steele Commager, 8th ed. (New York: Appleton-Century-Crofts, 1968), p. 65.

7. *Of the Fundamental Laws, or Politick Constitution of this Kingdom,* in *State Tracts* (1692), p. 33. See also the Commons Resolution of 28 January 1689, which justified the people's rejection of James II because he had violated the fundamental laws.

8. *The Advantages of the Present Settlement* (1699) mentions "the Fundamental Constitutions of the Kingdom" (p. 19); *Queries to the New Hereditary Right-Men* (1710) mentions "the Fundamental Laws" (p. 10). In *An Answer To a Question That No Body Thinks Of* (1713), Defoe derived fundamental rights from statute law.

9. *The Observator,* no. 24 (11-15 July 1702). See also no. 99 (31 March-3 April 1703).

10. *The Old English Constitution* (1714), p. 3. Though, it must be admitted, always in tandem with the Law of Nature and the Law of God.

11. *Reflections,* p. 37.

12. *The Observator,* no. 24.

13. *The Free-Holders Plea* (1701), p. 3. For Defoe's rejection of Parliament's omnipotence see *Some Reflections on a Pamphlet Lately Publish'd* (1697), p. ii.

14. Christopher Hill, "The Norman Yoke," in *Puritanism and Revolution* (New York: Schocken, 1958); Pocock, *The Ancient Constitution,* passim; Quentin Skinner, "History and Ideology in the English Revolution," *Historical Journal,* 8 (1965), 151-178.

15. Pocock, p. 53; Marchamont Nedham, *The Case of the Commonwealth of England Stated* (1650), p. 14. See also Zera Fink, *The Classical Republicans* (Evanston, Ill.: Northwestern University Press, 1962),

p. 159. Arguing the Whig position Tutchin asserted that William was falsely called a conqueror; see *Observator,* no. 15 and no. 99.

16. *The True-Born Englishman* (1701), in *A True Collection,* pp. 5-6, 14, 30; *Jure Divino* (1706), VII, 18-19; IX, 9, 11, 13; *Of Royall Educacion,* ed. Karl Bulbring (London: David Nutt, 1895), p. 6.

17. Skinner, pp. 162-165; Pocock, pp. 150-151.

18. For a superficial equation of Locke and Defoe see Charles Bastide, *John Locke: See Théories Politiques et Leur Influence en Angleterre* (Paris: E. Leroux, 1907), p. 347; George Smock, "John Locke and the Augustan Age of Literature," *Philosophical Review,* 55 (1946), 275-278; Kenneth MacLean, *John Locke and English Literature of the Eighteenth Century* (New Haven: Yale University Press, 1936), p. 147; *Locke's Second Treatise of Civil Government,* ed. J. W. Gough (Oxford: Basil Blackwell, 1946), p. xxviii. Perhaps the least misleading essay is A. E. Levett, "Defoe," in *The Social and Political Ideas of Some English Thinkers of The Augustan Age,* ed. F. J. C. Hearnshaw (London: G. G. Harrap, 1928), pp. 157-187. The latest examination of Defoe's politics is Jean Béranger, *Les Hommes de Lettres et la Politique en Angleterre de la Révolution de 1688 à la Mort de George 1er* (Bordeaux: Faculté des Lettres et Sciences humaines de l'Université de Bordeaux, 1968). Professor Béranger's tome is thorough, sensible, and, as Johnson said of Addison's translations, licentiously paraphrastical. In an attempt to show how Defoe's ideas are similar to those of Temple, Tyrrell, Halifax, Sidney, and Locke, he seems to overlook those which distinguish Defoe's from those of his contemporaries.

19. John Locke, *Two Treatises of Government,* ed. Peter Laslett (Cambridge: Cambridge University Press, 1967), p. 108. All citations will be from this edition.

20. Bertrand Russell, *A History of Western Philosophy* (New York: Simon and Schuster, 1945), p. 629.

21. See *The Shortest Way to Peace and Union* (1703), in *A True Collection,* p. 452; *Jure Divino,* p. xii; *Some Considerations on a Law for Triennial Parliaments* (1716), p. 18; cf. Locke and Defoe on the founding of Rome; *Two Treatises,* II, 102 (p. 353), and Defoe, *A General History of the Pyrates,* ed. Manuel Schonhorn (London: Dent, 1972), pp. 7, 590.

22. *Mock Mourners* (1702), in *A True Collection,* p. 50; *Review,* V, 406. At the very end of his life, Defoe was still attacking the effeminacy of the landed class, gentry and lords; see *The Compleat English Gentleman,* ed. Karl Bulbring (London: David Nutt, 1890).

23. *Les Hommes de Lettres,* p. 339 and footnote.

24. J. G. A. Pocock, "Machiavelli, Harrington, and English Political Ideologies in the Eighteenth Century," *William and Mary Quarterly,* 22 (1965), 568.

25. Tyrrell, *Patriarcha non Monarcha,* pp. 98-100; Philip Hunton, *A Treatise of Monarchy* (1689), pp. 23-25; George Savile, Marquess of

Halifax, *The Character of a Trimmer*, in *Miscellanies* (1700), p. 7; Philip Warwick, *A Discourse of Government* (1694), p. 41.

26. *Reasons Against a War with France* (1701), in *A True Collection*, pp. 190-191. "A just Ballance of Power is the Life of Peace." *The Two Great Questions Considered* (1701), in *A True Collection*, p. 356; *Review*, III, 245-268.

27. Pocock, "English Political Ideologies," p. 568; *Honour and Prerogative* (1713), pp. 13-14.

28. *The Free-Holders Plea* (1701); *Review*, IV, 607, 614, 630; VIII, 25; IX, 82; *Seldom Comes a Better* (1710), p. 10.

29. *The Advantages of the Present Settlement* (1689), p. 16.

30. *The True-Born Englishman*, in *A True Collection*, p. 39.

31. John Cotton, *Scarronides*, in *Genuine Works* (1715), pp. 2, 4, 24.

32. *A New Discovery*, in *A Second Volume*, p. 6.

33. Robert Filmer, *Patriarcha and other Political Writings*, ed. Peter Laslett (Oxford: Blackwell, 1949), p. 11; see also *Review*, III, 389-390.

34. *An Essay on Projects*, in *The Earlier Life and Works of Daniel Defoe*, ed. Henry Morley (London: George Routledge, 1889), p. 150; *Review*, I, 347; II, 383.

35. Alexander Pope, *Pastoral Poetry and An Essay on Criticism*, ed. E. Audra and A. Williams (London: Methuen, 1961), p. 155. See *Jure Divino*, II, 20. Defoe had presented Nimrod as the first tyrant earlier in *Reflections*, p. 10. For Nimrod's monarchy after the division of the earth to Noah's three sons see *The Protestant Jesuite Unmask'd* (1704), p. 11.

36. Temple, *An Essay*, p. 49; Tyrrell, *Patriarcha non Monarcha*, p. 116.

37. See Hugo Grotius, *Of the Rights of War and Peace* (1715), Book II, chap. xiv; III, viii; Thomas Hobbes, *Leviathan*, ed. Michael Oakeshott (Oxford: Blackwell, n.d.), chaps. xix, xx; Tyrrell, *Bibliotheca Politica* (1718), p. 103.

38. The vision of a warrior-prince and a hereditary monarch defusing the destructive tensions of the succession issue can be read in Defoe's most dramatic and overlooked pamphlet, *The Succession to the Crown of England, Considered* (1701). Ostensibly an objective examination of the claimants to the English throne following the death of the Duke of Gloucester, the tract is really an impassioned plea for the suitability of James Scot, Monmouth's son, as King of England. For Defoe, royal blood and military merit — Scot had fought well under William in Flanders in 1697 — could resolve all of the contemporary disputes and differences between England and Scotland, place a rightful English king on the English throne, and dispose forever of Stuart pretensions. He returned to this theme in the *Review*, III, 333-336. Perhaps it should be recalled that Defoe devoted his political career and allegiance to two men, King William and Harley, of rare courage and bravery; see Dennis Rubini, *Court and Country*, 1688-1702 (London: Rupert Hart-Davis, 1967), pp. 13, 210.

39. *Party Tyranny,* in *Narratives of Early Carolina,* ed. Alexander Salley (New York: C. Scribner's Sons, 1911), p. 235. Maximillian Novak, in his *Defoe and the Nature of Man* (Oxford: Oxford University Press, 1963), discusses this passage from a different point of view (pp. 59-60), and has some illuminating things to say about Defoe's psychology and his search for a hero (pp. 129-161).

40. *The Secret History of State Intrigues in the Management of the Scepter* (1715), pp. 14-15. *The Secret History of the Scepter* appears to be an earlier printing of the same work which ends abruptly on p. 48 and is twenty-four pages shorter. The new title page and the addition of one gathering in the later work is a bibliographical problem that needs some investigation. Defoe's vigorous assertion of a Filmerian position, royal blood and lineal descent, probably results from the particular occasion: the accession to the throne of George I and Defoe's attempt to sanction it by divine and parliamentary law.

41. Clayton Roberts, *The Growth of Responsible Government in England* (Cambridge: Cambridge University Press, 1966), p. 412.

42. *Mock Mourners* (1702), pp. 58-59, 63.

43. See *The Old Whig and Modern Whig Reviv'd* (1717).

44. Locke, *Two Treatises,* II, 49 (p. 319).

45. See William B. Stein, "Robinson Crusoe," *Centennial Review,* 9 (1965), 278; H. W. Hausermann, "Aspects of Life and Thought in *Robinson Crusoe,*" *Review of English Studies,* 11 (1935), 449.

46. *Robinson Crusoe,* ed. J. Donald Crowley (Oxford: Oxford University Press, 1972), p. 220. All citations will be from this Oxford English Novels edition.

47. *Anarchy of a Limited or Mixed Monarchy,* in *Patriarcha,* ed. Laslett, p. 289. Defoe, of course, is no defender of absolutism, Stuart or otherwise. Professor Novak reminds me that the patriarchal model for government was a possible Whig model until Locke's became the guiding one. Defoe's "Filmerian" echoes seem freakish or unexpected, but only because he tried to graft a Revelationless Lockeian branch to his scriptural root. For Defoe's view of Adam as a freeholder and king see *Review,* III, 389-390, 431.

48. Gerald Straka, *Anglican Reaction to the Revolution of 1688* (Madison: State Historical Society of Wisconsin, 1962), pp. 65-79; Robert Fleming, *A Discourse of Earthquakes* (1693), deals with the event in a completely religious manner. Defoe, of course, was aware of the positive and negative interpretations of natural phenomena; see *Review,* III, 325-327.

49. The Dutch invasion fleet sailed out 19 October. Fresh gales from the S.E. later veered a great deal about E. Westerlies and a fierce storm blew it back and disrupted this attack. On 1 November the new expedition sailed out steering a northward course. A strong east wind almost caused the fleet to overshoot its mark, but on 5 November, "on a sud-

den, to all our wonder, it calmed a little, and then the wind turned into the south; and a soft and happy gale of wind carried in the whole fleet in four hours' time into Torbay." Gilbert Burnet, *History of his Own Time* (1724), p. 788, quoted in Edward B. Powley, *The English Navy in the Revolution of 1688* (Cambridge: Cambridge University Press, 1928), p. 83.

50. Gerald Straka, "The Final Phase of Divine Right Theory in England, 1688-1702," *English Historical Review*, 77 (1962), 642.

51. *An Essay on the History and Reality of Apparitions*, Talboys ed. (Oxford, 1840), XIII, 38; for Symon Patrick see Straka, p. 643.

52. See Elizabeth Pope, *Paradise Regained* (Baltimore: Johns Hopkins Press, 1947); Thomas Manton, *Christs Redemption and Transfiguration* (1685), p. 17. For Defoe on Manton see *Dialogue Between a Dissenter and The Observator* (1703), p. 14; *Review*, V, 478.

53. Maximillian Novak, "Crusoe the King and the Political Evolution of his Island," *Studies in English Literature*, 2 (1962), 338.

54. For an examination of the sources see my dissertation, "Defoe's Sources and Narrative Method" (University of Pennsylvania, 1963), Chap. II.

55. *Royal Religion* (1704), in *A Second Volume*, p. 479.

56. Tyrrell, *Patriarcha non Monarcha*, pp. 16-17.

57. We do not know the exact date of birth of Defoe's first-born son, Benjamin, but a coincidence should be noted. Defoe married in 1684, and Benjamin was born in 1685 or 1686. Defoe, then, would have been twenty-five or twenty-six years older than his son, a figure curiously paralleling the Crusoe-Friday relationship.

58. *The Family Instructor* (1720), p. 53.

59. Locke, *Two Treatises*, II, 1 (p. 286).

60. George A. Starr, *Defoe and Spiritual Autobiography* (Princeton: Princeton University Press, 1965), pp. 120-125; J. Paul Hunter, "Friday as a Convert," *Review of English Studies*, 14 (1963), 243-248.

61. Hilton Kramer, reviewing a Frank Stella retrospective exhibition, in *The New York Times*, 5 April 1970, Section II, p. 19.

62. *The Farther Adventures of Robinson Crusoe* (1719), p. 47. All citations will be from this edition.

63. *Pseudodoxia Epidemica*, in *Works*, ed. Geoffrey Keynes (London: Faber and Gwyer, 1928), III, 54 (Book IV, chap. xii).

64. Filmer, *Patriarcha*, p. 5. See Locke, *Two Treatises*, II, 36 (p. 311); Defoe, *The Protestant Jesuite Unmask'd*, p. 11. Everett Zimmerman posits a psychological need for the continuation; see his "Defoe and Crusoe," *ELH*, 38 (1971), 377-396.

65. *Of Royall Educacion*, p. 32. Professor Novak minimizes Crusoe's kingly status in his "Crusoe the King," pp. 345, 347.

66. *Jure Divino*, passim; *A Letter from a Dissenter in the City* (1710), pp. 13, 15; *The Farther Adventures*, pp. 51-52, 54-55.

67. George Clark, *The Later Stuarts*, 2d ed. (Oxford: Clarendon, 1961), p. 153; George Sherburn, *The Early Career of Alexander Pope* (Oxford: Clarendon Press, 1934), p. 35.

68. Father, captain, and king have been used continually and interchangeably to define Crusoe in both volumes.

69. Starr, *Defoe and Spiritual Autobiography*, pp. 22-23.

70. Henry Ainsworth, *Annotations upon the first book of Moses, called Genesis* (1616), unpaged, on Genesis 45; Isidore Epstein, *The Jewish Way of Life* (London: E. Goldston, 1946), pp. 141 ff.

71. *The History of the Bucaniers of America* (1699), sig. A2v.

72. *A General History of the Pyrates*, pp. 6, 308-309. See also the dissertation by Joel H. Baer, "Piracy Examined: A Study of Daniel Defoe's *General History of the Pirates* and its Milieu" (Princeton, 1970).

73. 23 May 1724. Other puffs, presumably by Defoe, appeared on 6 June, 29 August 1724.

74. *The Compleat English Gentleman*, pp. 14, 36, 37; *An Essay upon Projects*, in *The Earlier Life*, ed. Morley, pp. 31, 133.

75. *Of Captain Misson*, intro. Maximillian Novak, Augustan Reprint Society, Pub. 87 (1961), p. i.

76. Baer, "Piracy Examined," Chap. V.

77. *Of Royall Educacion*, pp. 47-48.

78. See Defoe's biographies: *The History of the Wars, of His Late Majesty Charles XII, King of Sweden*. The Second Edition. (1720), and *An Impartial History of the Life and Actions of Peter Alexowitz, The Present Czar of Muscovy* (1723).

79. *A Survey of the Constitution and Interests of the Empire* . . . , in *Miscellanies* (1705), I, 17.

80. Pocock, *The Ancient Constitution*, p. 145.

81. I would like to thank Maximillian Novak for his continuing generosity and his pertinent and helpful suggestions here and elsewhere.

II

THE NIGHTMARES OF STREPHON: NYMPHS OF THE CITY IN THE POEMS OF SWIFT, BAUDELAIRE, ELIOT

C. J. Rawson

Professor of English and Comparative Literature, University of Warwick

This paper is partly concerned with exploring some aspects of Swift's poetic treatment of cities, and of those typical inhabitants of cities, the whore and the fine lady. Two other city poets, Baudelaire and Eliot, belong, so to speak, to the subplot. They are there to illustrate, by similarity or difference, certain features of Swift's writing, and of a poetic tradition to which he made some memorable contributions.[1]

I begin with the "Description of the Morning" ([1709] *Poems,* I, 123 ff.), a parody of poetical descriptions of dawn, as well as a "realistic" description of a town scene. It is one of Swift's relatively few poems in the heroic couplet, and puts it to subheroic use. The form is here not only parodied, but (perhaps more important) pointedly reduced to a banal flatness:

> Now hardly here and there an Hackney-Coach
> Appearing, show'd the Ruddy Morn's Approach.
> Now *Betty* from her Masters Bed had flown,
> And softly stole to discompose her own.
>
> (11.1-4)

This poem and its companion piece, the "Description of a City

Shower," belong to a proud tradition of city poems which includes Juvenal's third and Boileau's sixth satires (Boileau's satire is rather close to Swift's poems in several details, and has a vivid account of a "city shower"), Baudelaire's "Tableaux Parisiens," and Eliot's "Preludes" and "Morning at the Window." But Swift strikes a more sober and deadpan note than any of the others. There is no Juvenalian indignation, and none of Boileau's irritated grandiloquence. Nor is there the Baudelairian note of suffering self-involvement, the touch of self-glamourizing eloquence, the fascinated wonder at the "Fourmillante cité, cité pleine de rêves."[2]

Eliot's laconic notation of city squalors is perhaps closest to Swift's. He is known to have been deeply interested in Swift. He once intended to write an essay on Swift as a poet, among other studies of seventeenth- and eighteenth-century poets. This intention was not fulfilled. But he made, over the years, a number of memorable comments upon him. His imagination was impregnated with Swiftian presences and echoes.[3] It was Yeats and not Eliot who said in so many words that he was "haunted" by Swift,[4] but Eliot has revealed that Swift, in combination with Yeats, was a principal element in that "familiar compound ghost" who appears to Eliot in *Little Gidding*.[5]

Both poets, especially in their earlier works, in the "Description of a City Shower" or parts of the *Waste Land,* display a strongly localized sense of London, a rhetorical as well as a topographical feeling, mixed with irony, for its street-names and place-names, and also a sense that the decays of London evoke the fall of other great cities, notably Troy. And it is Eliot, in the "Preludes" and "Morning at the Window," who, of all the poets I have mentioned, most nearly approached the flat descriptive idiom of the "Description of the Morning." But even Eliot departs fairly readily from this flatness, dramatizing the comic scene into a sweeping mock-cynical pathos ("the damp souls of housemaids," the "aimless smile that hovers in the air"),[6] and allowing himself an unSwiftian release of lyric impulse and meditative luxury:

> I am moved by fancies that are curled
> Around these images, and cling:
> The notion of some infinitely gentle
> Infinitely suffering thing.[7]

The disciplines of parody help Swift to keep clear of such self-commitment and its sentimentalizing risks. But parody, and especially mock-heroic, often preserves a perverted residue of original grandeurs. Swift's mock-*descriptio* of Dawn, however, has the effect not so much of inflating or deflating, as of *leveling*. The commonplace of Aurora rising from Tithonus's bed gives way to an unfussily earthbound glimpse of Betty stealing from her master's bed to discompose her own. An almost novelistic episode, something out of Scarron or Fielding, is sketched out, passingly, with a graceful, laconic completeness.[8] Baudelaire's "Crépuscule du Matin" and Eliot's "Preludes" also evoke episodes that might, in a sense, be developed into fictions beyond the limits of the descriptive set piece: see Baudelaire's "bruns adolescents" tormented by unhealthy dreams, for example, or the suggestions in Eliot of an element of narrated activity ("You tossed a blanket from the bed, . . . " "His soul stretched tight across the skies . . ."). But there is nothing in either Eliot or Baudelaire of Swift's take-it-or-leave-it factuality. Eliot's shadowy and unnamed figures, and Baudelaire's generalized adolescents, both come charged with an authorial fervor of romantic agony.

But Swift's Betty should most strongly be contrasted with those solitary fallen women who appear in such post-Baudelairian city poems of Night and Dawn as Wilde's "Impression du Matin." There "one pale woman all alone," standing under a gaslight, is set against Whistlerian colors of fog and river, the central figure of a sentimental set piece. Betty is neither a central figure, nor sentimentalized. Swift's poem has no Wildeian luxuries of fascination or recoil, just as it preserves no grandeurs of mock-heroic (a later poem, "A Beautiful Young Nymph Going to Bed" [1731], is, like Wilde's, about a whore at the end of her night's work, and has some celebrated anatomical squalors which may call Baudelaire to mind, and to which I shall return). In the "Description of the Morning," Betty takes her place in a flat but animated world which includes a "Slipshod Prentice," Moll whirling her mop, a loud chimney sweep, turnkeys, bailiffs, proverbial "School-Boys . . . with Satchels in their Hands," and other citizens.[9] Introducing the poem in *Tatler*, No. 9, Steele said that Swift "described things exactly as they happen: he never forms fields, or nymphs, or groves, where they are not. . . . " This catches the mixture of

realism and parody well because it suggests the resolute avoidance, rather than the baroque exploitation, of traditional poeticisms. Roger Savage has said that, in this poem,

Warbling larks and tuneful linnets become coalmen and chimney-
sweeps; the shepherd-swain about to wake and sound his jovial pipe
becomes the turnkey counting his flock of thieves as they come in from
night-pasture. [10]

But these parodic patterns, though inescapable, are relatively
uninsistent. They are a token of certain stylistic refusals, but they
are transcended into a primary idiom of sober description. For
many Augustans, mock-heroic routines, and other stylizations,
acted as a strongly visible "dress of thought," covering (or distanc-
ing or modifying) the unsettling nakedness of fact. Swift was less
concerned than some with such signposted disguises, but he
shared the impulse, and it may be that for him also a dash of
parody seemed a desirable stylistic protection against, and even a
condition of release for, the rowdy indecorum of fact. But, if so,
the "dress" is very plain, and Swift clearly felt it even more important to avoid the excesses of *over*-dress (heroic and mock-heroic
alike) than the vulnerabilities of nudity.

By the late 1690s, as is well known, Swift had abandoned Cow-
leyan pindarics and "serious Couplets." He did not often return
to the less "serious" couplets of the "Description" poems either.
He experimented with various lighter, more deflating, or more
"popular" verse forms. In "The Discovery" ([1699] *Poems,* I, 61
ff.) and "A Ballad on the Game of Traffick" ([1702] *Poems,* I,
74-75), he explored variant kinds of witty quatrain, a stanza
which he was later to develop into a style anticipating or resembling some of T. S. Eliot's early *vers de société.* For example, the
satiric quatrains on financiers in "The Run upon the Bankers"
([1720] *Poems,* I, 239):

> Money, the Life-blood of the Nation,
> Corrupts and stagnates in the Veins,
> Unless a proper Circulation
> Its Motion and its Heat maintains,
>   (11.9-12)

are comparable, in meter as well as in tone and atmosphere, to the stanzas about dividends and Exchequer Bonds in Eliot's "The Hippopotamus" or "A Cooking Egg."[11]

Among his other metrical experiments were the sprawling garrulous rhythms of "Mrs. Harris's Petition" ([1701] *Poems*, I, 68 ff.), which anticipate Ogden Nash rather than Eliot:

> So next Morning we told *Whittle*, and he fell a Swearing;
> Then my Dame *Wadgar* came, and she, you know, is
>   thick of Hearing;
> *Dame*, said I, as loud as I could bawl, do you know what
>   a Loss I have had?
> Nay, said she, my Lord *Collway*'s Folks are all very sad.
>   (11.24-27)

But the "Petition" is also the first of several brilliant mimicries of servant-talk, looking forward not only to "Mary the Cook-Maid's Letter" ([1718] III, 985 ff.), but to famous feats of cliché-anthologizing, of demotic as well as of polite speech, in prose.[12] It is a talent which Eliot displayed very memorably at least once, in the second half of "A Game of Chess" in the *Waste Land*.[13]

Over the years, Swift became one of the masters in a great English tradition of serious light verse which includes Skelton, Butler, Prior, Byron, and Auden. Byron said, Swift "beats us all hollow, his rhymes are wonderful."[14] Swift recognized as much as the others that light verse could be made a vehicle of serious commentary, and that an avoidance of the more officially recognized "serious" styles did not necessarily imply triviality. "I have been only a Man of Rhimes, and that upon Trifles, never having written serious Couplets in my Life; yet never any without a moral View," he wrote in 1732 (*Correspondence*, IV. 52). Among the forms of light verse which he adopted instead, the principal one was the Hudibrastic,[15] which he developed into that sinewy, flexible style, with its conversational manner, its controlled digressiveness and its cheeky rhyming, so admired by Byron.

Swift's abandonment of the decasyllabic or "heroic" couplet (he used it less than Byron, for example) extended even to those satiric or mock-heroic or informally colloquial contexts to which Pope and other contemporaries were able triumphantly to adapt the form. In the 1730s, both Swift and Pope wrote apologias for their own satire, in imitation of Horace, *Sat.*, II, i, and their respective kinds of informality may usefully be contrasted. Swift's poem begins:

> Since there are persons who complain
> There's too much satire in my vein . . .
> ([1730] *Poems*, II, 489)

Pope's begins:

> There are (I scarce can think it, but am told)
> There are to whom my Satire seems too bold . . . [16]

Both are informal, easy, colloquial. But Swift's colloquial ease is that of brisk, dry chatter, whereas Pope's has a proud witty sweep, a formalized freedom and a kind of excited grandeur not unlike that of Yeats (Yeats's deep regard for Swift, and his dislike of Pope, may be paradoxically connected with this: did Yeats shy, in Pope, from an arrogant fervor too like his own?).[17] Pope's poem, though imitating Horace, is full of Juvenalian majesties of self-projection: "To VIRTUE ONLY and HER FRIENDS, A FRIEND," "Scriblers or Peers, alike are *Mob* to me" (11.121, 140).[18] Swift, on the other hand, though often called Juvenalian, keeps the attack in a low key ("Must I commend against my con-science / Such stupid blasphemy and nonsense" [11.37-38]), shortening his Horatian original so as to evade some high gestures, with a short dry angry boast coming only at the end (and through the mouth of his "adversary" or interlocutor at that). The metrical difference has much to do with these differences of tone, Pope's couplets preserving, within the informal idiom, much of their "heroic" flavor, Swift's Hudibrastics waiving all such claims from the start. Meter is, of course, only one contributory factor in the total effect, but it is fair to say that the initial choice of meter was already, in both poets, an expression of personality.

The Hudibrastic meter was not only a guard against "heroic" pretension in a limited sense. The fluent finalities of the high couplet gave it a certain tendency to orderly containment which Swift's temperament repudiated (although, as the ending of the "City Shower" or the lines on Walpole in "To Mr. Gay" show, he could himself transcend this tendency in order to do justice to the vitality of disorderly fact). In the face of life's teeming disorders, the order of art seemed to Swift a falsifying thing, and the confident accents of priests of the muses a kind of misplaced rhetoric. In a satire on Vanbrugh ([1703] *Poems,* I, 80) he wrote:

> And now he spreads his little Fans,
> (For all the Muses Geese are Swans)
> And borne on fancy's Pinions, thinks,
> He soars sublimest when he Sinks.
>
> (11.49-52)

This manuscript of "Vanbrug's House," like its fuller printed version (*Poems,* I, 105 ff.),[19] is full of characteristic Swiftian jokes against the republic of bad poets: garrets, castles in the air, poverty, soaring-and-sinking, a maggotlike destructiveness of ancient edifices of sweetness and light. The little parenthetic mock-courtesy of "(For all the Muses Geese are Swans)" is instructive. Its ironic point is, of course, that swans like Vanbrugh are actually geese, and there is no Yeatsian glow at the thought that swans might grow out of ugly ducklings: "For even daughters of the swan can share / Something of every paddler's heritage."[20] It seems possible that Swift's line mingled with Hans Andersen's story in Yeats's mind, to be sublimed not only by a grand reversal of valuations (openly soaring "sublimest when he Sinks"), but by Yeats's bold and somewhat Popeian decasyllabic sweep.

Swift made no Yeatsian claims for farmyard birds, but he did recurrently compare poets to them. In "The Progress of Poetry" ([1720] *Poems,* I, 230 f.), a poet is again compared to a farmer's goose who, if in funds, is too fat to fly, and if hungry, "singing flies, and flying sings, / While from below all *Grub-street* rings."[21] The sublime counterpart of Swift's goose is Baudelaire's albatross, proud and beautiful in the air, but unable to walk on the ground: the poet as a high lonely figure, ill adapted to society's earthbound ways. Baudelaire would not have shared Swift's contempt for that high place of poets, the garret, but that is a matter of period and of differing cultural attitudes. Swift resists high-flying *as such,* and part of him instinctively thought of poetry as high-flying. The Hudibrastic meter is a stylistic declaration of this resistance.

But Swift's most notorious poetic deflations are those which are directed against the idealizations of conventional love poetry, or which make use of excremental imagery as a comically or harshly degrading reminder of the animal facts; and there is an important group of poems which, like some of the city poems, have a signposted mock-pastoral element. Just as the city squalors are played off against poetic inventions of Arcadian innocence and peace, so the physical realities of the human animal are played off against the erotic idealism, and the stylized plangencies, of the pastoral universe of Strephons, Chloes, Celias and their like. And as in the city poems, more is usually at work than a simple parody of idealizing poeticisms.

"The Progress of Beauty" ([1719] *Poems,* I, 225 ff.) is the first of the Strephon-Celia poems. It is a piece of neometaphysical *vers de société,* some of whose language and cadence seems to look back to Marvell ("Twixt earthly Femals and the Moon / All Parallells exactly run," [11.9-10]), but which seems even closer in feeling to T. S. Eliot:

> When first Diana leaves her Bed
> Vapors and Steams her Looks disgrace,
> A frouzy dirty colour'd red
> Sits on her cloudy wrinckled Face.
>
> But by degrees when mounted high
> Her artificiall Face appears
> Down from her Window in the Sky,
> Her Spots are gone, her Visage clears.
> (11.1-8)

Until the last line and a half, which make it clear that Diana is the Moon, not a woman, she seems a figure from the world of Sweeney or Grishkin. The parallel between the moon and the unchaste woman (a reversal of "the conventional comparison of the chaste lady with the pure Diana")[22] is found again in Eliot's "Rhapsody on a Windy Night," where the moon and the streetwalker are made to blur into one another:

> The lamp hummed:
> "Regard the moon,

La lune ne garde aucune rancune,
She winks a feeble eye,
She smiles into corners.
She smooths the hair of the grass.
The moon has lost her memory.
A washed-out smallpox cracks her face, . . ."

The main and overt influences are Laforguian, and the haunting and ambiguous fluidities of interpenetration are far removed from the ruthless, clipped Marvellian logic of Swift's analogy. But the subject matter of the analogy in both poets is the same, and Eliot's last line has a certain imaginative kinship with the cracked face of the Diana-Celia of Swift's poem ("The Paint by Perspiration cracks, / And falls in Rivulets of Sweat, . . . Each Night a Bit drops off her Face," [11.37-38, 87]).[23]

Swift's poem elaborates its parallel between "earthly Femals and the Moon," so that all it says about Diana is applicable to Strephon's Celia. Its theme, a recurrent one in the whole group to which this poem belongs, is that if Strephon could see Celia as she got out of bed, "All reeking in a cloudy Steam, / Crackt Lips, foul Teeth, and gummy Eyes" (11.14-15), he would be horrified. Luckily, Celia can restore herself with cosmetics, so that "after four important Hours / Celia's the Wonder of her Sex" (11.53-54). But there comes a time when nothing is left for the cosmetic art to work on, and "The best Mechanick Hand must fayl" (1.79).

At this point, Celia is like the waning moon, and the waning is seen, surprisingly, but aptly as it turns out, as a mechanical disintegration (parts dropping off each night):

> And this is fair Diana's Case
> For, all Astrologers maintain
> Each Night a Bit drops off her Face
> When Mortals say she's in her Wain.
> (11.85-88)

This not only reverses the preceding image of mechanical or cosmetic patching up, but is in turn reversed by tentative but finally unfulfilled notions of a new mechanical reassembly. As, ashamed to be seen in her growing ugliness, "rotting Celia stroles the Street

/ When sober Folks are all a-bed" (11.103-104), she starts to de-
compose, and cosmetics are not enough:

> No Painting can restore a Nose,
> Nor will her Teeth return again.
>
> Two Balls of Glass may serve for Eyes,
> White Lead can plaister up a Cleft,
> But these alas, are poor Supplyes
> If neither Cheeks, nor Lips be left.
>   (11.111-116)[24]

This has a kind of horrific jauntiness, and the poem closes with
a gay mock-gallant appeal to the gods of love to "Send us new
Nymphs with each new Moon." The jauntiness is not present in a
more famous poem of twelve years later, "A Beautiful Young
Nymph Going to Bed" ([1731] *Poems,* II, 580 ff.). Here also a decaying whore is held together in working hours by means of artificial hair, eye, eyebrows, teeth, breasts, etc., which conceal "Her
Shankers, Issues, running Sores" (1.30), and she is also heavily
cosmeticized. Before retiring to sleep, she takes off her artificial
parts one by one, revealing the real presence beneath the patch-
work. The flayed woman of the *Tale* is brought to mind; but the
poem, though more circumstantial, is, as I have argued elsewhere,[25] less shocking because it is a leisurely formulaic elaboration, working out a clearly spelled out moral theme, rather than
generating a sudden "gratuitous" shock.

Nevertheless, the details are horrific, and the poem is often instanced as an example of unhealthy intensity and morbid body-
hatred on Swift's part. Ehrenpreis counters this view by citing several parallels which show that the main formula of an apparently
beautiful woman (or handsome man) held together by artificial
parts was a literary commonplace before and after Swift.[26] Swift's
description possibly outdoes most of the others in scabrous detail;
but this might be partly due to a desire to play the gimmick for all
it is worth, outdoing the competitors with a cheeky perfectionist
bravura. Such bravura would not be inconsistent with the dry, as
it were poker-faced, quality of Swift's enumeration.

On the other hand, Swift adds elements that do not seem to
exist in the analogues. He has his heroine wake up to find that
during the night

A wicked Rat her Plaister stole,
Half eat, and dragg'd it to his Hole.
The Crystal Eye, alas, was miss't;
And *Puss* had on her Plumpers p——st....
(11.59-62)

And while poor Corinna labors every morning to "recollect the
scatter'd Parts" (1.68), the poet's "bashful Muse" turns away,[27]
and the poem ends with a dry abruptness which surely subdues
any previous overtones of playful fantastication:

Corinna in the Morning dizen'd,
Who sees, will spew; who smells, be poison'd.
(11.73-74)

This extreme dryness, and the tart *literalness* of the outburst,
are relatively rare in Swift's verse. Even in the "Beautiful Young
Nymph," the eruption is very brief, a spasm of irritation (real or
rhetorical or both) as the cumulative force of the whole scabrous
enumeration gathers in the poet's mind in the conclusion. "Strephon and Chloe" and "Cassinus and Peter" ([both 1731, and published as a pamphlet with the "Beautiful Young Nymph" in 1734]
Poems, II, 584 ff.) are, almost throughout, much more animated
in manner and feeling. In the first, Strephon (along with many
other swains) woos the beautiful Chloe. Modern courtship is
described with a brisk headlong grace which calls to mind the
Byron of *Beppo* or *Don Juan:*

Think what a Case all Men are now in,
What ogling, sighing, toasting, vowing!
What powder's Wigs! What Flames and Darts!
What Hampers full of bleeding Hearts!
(11.33-36)

But the principal purpose of "Strephon and Chloe" is to expose
the foolish idealism of Strephon, who does not expect, and cannot
bear, to find a human reality behind his wife's fine clothes.
Chloe, unlike the heroines of "The Progress of Beauty" and the
"Beautiful Young Nymph," is not a withered hag, but only a nor-
mal girl, who, after the eating and drinking of her wedding day,
will naturally have some unromantic bodily needs. Strephon had
been shy of touching this goddess, but he now

> Cry'd out, ye Gods, what sound is this?
> Can *Chloe,* heav'nly *Chloe* — ?
> (11.177-178)

As the smell grows and he recognizes that she is "As *mortal* as himself at least" (1.186), he is himself emboldened "To reach the Pot on t'other Side" (1.190). The result is a situation out of slapstick farce:

> And as he fill'd the reeking Vase,
> Let fly a Rouzer in her Face.
> (11.191-192)

This devolution into farce marks a decisive and vigorous change. The "little *Cupids*" who had attended on the lovers with an aerial delicacy out of *The Rape of the Lock,* now vanish forever, taking with them the brittle idealisms of the polite world (11.193 ff.). (Their feelings of shame reappear, much transformed, in the two golden Cupidons of the *Waste Land,* [11.80-81].) The marriage is vulgarized, not improved. If there is some dubious gain in the fact that the couple "learn to call a Spade, a Spade,"[28] the advantages of seeing them freed "from all Constraint" are hardly seductive (11.203 ff.). Smelly intimacies, coarse words, and free farting replace decency as well as pretence:

> For, Beauty, like supreme Dominion,
> Is best supported by Opinion;
> If Decency brings no Supplies,
> Opinion falls, and Beauty dies.
> (11.223-226)

But if "Decency " itself is a mere social fiction, Swift would nevertheless not do without it. The ambiguity, or impasse, is characteristic. Between the civilized lie and the beastly truth, the middle way is hard to find. The poem may seem to warn the Strephons against poetic fictions which impute aethereality to the fair sex. But the moral is not quite as cosy as the commonsense critics would have it. If Strephon had known the bodily facts beforehand, the marriage, far from being started on a sounder basis, would probably not have occurred at all:

O *Strephon,* e'er that fatal Day
When *Chloe* stole your Heart away,
Had you but through a Cranny spy'd
On House of Ease your future Bride,
In all the Postures of her Face,
Which Nature gives in such a Case;
Distortions, Groanings, Strainings, Heavings;
'Twere better you had lickt her Leavings,
Than from Experience find too late
Your Goddess grown a filthy Mate.
Your Fancy then had always dwelt
On what you saw, and what you smelt;
Would still the same Ideas give ye,
As when you spy'd her on the Privy.
And, spight of *Chloe*'s Charms divine,
Your Heart had been as whole as mine.
                                    (11.235-250)

When Swift asks near the end of the poem, "What Edifice can long endure, / Rais'd on a Basis unsecure?" (11.299-300), he does not primarily mean a more clearheaded acceptance of the facts of the body. He means that the body must take second place to Sense, Wit, Decency, Prudence, Good Nature (11.307-309). The "Decency" which was earlier identified with sentimental or truth-evading conventions (11.225, 252), is now identified with a good decorum which must surely keep the cloacal necessities just as firmly out of sight.

Reality and artifice, in other words, are at their usual tug of war. We must in some sense face the reality of the flayed woman and the gutted beau, but decency and civilization demand that they also be kept out of sight. It is sentimental of the critics to say that Swift resolved the dilemma by some kind of "compromise" or middle way; it is the fact that he never resolved it at all which gives his work its particular urgency and truth. The imbecile "author" of the "Digression concerning Madness," extolling "the Assistance of Artificial *Mediums,* false Lights, refracted Angles, Varnish, and Tinsel," is the very same who, in the next sentence, speaks more than he knows for his satirist-creator when he says that the art "of *Unmasking* . . . has never been allowed fair Usage, either in the *World* or the *Play-House*" (*Works,* I, 109).

In some ways Swift's foolish "author" resembles the Baudelaire of "L'Amour du mensonge":

> Mais ne suffit-il pas que tu sois l'apparence,
> Pour réjouir un coeur qui fuit la vérité?
> Qu' importe ta bêtise ou ton indifférence?
> Masque ou décor, salut! J'adore ta beauté.

Such outrageous paradoxes are for "moderns" to wallow in. Baudelaire in other moods, like Swift's "author," enjoyed digging beneath surfaces to the squalors within. The famous prefatory poem addressed to the *hypocrite lecteur* speaks of our fondness for the repugnant realities of life's Satanic puppet show:

> C'est le Diable qui tient les fils qui nous remuent!
> Aux objets répugnants nous trouvons des appas.

But where Baudelaire embraces with eloquent sensuousness the visceral squalors of flayed women and decaying nymphs, Swift's "author" cannot take more than a limited dose of such pungent realities. When he tries to dissect "the Carcass of *Humane Nature,*" he quickly finds that it "*smelt* so strong, I could preserve it no longer" (*Works,* I.77). The Baudelairian cherishing of our uglinesses of mind and body, "Comme les mendiants nourrissent leur vermine," is not for him. But nor is it for Swift himself, who would not deny the existence of the vermin or the beggars (and offers some grim descriptions of both), but would not encourage anything that increased their visibility in everyday life or allowed their open presence to impair the hardwon decencies of civilized existence.

Like Baudelaire, Swift thought of life as a shoddy spectacle, puppet show or bad play, full of falsehood and disguise, yet all too wretchedly real. The blurring of world and playhouse into unexpected interpenetrations occurs in "Strephon and Chloe," as in the *Tale of a Tub,* but in a lower and frankly more farcical key. The awakening to an ugly reality (Strephon farting in Chloe's face as he fills the pot) happens paradoxically through a stylized chamberpot accident which comes straight out of slapstick comedy. When Pope called Swift "an Avenging Angel of wrath," he spoke at the same time of Swift's breaking his "Vial of Indignation over the heads of the wretched pityful creatures of this World" (*Correspondence,* III, 108).[29] Sublimities of punitive fury were aptly seen as going hand in hand with a farcical indignity. Swift's own saying that life was "a Farce . . . in every sense but the most important one, for it is a ridiculous tragedy, which is the worst kind of composition," (*Correspondence,* III, 456) similarly contains other elements than the grandiose poignancy we tend to see in it. If truth is painful, and indecorous, like a play in bad taste, it is also "ridiculous," funny — and, in some paradoxical ways, just as artificial.

If the chamberpot farce in "Strephon and Chloe," like the satirist's vials of indignation broken on the heads of mankind, is a means of awakening us to reality, that particular reality, in the poem at least, is rejected by Swift. Its faecal intimacies are not much better than the glamorized vacuities which they replace, though clearly more physical or "organic." But later in the poem, as sometimes in Baudelaire, it is to the "mechanisms" of the puppet show that life (disguise *and innards* both) is compared:

> Why is a handsome Wife ador'd
> By ev'ry Coxcomb, but her Lord?
> From yonder Puppet-Man inquire,
> Who wisely hides his Wood and Wire;
> Shows *Sheba*'s Queen completely drest,
> And *Solomon* in Royal Vest;
> But, view them litter'd on the Floor,
> Or strung on Pegs behind the Door;
> *Punch* is exactly of a Piece
> With *Lorraine*'s Duke, and Prince of *Greece.*
> (11.283-292)

Tangible excrement and the idiot void, human viscera and bits of string are closer to one another in this vision than we think, or than Swift might openly claim. Appearance and Reality (those sturdy handmaids of the critic) are locked in an unnatural embrace, and Swift finally knows (unlike the critics) that he cannot separate them. Still less can he decide which to prefer, for Appearance is not only "false Lights" but "Decency," and Reality is frank "unmasking" *and* the Yahoo beast.

If it seems complacent to see in this a simple fondness for

middle ways and golden means, it is also facile to overemphasize morbidity and disgust. The verse of "Strephon and Chloe" has a witty *élan,* which stops well short of Rabelaisian expansiveness, but which neither seems frozen to a morbid constraint, nor buried in indulgent sensualities of squalor. A live, intelligent, and not unjoyful vitality animates the portrayals, not only of vacuous courting rituals ("ogling, sighing, toasting, vowing!" [1.34]), but also of excremental fact ("Distortions, Groanings, Strainings, Heavings" [1.241]).

A similar degree (if not quite the same kind) of animation occurs in "Cassinus and Peter" ([1731] *Poems,* II, 593 ff.). In this lighthearted amalgam of mock-pastoral and undergraduate fun (the two heroes are "Two College Sophs of *Cambridge* Growth" [1.1]), the ironic contrast between erotic idealization and excremental fact is established more crudely or formulaically. Peter visits Cassinus and finds him dejected, a dejection connected with his beloved Cælia, but whose exact cause neither Peter nor we can discover for over a hundred lines. After a protracted mock-suspense, as Cassinus grows more and more frantic and Peter more and more curious, the famous punch line occurs at the close:

> Nor wonder how I lost my Wits;
> Oh! *Caelia, Caelia Caelia* sh——.
> (11.117-118)

As in "Strephon and Chloe," the verse has a Byronic lightness, playful rhyming, a brisk animation of movement. It lacks the more many-sided sharpness of "Strephon and Chloe," however, and much of its vigor lies in the zany elaboration of mystery and the comic drop of the final revelation. The last line has become famous because it shocked Lawrence, Huxley, and others into healthy-minded denunciations of Swift's bowel-hatred and misogyny.[30] The verve, and the formulaic arrangement itself, of this poem make very clear not only Swift's fun, but the exposure of Cassinus as a bit of an ass. The irony spells out not bowel-hatred, but the fatuous naivety of the bowel-hater.

But Huxley and others were talking not only of this poem, but of its more famous predecessor, "The Lady's Dressing Room"

([1730] *Poems,* II, 524 ff.), where the offending line also occurs
(1.118). Strephon steals into Celia's room and discovers the detri-
tus of her toilette, "various Combs for various Uses, / Fill'd up
with Dirt" (11.20-21), a paste composed of "Sweat, Dandriff,
Powder, Lead and Hair" (1.24),[31] "Ointments good for scabby
Chops" (1.36), a basin for spitting and spewing, dirty towels,
petticoats, handkerchiefs, stockings, tweezers. These things are
enumerated with a headlong exuberance which, despite the
squalor of the material, is prevented in various ways from acquir-
ing the aggressive disturbance of some satiric enumerations in
Gulliver's Travels, where catalogs of abundance tend to suggest,
or to mimic, irrepressible energies of evil. Here, on the other
hand, an urbane elegance of descriptive notation, a lively exacti-
tude of reportage, the metrical lightness, the early signposting of
the parody of idealistic inflation and gallant compliment ("Strephon... / ...swears how damnably the Men lie, / In calling
Celia sweet and cleanly," [11.16-18]) keep any undue intensities
at bay.

A Gulliverian image in the poem helps to define its essential
difference from Gulliverian acerbity:

> The Virtues we must not let pass,
> Of *Celia's* magnifying Glass.
> When frighted *Strephon* cast his Eye on't
> It shew'd the Visage of a Gyant.
> A Glass that can to Sight disclose,
> The smallest Worm in *Celia's* Nose,
> And faithfully direct her Nail
> To squeeze it out from Head to Tail;
> For catch it nicely by the Head,
> It must come out alive or dead.
> (11.59-68)

This repeats a joke which occurs several times in *Gulliver,* where
the relative sizes of Lilliputians, Brobdingnagians, and Gulliver
himself enforce some ironies of visual perspective:[32] Brobdingnagian women drive home to Gulliver how human ladies would
look to a Lilliputian eye: the Nurse with her "monstrous Breast
...The Nipple...half the Bigness of my Head...the Dug so
varified with Spots, Pimples and Freckles, that nothing could
appear more nauseous" (*Works,* XI, 91); the Beggar "with a Can-

cer in her Breast, swelled to a monstrous Size, full of Holes, in two or three of which I could have easily crept, and covered my whole Body," and the lice of the Beggars, with their limbs distinctly visible, "and their Snouts with which they rooted like Swine" (*Works,* XI, 112-113), etc. . . . There is comedy here too. Gulliver, the projector, would have done some dissecting of one of these lice "if I had proper Instruments (which I unluckily left behind me in the Ship) although indeed the Sight was so nauseous, that it perfectly turned my Stomach" (*Works,* XI, 113). But the last words show how quickly the comedy blackens. Grotesqueries like that of the Maid of Honour who used to set Gulliver "astride upon one of her Nipples" (*Works,* XI, 119) have a Rabelaisian extravagance, but it is Rabelais, as Coleridge said, "in a dry place,"[33] and charged with astringency and revulsion. (It is interesting that Baudelaire, so much more often than Swift given to indulgences of revulsion, has, in "La Géante," a similar erotic fantasy involving a young giantess, but full of a genial, tender and undisgusted longing to enjoy and explore the magnificent geography of her body.) And Swift's humor on this theme in *Gulliver's Travels* is closely related to some Kafkaesque horrors, like that of the huge rat in the first chapter of book II which might have torn Gulliver to pieces (*Works,* XI, 93).

The metaphorical worms in Celia's nose are hardly to be compared with the lurid nausea of the Beggar's breast, or even with the tart disgust of the Nurse's "Spots, Pimples and Freckles." They belong much more closely to a world of Hudibrastic fun.[34] The passage from the poem is something of a set piece, with (surprisingly) a quality of light, almost balletic, animation:

> And faithfully direct her Nail
> To squeeze it out from Head to Tail;
> For catch it nicely by the Head,
> It must come out alive or dead.
> (11.65-68)

This animation is quite special. The worms have neither the energetic bestiality of the Gulliverian lice, nor for example the teeming and deathly splendors of the "noirs bataillons / De larves" which come out of the stomach of Baudelaire's "Charogne," that "carcasse superbe" which opens up like a filthy-smelling flower.

Here, as the poet compares the carrion by the wayside to the fate of his mistress, the serenities of "La Géante" are wholly absent.

The theme of worms doing their business on the dead is one to which Baudelaire often returned, sometimes with surprising self-identifications, often with a queer tenderness, and always with a special and vivid intensity. In "Je t'adore à l'égal de la voûte nocturne," Baudelaire compares his pursuit of his cold mistress to worms attacking a corpse; in "Remords Posthume," the guiltlike worm will eat away at the skin of the mistress's corpse; in "Le Mort Joyeux," the poet invites the worms, "noirs compagnons, . . . Philosophes viveurs, fils de la pourriture," to take him freely; in "La servante au grand coeur," the lovely passage beginning, "Les morts, les pauvres morts, ont de grandes douleurs," which speaks of the dead with an almost sensuous nostalgic compassion, has a vivid line about their "Vieux squelettes gelés travaillés par le ver."

Swift's animation in the passage about Celia's nose is that of deadpan humor. Baudelaire's is of horrified enchantment. The difference of subject matter accounts for much of the difference. The special dryness with which Swift can play with a metaphorical fantasy of worms eating away at the human frame is something of which Baudelaire would have been incapable. In *A Full and True Account of the Solemn Procession to the Gallows, at the Execution of William Wood, Esquire and Hard-ware-man, Written in the Year 1724,* we read:

> We hear the Body is not yet interred; which occasions many Speculations. But what is more wonderful, it is positively assured by many who pretend to have been Eye-witnesses; that there does not appear the least Alteration in any one Lineament or Feature of his Countenance, nor visible Decay in his whole Frame, further than what had been made by Worms long before his Execution. The Solution of which Difficulty, I shall leave among Naturalists. (*Works,* X, 149)

Swift delights in this "antinatural" problem for "Naturalists": its "Solution" is, of course, that the dead "Wood" is a wooden effigy. Swift the joker and Wood the victim aptly share the wooden or deadpan expression of the stage comic.

There are, in Swift, both worms and carcasses which, unlike those of Wood's effigy, or of Celia's nose in "The Lady's Dressing Room," *are* charged with a special intensity: "*Wisdom* is . . . a

Nut, which . . . may cost you a Tooth, and pay you with nothing but a *Worm*" (*Works,* I, 40); the dissected "Carcass of *Humane Nature,*" which "*smelt* so strong, I could preserve it no longer" (*Works,* I, 77); the flayed woman and stripped beau in the "Digression concerning Madness" (*Works,* I, 109-110). These things, however, are not only partly controlled in each case by a note of parodic playfulness, but also (insofar as, very powerfully, they transcend the parody) have a vitality of harsh sudden shock rather than of protracted indulgence.[35] And the shock is largely conceptual, with relatively little visual elaboration. In the "Beautiful Young Nymph," where elaboration of visual detail *does* exist, it exists largely, as we have seen, as a formulaic accumulation, where most of the effects are predictable in principle, and where supercharged intensities based on *surprise* are therefore rare. Perhaps the only such intensity of suddenness is the laconic eruption which brings all contemplation of the carcass, and indeed the poem itself, to an end ("Who sees, will spew; who smells, be poison'd").

The "Beautiful Young Nymph" may be contrasted with one of Baudelaire's poems about the "affreuse Juive," Sara. The poem, "Je n'ai pas pour maîtresse une lionne illustre," resembles Shakespeare's "My mistress' eyes are nothing like the sun" both in the rhetorical reversal of its opening line, and in its peculiar combination of erotic tenderness and sensual recoil or disgust. Like Swift's poem, it is about a whore who strolls the streets, suffers from hunger, diseases and tormented dreams, is heavily covered in make-up, wears "artificial Hair" and has "flabby Dugs" (Swift, *Poems,* II. 581-583; Baudelaire, *Oeuvres Complètes,* pp. 196-198). But where Swift coolly recoils from the squalor, Baudelaire lavishes a rich, erotically charged devotion on the woman ("ma reine, ma duchesse, / . . . qui dans ses deux mains a réchauffé mon coeur"), showering kisses on her balding brow (more peeled than a leper) and sucking and biting her sagging breasts. The poem illustrates closely Baudelaire's famous statement in "Au Lecteur" about our fateful sensuous fascination with such "objets répugnants" in their most specifically sexual manifestations ("Ainsi qu'un débauché pauvre qui baise et mange / Le sein martyrisé d'une antique catin").

There is no *fascination* of hate in Swift's portrayal of the crippled old hag in the "Beautiful Young Nymph," but none also of the queer fascinated tenderness with which Baudelaire writes of the misshapen hags (once beautiful women, mothers, courtesans, or saints) in "Les Petites Vieilles," for example when he notes their shrivelled smallness in old age and death:

> - Avez-vous observé que maints cercueils de vieilles
> Sont presqu'aussi petits que celui d'un enfant?

This tenderness is not unconnected with the more positively erotic charge of feeling in "Une Charogne," where the poet tells his mistress that one day she will resemble the putrefying carcass, and especially when the carcass itself is seen with its legs in the air, "comme une femme lubrique." The "Shankers, Issues, running Sores" of the "Beautiful Young Nymph" are (if the paradox may be permitted) almost aseptic, and certainly cool, by comparison.

Baudelaire responded to such things with a warmth of self-involvement, and a quality of entranced sensuousness unthinkable in Swift:

> Dans les plis sinueux des vieilles capitales,
> Où tout, même l'horreur, tourne aux enchantements...

This grand opening of "Les Petites Vieilles" shows that in Baudelaire's vision, as in Swift's, the teeming squalors of great cities, and those of the decaying human body, were closely related. But Swift refused the *enchantments,* whether of cities or of carcasses. Baudelaire, not surprisingly, thought of Swift as a "farceur froid";[36] and Swift might have scorned not only these grandeurs, but some of the humorless dandy rigidities of Baudelaire, dismissing him as a "modern" and a beau. Swift's self-implication in the frailties and corruptions revealed by his own satire is insistent and profound, like Baudelaire's: but it differs greatly from Baudelaire's in its character. Swift would certainly recognize, wryly, that is "his *Brain,* his *Heart,* and his *Spleen*" were "laid open," like those of the Beau in the "Digression concerning Madness" (*Works,* I, 110), the operation would likewise alter his appearance for the worse. But when Baudelaire proclaims his identity with the hanged man in "Un Voyage à Cythère" (with his innards, opened by birds of prey, pouring out into his thighs), he indulges in quite unSwiftian luxuries of self-immolation:

> Ridicule pendu, tes douleurs sont les miennes!...

> Dans ton ile, o Venus! je n'ai trouvé debout
> Qu'un gibet symbolique ou pendait mon image....

Later critical tradition has sometimes seen Swift as a Byronic or Baudelairian hero, taking to himself, like Byron's Prometheus, "the sufferings of mortality," lonely and proud as the vulture devours his innards.[37] In *his* poem *Prometheus* ([1724] *Poems,* I, 343 ff.), Swift treats that hero not as a noble rebel, but as a squalid thief, alias William Wood, for whom he recommends an updated form of Promethean torment, the gallows (the fate, oddly, of Baudelaire's hero),

> Where, if we find his *Liver* grows,
> For want of *Vultures,* we have *Crows.*[38]
> (11.75-76)

(When Byron wrote on Ireland's oppression in "The Irish Avatar" [11.45 ff], it was one of Ireland's champions, Grattan, and not an oppressor like Wood, whom he identified with Prometheus.)[39] Characteristically, Swift's lines show him not only steering clear of those Romantic grandeurs of the suffering self which Yeats and others imputed to him ("Swift beating on his breast in sibylline frenzy blind / Because the heart in his blood-sodden breast had dragged him down into mankind"),[40] but also rewriting the old Titanic myth in a very low key.

Even in mock-heroic, Swift shied from those grandeurs which might rub off on the mockery. He seldom wrote sustained mock-heroic, on the model of *The Dunciad,* and his rare and sporadic moments of mock-heroic inflation are rigorously prevented from disturbing the radical flatness of his manner. When Strephon, in "The Lady's Dressing Room,"[41] wishes that Celia may

> better learn to keep
> 'Those Secrets of the hoary deep',
> (11.97-98)

a stately Miltonic enjambment (*Paradise Lost,* II, 891) is wittily assimilated into Swift's light octosyllabic measure, while Milton's "dark/Illimitable Ocean without bound" (II, 891-892) shrinks to the mysteries of a girl's chamberpot. The buoyant mock-heroic inflations of Pope's Miltonizing "vast profound"[42] are completely absent, just as "*Fleet-Ditch's* oozy Brinks, / Surrounded with a Hundred Stinks" in the "Beautiful Young Nymph" (11.47-48) lack the rolling amplitude of Pope's riverine pageant, in the *Dunciad,* (II, 271-272),

> . . .where Fleet-ditch with disemboguing streams
> Rolls the large tribute of dead dogs to Thames.[43]

Fleet-ditch is part of the mock-heroic geography of London,[44] and its "oozy Brinks" serve Augustan poets as a polluted modern version of great mythological waters, archetypal rivers and seas. In Swift, such waters easily shrink, as he made Milton's illimitable ocean shrink, to the size of a privy. The poet in "The Lady's Dressing Room" compares Celia to Venus rising from the sea:

> Should I the Queen of Love refuse,
> Because she rose from stinking Ooze?
> (11.131-132)

The poet's taunt to Strephon acquires its quasi-heroic coloring by imagining the heroic or mythological prototype as itself containing modern squalors, not as a grandeur from which we have lapsed (contrast Baudelaire's Cythère, which preserves in its modern degradation not only the "superbe fantôme" of ancient Venus, but also the splendors and miseries, the ironic or paradoxical sublimities, of the hanged young man).[45] Swift's couplet (one of several witty perversions of the Venus story)[46] has, however, a special bracing quality: Venus remains Venus, though she rises from the privy each day.

The whole question of misogyny, body-hatred, obscenity must be viewed in the context of Swift's temperamental dislike of "lofty" writing. Virtually all the examples we have examined occur in contexts of parody, and there may be a correlation between Swift's insistence on the "low" bodily functions, and the deflations or self-deflations of parody. This correlation is doubtless not a simple one, just as Swift's parody and the motives behind it are seldom simple. But it is an apt coincidence that the same friend who elicited the playful denials of misogyny in "The Journal of a Modern Lady" also inspired the poem in which Swift most fully repudiates the "lofty Stile." In "An Epistle to a Lady, Who Desired the Author to make Verses on her, in the Heroick Stile" ([1733] *Poems*, II, 628 ff.), Lady Acheson begs Swift to suspend his "paultry *Burlesque* Stile...Turning all to Ridicule" (11.50-52) and to "Sing my Praise in Strain sublime" (1.57). Swift's reply begins with a few bantering compliments, conceding her social and domestic qualities, but also saying (the theme is familiar in Swift's serious writing about women) that she must also learn "with good sense to entertain us" (1.114). He then enters into a long account of his unfitness in "a Stile sublime" (1.258), concluding on a characteristic note of cheeky friendliness about her intellectual deficiencies. Towards Lady Acheson, the tone, as George P. Mayhew has said, is "one of *raillery*, which turns seeming blame to praise sincerely meant."[47]

The second half of the poem (11.133 ff.) deals with Swift's rejection of the "lofty Stile" (11.140, 218). It contains at the same time a strong attack on Walpole and his ministry which is somewhat out of keeping with the genial levity of the first half, and is believed to have been written at a different time (1732-1733, as against 1728-1730).[48] Walpole was reputedly so angered by this poem and by "On Poetry: A Rapsody" (1733) that he contemplated arresting Swift.[49] The intensities of the second half are not only at variance with the first half, but also with the more bantering portions within the second half itself—notably the poem's concluding lines, with their renewed "raillery" of Lady Acheson, which may perhaps have been drafted earlier, together with the first half. Moreover, the corrosive political attack is woven into the parade of lighthearted self-analysis in a way which further complicates or confuses the tone, and which is not altogether free of the lofty postures that Swift pretends to decline. From one of the opening couplets of the second half, "I, as all the Parish knows, / Hardly can be grave in Prose" (11.137-138), to the next couplet, "Still to lash, and lashing Smile, / Ill befits a lofty Stile" (11.139-140), a small tightening of feeling occurs. And very soon, the lightheartedness which Swift boasts of turns into a harsh and

jeering scorn: "I can easier scorn than hate" (1.144); "All their
Madness makes me merry" (1.164); "Like the ever-laughing Sage,
/ In a Jest I spend my Rage" (11.167-168); "I would hang them if
I cou'd" (1.170); "Not by Anger, but a Sneer" (1.228). It is as
though the chatty Byron of *Beppo* or *Don Juan* had turned,
within the same poem, into the graver and more sinister Byronic
hero of *Lara,* that "hater of his kind" whose gay smile, "if oft
observed and near, / Waned in its mirth, and wither'd to a sneer"
(I, xvii).

Unlike Byron, Swift was not temperamentally able to sustain
romantic self-projections of the *Lara* type. He must have sensed
that he was coming dangerously close to such a posture, and that
the urbane banter to Lady Acheson was not sufficient to undercut it. Accordingly, there are some more decisive drops into
quasi-farcical or knockabout humor ("Switches better guide than
Cudgels;" "a little gentle Jerking / Sets the Spirits all a working,"
11.202, 205-206), often charged with coarseness:

> Let me, tho' the Smell be Noisom,
> Strip their Bums; let CALEB hoyse 'em;
> Then, apply ALECTO's Whip,
> Till they wriggle, howl, and skip.
> (11.177-180)

The scourge of infamy yields to the humbler role of muckraker, a
reduction of dignity without reduction of anger. A queer intimacy is established, in which satirist, victim, and reader all par-
take, the teasing, harsh intimacy of an enclosed, fetid atmosphere.

This intimacy exists also in *Gulliver's Travels,* where a "lofty
Stile," or at least a Swiftian commitment to "Timons manner,"
(*Correspondence,* III, 103) is also avoided, and where scatological play and exposure also take place at close quarters. For example, Gulliver's explanation in I. ii that he has given us an unimportant detail about his bodily functions because his maligners
have attacked his character "in Point of Cleanliness" alludes, like
the verse "Panegyric on the Reverend D——n S——t" ([1730]
Poems, II, 491 ff.), to accusations against Swift of excessive scatological indecency. But, in fact, Swift is cheekily doing the very
thing he is denying against the critics, and saying that this proves

that he isn't like that really.[50] There is about this kind of joke an aggressive defiance of the reader, an invitation to embarrassment in case the mere scatology, on its own, failed to shock. Much of the excremental element in *Gulliver,* as well as related passages of so-called body-disgust or sexual revulsion, and the celebration of what the "Panegyric" called "The *Horse's Countenance Divine*" (1.176), suggests not so much an excremental obsession as a concern with shaking us out of our "healthy" sensibilities. *Hypocrite lecteur.*

Swift's scatology is undoubtedly aggressive. But the aggression, fierce as it sometimes is, may, in other words, be less against the bowels or the sexual parts than against that highly personalized representative of mankind, the reader: against his squeamishness, his complacent normality, his shoddy idealisms and self-deceptions, his attachment to the human form divine, and his belief in the rationality of the human mind, in short, against all those serene peaceful states that Swift wants to "vex" the world out of.

I do not mean by this merely a conscious or official didacticism. Critics remind us that dung is a time-honored element not only in satiric but in homiletic tradition; that Swift as a churchman wished to instill in us a proper humility, and warn us against sins of the flesh; that he wished us to see truth clearly and without delusion; that he was exhorting us to a middle course between this and that form of excess; or advocating hygiene; or playing with scientific notions of the relativity of vision (e.g., a propos of the huge cancers in the breasts of the Brobdingnagian ladies); or parodying some foolish literary conventions. It would be difficult to say that these views do not all contain some truth. But one sometimes feels that the hysterias of revulsion displayed against Swift by Thackeray or Lawrence, or the equally dispiriting pedantries of the psychoanalysts, are preferable to these calmer hysterias and pedantries of present-day "golden mean" fetishists and other common-sense explainers-away.

These current academic explanations of alleged conscious or "official" purposes always ignore the peculiar energies of Swift's manner, the sudden intensities, the redirections of irony, the needling intimacy, the unsettling exuberance, the laconic asperities. Certainly, Swift took seriously the didactic obligations of the

satirist, but when he made Gulliver say to the reader "my principal Design was to inform, and not to amuse thee," he introduced
a special tease into the old Horatian tag about pleasure and instruction. For Gulliver is here protesting not his (undoubted)
reformative leanings, but his factual truth, "plain Matter of
Fact" as opposed to wild travelers' tales (*Works*, XI, 291): and by
the end of *Gulliver's Travels*, such a joke has a dry disturbing
ring. Critics often shy from the exact implications of another of
Swift's variations, this time in his own name, on Horace's tag:
"the chief end I propose to my self in all my labors is to *vex* the
world rather then divert it" (*Correspondence*, III, 102; my
italics). *Vex* relates closely to the mood of the "Epistle to a Lady":
"Till they wriggle, howl, and skip" (1.180), "a little gentle Jerking, / Sets the Spirits all a working" (11.205-206). We should not
be misled by "gentle." The word carries a touch of sadistic glee
insofar as it is not simply a contrast to the "Bastings heavy"
(1.203) of a more pretentious loftiness of denunciation.[51]

Many of Swift's scatological poems are more lighthearted in
manner than the "Epistle to a Lady," or than *Gulliver*. Poems
like "The Lady's Dressing Room" and "Cassinus and Peter" are
said by Huxley to be a childish bowel-hating "refusal . . . to accept
the physical reality of the world."[52] These poems are actually
pleas for seeing reality straight, rather than through a rosy film of
false poeticizing. But Huxley's real mistake, it seems to me, lies in
giving a melodramatic gloss to an issue which Swift almost always
kept in a low key. The point about "*Celia, Celia, Celia* shits" is
not so much that Swift is entirely unmoved, but that any Hux-
leyan revulsion Swift may have felt is disguised in the comedy of
Strephon's or Cassinus's plaintiveness, or undercut by the witty
élan of the verse. But this *élan*, this lightheartedness, not only
parodies solemnity. It also serves to shield Swift from seeming
solemn, even in his mockery of solemnity. Like other forms of
ironic indirection, it is partly a playing for victory (flinging dung
more because it shocks the reader than obsesses Swift), and partly
a concealment or defense against the vulnerabilities of an over-
exposed sincerity as well as against the risks of self-importance.
One of the final objections to a "lofty Stile" made in the "Epistle
to a Lady" was that "I Shou'd make a Figure scurvy" (1.219), and
perhaps this playful admission should be taken as seriously as the

purpose (also playfully expressed) of vexing rather than diverting the world.

A dimension of stylistic undercutting, chiefly through parody, exists even in Swift's most personal poems, those which he wrote to Esther Johnson (Stella) on her birthdays and at other times, between 1719 and her death in 1728. In "To Stella, Who Collected and Transcribed his Poems" ([1720] *Poems*, II, 727 ff.), he wrote:

> Thou *Stella,* wert no longer young,
> When first for thee my Harp I strung:
> Without one Word of *Cupid*'s Darts,
> Of killing Eyes, or bleeding Hearts:
> With Friendship and Esteem possesst,
> I ne'er admitted Love a Guest.
>
> (11.9-14)

How true the last line is, nobody knows. Swift's relationship with Stella, whom he probably first met in Temple's household in 1689 when she was very young, has never been satisfactorily understood. The mystery surrounding it (which, like the larger questions about Swift's sexual character, has been much sensationalized) seems partly the result of the same temperamental guardedness which produced the protective obliquities of parody, and the self-concealing deflations of Swift's whole ironic manner. The signposted disavowal of "*Cupid*'s darts" and other gestures of love poetry is part of an exercise which began when, in 1719, he first gave Esther Johnson her poetic name of Stella, in a half-mocking allusion to the heroine of Sidney's poems. The joke could disengage Swift from some vulnerabilities of high sentiment, while not impairing the deep tenderness he clearly felt. As Herbert Davis said, "paradoxically it could at the same time hide and flaunt the truth that she was 'the star whereby his course was only directed.'"[53]

An important theme of these poems, along with the denial of romantic love, is that of a "Friendship and Esteem" based on mutual respect for moral and intellectual qualities. Swift believed profoundly that these were the only sure basis for a durable relationship between men and women, within or outside marriage. He argued that for this purpose women must cultivate the same intellectual interests as men, meeting them on terms of intelligent conversation and of mutual respect,[54] and abandoning the mindless seductions of female affectation. This doctrine, most fully stated in the prose "Letter to a Young Lady, on her Marriage, Written in the Year 1723" (*Works,* IX, 83-94), occurs again and again in his writings to and about Stella, as well as in the earlier *Cadenus and Vanessa* (1713). His relationship with both Stella and Vanessa involved a "tutorial" role on his part. Some of his most moving praise of Stella deals with her success in living up to these exacting "male" standards (*Poems,* II, 725-726, 734-736; *Works,* V, 228 ff.).

There is nothing unique or necessarily abnormal in this praise of a woman for her "male" qualities. At a time when women were conventionally expected to be social ornaments, rather than intelligent beings, Swift was speaking not of virtues which women necessarily lacked (his point was to assert the opposite), but which society pretended they lacked or discouraged them from possessing. Occasionally, as in "To Stella, Visiting me in my Sickness," ([1720] *Poems,* II, 722 ff.), he allows a formulaic distinction, in order to praise Stella for combining the best of both sexes:

> Say, *Stella,* was *Prometheus* blind,
> And forming you, mistook your Kind?
> No: 'Twas for you alone he stole
> The Fire that forms a manly Soul;
> Then to compleat it ev'ry way,
> He molded it with Female Clay:
> To that you owe the nobler Flame.
> To this, the Beauty of your Frame.
> (11.85-92)

The light and chatty compliment is perhaps, at worst, less patronizing than Pope's compliment to Martha Blount (was it modeled on Swift's lines?):

> Heav'n, when it strives to polish all it can
> Its last best work, but forms a softer Man.[55]

It is possible that these backhanded gallantries to Stella, together with the disavowal of romantic love and the celebration of intellectual companionship, were Swift's way of saying to Stella *not* that he did not love her, but only that his love was deeper, more soundly based, and freer of cant, than poems normally say. Like the parodic elements, they disengage Swift from the foolishness of cant, and from the vulnerabilities of naked disclosure. We cannot tell exactly what flavor the romantic appellation of Stella had for them both, but the joke would have no point, or might seem merely cruel, if they were not lovers, or at least in love, in some (still puzzling) sense.[56] The Stella poems have this distinctive feature, that the antiromantic elements are often not denials of the conventions of love poetry, so much as revalidations by means of a saving "realism." Even when, as in the birthday poem of 1721 (*Poems,* II, 734 ff.), he asserts that Stella's intellectual qualities will outlast the prettiness of poetic heroines, a gruff tenderness gives literal value to the mock-romantic talk of Stella's angel face and mind:

> Now, this is Stella's Case in Fact;
> An Angel's Face, a little crack't;
> (Could Poets or could Painters fix
> How Angeles look at thirty six)
> This drew us in at first to find
> In such a Form an Angel's Mind
> And ev'ry Virtue now supplyes
> The fainting Rays of Stella's Eyes...
>   (11.15-22)

Behind this lies a lightly sketched mock-mythology, in which Stella, young, was a pastoral heroine, "The brightest Virgin of the Green" (*Poems,* II, 721), or perhaps "Beauty's Queen," whom some youthful poet might have "sweetly sung" (*Poems,* II, 757). These last words are from the very moving birthday poem of 1725, in which Swift says that age has given her wrinkles, but dimmed his sight so that he cannot see the change:

> No Length of Time can make you quit
> Honour and Virtue, Sense and Wit,
> Thus you may still be young to me,
> While I can better *hear* than *see;*
> Oh, ne'er may Fortune shew her Spight,
> To make me *deaf,* and mend my *Sight.*
>   (11.49-54)

In his copy of the volume in which this poem appeared, Swift
wrote fifteen years later, against the last line: "now deaf 1740."

Stella died in 1728. Swift gave release to his grief in a prose
piece "On the Death of Mrs. Johnson," begun the night of her
death. It is one of the most moving things he ever wrote:

> This day, being Sunday, January 28th, 1727-8, about eight o'clock at
> night, a servant brought me a note, with an account of the death of the
> truest, most virtuous, and valuable friend, that I, or perhaps any other
> person ever was blessed with. She expired about six in the evening of this
> day; and, as soon as I am left alone, which is about eleven at night, I
> resolve, for my own satisfaction, to say something of her life and charac-
> ter.
> She was born at Richmond in Surrey on the thirteenth day of March,
> in the year 1681. Her father was a younger brother of a good family in
> Nottinghamshire, her mother of a lower degree; and indeed she had
> little to boast of her birth. I knew her from six years old, and had some
> share in her education, by directing what books she should read, and
> perpetually instructing her in the principles of honour and virtue; from
> which she never swerved in any one action or moment of her life. She
> was sickly from her childhood until about the age of fifteen: But then
> grew into perfect health, and was looked upon as one of the most beau-
> tiful, graceful, and agreeable young women in London, only a little too
> fat. Her hair was blacker than a raven, and every feature of her face in
> perfection.... (*Works*, V, 227)

There is no question, in such a passage, of tricks of style. The
writing has the flat dignity of pain, a brokenhearted matter-of-
factness, giving each meticulous detail (the time of death, the
date of birth) a kind of stunned significance. But this profound,
unguarded genuineness preserves all the lineaments of Swift's
parodic manner. The factuality of, "Her father was a younger
brother of a good family in Nottinghamshire," is very close to the
poker-faced idiom of the opening of *Gulliver:* "My Father had a
small Estate in *Nottinghamshire;* I was the Third of five Sons."
The sentences of heartfelt praise are laced with literal-minded
admissions that seem the nonsatiric counterpart to the deflations
in the burlesque poems: "indeed she had little to boast of her
birth,"[57] "only a little too fat."

The latter may be compared with the affectionate quasi-
parodic literalness with which Fielding describes Sophia Western:
"a middle-sized woman; but rather inclining to tall" etc. (*Tom
Jones*, IV, ii). The parallel is reinforced by the fact that Fielding

tells us that Sophia resembled a, now dead, woman very dear to him (actually his late wife). Fielding's heavyheartedness on this point is distanced by time, and by a comic context. He sets his fresh realistic portrait off against the blowsy extravagance of a burlesque preamble which mocks the "sublime" introductions of heroines in romances. Though he makes it clear that Sophia (like Stella in Swift's account) is very beautiful, the drop into the real is the climax of a stylistic deflation as decisive as any in Swift's burlesque poems, though doubtless more genial. It differs from these poems in that their heroines do not necessarily remain beautiful after the rant has been punctured. But it differs from the account of Stella, not because that account is free of hyperboles of celebration, but because these remain wholly unpunctured. The touch of romance jargon in: "[she] was looked upon as one of the most beautiful, graceful, and agreeable young women in London. . . . Her hair was blacker than a raven, and every feature of her face in perfection," is not at all devalued by the insertion of "only a little too fat" in the middle. The example illustrates the force of his commitment to literal truth, and his guardedness even with those stylistic sublimities to which he wants to give literal value. It shows also how deep a part of his personality is involved in the more stylized undercuttings of the burlesque poetry.

Again, the hyperbole of "truest, most virtuous" is not undercut but *revalidated* by its context, so that we are disposed to think of it as nothing but the sober truth. The same effect was already present in the earliest poems to Stella, for example "To Stella, Visiting me in my Sickness" ([1720] *Poems,* II, 722 ff.):

> Ten thousand Oaths upon Record,
> Are not so sacred as her Word:
> The World shall in its Atoms end,
> E'er *Stella* can deceive a Friend.
> (11.55-58)

In these deeply felt passages all impulse to parody is waived, or transcended. The fact that the potential, or the raw material, for parody is so freely proferred suggests the extent of Swift's readiness, where Stella is concerned, to drop his ironic guard. There are, of course, several lighthearted poems, like the birthday poem of 1723 or the same year's "Stella at Wood-Park" (*Poems,* II, 740 ff.). The latter is a banter on Stella getting used to high living at Wood-Park (Charles Ford's house), and then returning to Dublin and homelier fare, with Swift for company. But at the end, the poem takes an uncharacteristic turn, not into deflation, but to a cancellation of the mockery (11.73 ff.). The final witty twist is a tender compliment (very different from the satiric mock-gallantries of the burlesques or even the friendly ones to Lady Acheson) in which Swift says that for him, although "my Raillery were true, / A Cottage is *Wood-Park* with you" (11.91-92). Conversely, when Swift warns Stella of certain faults in her character, as in "To Stella, Who Collected and Transcribed his Poems" (11.83 ff.), there is a frank, tender firmness which, though lightly carried, differs radically from the witty badinage to Lady Acheson in the "Epistle to a Lady" and other Market Hill poems.

In his tributes to Stella's selfless nursing of him in his illness (*Poems,* II, 722 ff. and, especially, II, 754-755), affectionate humor modulates into an unusual, soberly introspective gravity. Even more moving are the poems in which he expresses anxiety for her in her last illness. The verses written while his crossing to Ireland was delayed at "Holyhead. Sept. 25. 1727" (*Poems,* II, 420-421) have an unusual self-exposing starkness:

> I never was in hast before
> To reach that slavish hateful shore
> Before, I always found the wind
> To me was most malicious kind
> But now, the danger of a friend
> On whom my fears and hopes depend
> Absent from whom all Clymes are curst
> With whom I'm happy in the worst
> With rage impatient makes me wait
> A passage to the land I hate.
> (11.19-28)

In the last of the birthday poems ([1727] *Poems,* II, 763 ff.), written a few months before the Holyhead verses, the opening badinage strikes a note of tender, mock-cantankerous desperation:

> This Day, whate'er the Fates decree,
> Shall still be kept with Joy by me:
> This Day then, let us not be told,

> That you are sick, and I grown old,
> Nor think on our approaching Ills,
> And talk of Spectacles and Pills;
> To morrow will be Time enough
> To hear such mortifying Stuff.
>   (11.1-8)

Swift then announces a new found sobriety:

> From not the gravest of Divines,
> Accept for once some serious Lines.
>   (11.13-14)

The poem proceeds to some serious meditations on past and
future, on Stella's virtue and her "Life well spent" (1.36). There is
a spare eloquence about this which is paradoxically heightened,
not reduced by the light octosyllabic meter. But it is at the end of
the poem, where a final complimentary turn occurs, that the
most poignant effect is achieved. A hint of neatly executed gal-
lantry is transfigured into the most soberly and urgently truthful
praise of all:

> O then, whatever Heav'n intends,
> Take Pity on your pitying Friends;
> Nor let your Ills affect your Mind,
> To fancy they can be unkind.
> Me, surely me, you ought to spare,
> Who gladly would your Suff'rings share;
> Or give me Scrap of Life to you,
> And think it far beneath your Due;
> You, to whose Care so oft I owe,
> That I'm alive to tell you so.
>   (11.79-88)

Stella was the only person who drew from Swift such stark un-
embarrassed sincerities.

NOTES

1. The following editions of Swift's writings have been used and are
referred to in the text in abbreviated form: *Correspondence,* ed. Harold
Williams, 5 vols. (Oxford: Clarendon Press, 1963-1965); *Poems,* ed.

Harold Williams, 3 vols., 2d ed. (Oxford: Clarendon Press, 1958); *Works* [*Prose Works*], ed. Herbert Davis and others, 14 vols. (Oxford: Blackwell, 1939-1968). The dates given for each poem are dates of composition as suggested by Williams and may or may not be the same as the dates of publication.

Quotations from Pope's poems use the text and lineation of the Twickenham edition. Page references are not supplied for these, nor for the poems by Baudelaire and Eliot, all of which are easy to find in any collected edition. Texts of Baudelaire are from *Oeuvres Completes,* ed. Y.-G. Le Dantec, revised by Claude Pichois (Paris: Pléiade, 1961); texts of poems by Eliot are from *Collected Poems 1909-1935* (London: Faber and Faber, 1951), and *Four Quartets* (London: Faber and Faber, 1950).

2. "Les Sept Vieillards."

3. See Maurice Johnson, "T. S. Eliot on Satire, Swift, and Disgust," *Papers on Language and Literature,* 5 (1969), 310-315. Some of Eliot's statements are reprinted in *Jonathan Swift. A Critical Anthology,* ed. Denis Donoghue (Harmondsworth: Penguin, 1971), pp. 128-135. For some parallels and resemblances between Eliot and Swift, see below pp. 58-61, 64-65, and nn. 5, 11, 13, 23.

4. "Swift haunts me; he is always just round the next corner." Introduction to *The Words upon the Window-Pane,* in *Explorations,* ed. Mrs. W. B. Yeats (London: Macmillan, 1962), p. 345.

5. In a letter to Maurice Johnson, 27 June 1947: see Johnson, "The Ghost of Swift in Eliot's *Four Quartets,*" *Modern Language Notes,* 64 (1949), 273; *The Sin of Wit. Jonathan Swift as a Poet* (Syracuse: Syracuse University Press, 1950), pp. 130-131. See also Grover Smith, *T. S. Eliot's Poetry and Plays* (Chicago: University of Chicago Press, 1962), pp. 290, 328n. Eliot seems to have put a different emphasis on the importance of the Swiftian presence in speaking or writing to different persons. Richard Ellmann, *Eminent Domain* (New York: Oxford University Press, 1967), pp. 94, 144n, reports that Eliot told Kristian Smidt that although "the figure blends various writers, especially Yeats and Swift, it is primarily and recognizably Yeats." Kristian Smidt's recent book, *The Importance of Recognition: Six Chapters on T. S. Eliot* (Tromsø: A. S. Peder Norbye, 1973), pp. 44, 46n, 81, suggests a still firmer emphasis on Yeats.

6. "Morning at the Window."

7. "Preludes."

8. And compare the burlesque night piece which opens *Tom Jones,* X, ii, where Susan the chambermaid is about to retire "to the arms of the fond, expecting ostler."

9. For an earlier example of lines about morning, in which elements of formal *descriptio* mingle comically with scenes of everyday unromantic activity, and in which several characters similar to Swift's appear (including the slow-paced schoolboy with his satchel), see Charles Cotton's, "Morning Quatrains," in *Poems,* ed. John Buxton (London: Routledge, 1958), pp. 1-5, cited by Maurice Johnson, *The Sin of Wit,* pp. 14-15.

10. Roger Savage, "Swift's Fallen City: 'A Description of the Morning,'" *The World of Jonathan Swift,* ed. Brian Vickers (Oxford: Blackwell, 1968), p. 177.

11. Maurice Johnson, *The Sin of Wit,* pp. 111-112, notes that the line *"Carminative* and *Diuretick,"* in "Strephon and Chloe," ([1731] *Poems,* II, 588, 1.133) has an affinity with "the polysyllabic 'Mr. Eliot's Sunday Morning Service.'" For another suggested parallel, see Richard C. Turner, "Burbank and Grub-Street: A Note on T. S. Eliot and Swift," *English Studies,* 52 (1971), 347-348.

12. Swift began collecting materials for the *Complete Collection of Genteel and Ingenious Conversation* ([1738] *Works,* IV, 97 ff.) in 1704 or earlier. On this work, and on Swift's interest in linguistic fashions and affectations, see Herbert Davis's introduction in *Works,* IV, xxviii ff. See also *A Full and True Account of the Solemn Procession to the Gallows, at the Execution of William Wood, Esquire, and Hard-wareman,* ([1724] *Works,* X, 143 ff.).

13. According to the second Mrs. Eliot, "Eliot said this passage was 'pure Ellen Kellond,' a maid employed by the Eliots, who recounted it to them," *The Waste Land: A Facsimile and Transcript of the Original Drafts, Including the Annotations of Ezra Pound,* ed. Valerie Eliot (London: Faber and Faber, 1971), p. 127n.

14. *His Very Self and Voice. Collected Conversations of Lord Byron,* ed. Ernest J. Lovell, Jr. (New York: Macmillan, 1954), p. 268.

15. For some qualifications on the extent of Butler's influence on Swift, see C. L. Kulishek, "Swift's Octosyllabics and the Hudibrastic Tradition," *Journal of English and Germanic Philology,* 53 (1954), 361-368.

16. Pope, *The First Satire of the Second Book of Horace Imitated* (1733), 11.1-2. I make a brief comparison of these two poems in "The Proper Study of Pope," *Times Literary Supplement,* 14 March 1975, p. 275. The discussion goes on to compare Swift, Pope, and Yeats as poets.

17. On 7 April 1930, Yeats wrote to Lady Gregory: "I am reading Swift, the *Diary to Stella,* and his correspondence with Pope and Bolingbroke; these men fascinate me, in Bolingbroke the last pose and in Swift the last passion of the Renaissance, in Pope, whom I dislike, an imitation both of pose and passion" *Letters,* ed. Allan Wade (London: R. Hart-Davis, 1954), p. 773. In a manuscript book of 1921, referred to in Donald T. Torchiana's *W. B. Yeats and Georgian Ireland* (Evanston: Northwestern University Press, 1966), p. 114, Yeats deplored the rigid Roman influence introduced into English letters by Milton, Dryden, and Pope. In his Introduction to *The Oxford Book of Modern Verse 1892-1935* (Oxford: Clarendon Press, 1936), pp. xxi-xxii, Yeats speaks of the early T. S. Eliot as "an Alexander Pope, working without apparent imagination . . . satirist rather than poet." See also *A Vision* (London: Macmillan, 1961), p. 296. There are some excellent brief remarks about "the arrogance of formal mastery" in the late poems of Pope and

of Yeats in Martin Price, *To the Palace of Wisdom* (Garden City, N.Y.: Doubleday, 1965), pp. 166-168.

18. The first of these lines translates 1.70 of Horace's poem. Horace is talking about Lucilius, Pope about himself. On this question, and on the Juvenalian qualities of Pope's Horatian imitation, see G. K. Hunter, "The Romanticism' of Pope's Horace," *Essays in Criticism,* 10 (1960), 390-404.

19. A third satirical piece on Vanbrugh is "The History of Vanbrug's House" ([1706] *Poems,* I, 85 ff.).

20. Yeats, "Among School Children," *Collected Poems* (London: Macmillan, 1952), p. 243.

21. For a variant of this fable, see the "Poet, starving in a Garret," in "To Stella, Who Collected and Transcribed his Poems," 11.25 ff. (*Poems,* II, 728-729), written in the same year as "The Progress of Poetry."

22. Kathleen Williams, *Jonathan Swift and the Age of Compromise* (Lawrence: University of Kansas Press, 1958), p. 149. See also Christine Rees, "Gay, Swift, and the Nymphs of Drury-Lane," *Essays in Criticism,* 23 (1973), 17. This essay has an enlightening discussion of several of the poems and themes with which I am concerned (esp. pp. 14-20).

23. Eliot's "Rhapsody" (Swift, incidentally, also used this word for the ironic title of one of his best-known poems) continues with references to "female smells in shuttered rooms" and other sleazy properties which would not be out of place in Swift's poems. Cf. also the passage about the "hearty female stench" in Eliot's cancelled pastiche of Pope in the typescript of the *Waste Land*'s "Fire Sermon," *The Waste Land. A Facsimile and Transcript of the Original Drafts,* pp. 23, 39. The "passage was written in imitation of *The Rape of the Lock*," as Mrs. Eliot says (p. 127n.). Pound told Eliot to scrap it, "for you cannot parody Pope unless you can write better verse than Pope—and you can't," (p. 127n, cited from Eliot's Introduction to Pound's *Selected Poems* [London: Faber and Faber, 1948], p. 18; see also Eliot's *Paris Review* interview, *Writers at Work, Second Series,* ed. Van Wyck Brooks [London: Secker & Warburg, 1963], p. 83. For Yeats's comment that Eliot was "an Alexander Pope...satirist rather than poet," see above, n. 17). And in the verse-paragraph which includes the "hearty female stench," Pound objected to a particular coupleteering "trick of Pope" (p. 39). But much that disappeared at Pound's insistence, though written in "Popeian" couplets, was more like Swift than Pope. The "brisk Amanda" with her "coarsened hand, and hard plebeian tread," who attends on the heroine Fresca's awakening, would be at least as much at home in the "Description of the Morning" as in Pope's *Rape* (pp. 23, 39).

In ensuing lines about Fresca herself, various details of scene or atmosphere take us back to Swift's satires of female polite conversation or to his Celia poems almost as much as to Pope's Belinda (pp. 23, 27, 39-41). Then, in the scene of the typist and the "young man carbuncular," a draft passage about "drying combinations...stockings, dirty camisoles, and stays," from which Pound urged the deletion of the last two words (p. 45) and which nevertheless survived in the finished poem as "drying combinations...Stockings, slippers, camisoles, and stays" (11.225-227), likewise has more in common with some items in the "Inventory" of "The Lady's Dressing Room" (11.10 ff.) than with, say, the "Puffs, Powders, Patches, Bibles, Billet-doux" of *Rape of the Lock*, I, 138. "The Lady's Dressing Room" and related poems by Swift have of course their own ironic relationship with the *Rape*, as Murray Krieger has shown in *The Classic Vision: The Retreat from Extremity in Modern Literature* (Baltimore and London: The Johns Hopkins Press, 1971), pp. 260-268; and see below, pp. 68, 73. After the seduction of the typist, the young man went on to "urinate, and spit" before Pound removed the detail as "proba[b]ly over the mark" (*Waste Land Facsimile*, p. 47). Pound's deletion of the Fresca passage and of other lines in the original "Fire Sermon" were in nearly all cases for the better, but he threw out a certain amount of Swift in the course of eliminating Pope, whether he knew it or not.

24. 11.113-116 and some earlier passages in the poem were omitted when the poem was first printed in the Pope-Swift *Miscellanies, The Last Volume*, 1727. See *Poems*, II, 221-222, and textual commentary, *Poems*, II, 226-229.

25. C. J. Rawson, *Gulliver and the Gentle Reader. Studies in Swift and our Time* (London and Boston: Routledge, 1973), pp. 34-35.

26. Irvin Ehrenpreis, *The Personality of Jonathan Swift* (London: Methuen, 1958), pp. 43-46.

27. Cf. Spenser, *Faerie Queene*, I, viii, 48: "My chaster Muse for shame doth blush to write." This occurs in the horrific portrait of Duessa, at I, viii, 46-48, which has a number of details in common with Swift's poem, and shares its theme of a fair exterior revealed as being a cover for appalling ugliness.

28. The phrase is used not only in "Strephon and Chloe," 1.204, but in a short prose piece, probably by Swift, defending a related poem, "The Lady's Dressing Room." See *Works*, V, 340.

29. Two months later, on 14 December 1725, in the same celebrated series of letters alluding to the composition of *Gulliver's Travels*, the "misanthropy" of Swift, and the kind of satire which "vexes," Pope returned to a similar image: "Not that I have much Anger against the Great, my Spleen is at the little rogues.... It would vexe one more to be knockt o' the Head by a Pisspot, than by a Thunderbolt. As to great Oppressors (as you say) they are like Kites or Eagles, one expects mischief from them: But to be Squirted to death (as poor Wycherley said to me on his deathbed) by *Potecaries Prentices*, by the under Strappers of Under Secretaries, to Secretaries, who were no Secretaries—this would provoke as dull a dog as Ph[ilip]s himself" (*Correspondence*, III, 120). Pope is voicing to Swift sentiments which were probably more character-

istic of Swift than of Pope himself: that satire had more to do with un-
dignified exposure than with grand denunciation; that the most effective kind of "vexing" came from pettier rather than grander sources,
etc. The *hauteur* which grants greater nuisance-value to "the under
Strappers of Under Secretaries, to Secretaries, who were no Secretaries"
than to the truly powerful is only part of the significance of Pope's letter
for the student of Swift. It conveys indirectly a point which Swift was to
make himself in his "Epistle to a Lady" ([1733] *Poems,* II, pp. 634-638,
11.137-248), that needling and humbling irritations are more vexing
than more openly angry onslaughts, and perhaps by implication that
the "great Oppressors" are best attacked by means which concede no
"greatness" to them. A peculiar identity develops in the two passages
from Pope's letters between the satirist who breaks vials on the heads of
his victims, and satiric victims who annoy the satirist more by dropping
pisspots on his head than do "the Great" by their "greater" misdeeds.

30. D. H. Lawrence, Introduction to *Pansies,* in *A Propos of Lady
Chatterley's Lover and other Essays* (Harmondsworth: Penguin, 1961),
pp. 10-11, and the account of Lawrence's views in Burton S. Kendle,
"D. H. Lawrence: The Man Who Misunderstood Gulliver," *English
Language Notes,* 2 (1964), 42-46; Aldous Huxley, "Swift," in *Do What
You Will* (London: Chatto and Windus, 1939), pp. 93-106. See also
Milton Voigt, *Swift and the Twentieth Century* (Detroit: Wayne State
University Press, 1964), pp. 126 ff; and Athar Murtuza, "Twentieth-
Century Critical Response to Swift's 'Scatalogical [*sic*] Verse.' A Check-
list," *Bulletin of Bibliography,* 30 (1973), 18-19 (an incomplete listing
of this inexhaustibly tedious and inescapable topic). The most recent
significant discussions of the scatological elements in Swift are Jae Num
Lee, *Swift and Scatological Satire* (Albuquerque: University of New
Mexico Press, 1971), and Thomas B. Gilmore, Jr., "The Comedy of
Swift's Scatological Poems," *PMLA,* 91 (1976), 33-43 and 464-467 (the
latter an exchange of views between Donald Greene, Peter J. Schakel
and Gilmore).

31. Contrast the "Puffs, Powders, Patches, Bibles, Billet-doux" of
Belinda's toilet in *Rape of the Lock,* I, 138, which show satire without
the ingredient of revulsion, however comic; and see the whole scene in
Rape, I, 121 ff. See also above, n. 23.

32. On the scientific background to this, see Marjorie Nicolson's
study, "The Microscope and English Imagination," in her *Science and
Imagination* (Ithaca: Cornell University Press, 1956), pp. 155-234, especially pp. 193-199.

33. S. T. Coleridge, *Table Talk,* 15 June 1830.

34. Cf. *Hudibras,* II, iii, 317-320, 377-378.

35. See above, p. 66 and n. 25.

36. Baudelaire, "Mon Coeur Mis a Nu," *Oeuvres Complètes,* p. 1296
(xl). In "Yeats and the Rhetoric of Defilement," *Review of English Literature,* 6, no. 3 (July 1965), 48-49, Jean Alexander distinguishes inter-

estingly between Swift, Baudelaire, and the Marvell of "To His Coy Mistress." In "Une charogne," she argues, Baudelaire "uses putrefaction both as a refinement of sensuous pleasure and as an instrument of sexual power. . . . Marvell snatched the beloved back from the tomb and its worms, but Baudelaire thrusts her body prematurely into dissolution. One might say that Baudelaire is as destructive as Swift, were it not for his perverse sensuous pleasure in the sight and smell of rot and the grotesque, obscene posture of death. In Swift's use of defilement in the second and especially the fourth books of *Gulliver's Travels,* the sexual indignities and smearing with excrement are intended to destroy every idealization of the human body and its functions; further, they are intended to destroy the erotic impulse itself. In contrast, the erotic impulse is violently displaced in Baudelaire's poetry: instead of desire shrivelling before the image of love defiled, the desirable object ('une femme lubrique / Brûlante . . .') lends its excitement to the image which would defile it. Thus desire is not destroyed, but the natural order of desires is shattered and the poet replaces it with his own perverse constructions."

37. E.g., Thackeray, *English Humourists of the Eighteenth Century* (London: Macmillan, 1910), p. 19: "what a vulture that tore the heart of that giant!" Thackeray is not, of course, being wholly friendly to Swift.

38. That such neo-Promethean immolations did not in Swift's eyes dignify a victim, is confirmed by an angry marginal note on Henry VIII: ". . . I wish he had been Flead, his skin stuffed and hangd on a Gibbet, His bulky guts and Flesh left to be devoured by Birds and Beasts. . ." (*Works,* V, 251). For other references to Prometheus in Swift's poems, see *Poems,* I, 266; II, 659, 726. For a seventeenth-century satirical allusion in which Prometheus is thought of primarily as a thief, see the attack on Dryden, *A Panegyric on the Author of Absalom and Achitophel,* 1681, 1.54: "Thy soaring heights Prometheus' thefts excel," *Poems on Affairs of State, vol. 2: 1678-1681,* ed. Elias F. Mengel, Jr., (New Haven and London: Yale University Press, 1965), 503.

39. I owe the reference to Raymond Trousson, *Le Thème de Prométhée dans la Littérature Européenne* (Geneva: Droz, 1964), II, 344. On the Romantic development in which Prometheus "incarne le poète paria et préfigure ainsi l'albatros" of Baudelaire, see Trousson, II, 300. Baudelaire himself sometimes mocked the Promethean pretensions of others (Trousson, II, 299n, 378; Baudelaire, *Oeuvres Complètes,* pp. 596-598, 1262), but was attracted to the myth, and returned with a particular fascination and self-involvement to images of devouring by birds of prey, not only in "Un Voyage à Cythère" but in "Le Mort Joyeux."

40. Yeats, "Blood and the Moon," *Collected Poems,* p. 268.

41. The poem is not without its own Promethean flippancies: Celia's closestool is compared with "*Pandora's* Box" (1.83).

42. *Dunciad,* I, 118. Pope's note to the passage as a whole refers us to

the devil's progress through Chaos (*Paradise Lost,* II, 927 ff.). See also the "vast profunditie" of *Paradise Lost,* VII, 229. A significant fact is that Pope also uses "vast profound" in serious heroic contexts in *Iliad,* VIII, 162 and *Odyssey,* IV, 777; VIII, 34; and XIII, 185. See Arthur Sherbo, "No Single Scholiast: Pope's *The Dunciad,*" *Modern Language Review,* 65 (1970), 505. The example adds confirmation of the closeness of Pope's mock-heroic to those primary heroic grandeurs which it mimics.

43. Again Pope also wrote a straight heroic version, in *Odyssey,* IV, 480: "the deep roar of disemboguing Nile." The whole passage from *The Dunciad* (II, 271 ff.) may also be contrasted with the closing lines of the "City Shower." It is true that Swift talks of a "huge Confluent" (1.59), but his overriding effect is not of a large majestic movement but of an animated crowd of little things: "Drown'd Puppies, stinking Sprats, . . . Dead Cats and Turnip-Tops" (11.62-3). See *Times Literary Supplement,* 14 March 1975, p. 275.

44. Cf. Garth, *Dispensary,* III, 125-126, and Gay, *Trivia,* II, 168 ff. On Fleet-ditch and its literary associations and significance, see Pat Rogers, *Grub Street: Studies in a Subculture* (London: Methuen, 1972), pp. 142-174. See also Ian Donaldson, "The Satirists' London," *Essays in Criticism,* 25 (1975), 116, 122n.

45. The theme of the modern degradation of the island of Venus to a barren British colony is to be found in Baudelaire's source, Nerval's article "Voyage à Cythère," published in *l'Artiste,* 30 June and 11 August 1844 and subsequently absorbed into his *Voyage en Orient;* and also in Victor Hugo's "Cérigo," a poem inspired by Baudelaire's. But it is in Baudelaire that the memory of Venus's "superbe fantôme" is at its richest, and (although the episode of the hanged man was probably invented by Nerval) it is only in Baudelaire that the poet's self-identification with the "Ridicule pendu" occurs. See Baudelaire, *Oeuvres Complètes,* p. 1555; Nerval, *Oeuvres,* ed. Albert Béguin and Jean Richer (Paris: Pléiade, 1961), II, 63-72, 1292-1296; Hugo, *Oeuvres Poétiques,* ed. Pierre Albouy (Paris: Pléiade, 1967), II, 704-706, 1587-1589; Paul Maury, "Cérigo ou Un Épisode de l'Hellénisme en France," *Mercure de France,* 183 (1925), 392-400; Georges Collas, "Victor Hugo et Baudelaire," *Revue d'Histoire Littéraire de la France,* 36 (1929), 268-269.

46. See "The Progress of Marriage" ([1722] *Poems,* I, 289 ff., lines 107 ff.), for a different one. And see *The Bubble* ([1720] *Poems,* I, 248 ff., 11.93-96), where Venus dives *into* the sea for pearls and coral—a jibe at female investors in the South Sea Bubble.

47. George P. Mayhew, *Rage or Raillery. The Swift Manuscripts at the Huntington Library* (San Marino: Huntington Library, 1967), pp. 95, 111.

48. See Williams in *Poems,* II, 629, and Mayhew, pp. 111-112.

49. *Poems,* II, 629. The printer, bookseller and others were actually taken into custody (*Poems,* II, 629, 640).

50. I discuss the passage more fully in *Gulliver and the Gentle Reader*, pp. 6-7.

51. Swift's appeal to Horace's view that "Ridicule has greater Pow'r / To reform the World, than Sour" (11.199-200) should not mislead us into thinking that Swift's own forms of ridicule are often of an urbane Horatian sort. It is true that elsewhere, notably in his praise of the *Beggar's Opera* in *Intelligencer*, No. III, Swift similarly celebrates humor, which is "the best Ingredient towards that Kind of Satyr, which is most useful, and gives the least Offence; which, instead of lashing, laughs Men out of their Follies, and Vices; and is the Character that gives *Horace* the Preference to *Juvenal*" (*Works*, XII, 33). Such an emphasis would doubtless seem particularly appropriate in a friendly celebration of a relatively genial work like the *Beggar's Opera*, but there is no reason to suppose that Swift was not sincere in voicing his allegiance to some official pieties about the satirist's art. Some important passages of the "Epistle to a Lady," however, as well as *Gulliver's Travels* and the great Irish tracts, lack this note of easy and inoffensive laughter and are truer to Swift, revealing him in a more total creative engagement of his whole personality. The *Intelligencer's* reference to the satirist's "*publick Spirit*" which prompts "Men of *Genius* and Virtue, to mend the World as far as they are able" (XII, 34), likewise expresses a conventional piety sincerely. But it similarly bears a less than total relationship to Swift's more sombre satiric energies and motivations and to his many ironies (themselves hard to evaluate exactly) about the world's unmendability.

52. Aldous Huxley, *Do What You Will*, p. 99.

53. Herbert Davis, *Jonathan Swift. Essays on his Satire and Other Studies* (New York: Oxford University Press, 1964), p. 37.

54. For some predecessors in this attitude to women, see James W. Johnson, *The Formation of English Neo-Classical Thought* (Princeton: Princeton University Press, 1967), p. 119. See also Irvin Ehrenpreis, "Letters of Advice to Young Spinsters," in *Stuart and Georgian Moments*, ed. Earl Miner (Berkeley, Los Angeles, London: University of California Press, 1972), pp. 245-269, which compares Swift's attitude with earlier and later attitudes.

55. *Of the Characters of Women: An Epistle to a Lady* (1735), 11.271-272. Pope knew the Stella poems, most of which were first printed in the joint Pope-Swift *Miscellanies, The Last Volume*, 1727. A few lines later in his own poem, he equivocates on Martha Blount's age in a way which recalls another of the Stella poems (1.283, and Twickenham note). For a recent discussion of Pope's lines, and a brief and not very searching comparison with Swift, see Felicity A. Nussbaum, "Pope's 'To a Lady' and the Eighteenth-Century Woman," *Philological Quarterly*, 54 (1975), 451-454.

56. Writing to the Rev. James Stopford on 20 July 1726, Swift expressed his deep anxiety about Stella's health, adding: "believe me that violent friendship is much more lasting, and as much engaging, as vio-

lent love," (*Correspondence*, III, 145). The word "love" is not conceded, but what Swift meant by "violent friendship" is not clear and probably never will be. Theories of a secret marriage between Swift and Stella have often been entertained, and much gossip about their relationship plagued them in their own lifetime.

57. Swift speaks of his own birth much as he does of Stella's (and of Gulliver's) in a letter to Bolingbroke, 31 October 1729: "My Birth although from a Family not undistinguished in its time is many degrees inferior to Yours . . . a Younger Son of younger Sons" (*Correspondence*, III, 354).

III

POPE'S MEANINGS AND THE STRATEGIES OF INTERRELATION

Ralph Cohen

William R. Kenan, Jr. Professor of English, University of Virginia

In the last fifty years a considerable body of work has appeared exploring theoretically and practically *how* Augustan poems mean. A case has been made that "meanings" are not merely carried by the referential dimension of words, but by rhyme, syntax, imagery, allusion, indeed by the whole range of rhetorical features. Thus the eighteenth-century criteria of "clarity" and "decorum" have been redefined as complex procedures, decipherable by turning not only to the explicit meaning of words but to what William Wimsatt has called the "alogical" procedures of verse.[1] This view of meaning was, in part, supported by the linguists' demonstration that any communication, including poetry, involves an addresser, an addressee, a code, a message, a message context, and a means of transmission (contact).[2] Modern critics of eighteenth-century poetry have argued that its message pertains to Augustan support of humanistic values, and they have focused their analyses on problems of language and rhetoric, of the social, political, and historical dimension of meaning, and of the character and expectations of the audience.

Their approaches have shown that Pope's poetry is subtle, witty, and deals with social values, that it connects pastoral retirement with urban politics, wit with seriousness. To explain these, however, they have offered either *ad hoc* generalizations or an organic theory of poetry. In this paper I offer an explanation of Pope's poetry as composite. The ideas of interrelation to which I limit myself are those which explain Pope's manner of relating poetry to society, to his self-conscious processes of composition, to his artistic and didactic procedures of diction and rhetoric, and to his principles of connection.

Since my approach builds upon the work of earlier critics while offering a somewhat different view of the nature of a literary work, I wish first to outline their insights. Geoffrey Tillotson, after his early studies of Pope's poetry,[3] offered hypotheses about the relation of Pope's language to social class:

For the Augustans things in general were more thoroughly departmentalized than for us, and this was partly because of the deeper divisions among the social classes. In particular it greatly mattered to the poets that the reading public included aristocrats as their first patrons.[4]

It should be noted that John Arthos's identification or description of personified generalizations—"scaly breed," "feathered tribe"—were placed within an explanatory hypothesis—the relation of poetic language to conventional or scientific terminology.[5] But not only Pope's periphrases mix natural description with metaphor; his nature imagery as a whole reflects the uncertain relations between man and his environment.

With regard to the nonreferential features of language, for example, Maynard Mack noted that Pope used names as metaphor, juxtaposition as analogy. He pointed to modes of imaging that he called "more reticent" or "restrained" than earlier uses, and he suggested that the great pervasive metaphor of Augustan poetry was the mock-heroic:

it was a metaphor that could be made to look two ways. If the heroic genre and the heroic episodes lurking behind *The Rape of the Lock* diminish many of the values of this society, they also partially throw their weight behind some others. Clarissa's speech is an excellent case in point.[6]

Maynard Mack also noted a number of patterns and devices of complication "that help supply the kind of unity in Pope's poems which he is popularly not supposed to have."[7] Mack's hypothesis assumed that Pope's metaphors were defined by Coleridge's definition of the power of imagination,[8] and the unity of his poems was self-contained or organic:

There is the implicit theme, usually announced in a word or phrase toward the outset of the poem, and while seldom developed in recurrent imagery, as in Shakespeare, almost always developed in recurrent references and situations. There is also, often, a kind of pattern of words that reticulates through a poem, enmeshing a larger and larger field of associations—for instance, words meaning light in the *Essay on Criticism,* or the word "head" (and, of course, all terms for darkness) in the *Dunciad.* And there are a great many more such unifying agents.[9]

Maynard Mack applied Coleridgean terms like "balance" and "reconcilement" of opposites[10] to Pope's poetry, and he found that it possessed a unity governed by reticulation of recurrent words and associations. The unity of a Pope poem surely involves reticulation, but this is aligned with procedures such as association, analogy, logical connections, and so forth, that can be called "combination" in contrast to Coleridgean organicism.

Just as the analysis of diction and metaphor involved constructs explaining the features by reference to the critic's views of language and society, or his views of poetic and scientific language, so, too, the function of allusion formed part of a construct. Reuben Brower declared:

For Dryden and for Pope allusion, especially in ironic contexts, is a resource equivalent to symbolic metaphor and elaborate imagery in other poets. Through allusion, often in combination with subdued metaphors and exquisite images, Pope gets his purchase on larger meanings and evokes the finer resonances by which poetry (in Johnson's phrase) "penetrates the recesses of the mind."[11]

These "larger meanings" were, of course, Pope's sense of a great classical, humanist tradition and the need for its restoration. But Brower claimed, as did the other critics, that the view of allusion he proposed was understood by eighteenth-century readers, and that this was one of the forms of continuity in our interpretation of the poetry. He, therefore, characterized the audience as one that would support his hypothesis:

They could agree with Pope that Nature and Homer were the same, because they shared a belief in the unchanging characteristics of human beings and, underlying that, a conviction that there was a stable order in the nature of things, the Great Nature that included both man and the universe. For the eighteenth-century reader Homer was the grand example of fidelity to this higher truth of "general nature."[12]

These views of meaning that I have been describing are representative of those that have redeemed the poetry of Dryden and Pope. They demonstrated that the poetry of statement was not prose but highly subtle poetry, dealing not with trivial but with serious matters. Dominated as these critical constructs were by Matthew Arnold's attack on the two writers as wit-writers rather than soul-writers, as classics of our prose and not our poetry,[13] the criticism may be said to have restored Dryden and Pope as classics of poetry *for Matthew Arnold*. They were indeed shown to be writers with a vision of civilization, poets of high seriousness and moral fervor. Thomas Edwards puts it this way:

We deny that Pope was, in Arnold's sense, the high priest of an age of prose and reason by substituting for "prose and reason" qualities more to our taste — and to Arnold's, some of them. We find "imagination" in the wit of his imagery, organizational control rather than pedantry in his allusions, moral and metaphysical seriousness in his "social" attitudes and ironies; in general he serves as a useful corrective to a too narrow idea of poetry.[14]

These critics altered the Victorian reading of eighteenth-century poetry; they reestablished a basis for examining this poetry. But in doing so they accepted, perhaps inevitably, the premise of the organic nature of the individual poem, the belief that inherited culture is overt rather than covert, the view of a work as a whole rather than a combination of parts associatively connected, and the view of a unified audience as preparatory for and responsive to, but not shaped by, the literary work.

These premises (but not the insights that accompanied them) need, I believe, to be revised. If the knowledge of Augustan poetic language and thought is to be made usable for yet another body of critical readers, they must be placed within hypotheses that accord more convincingly (obviously I speak out of my immodest conviction) with the nature of eighteenth-century poetry: namely, that these poems are combinations of parts associatively connected to achieve particularized generic ends. Although critics have noticed such interconnections in diction, imagery, and subject matter, they have lacked a comprehensive theory to explain them. In fact, even the audiences for whom the poems were written recognized only some of these procedures.

Because the hypothesis of audience expectation has been held by esteemed critics, I wish to begin my argument for reinterpretation by examining a clear statement of it with reference to *Absalom and Achitophel:*

the meaning of the passages in Dryden's masterpiece that deal with Achitophel seem to me limited by what the author might have expected his reader to find, by what the reader might reasonably attribute to the author, by what either might be expected to know of Achitophel or of Shaftesbury, by what the words of the poem are likely to have meant to Dryden and his audience.[15]

Now there is every reason to assume that an author has certain expectations of his readers; the "engagement" that Wordsworth spoke about was operative in the prefaces and prologues of eighteenth-century literary works.[16] But what precisely were the author's expectations of his readers? Such expectations are not and cannot be completely fulfilled since their completion is dependent upon the reader's specific response to a poetic tradition, to the implications of poetic form, to the manner of presenting characters, alluding to other works and to contemporary events.[17] What could Dryden have expected his audience — which was of varied political opinions — to find in *Absalom and Achitophel?* Aside from the reference to contemporary figures and to the Homeric and biblical narratives, what could their expected response have been to a mock-heroic poem? How did they anticipate or respond to images of space and time, to Zimri, to the newness of the form? Is it not the point of this theory of meaning that the audience *expected* more than they could define?

The appeal to authorial expectations of readers is not a matter that lends itself easily to careful examination, but when it does, it reveals the limits of the author's knowledge of his own work and his audience. The very idea of "expectations" — if it is to be entertained, for it is surely not an eighteenth-century way of talking about literature — cannot be restricted to the expectations of the *primary* audience of the work. If the work is to have any further existence, it would have to depend on satisfying expectations that are shaped by the poem.

The audience of Pope's *Iliad,* according to Reuben Brower, expected the poem to satisfy a certain standard of aristocratic manners, a certain standard for the heroic poem, and certain conventions that distinguished poetry from prose.[18] But the appeal to "audience" as a homogeneous entity with homogeneous expectations raises difficulties. For an "audience" is not a single responder, and even though it may share some expectations, it does not share the qualitative responses to expectations. This is especially true in a period in which the audience is changing, as Addison notes in considering the audience of *The Spectator.*[19] Later audiences cannot be limited by the expectations of the first audience, and they cannot read the work as though they are that audience. If they try to do so, the poem becomes a museum piece, not a work with contemporary value. Indeed, one point about authorial expectations is that the author needs to engage his initial audience by *defeating* some of their expectations.

Did the author know how his meaning was achieved? In the sense that "knowing" is a conscious awareness of what one is doing, there is ample reason to doubt that authors' knowing is more extensive than that of critics who comment on the work. Only if we consider the writing itself equivalent to knowing does this hypothesis seem reasonable. And as William Wimsatt indicates, the evidence does not support this view:

[N]either in his *Essay on Criticism,* nor in his remarks to Spence, nor in his letters, even the elaborate letter on versification to Walsh, has Pope anything substantial to say about the system of artful figures which later critics have considered characteristic of his couplets.[20]

It should be noted that in *An Essay on Criticism* Pope argued that Virgil composed his poem without a knowledge of what the conventions were. It was only after the composition was completed that he discovered with amazement that "Rules as strict his labour'd Work confined, / As if the *Stagyrite* o'erlook'd each Line." And although his own work seeks to instill critical and poetical consciousness, it is clearly limited as a description of this state by eighteenth-century hypotheses.

Should the modern critic be limited by what the words of the poem meant to the poet or his original audience if these *could* be

determined? To assume that the reading by an educated contemporary in some way constitutes the necessary and sufficient
grounds for interpretation rests on a mistake. The fact that readers are first readers does not make their reading valid. Contemporaries can help describe probable usages and meanings, but
the constructs into which these are placed must be limited by
views of their traditions. Such readers are as much in the stream
of time as modern readers; they see limited aspects of a text as do
subsequent readers. Using the first readers of a poem as a hypothetical standard cannot be sufficient to validate an interpretation since a poem, especially an effective poem, extending
beyond the poet's conscious endeavors, possesses ways of using
and developing traditions, allusions, and conventions that the
contemporary reader does not grasp.

The great effort of the critics who have redeemed Pope for us
has been to explain how his language has continued to make his
thoughts and feelings significant. None of them wish to deny the
need to know what the words meant in the eighteenth century.
But no Bailey's or Johnson's dictionary can explain how the words
interact in a poem to subtilize their meaning. The meaning is
part of the tone, attitude, syntax, imagery, and sound as these
are interwoven. Awareness of or familiarity with contemporary
usage can prevent anachronisms or misinformation, but it does
not provide an interpretation, for interpretation is governed by
critical hypotheses. The fact that contemporary critics, like
Addison and Dennis, can respond differently to *The Rape of the
Lock,* and that Arabella Fermor can respond first positively then
negatively to the poem, indicates that intelligent contemporary
readers do not possess privileged interpretations.[21]

Eighteenth-century poems did not pose interpretative problems
for contemporary critics, but offered forms of education, controversy, persuasion, admiration, etc. The didactic tendency of this
poetry has been recognized especially in satire, georgic, and epistle by some modern critics.[22] But the placing of epigrams in odes
or other lyric forms, the use of maxims in elegies and epitaphs, in
fact, the omnipresence of interrelating parts of varied forms and
subjects has not been noticed, or, if it has, it has been seen as in-
adequate or as a breakdown of proper form.[23] When varieties of
diction or "style" have been found successful in Pope's poetry,
they have been explained by highly questionable arguments.

Critics have noted that varieties of diction occur within the Popeian poem, or that varieties of style are characteristic of *The Dunciad* or even of satire as a genre. F. R. Leavis, referring to "Elegy to the Memory of an Unfortunate Lady," noted that Pope could pass from satiric ridicule to resonant and decorous elevations because he was at "one with a society to which these [moral, aesthetic, and utilitarian certitudes] were obvious but important truths."[24] Maynard Mack, commenting on Pope's use of witty and ingenious images in the same poem, drew attention to what he considered the infrequency of such combinations:

Pope rarely uses these extensive collocations of witty and ingenious images, and . . . when he does, it is almost always to establish something that his poems intend to disvalue — here a death-in-life theme, contrasting with a life-in-death theme built up around the lady.[25]

These critics place their remarks — as Maynard Mack's on combinations of retirement and satiric poetry — within a context of reality responses or organicism. But neither of these can do justice to the fact that Pope's poems are "wholes" in the sense of associated parts. They combine widely diverse parts held together by implicit modes of connection or interrelation.

Pope was certainly not "at one" with his intellectual environment, and even if he were, the procedure applies to poets who attack Pope and do not share his "at oneness." The interrelations of imagery and diction, satire and sublimity, are only a very few of the combinations that give life and vigor and meaning to Pope's poetry. These interrelations are carried in a series of analogies or equations which begin with the view of poetry as composed of a changing body and an unchanging soul. The interrelations form a set of changing contexts — change-sameness, energy-dullness, motion-rest, war-peace, pastoral-satire, vice-virtue — but all the contexts rest on an underlying concept. The interrelations can occur in all the aspects of a structure from the lexical to the metaphysical, and they provide the basis for understanding the concepts of "mean," of "ruling passion," of the "whole."[26]

The social basis of this procedure lies in Pope's awareness of the social and intellectual change in his time and his belief in the need for wariness in such a period. The aristocratic, humanistic values for which he stands are hedged by his uncertainty in defining and identifying these values in practice. Pope relates them to his concept of "spirit" or continuity, but they become ambiguous limits and offer specific but shifting boundaries. The anxiety that makes Ariel uneasy in *The Rape of the Lock,* that requires constant and subtle discrimination in *An Essay on Criticism,* that leads to ultimate assertions of humility and authority in the *Epistle to Dr. Arbuthnot*—this anxiety is at the source of Pope's need for consciousness. It is this consciousness that makes it possible to grapple with the problem of continuity and change.

One of the key passages in Pope which explains the process of interrelation in nature and art appears in *An Essay on Criticism.*

> First follow NATURE, and your Judgment frame
> By her just Standard, which is still the same:
> *Unerring Nature,* still divinely bright,
> One *clear, unchang'd,* and *Universal* Light,
> Life, Force, and Beauty, must to all impart,
> At once the *Source,* and *End,* and *Test* of *Art.*
> *Art* from that Fund each *just Supply* provides,
> Works *without Show,* and *without Pomp* presides:
> In some fair Body thus th' informing Soul
> With Spirits feeds, with Vigour fills the whole,
> Each Motion guides, and ev'ry Nerve sustains;
> *It self unseen,* but in th' *Effects,* remains.
>   (68-79)[27]

"Nature" gives each work the power, vigor, and life appropriate to it. Art works by selecting from nature the powers appropriate to its particular form. The "unchang'd" universal light is a principle of the cosmos as well as of art; it is present in all existence as the source of life, as the continuing energy or force in life, and as beauty which is its appropriate effect. Art works without revealing the underlying soul that feeds, fills, guides, and sustains it. And because the soul works without show and without pomp— "*It self unseen,* but in th' *Effects,* remains"—it provides men with the model for modesty, for stooping, for self-conscious acceptance of limitations. The test of one's artistic judgment is the correlation of how one means with how one learns.

In the *Epistle to Burlington* Pope wrote:

> He gains all points, who pleasingly confounds,
> Surprizes, varies, and conceals the Bounds.
>   (55-56)

Although in this couplet Pope was writing of garden-design, he clearly considered this form of art, like poetry, governed by the general principle of God's underlying power. The analogies between man and nature, between politics and pastoralism, have been pointed out by Earl Wasserman, by Maynard Mack, and others. It is not surprising that *An Essay on Criticism, Windsor Forest,* and *The Rape of the Lock* should have such mixtures of subject matter and that they should resemble one another in the interrelations of their parts.

The need for modesty and modulation arises in Pope because these attitudes are the expressions of a life without show and without pomp. Thus negation and its analogues—restraint, control, boundedness, shrinking, etc.—becomes forms of virtue; they are types of discipline, of action, that restrain self-love, that make possible the shifting boundaries of self-inquiry without succumbing to vice:

> Virtuous and vicious ev'ry Man must be,
> Few in th' extreme, but all in the degree.
> (*Essay on Man,* 231-232)

Moderation and *modesty* were movable concepts, relational but not relative. Pope denies the fusion of virtue and vice, even though they may seem at times to overlap. Virtue and vice are identifiable by their consequences, but even the virtuous man is limited by his mortality.

This is the praise Pope gives in the epitaph to "modest," "mod'-rate" John Lord Caryll (1711). Addressing the "Exalted Souls" who come through their learning to consider themselves above mankind, he writes:

> Then, when you seem above mankind to soar,
> Look on this marble, and be vain no more!
> (16-17)

The view of modesty, of limits, of the consciousness of self are developed by Pope with reference to composition and criticism in *An Essay on Criticism.* Pope knows that there are critics who, like Aristotle and Quintilian, are not poets but can, nevertheless, provide reliable guides for them. He recognizes that poets, like

Homer and Virgil, are critics because their works are poetic models.[28] But the best critic composes model poems that contain model precepts. And this is the aim Pope sets himself. He presents the reader with a poem that is both a model of a particular poetic kind and a series of statements about how to compose and criticize such a model. This form of critical writing which illustrated what it explained was practiced by Horace, Vida, Boileau, and others; Pope converted this type of poem into his version of the genre by his strategies of interrelation.[29] In the *Essay on Criticism* he had written: "Let such teach others who themselves excell, / And *censure freely* who have *written well*" (15-16). Of Horace, one of his models, he wrote:

> He, who Supream in Judgment, as in Wit,
> Might boldly censure, as he boldly writ,
> Yet *judged* with *Coolness* tho' he sung with *Fire;*
> His *Precepts* teach but what his *Works* inspire.
>   (657-660)

And Longinus was "himself that great *Sublime* he draws" (680).

Pope found in Horace a body of precepts for poetry that conjoined cool judgment with inspirational flights.[30] Pope applied these precepts with judgment to his own poetic power, while disdaining the dullness of others. *An Essay on Criticism* is composed with the self-consciousness of a historical tradition and the poet's and critic's role in applying this tradition to his own time. The double role of the poem — as model and as statement — becomes for Pope a method of mixing praise with satiric attack, of urging continuity while demonstrating change.

Consider the following passage not in its interrelations with Horatian principles, but in terms of the interrelation of "all things" that Pope sees as limited. And consider also the underlying implications of "Limits fit."

> Nature to all things fix'd the Limits fit,
> And wisely curb'd proud Man's pretending Wit.
> As on the *Land* while *here* the *Ocean* gains,
> In *other Parts* it leaves wide sandy Plains;
> Thus in the *Soul* while *Memory* prevails,
> The solid Pow'r of *Understanding* fails;
> Where Beams of warm *Imagination* play,

The *Memory*'s soft Figures melt away.
One *Science* only will one *Genius* fit;
So *vast* is Art, so *narrow* Human Wit;
Not only bounded to *peculiar Arts,*
But oft in *those,* confin'd to *single Parts.*
Like Kings we lose the Conquests gain'd before,
By vain Ambition still to make them more:
East might his *sev'ral Province* well command,
Wou'd all but *stoop* to what they *understand.*

(52-67)

In this passage "Nature" is the power that establishes divinity of operation, but controls the diversity within limits. The curbing of man's "pretending Wit" applies to a wide variety of actions just as the tides move over different areas of the shore. The oceans and the plains, the faculties of the mind, the authority of the conqueror over the conquered — all are controlled by limits. They are interrelated not only in the imagery of power ("gain'd," "prevails," "melt away"), but in the way limit is defined. "Nature" sets the limits for elemental ocean and plains; it sets the limits to the innate capacities of man; it sets limits to the actions of men as conquerors or independent actors; and when these ignore the limitations, they suffer the consequences. The concluding image of conquest or power sums up the nature of proper authority; it must acknowledge curbs, concede its limits. To command involves a consciousness of vain ambition, a willingness to stoop to "understanding."

This passage relates the contexts of change — of the incursion of ocean upon land, of memory that excludes understanding, of authority that stoops — to the concept of the unchanging. As early as the first decade of the eighteenth century, Pope included in his addition to Wycherly's poem, "The Various Mix'd Life," the following lines about "the Stream of Life":

Around in sweet Meanders wildly range,
Kept fresh by Motion, and unchang'd by Change.

(24-25)

Similar distinctions between the concept and context of change appeared in the *Essay on Man:*

> All are but parts of one stupendous whole,
> Whose body, Nature is, and God the soul;
> That, chang'd thro' all, and yet in all the same,
> Great in the earth, as in th' aethereal frame.
>
> (I, 266-270)

The relations between change and sameness apply to wit, to politics, to the self, to the natural environment, to the cosmos. In *Windsor Forest,* for example, Pope described the natural world as harmoniously confused:

> Where Order in Variety we see,
> And where, though all things differ, all agree.
>
> (15-16)

An analogical view appears in *An Essay on Man:*

> Extremes in Nature equal ends produce,
> In Man they join to some mysterious use;
> Tho' each by turns the other's bound invade,
> As, in some well-wrought picture, light and shade,
> And oft so mix, the diff'rence is too nice
> Where ends the Virtue, or begins the Vice.
>   Fools! who from hence into the notion fall,
> That Vice or Virtue there is none at all.
>
> (205-212)

Pope draws attention to the distinction between extremes in nature and in human nature. In the cosmos each extreme can produce positive as well as negative effects, but in human behavior extremes are often so mixed as to make it difficult to distinguish vice from virtue. But Pope's point here and elsewhere is that distinctions can and need to be made. It is in the discrimination of the invaded bounds that the responsibility of the critic lies, between an invasion that leads to liberty and one that leads to destruction of liberty.

Pope's statements often refer to two worlds—the metaphysical and the actual; this has been persuasively argued by Earl Wasserman, but his further claim that in the actual world Pope sees virtue as a mean between opposing vices seems far less convincing.

With wonderful ingenuity and, so far as I know, with great originality, Pope has brought together two loosely related ideas deeply rooted in Western thought: *concordia discors,* or the supernatural harmony of the contradictory extremes of this world; and the Aristotelian ethical tradition of *mediocritas,* or the definition of virtue as the mean between opposing vices.[31]

Overlooked in this presentation is Pope's relational view, an understanding of his poems as composite sequences of parts related by means of connection or association. A historical topos such as *concordia discors* will inevitably be drawn into the poem's relational procedure. Pope does not proceed by opposing human forces, but by establishing a range of relation within which such forces can operate. When Pope refers to the "middle state," he can mean that it involves neither arbitrary punishment of a butler for "one bad Cork" nor keeping a servant who is always slovenly and careless.[32]

In dealing with the development of a traditional idea, it is necessary to note Pope's procedure in continuing yet changing it. To neglect this is to overlook that for him ideas and actions rest on an unstated generalization about God's presence. In the *Essay on Man* Pope found that extremes in man join "to some mysterious use," whereas in the *Epistle to Bathurst* these extremes "concur to gen'ral use":

> Extremes in Nature equal good produce,
> Extremes in Man concur to gen'ral use.
>   (163-164)

In the *Essay on Man* the couplet was joined with couplets relating the mystery of human behavior to the images of invasion of the bounds of vice and virtue and the delicate mixing of light and shade in a painting. The relationship of vice and virtue belongs, as in the *Essay on Criticism,* with a discrimination of boundaries and the discipline of art. In the *Epistle to Bathurst* this couplet is related to the Power "who bids the Ocean ebb and flow," to the metaphysical basis of the cycle of life and death, of the power that "on Change Duration founds."

Pope converts the topos of *concordia discors* into a movable relation that has both shifting boundaries and changing relations within the boundaries. The limits remain for Pope undiscovered though there is no doubt that they exist. Within the bounds, relations can be complementary, contradictory, or subtly conjoined.

Thus Pope's "mean" is part of his view of nature, of man, and of society. With regard to nature, there is the underlying soul or spirit that controls all and provides a harmony that man cannot grasp. Man can, however, recognize overt harmony in the seasons or in his environment. With regard to man, each individual is dominated by an inborn ruling passion; although in single actions the ruling passion is elusive, it is detectable by examining many and varied actions. With regard to society, the observer recognizes contradictory human actions that do not often lead to a harmony of general interest, but he must trust that a future life will bring harmony.

The concept of actual bounds, therefore, should be understood as shifting within the designation of absolutes not clearly perceived. True harmony exists on a metaphysical level; actual harmony may exist, though it rarely does, in human actions, and it is recognizable by the discriminating participant or observer. Pope unfolds these views by particular functions of language and rhetorical procedures.

Pope's diction has been well served by the critics who have traced its ambiguities and subtleties. The explanation of the diversity of meanings, however, demands a hypothesis more comprehensive than the contextual one, and I have proposed the relation between context and concept. The context functions as the body, with the common basis of varied functions serving as the "soul." In rhetoric, this procedure is metonymy.[33]

The most obvious example of Pope's metonymy is his variant of a Miltonic procedure, using differing inflected forms of the same word. Although such practices are identified in rhetoric by varied terms, I call them metonymy because they share common functions.

> All spread their charms, but charm not all alike
> (*Essay on Man*, II, 127)

and

> Grows with his growth and strengthens with his strength
> (*Essay on Man,* II, 136).[34]

The relation between identical terms ("all" and "with his") and changing terms ("charms," "charm," "grows," "growth," "strengthens," "strength") connects process with product, unity with multiplicity. In the first example, "charm" is a plural term, emphasizing the similarity among all "charms," but "charm" as verb is distributive, drawing attention to the different processes involved in "charming."

Pope's use of the multiple meanings of particular terms has been amply demonstrated by William Empson, E. N. Hooker, G. Tillotson,[35] and others. And his consciousness of this procedure can be demonstrated in such a key term as "correct." Walsh urged Pope in 1703 (?) to follow "correctness,"[36] and Pope referred to this in *The First Epistle of the Second Book of Horace Imitated* (1736-1737):

> Late, very late, correctness grew our care,
> When the tir'd nation breath'd from civil war.
> (272-273)

But in the *Epilogue to the Satires Dialogue I* (1738) the speaker accuses him of growing correct in place of writing with rapture:

> You grow *correct* that once with Rapture writ,
> And are, besides, too *Moral* for a Wit.
> (3-4)

Correctness in the first context is part of a historical exposition that makes "correctness" consistent with energy and fire; and wit in the second is governed by the same concept of correctness and fire and attributes the separation of correctness from rapture to Pope's "Decay of Parts, alas" (5).

Nevertheless, Pope's multi-meaning language does not depart from the principle of sameness in difference. If one selects an early usage and a later one to test this, the principle of metonymy will be clear. In his translation of Ovid's "The Fable of Vertumnus and Pomona" occurs the passage:

> Force he prepar'd, but check'd the rash Design;
> For when, appearing in a Form Divine,
> The Nymph surveys him, and beholds the Grace
> Of charming Features and a youthful Face,
> In her soft Breast consenting Passions move,
> And the warm Maid confess'd a mutual Love.
> (118-123)

In *An Essay on Criticism* the phrase "checks the *bold* Design" (my italics) occurs in the following passage:

> When first young *Maro* in his boundless Mind
> A Work t' outlast Immortal *Rome* design'd,
> Perhaps he seem'd *above* the Critick's Law,
> And but from *Nature's Fountains* scorn'd to draw:
> But when 't examine ev'ry Part he came,
> *Nature* and *Homer* were, he found, the *same:*
> Convinc'd, amaz'd, he checks the bold Design,
> And Rules as strict his labour'd Work confine,
> As if the Stagyrite o'erlook'd each Line.
> Learn hence for Ancient *Rules* a just Esteem.
> (130-139)

In examining the context of "check'd the rash Design," it is apparent that this lyrical passage is dependent on the rejection of disguise. For when the young god appears in his own form, his grace, charm, and youth move the mind. Thus neither disguise nor violence reveals the grounds for love. And in the *Essay on Criticism,* the "bold Design" embodies beauty and spirit so that there is an equation between the recognition of godlike grace and the recognition of proper artistic principles of design. Although "check'd" in the first example has reference to Vertumnus's curbing or restraining his plan, and "checks" in the second refers to Virgil's confirming his design by comparing it to an original, both usages belong to the procedure of seeing into or beyond the surface—though changed, yet the same.

The relational procedure governing the diction has significance for the chronological study of Pope's works. In these, a shift takes place from the early ceremonial or playful relationships to those involving "characters." The early relations between nature and mythology, the altar and the religious or irreligious prayers, the games and social occasions, function to show pomp or modesty.[37] In the later works, these ceremonials and games move to subordinate positions, making the actors dominant. Another aspect of change occurs in Pope's insertions of his corrections and additions to Wycherley's poem. There his contribution is subordinated to Wycherley's, but in the poems imitative of Horace, Horace's work is subordinated to Pope's reworking of it. The shift that takes place is defined by Pope's parody of tradition and his use of characters to indicate the disharmonious relations among men and the uncertainty in locating an underlying spirit or concept.

The problem of change and continuity is one of the persistent themes in Pope's work, and I have tried to indicate its extensiveness. Pope absorbs and reworks Ovid's transformations, making them part of the world of change in sameness. The sources for this lie in Pope's political and personal awareness of the price one pays for peace, so that much of change is endured rather than welcomed. But in insisting on his personal independence and liberty, he nevertheless admitted that the boundaries of his possibilities were controlled not by himself but by his intellectual and political environment. Thus neither the country nor the city, neither retirement nor politics, could do any more than provide the compromises that finally led him to his desperate cry: "Universal Darkness buries all!"

The interrelationship of Pope's early work to his later can be observed in his process of composition. In "The River," composed in imitation of Cowley's poem in 1701, although published in 1717, Pope wrote:

> While mankind boasts superior sight,
>   With Eyes erect the heav'ns to see;
> The starry eyes of heav'n delight
>   To gaze upon themselves in thee.
>
> A second sun thou dost present,
>   And bring new heav'ns before our eyes;
> We view a milder firmament,
>   And pleas'd, look downward to the skies.
>   (9-16)

The pastoral image of reflected heavens is naturalized in the everflowing river; the second sun and the second sky are "a milder firmament" observed by man looking down at the river, thus made subordinate rather than superior to man. The reflective image is thus related to joy, love, and self-love or pride (the Narcissus image and its analogies recur in Pope's poetry),[38] to the transitory river so that, in typical Popeian fashion, the eternal heavens are also seen in a transient aspect. The image of reflection is a surface and illusory one. The concept governing it implies levels in the water — surface and bed — as there are levels in the universe. The river is not only a form of reflection, it is also a source of nourishment for flowers and vines that man converted to polluting drink. The interrelation of pastoral reciprocity or harmony and ultimate vice is rehearsed again in the *Essay on Criticism*. The great poets arrived on Parnassus's top with the generous critics encouraging their raptures, "But following Wits from that Intention stray'd." The drive for imitation rather than support arose from envy, ambition, and self-deceit. Thus the reflective or imitative passage was related to social behavior, as in the Narcissus references. But why these should arise in a condition that is idyllic is a problem that Pope avoided here but came to recognize as insoluble, the source of a continuing anxiety.

In *Windsor Forest* the Ovidian passage of the transformation of Lodona is concluded with the following mimetic or reflective passage:

> In her chast Current oft the Goddess laves,
> And with Celestial Tears augments the Waves.
> Oft in her Glass the musing Shepherd spies
> The headlong Mountains and the downward Skies,
> The watry Landskip of the pendant Woods,
> And absent Trees that tremble in the Floods;
> In the clear azure Gleam the Flocks are seen,
> And floating Forests paint the Waves with Green.
> Thro' the fair Scene rowl slow the lingring Streams,
> Then foaming pour along, and rush into the *Thames*.
> (209-218)

If the reflective scene is usually related to ideal pastoral, to man's fall, here strife leads to a peaceful stream which pictures a "watry Landskip." The stream is the goddess dissolved and the one in which "oft the Goddess laves." It is mythological stream and a natural one, one in which at one moment the reflection can be seen and at another it disappears amid the foaming and rushing current.

The narrative of pursuit followed by the reflective pastoral concluding with sudden violent movement provides still another analogy for the principle of change and continuity. In addition the passage draws attention to a self-consciousness both in the narrative and in the description. The narrative has the goddess lamenting her situation, and the description carries this consciousness to the reader by positing a "musing Shepherd" observing the slow-moving "floating Forests," and this scene is suddenly replaced by a rushing and foaming river.

The self-consciousness of the goddess which results from an inability to rest content with her changed state is an analogue to Pope's poems as they relate to each other. I have indicated the frequency of reflective images, and other critics have noted Pope's frequent imagistic returns. But there is yet another type of interrelation which is not dictional or imagistic; it consists of Pope's incorporation of passages originally written as independent pieces or parts of poems into later works.

In *An Essay on Criticism* Pope's self-consciousness was tied to attacks on lack of modesty, on false pretensions, on all those faults that stemmed from show and pomp. But the process of composition related self-consciousness to the need to establish continuity of expression, of art. The passages establish a basis for analogical or equational relationships whether these are the types of situations that can be considered means or the types of reflective images that can be the basis of narcissistic self-deceit or self-conscious awareness of loss or transience.

The procedure that I pursue should not be confused with the use of selected contexts; rather, it is based on the assumption that the understanding of a reflective image or an idea of *concordia discors* can only be explained by recognizing that the *context* requires an assumption about repetitive or relational or equational uses of a device wherever it occurs in Pope's poetry. Since a poem is a series of parts, it is necessary to recognize that all the poems must also be considered as parts. Thus the understanding of any one part requires not merely a study of its connection in a single poem, but its connection with similar parts in other poems.

One of the earliest instances of self-expropriation is the poem addressed to Elkanah Settle (written about 1702) and published in 1712. Pope included four of its lines in *The Dunciad* (1728) and two, slightly altered, in "The Second Satire of Dr. John Donne . . . Versifyd" (written 1713). The original lines were:

> Wit, past thro' thee, no longer is the same,
> As Meat digested takes a diff'rent Name.
> (11-12)

Donne's lines read:

> For if one eate my meate, though it be knowne
> The meat was mine, th' excrement is his own.
> (29-30)[39]

The lines in Pope's versification were:

> Sense, past thro' him, no longer is the same,
> For food digested takes another name.
> (33-34)

And Pope returned to this transformation image in *Epilogue to the Satires: Dialogue II:*

> If one, thro' Nature's Bounty of his Lord's,
> Has what the frugal, dirty soil affords,
> From him the next receives it, thick or thin,
> As pure a Mess almost as it came in;
> The blessed Benefit, not there confin'd,
> Drops to the third who nuzzles close behind;
> From tail to mouth, they feed, and they carouse;
> The last, full fairly gives it to the *House*.
> (173-180)

Pope's conscious use of his early verse for incorporation into later poetic efforts is obviously an attempt at continuity and changing sameness. But the range and variety of the interrelations include parody and the placing of passages belonging to one type of verse into another. The best-known example of Pope's "parody" is his use of the Sarpedon episode from the *Iliad* (translated and published in 1703). A variant of this translation was incorporated into *The Rape of the Lock* in 1717 as Clarissa's speech and noted as a parody by Pope. He remarked that it "opens more clearly the *Moral* of the Poem."[40] Thus parody became in this instance a form of moral discourse in a mock-heroic poem.[41] As for the original passage, it found its nonparodic place (with slight alterations) in Pope's translation of the *Iliad* (1715-1720). And it should be noted that the translation itself was published several books at a time and was, therefore, characteristic of the parts procedure discussed above. But the characteristic artistic procedure was here related to financial advantage.

The equational or proportional relationships between Clarissa's admonitions and an earlier passage in the "Epistle to Miss Blount, with the Works of Voiture" (1710, 1712) and a later one in *Epistle II. To a Lady* (1732-1734, 1735), is footnoted by the editor. F. W. Bateson who edited *Epistle II. To a Lady* notes that it contains couplets from "Sylvia, a Fragment" (published 1727), from "Stanzas. From the French of Malherbe" (1710, 1717), from "Epigram" (1730), and lines from other works.[42] Pieces of Pope's poetry reappear sometimes in poems of the same kind, as some of the "Fragment of a Satire" is part of the *Epistle to Dr. Arbuthnot,* sometimes in poems of other kinds—statements about extremes appear in the georgic *Windsor Forest,* the philosophical *Essay on Man,* the *Epistle to Bathurst.* And Pope's couplet from the *Essay on Criticism* (slightly revised) reappears in an imitation of Horace:

> But [True] Ease in Writing flows [comes] from Art, not Chance,
> As those move easiest who have learn'd to dance.
>
> (178-179)

To point out the role of critical consciousness in the poetry of Pope is to note that the key incident in *The Rape of the Lock* depends on this phenomenon, for the earthly lover lurking at Belinda's heart, though not consciously acknowledged, prevents Ariel from exercising his protective power. Insofar as Pope conceived of poetry as a form in which artistry was achieved not by statements but by effects, the poem possessed but did not announce or expound its skill. This was to be made explicit only in a work which was both a poem and an explanation of how a poem was to be criticized. The emphasis on the unseen force, energy, and spirit must be considered, as some critics have recognized, as a readjustment of the relation between mimesis and energy.[43]

This point is evident in the assumption that craft, wisdom, power, and energy in art as in human behavior lead to subtleties that constantly require discrimination on the part of the reader. For craft may be regularly dull just as subtlety may be extravagant. In the *Essay on Criticism* Pope wrote:

> True Ease in Writing comes from Art, not Chance,
> As those move easiest who have learn'd to dance.
>   (362-363)

In "Discourse on Pastoral Poetry" (1704, 1717) he wrote:

> But with a respect to the present age, nothing more conduces to make these composures natural, than when some Knowledge in rural affairs is discover'd. This may be made to appear rather done by chance than on design, and sometimes is best shewn by inference; lest by too much study to seem natural, we destroy that easy simplicity from whence arises the delight.[44]

And in the *Epistle to Burlington* (1730-1731):

> Let not each beauty ev'ry where be spy'd,
> Where half the skill is decently to hide.
>   (53-54)

And in *Epistle II, i:*

> Even copious Dryden, wanted, or forgot,
> The last and greatest Art, the Art to blot.
>   (280-281)

These passages, revealing the continuity of Pope's concern with consciousness, deal with the artist's craft in creating an ease for the reader that disguises the effort of the writer. This concern with the poetry not on the printed page, with the discarded verse, is correlative to Pope's sense of how "nature" works without show and without pomp, recognizable only in its effects. It is analogous to his view that the "limits fit" are dependent upon the writer and his society, that no limits can be specified as absolute, only the existence of limits.

The interrelations here are with the principle of curbing one's

imagination. To discard, to blot, to refine, to keep the beauties
in modest array—these are analogous to the principle of modesty,
of "stooping" to one's understanding. Limits always exist, but
they are not always the same. The ideal limits reached by the sublime Homer and Virgil were the result of a harmonious comple-
mentarity between critic and poet. But the possibilities of sublime
art were eliminated with the clash between poets and critics, and
this was the situation in Pope's time as well.

Pope's sublime passages exist as moments to introduce the need
for consciousness of what could be or once was, and they led into
passages attacking all who were responsible for the cultural corruption. Pope attributed to these conditions some of his limitations as an artist. From this conclusion followed his frustration
and bitterness with those responsible for the worst of times. To
illustrate how the interrelated poetic styles and forms serve to
explain Pope's personal satire, it is appropriate to examine the
epigram that concludes the discussion of unanticipated graces
and the hymn that follows it:

> Those oft are *Strategems* which *Errors* seem,
> Nor is it *Homer Nods,* but *We* that *Dream.*
>   Still green with Bays each *ancient* Altar stands,
> Above the reach of *Sacrilegious* Hands,
> Secure from *Flames,* from *Envy's* fiercer Rage,
> Destructive *War,* and all-involving *Age.*
> See, from *each Clime* the Learn'd their Incense bring;
> Hear, in *all Tongues* consenting *Paeans* ring!
> In Praise so just, let ev'ry Voice be join'd,
> And fill the *Gen'ral Chorus* of *Mankind!*
> Hail *Bards Triumphant!* born in *happier Days;*
> *Immortal* Heirs of *Universal* Praise!
> Whose Honours with Increase of Ages *grow,*
> As Streams roll down, *enlarging* as they flow!
> Nations *unborn* your mighty Names shall sound,
> And Worlds applaud that must not yet be *found!*
> Oh may some Spark of *your* Caelestial Fire
> The last, the meanest of your Sons inspire,
> (That on weak Wings, from far, pursues your Flights;
> *Glows* while he *reads,* but *trembles* as he *writes*)
> To teach vain Wits a Science *little known,*
> T' *admire* Superior Sense, and *doubt* their own!
>   (181-200)

In moving from the epigram to the sublime hymn, Pope means to assert the continuity of the values of the old Bards for his time, the proper role of the critic as handmaid to the poet, his own ability to rise, even if only for a short flight, to the demands of his subject. But the passage concludes with a descent into self-deprecating personal statement and a final epigram that asserts his superiority to "vain wits."

> To each vain Wits a Science *little known,*
> T' *admire* Superior Sense, and *doubt* their own!

Pope's movement from wit to the sublime to modest personal statement to epigrammatic disdain of critics who lack the consciousness to doubt their own sense, reveals the procedure by which the critic is conscious of his limitations. His attack upon others who are too vain to acknowledge their own limitations stems from his realization that in doing so, they make it impossible for a society hospitable to great poetry to develop. In a sense they condemn the poet to minor flights. It is for this reason that the disdain combines with personal animus and becomes in *The Dunciad* a furious assault. But the shift in styles is not a mere convention; it functions for Pope as an instructive device, as a demonstrative exhibit of his own talents, as a method for giving comprehensiveness to the didactic form, as a way of demonstrating the distributive or combinative quality of the poem, and, finally, as a procedure for indicating that the ideal of great poetry is, in its contemporary effects, achievable only fragmentarily, rarely, and, even then, against great odds.

Pope's procedures of mixed styles and mixed forms serve to clarify how variety can be sustained, and his attack on the neglect of self-consciousness in poets and critics illustrates those in whom the "*Universal* light" is concealed. Thus the *Essay on Criticism* reveals that the great tradition has diminished in Pope's time; it reveals, too, the poet's efforts, carried on in a minor key, to make his contemporaries conscious of the means for its recovery. His great effort, therefore, is devoted to attacking those who have perverted or continue to subvert the great tradition. One function of mixing forms in Pope's poem is to draw attention to this subversion as a form of madness.

To see Pope's poetry as interrelated is to see it as a combination of parts dependent on their connections. These interrelations refer not only to a single poem's ordering of its parts, but to the relation of parts of one poem to another. His very process of composition stemmed from an awareness of the need for continuity of concept while altering contexts. The contexts, however, are related to one another in terms of analogy, association, contrast, reciprocity; their differences can be understood as varied instances of a common underlying force or spirit. The variety of contexts is both a wit device and a challenge to the reader's discrimination. This challenge is minimized, overlooked, or denied by critics who place the religious or universalizing concept at the forefront of this poetry; they are right to recognize its importance, but wrong to disregard its relation to varied contexts.

The epitome of Pope's strategies of interrelation is his last version of *The Dunciad* (1743), his greatest poem. It subdues, parodies, and ridicules the playful, ceremonial views of his earlier poetry. Pope's consciousness of his own former aims and work is matched by his consciousness of intellectual corrupters who treat perverted behavior as a form of virtue and take pride in being honored members of the monarchy of dullness.

The prose commentary treats the narrative as reality supporting the poetry but neglecting its tone, a tone which joins the living with the dead, truth with fiction, the natural with the unnatural. As the characters of Book IV address the Goddess of Dullness, they create a chorus of dissonance; and the chorus is united by its absence of that spirit or energy which is the driving force of life and art. The dullards attend to the smallest detail, but they do not see its relation to a whole. Details as small as a hair were seen by Pope as full of soul and spirit — "as full, as perfect, in a hair as heart" (*Essay on Man*, I, 276). But the corrupters see only a hair and its pores, details with no proper relations. For them, the spirit has departed:

> The critic Eye, that microscope of Wit,
> Sees hairs and pores, examines bit by bit:
> How parts relate to parts, or they to whole,
> The body's harmony, the beaming soul,
> Are things which Kuster, Burman, Wasse shall see,
> When Man's whole frame is obvious to a *Flea*.
> (*Dunciad*, IV, 233-238)

NOTES

1. "Rhetoric and Poems: Alexander Pope," *The Verbal Icon* (Lexington: University of Kentucky Press, 1954), p. 180. Wimsatt discusses alogical and counterlogical procedures in other essays in this book: "One Relation of Rhyme to Reason" and "Verbal Style: Logical and Counterlogical." The reconsideration of Dryden and Pope began with Mark Van Doren, *The Poetry of John Dryden* (New York: Harcourt, Brace and Howe, 1920), followed in 1922 by T. S. Eliot's essay on Dryden.

2. Roman Jakobson, "Closing Statement: Linguistics and Poetics," *Style in Language,* ed. Thomas A. Sebeok (Cambridge: M.I.T. Press, 1960), p. 353. The combination of linguistic and formalist premises of the Prague Linguistic Circle were widely circulated in this country through *Theory of Literature* by René Wellek and Austin Warren (New York: Harcourt, Brace, 1949).

3. *On the Poetry of Pope* (Oxford: Clarendon Press, 1938). For a study of the views of James Thomson's diction by Tillotson and his contemporaries, see *The Art of Discrimination* (Berkeley and Los Angeles: University of California Press, 1964), pp. 357-364.

4. "More About Poetic Diction," *Augustan Studies* (London: Athlone Press, 1961), pp. 64-65.

5. *The Language of Natural Description in Eighteenth-Century Poetry* (Ann Arbor: University of Michigan Press, 1949).

6. "Wit and Poetry and Pope: Some Observations on His Imagery," *Pope and his Contemporaries: Essays Presented to George Sherburn,* ed. James L. Clifford and Louis Landa (Oxford: Clarendon Press, 1949), reprinted in *Eighteenth-Century English Literature,* ed. James L. Clifford (New York: Oxford University Press, 1959), pp. 36-37.

7. Ibid., p. 32.

8. Ibid., p. 36.

9. Ibid., p. 33.

10. Ibid., p. 36.

11. *Alexander Pope: The Poetry of Allusion* (Oxford: Clarendon Press, 1959), p. viii.

12. Ibid., pp. 106-107.

13. "Thomas Gray" (first printed 1880), *Essays in Criticism, Second Series* (London, 1896), p. 95; "The Study of Poetry" (first printed 1880), ibid., pp. 41-42.

14. "Visible Poetry: Pope and Modern Criticism," *Twentieth-Century Literature in Retrospect,* ed. Reuben A. Brower, Harvard English Studies 2 (Cambridge, Mass.: Harvard University Press, 1971), pp. 303-304.

15. Irvin Ehrenpreis, "Explicitness in Augustan Literature," *Literary Meaning and Augustan Values* (Charlottesville: University of Virginia Press, 1974), p. 39. It should be noted that in detailing the shared assumptions of the eighteenth-century audience, Earl Wasserman and

Reuben Brower listed those characteristics that supported their premises. Earl Wasserman, *The Subtler Language* (Baltimore: Johns Hopkins Press, 1959), pp. 10-11. "In varying degrees, ranging from conviction to faith and to passive submission, man accepted, to name but a
few, the Christian interpretation of history, the sacramentalism of
nature, the Great Chain of Being, the analogy of the various planes of
creation, the conception of man as microcosm, and, in the literary area,
the doctrine of the genres. These were cosmic syntaxes in the public
domain; and the poet could afford to think of his art as imitative of
'nature,' since these patterns were what he meant by 'nature.' He could
expect his audience to recognize his employment of these cosmic syntaxes, could transform language by means of them, and could survey
reality and experience in the presence of the world these syntaxes
implied. Poetry was, in the sense in which the word has been employed
here, essentially lyric, the poet's task being to 'imitate nature' by giving
poetic reality to nature's principles." Brower, *Allusion,* pp. 106-107:
"They could agree with Pope that Nature and Homer were the same,
because they shared a belief in the unchanging characteristics of human
beings and, underlying that, a conviction that there was a stable order
in the nature of things, the Great Nature that included both man and
the universe. For the eighteenth-century reader Homer was the grand
example of fidelity to this higher truth of 'general nature.'"

Note also that F. R. Leavis, *Revaluation* (New York: G. W. Stewart,
1947), declares that the Augustans "were in complete accord about fun-
damentals" (p. 77). Martin Price, discussing the *Essay on Man* finds
that the central contradictions of the poem "lie in the conflict between
an aesthetic vision and a moral one," *To the Palace of Wisdom* (Garden
City, N. Y.: Doubleday, 1964), p. 142.

16. "Preface to *Lyrical Ballads*" (1800), *Wordsworth's Literary Criticism,* ed. Nowell C. Smith (London: H. Frowde, 1905), p. 13.

17. For a presentation of this argument, see Hans Robert Jauss, "Literary History as a Challenge to Literary Theory," *New Directions in
Literary History,* ed. R. Cohen (Baltimore: Johns Hopkins Press, 1974),
esp. pp. 13-31.

18. Brower, *Allusion,* p. 106.

19. *The Spectator,* ed. Donald F. Bond (Oxford: Clarendon Press,
1965), I, no. 4 (March 5, 1711), 18-22, and no. 10 (March 12, 1711),
44-47.

20. Wimsatt, *Verbal Icon,* p. 176.

21. John Dennis, *Remarks on Mr. Pope's Rape of the Lock* (1728),
The Critical Works of John Dennis, ed. E. N. Hooker (Baltimore: Johns
Hopkins Press, 1943), II, 321-352. "Introduction," *The Rape of the
Lock and Other Poems,* ed. Geoffrey Tillotson, *The Twickenham Edi-
tion of the Poems of Alexander Pope,* II (London: Methuen, 1940),
89-91.

22. Rosalie Colie, *The Resources of Kind* (Berkeley, Los Angeles,
London: University of California Press, 1973). John E. Sitter, "Generic

Confusion," *The Poetry of Pope's Dunciad* (Minneapolis: University of Minnesota Press, 1971), pp. 6-50.

23. R. Cohen, "On the Interrelations of Eighteenth-Century Literary Forms," *New Approaches to Eighteenth-Century Literature,* ed. Phillip Harth (New York: Columbia University Press, 1974), pp. 33-78.

24. *Revaluation,* p. 80. See also pp. 71 and 77.

25. Mack, "Wit and Poetry and Pope," p. 23.

26. Earl Wasserman's reference to "cosmic syntaxes," *The Subtler Language,* p. 5, assumes that poetic language creates an "intra-referential system within the poem" (p. 9).

27. *Pastoral Poetry and An Essay on Criticism,* ed. E. Audra and Aubrey Williams, *The Twickenham Edition of the Poems of Alexander Pope,* I (London: Methuen, 1961), 246-248.

28. *Essay on Criticism,* 11. 130-140.

29. I use the expression "Augustan didactic" to differentiate Augustan (including Pope's) didactic functions from those used by earlier writers. Some of these functions include the use of modifiers to control the meanings of nouns and verbs, the relation of the natural scene to history, the reduction of inherited forms by modifying them with epigram and other forms of wit. But this is not the place for this presentation. The interrelations in this essay present Pope's contributions to the didactic procedures.

30. Horace, *Satires,* Book I, Satire 4.

31. *Pope's Epistle to Bathurst* (Baltimore: Johns Hopkins Press, 1960), p. 36.

32. *The Second Satire of the Second Book of Horace Paraphrased,* 11. 61-66.

33. For a discussion of *metonymy* in *The Seasons,* see my *The Unfolding of the Seasons* (Baltimore: Johns Hopkins Press, 1970), p. 52.

34. Some other examples in the *Essay on Man* are: I, 46: "All that rises, rise in due degree"; I, 273: "Lives thro' all life, extends thro' all extent"; III, 15-16: "See dying vegetables life sustain, / See life dissolving vegetate again"; III, 168: "And turn'd on Man a fiercer savage, Man"; III, 273-274: "For, what one likes if others like as well, / What serves one will, when many wills rebel"; IV, 59-60: "In who obtain defence, or who defend, / In him who is, or him who finds a friend"; IV, 96: "Best knows the blessing, and will most be blest."

35. William Empson, *Seven Types of Ambiguity* (London: Chatto and Windus, 1930), pp. 70-71; and "Wit in the *Essay on Criticism*" (1950), in *The Structure of Complex Words* (New York: New Directions, 1951); E. N. Hooker, "Pope on Wit: The *Essay on Criticism*" (1951), *Eighteenth-Century English Literature,* ed. James L. Clifford (New York: Oxford University Press, 1959), pp. 42-61. "Nature" is discussed by Geoffrey Tillotson, *Pope and Human Nature* (Oxford: Clarendon Press, 1958), pp. 1-26; and J. M. Cameron, "Mr. Tillotson and Mr. Pope," *The Night Battle* (Baltimore: Helicon Press, 1962), esp. pp. 175-190.

36. Joseph Spence, *Observations, Anecdotes and Characters of Books and Men,* ed. James M. Osborn (Oxford: Clarendon Press, 1966), I, 32: "[when] about fifteen, I got acquainted with Mr. Walsh. He encouraged me much, and used to tell me there was one way left of excelling, for though we had several great poets, we never had any one poet that was correct — and he desired me to make that my study and aim." See also *Essay on Man,* IV, 381-382: "Correct with spirit, eloquent with ease / Intent to reason, or polite to please."

37. For nature and mythology, see "The Fable of Dryope," "The Fable of Vertumnus and Pomona," *Windsor Forest, The Dunciad,* etc. For the altar and religious or irreligious prayers, see *Essay on Criticism,* 11. 181-184, 622-625; *Eloisa to Abelard,* passim; *The Rape of the Lock,* I, 121-128; II, 35-46; III, 105-108; *The Dunciad* I, 155-162, 243-256; *Epistle to Bathurst,* 11. 291-293; *Essay on Man,* III, 263-264.

38. See Pope's imitation "Cowley: The Garden"; "Polyphemus and Acis," 11. 25-28; *The Rape of the Lock,* I, 125-126; *Windsor Forest,* 11. 211-216. To these images should be added those in which the self becomes entranced with itself as in the story of Balaam in *Epistle to Bathurst,* esp. 11. 375-378; *Epistle to Dr. Arbuthnot,* 11. 209-214; or the paid poets who reflect their patrons. See also man's rejection of himself in his species, *Essay on Man,* III, 165-168; also *The Dunciad,* IV, 533-536, and IV, 790.

39. John Donne, "Satyre II," *The Satires, Epigrams and Verse Letters,* ed. W. Milgate (Oxford: Clarendon Press, 1967), p. 8.

40. Tillotson, *The Rape of the Lock,* II, 195 f.7.

41. Samuel Johnson defined *parody* as "a kind of writing, in which the words of an author or his thoughts are taken, and by a slight change adapted to some new purpose." The burlesque or mimicking of Sarpedon is subordinated in Pope's parody to the common sense precepts.

42. *Epistles to Several Persons* (Moral Essays), ed. F. W. Bateson, *Twickenham Edition,* III-ii (London: Methuen, 1951), 65 ff., 216-217; 66 ff., 231-232; 67 ff., 241-242. Also 68 ff., 253-256. This procedure of Pope is so extensive that these few concentrated examples cannot possibly convey the frequency of such interrelations. They merit a separate essay.

43. The energy governing Pope's poetry and the abandonment of the view that it was merely mimetic was recognized by most of the critics discussed at the beginning of this paper. Some recent critics of Pope — Patricia M. Spacks, John Sitter, John Paul Russo — have added to our knowledge of Pope's imagery, organization, and aims by working within the earlier hypotheses.

44. E. Audra and Aubrey Williams, *Pastoral Poetry,* I, 26-27.

IV

FROM ACCIDIE TO NEUROSIS: *THE CASTLE OF INDOLENCE* REVISITED

Donald Greene

Bing Professor of English, University of Southern California

In 1916 George Saintsbury published a book about eighteenth-century English literature bearing the curious title *The Peace of the Augustans*. The book itself is a strange one. Saintsbury, then an old man in a new and frightening world, created in it an imaginary eighteenth century in which he found the security lacking in the Europe of 1916. The title is curious because, first, one does not read far in the English literature of the eighteenth century before discovering many expressions of deep distrust of the despotism of Augustus Caesar's Rome and contempt for the sycophancy of the great writers of the Augustan establishment.[1] And it is hard to conceive how anyone familiar with British political and social history of the eighteenth century, its wars and riots and invasions, and with the tirades against it by those angry young men—who grew even angrier as they grew older—Swift, Pope in *The Dunciad* and later satires, Johnson in *London* and his political writing of the thirties and fifties, could see it as pre-eminently a time of peace. But the notion assuaged a personal need of Saintsbury's. The myth was not entirely of Saintsbury's invention: one finds something like it in the deservedly forgotten earlier school textbooks of English literary history that began to

131

appear in the mid-nineteenth century. But Saintsbury encapsulated the myth in a memorable phrase which has helped it, in spite of the erosion of its underpinnings by serious modern scholarship, to maintain currency in some quarters even today.

That Englishmen somehow enjoyed more "peace" in the eighteenth than in other centuries seems a priori unlikely, human nature being what it is. True, verses expressing a complacent optimism about things as they are, or as people would like to think they are, were popular, as they have been in other times — verses like Pomfret's *The Choice* and others in the "Happy Man" tradition.[2] Probably the most widely read and loved verse of the twentieth century has been that of Edgar Guest, Rod McKuen, and their like (as for prose, a best-seller in the 1970s bears the reassuring title *I'm O.K., You're O.K.*). Yet few thoughtful people would be inclined to call such phenomena evidence of the "peace of the twentieth century" — rather, perhaps, they illustrate a vain longing for the peace that continues to evade us. And if we take the trouble to look carefully at the more serious writing of eighteenth-century Britain, we find its inhabitants vexed with much the same woes of the human condition as those of the seventeenth, nineteenth, twentieth, or any other century.

> How small of all that human hearts endure
> That part which laws or kings can cause or cure![3]

Samuel Johnson wrote, implying not, as Macaulay foolishly suggested, that he thought public affairs unimportant — his voluminous and energetic political writings show he was well aware that legislators and other politicians can cause a great deal of curable or preventable human misery — but that, great as such misery may be, it is still minuscule compared with that the human individual inflicts on himself.

I should like in this paper to consider an eighteenth-century work dealing with one widespread form of such misery, James Thomson's *The Castle of Indolence*. The subtitle of the standard biography of Thomson is "The Poet of *The Seasons*,"[4] and it is true that, from its very beginning down to Ralph Cohen's two large volumes, criticism of Thomson has been dominated by the earlier poem, which has provided a rich mine for the historian of ideas. But it is a pity the popularity of *The Seasons* has so overshadowed the later and more mature poem, which many have found more readable and whose content, as I wish here to argue, is at least equally worthy of being taken seriously. Few who have commented on *The Castle of Indolence* have gone so far in its praise as Bonamy Dobrée, who wrote, "It is possible to say that this is Thomson's best poem, though it is not his most important" —a rather hard saying.[5] Dobrée is praising its versification, its "sensuous music." But what Thomson is trying to tell us in the poem, Dobrée, like almost every other critic (with the exception of A. D. McKillop, whose discussion I should like to consider later), treats as negligible. A more typical remark is George Sherburn's, which, though commending its "Spenserian melody and descriptive techniques," complains that its content is "somewhat deficient in action (it tells merely how the Wizard Indolence enticed pilgrims into his castle and how the Knight of Arts and Industry liberated them)."[6] Sherburn ignores the dangers of criticism by means of capsule plot summaries. One might equally well dismiss Henry James's *The Ambassadors* as being deficient in action—it tells merely how the Witch Mme. Vionnet enticed the pilgrim Chad into her castle, and how the Knight Strether failed to liberate him.

To some extent the poem has been the victim of the biographical or intentional fallacy, often called a piece of "dainty filigree" of versification. It was said to have originated as a joke among Thomson and his friends about their laziness, much as *The Rape of the Lock* used to be thought of as no more than a private joke among Pope, Caryll, and the Fermor and Petre families—until Cleanth Brooks took the trouble, apparently for the first time, to read what was actually being said in the poem, and discovered it was about what its title said it was about—namely, rape.[7] Thomson's poem may have started as a joke, but we should note how the account given by Thomson's early biographer continues:

It was at first little more than a few detached stanzas in the way of raillery on himself, and on some of his friends. . . . But he saw very soon that the subject deserved to be treated more seriously, and in a form fitted to convey one of the most important moral lessons.[8]

I should like in this paper to try to put the subject of the poem into its moral and psychiatric—indeed, theological—context, and to show that it does deserve to be treated seriously.

Why has it not been so treated? First, perhaps, because of the light touches of humor one often finds in it—for instance, the charming and often quoted line by Thomson about himself, "A bard here dwelt, more fat than bard beseems."[9] But recent study of Jane Austen, not to mention *The Rape of the Lock,* has surely shown us that exquisitely delicate humor is by no means incompatible with profound seriousness of moral purpose. And second, because laziness, irresponsibility, obesity seem to many a subject for light humor, not serious moral reflection, though the example of Falstaff might give them pause. The poem after all opens grimly enough:

> O mortal man, who livest here by toil,
> Do not complain of this thy hard estate;
> That like an emmet[10] thou must ever moil
> Is a sad sentence of an ancient date:
> And certes there is for it reason great;
> For, though sometimes it makes thee weep and wail,
> And curse thy stars, and early drudge and late,
> Withouten that would come an heavier bale,
> Loose life, unruly passions, and diseases pale.
>
> (I,i)

Clearly there is more here than a clever pastiche of Spenser's versification. Thomson has something to say to us, and what he is saying, if true, is important: "We complain about the curse of having to work, the punishment of the Fall—'In the sweat of thy brow, thou shalt earn thy bread.' And yet we should be grateful for this 'curse,' since otherwise we should suffer much worse affliction." Had Sartre or Camus written this, we might be applauding its remarkably modern, hard-nosed "existentialist" view of the "absurdity" of the human condition, or something of the sort.

Thomson knew what he was talking about; it is a poem of personal experience. The story was told of his friend, the musicologist Charles Burney, coming to call on Thomson—this was when he was a man in his thirties and reasonably successful in life. Burney found him at two in the afternoon still in bed, "with the curtains closed and the window shut." Burney asked the poet why he did not get up. Thomson thought this proposition over for a while and finally explained, "Why, mon, I had not motive to rise."[11]

We smile: it is a ludicrous story. And yet what a pathetic one! About the same time, another younger, talented writer, Samuel Johnson, lay groaning in his bed all morning, unable to rise, his will paralyzed, and had to be coaxed to dictate to a friend a translation he had undertaken, on the plea that the printer and his family were starving through his negligence.[12] In Robert Penn Warren's *All the King's Men,* the narrator, when he experiences trauma — when his marriage breaks up, when he learns of the dishonesty of the man he has taken as his ideal of integrity — goes into what he calls "the Great Sleep":

Sometimes sleep gets to be a serious and complete thing. You stop going to sleep in order that you may be able to get up, but get up in order that you may be able to go back to sleep.... He would come home in the evening, and because he knew that he could not work he would go to bed immediately. He would sleep twelve hours, fourteen hours, fifteen hours, feeling himself, while asleep, plunge deeper and deeper into sleep like a diver groping downward into dark water.... Then in the morning he would lie in bed, not wanting anything, not even hungry, hearing the small sounds of the world sneaking and seeping back into the room.... Then he would think: If I don't get up I can't go back to bed.[13]

This desire for unconsciousness, because life with full consciousness is too much to bear, is surely a form of death wish, as are such other varieties of escape from full consciousness as alcoholism and drug addiction. Johnson was once asked, apropos of drunkenness, "I wonder what pleasure men can take in making beasts of themselves." He answered with simple wisdom, "He who makes a beast of himself gets rid of the pain of being a man."[14] So with the escape routes of somnolence and lethargy. Comic as their victims may seem — as the victims of schizophrenia and catatonia seemed to earlier ages — we might ponder a fragment of dialogue in Evelyn Waugh's *Brideshead Revisited,* concerning the young alcoholic wreck, Sebastian Flyte:

"I suppose he doesn't suffer?"
"Oh, yes, I think he does. One can have no idea what the suffering may be, to be maimed as he is — no dignity, no power of will."[15]

Perhaps the power of Thomson's poem comes from the fact that Thomson — the fat, lazy, complaisant Jemmy Thomson, who

never quite realized the potential his friends saw in him—knew
something of such suffering.

It is not only in the language and versification that the poem is
indebted to Spenser, who knew a good deal about the mental and
moral ills that afflict the human race. The rhetoric of the Wizard
Indolence, in his long persuasive speech setting forth the joys of
detachment from life, is close to that of Despair in Book I of *The
Faerie Queene:* "Ease after pain, port after stormy seas, / Sleep
after toil, death after life, doth greatly please."[16] The student of
older literature has met the Wizard himself many times before
under the names of Sloth, Idleness, and Accidie (or Acedia). The
most easily accessible full account is that by Chaucer's Parson.
Accidie, he tells us, is the deprivation of "the love of all good-
ness." Accidie "dooth alle thyng with anoy [ennui], and with
wrawnesse [fretfulness], slakenesse, and excusacioun, and with
ydelnesse and unlust." "Accidie is lyk hem that been in the peyne
of helle, by cause of hir slouthe and hir hevynesse." It entails
lethargy and somnolence and damage to one's temporal well-
being through lack of care. Its most advanced stage is "wanhope,
that is despair of the mercy of God."[17] In *Piers Plowman,* Sloth is
given an amusing speech of self-revelation. In *The Pilgrim's
Progress* we meet him under various names, the most memorable
being Giant Despair. In Spenser, Sloth is the chief of the counsel-
lors of Lucifera—pride, as always the prime, the original sin, of
which the others are emanations. Sloth rides before her coach on
his symbolic animal the ass—"sluggish Idelnesse, the nourse of
sin," "still drowned in sleep and most of his days dead.... From
worldly cares himself he did esloyne [separate].... From every
work he challenged essoyne [exemption].... His life he led in
lawless riotesse / By which he grew to grevous malady."[18]

Morton Bloomfield, the modern authority on the seven cardi-
nal sins, argues that Spenser was the last important English writer
to make use of this concept, popularized in the sixth century by
Pope Gregory the Great, though originating earlier. Gregory had
reduced the previous eight to seven by astutely telescoping *tristitia*
into *acedia.* "Protestantism," Bloomfield writes, "tended to claim
that all sins were deadly": it might have been better to say that
Protestantism regards *sin,* whose wages is death, as not so neatly
divisible. If, as Bloomfield suggests, the popularity of the neat list

of seven had something to do with its convenience for priests hearing confession—one could tick them off on one's fingers—it is understandable that Protestantism, which discarded auricular confession and the sacrament of penance, would have found little use for it; so that, as Bloomfield says, "In the eighteenth century, the [Seven] Sins, except in Catholic countries, were practically forgotten, except by antiquaries."[19]

But it would be naive to think that with the abandonment of the formal list of seven sins, the realities for which their names stood disappeared or even diminished,[20] or that writers in the eighteenth century ceased to be concerned with those realities. The medieval names had been *descriptions* of a condition—sloth (slowness), idleness, accidie (from Greek ἀκήδια, a lack of care, a deficiency of emotional involvement). In the late Middle Ages and Renaissance, names derived from Aristotelian and Galenic medicine,[21] which designated a supposed physical *cause* for the condition began to be substituted for these: melancholy—there is an excess proportion of black bile in the mixture of four humors that governs one's emotional life; spleen—the organ which produces black bile is overactive; hypochondria—the hypochondria (singular, hypochondrium) are the segments of the ventral cavity that contain the spleen; the vapors—those generated by the spleen and ascending to affect the brain. The opposition between the two different approaches to the problems of mental and emotional disturbance—on the one hand, the psychological and moral (not to say theological), on the other, the physiological, replete with chemotherapy and prefrontal lobotomies—is not so modern as we may think.

A sequel to Bloomfield's book needs to be written, trying to trace the subsequent history of the Sins, under different names, from the Renaissance to the present. It would note such instances as Jaques's sardonic classification of the melancholies in *As You Like It* and Burton's encyclopedic study of them, called, in deference to the new "scientific" approach, an "anatomy." It would note Pope's Cave of Spleen, with its interesting anticipation of Freud—where "maids, turned bottles, cry aloud for corks."[22] It would point out that Swift described *A Tale of a Tub* as "a treatise writ against the spleen"[23] and that Sterne described the purpose of *Tristram Shandy* in the same words.[24] Swift's Yahoo, whom "a fancy would sometimes take...to retire into a corner, to lie down and howl and groan and spurn away all that came near him, although he were young and fat and wanted neither food nor water," Gulliver says, exhibits "the true seeds of spleen."[25] Nowadays we should call the poor creature the victim of neurotic depression and send him to be psychoanalyzed or perhaps prescribe amphetamines or electric shock: Swift has a different remedy. Johnson's Happy Valley in *Rasselas,* where everyone's physical wants are provided for without any effort on his part, and where no one is happy, is Thomson's *Castle* over again. There is Johnson's Latin poem Γυωϑι Σεαυτον, in which he vividly describes the depression and lethargy that seize him after he has completed the laborious task of revising his *Dictionary,* the troubled state of his mind where "empty forms, fleeting shadows, lonely shapes of things flit through the void," and he longs for another dictionary to drudge at—almost a replica of the first stanza of Thomson's poem.[26] Much more could be cited to show that the eighteenth century, whatever the myths about its self-satisfied complacency, was as familiar with accidie as the Middle Ages, with melancholy as the Renaissance or the Romantics, with doubt as the Tennyson of *In Memoriam* and the Arnold of "Dover Beach," with *Angst* as Auden's Age of Anxiety.[27] The names change from one generation to the next, and each generation gets a gloomy satisfaction from the thought that it is the victim of something new and fashionable—itself a manifestation of the senior sin, pride. But the clinical descriptions of the condition, from Chaucer to Auden, seem indistinguishable.

Thomson's *Castle* is only one of a number of eighteenth-century literary works illustrating the condition. There are those of James Boswell. Not only are his *Journals* filled with intimate, detailed, and boring accounts of his own moods and vagaries— neurosis, virtually by definition, is boredom—he also wrote and published a set of periodical essays, named, after himself, *The Hypochondriack,* many of which he devotes to discussion of the nature of hypochondria, and to such related subjects as fears, excess, suicide, and alcoholism ("an Hypochondriack," he writes, "is under peculiar temptations to participate freely of wine").[28] Boswell displays little concern with the etiology of the condition: it may be physiological, or it may be that "the mind is sick"; he even entertains the hypothesis, rare in the eighteenth century, that "the malady is sometimes owing to the influence of evil spirits." But of the various symptoms and manifestations he writes eloquently, from long experience—and with relish: Boswell is one of those, sometimes thought to be indigenous to the late eighteenth and early nineteenth centuries, but easily to be found in any other, who feel their proneness to "melancholy" gives them a certain cachet. Johnson does his best to bludgeon him out of this in his letters replying to Boswell's more hypochondriacal ones: "You are always complaining of melancholy, and I conclude from those complaints that you are fond of it. No man talks of that which he is desirous to conceal," and, probing beneath the surface, "there lurks, perhaps, in every human heart a desire for distinction, which inclines every man first to hope, and then to believe, that Nature has given him something peculiar to himself."[29] Accidie, like the rest, has its roots in Pride.

Of the two long eighteenth-century poems entitled *The Spleen*,[30] that by Matthew Green (1737) takes a lighthearted approach, reinforced by his jaunty octosyllabic couplets—though, to be sure, he coins the striking phrase "the daymare Spleen." He disclaims any intention "to write a treatise on the Spleen." Instead, he describes in lively detail the kind of life he says he lives, designed to drive away spleen, a fairly run-of-the-mill performance in the "Happy Man" tradition; not very convincing perhaps—one is left with an uneasy feeling that he protests too much; it isn't as simple as all that. Far more searching are the Pindarics of Anne Finch (*née* Kingsmill), Countess of Winchilsea (1701). She begins by describing the Protean nature of spleen:

> What are thou, Spleen, which ev'rything dost ape?
> Thou Proteus to abus'd mankind,
> Who never yet thy real cause could find
> Or fix thee to remain in one continued shape?

In Burtonian fashion she describes its varied manifestations:

> Now a Dead Sea thou'lt represent
> A calm of stupid discontent—

sometimes an irrational rage, a panic fear, sometimes insomnia, nightmare, hallucination. But at the heart of her poem is a vigorous rejection of the theory that the condition has a physical cause.

With wholehearted conservatism, she insists on the theological explanation:

> Falsely the mortal part we blame
> Of our depress'd and pond'rous frame
> Which, till the first degrading sin—

the Adamite act of pride in the Garden—

> Let thee, its dull attendant, in. . . .

Like Thomson, she makes it clear that she is writing from personal experience:

> O'er me, alas! thou dost too much prevail:
> I feel thy force whilst I against thee rail:
> I feel my verse decay, and my crampt numbers fail—

like Wordsworth in the *Immortality Ode* and at the beginning of *The Prelude:*

> Thro' thy black jaundice, I all objects see,
>   As dark and terrible as thee.
> My lines decried, and my employment thought
> An useless folly, or presumptuous fault.

She has an interesting theory, which Pope, in the *Essay on Man,* also seems to draw on ("Die of a rose in aromatic pain"), though possibly not original to either. Before the Fall, man was capable of full, robust response to the wealth of pleasurable sensory experience available to him. Now, like a delicate Victorian lady suffering from the vapors, he shrinks from such contact with the full spectrum of reality:

> Nor, whilst in his own heaven he dwelt,
> Whilst Man his Paradise possest,
> His fertile garden in the fragrant east,
> And all united odours smelt,
> No armed sweets, until thy reign [i.e. Spleen's]
> Could shock the sense, or in the face
> A flush't unhandsome colour place.
> Now the jonquil o'ercomes the feeble brain;

> We faint beneath the aromatic pain,
> Till some offensive scent thy pow'rs appease,
> And pleasure we resign for short and nauseous ease.

It is a pretty conceit—in our perversity we substitute the "short and nauseous ease" of a whiff of sal ammoniac or asafetida (nowadays it would be "pot" or "speed") to assuage our spleen, renouncing the joy of contact with the real world around us.

This account of hyperesthesia, as we might call it, lends itself easily to some sort of theory of a disorder of the nervous system; and in spite of Lady Winchilsea's firm rejection of a physical, in favor of a moral or theological, cause for the condition, and of her slap at the willingness of doctors to profit from their ignorance of its causes—

> Tho' the physician's greatest gains,
> Altho' his growing wealth he sees
> Daily increased by ladies' fees,
> Yet dost thou baffle all his studious pains.
> Not skillful Lower thy source could find
> Or thro' the well-dissected body trace
> The secret, the mysterious ways
> By which thou dost surprise, and prey upon the mind—

in spite of all this, Dr. William Stukeley, in 1723, prefixed Lady Winchilsea's poem to the printed version of his lectures to the Royal College of Physicians, *On the Spleen.*

Stukeley goes in great detail into the anatomy and vascular supply of the organ, providing a large foldout engraving of it, and seems, somewhat reluctantly, to accept the older theory that the bile—or its vapors—have something to do with the emotional conditions described by Lady Winchilsea. But Stukeley stresses his observation that the spleen is well supplied with nerves. Perhaps through these are transmitted the pathological symptoms which, says Stukeley, "most frequently attack scholars and persons of the soft sex most eminent for wit and good sense."[31] It is noteworthy, too, that in paying tribute to contemporary medical researchers who, were it possible, might have been thought able to track down a physical cause for "the Spleen," Lady Winchilsea chose Richard Lower, noted for his pioneering work in the anatomy of the nervous system.[32]

Two years later (1725) Sir Richard Blackmore, M.D., in his *Treatise of the Spleen and Vapours, or Hypocondriacal Affections*, goes farther and roundly denounces Aristotle and the ancients for believing that the spleen itself has anything to do with it: the condition stems from the nerves and the animal spirits — the nerves are lax and the animal spirits, the invisible fluid that circulates through them, weak and volatile — "low," in fact. Six years after this (1731) Dr. George Cheyne gives the nerves top billing in the subtitle of his *The English Malady, or a Treatise of Nervous Diseases of all Kinds, as Spleen, Vapours, Lowness of Spirits, Hypocondriacal and Hysterical Distempers.*[33] The viscera and its fluids being thoroughly discredited, since on dissection no one can find any physical evidence of a mechanism connecting them with the observed emotional conditions, the nerves are left with the field to themselves. What in the Middle Ages had been the product of original sin, and in the Renaissance of the contents of the abdomen, was now seen as a pathological state of the nervous system.[34]

This verdict was made official, so to speak, in the later eighteenth century, when the Scottish physician, Dr. William Cullen, in his reclassification of diseases,[35] ignored the humors completely, and postulated a new class of ailments, the "neuroses," a word Cullen seems to have invented. These included not only such organic conditions as epilepsy, but also the emotional conditions we have been considering. Although "neurasthenia" (literally, weak nerves) was a popular designation for their alleged cause in the late nineteenth and early twentieth centuries,[36] and although the term "nervous breakdown" is still sometimes heard, "neurosis" came in the mid-twentieth century exclusively to denote these conditions. "Neurotic," from having been used in the 1890s, when it became popular, as a neutral medical term, then took on a strong pejorative connotation, as in "You're behaving neurotically."

The present state of affairs is perhaps best represented by the interesting definition of "neurotic" given in *Webster's Third New International Dictionary* (1961), "Tending to respond to present life situations on the basis of their resemblance to early childhood experiences or on the basis of an idealized concept of the self rather than in terms of the requirements of immediate reality." It is noteworthy that Webster diplomatically allows the reader to choose between an orthodox Freudian position — "early childhood experiences" — and a more advanced, "post-Freudian" one — "an idealized concept of the self." For illustrations of its use, however, Webster relies on two post-Freudians: Karen Horney ("A neurotic personality has become estranged[37] from large parts of this world"), and Gordon Allport ("The very nature of the neurotic disorder is tied" — prepare for a surprise — "to pride").

The wheel has come full circle. The nervous system has been consigned to limbo, to join such other parts of the human frame as the spleen and the hypochondria. We are back where Lady Winchilsea and Spenser and Chaucer and Pope Gregory started — in the Garden after the Fall. The moral seems to be that however many ingenious names are devised that indicate a deterministic, physiological origin for the condition — an illness for which its possessor is not responsible and therefore not morally accountable for his behavior — the public voice will inevitably transform them into terms bearing a moral connotation, with the implication that if the individual wants to do something about correcting the condition, he can.

We return at last to revisit briefly the Castle of Indolence, though it deserves the more thorough tour that a close and sensitive reading of the text will provide. Its setting is a delightful pastoral landscape — "a pleasing land of drowsyhead" — described with lush onomatopoeia:

> Meantime unnumbered glittering streamlets played,
> And hurled everywhere their waters sheen;
> That, as they bickered through the sunny glade,
> Though restless still themselves, a lulling murmur made.
> . . . .
> And where this valley winded out below,
> The murmuring main was heard, and scarcely heard, to flow.
> (I,iii; I,v)

At the same time, Thomson skillfully introduces a vaguely ominous note:

> Full in the passage of the vale, above,
> A sable, silent, solemn forest stood;
> Where naught but shadowy forms were seen to move,

> As Idless fancied in her dreaming mood.
> And up the hills, on either side, a wood
> Of blackening pines, aye waving to and fro,
> Sent forth a sleepy horror through the blood.
>
> (I,v)

These early stanzas of description are worthy to be ranked, among dream landscapes, with those of Tennyson's "The Lotos-Eaters" and Coleridge's "Kubla Khan."

The eleven-stanza oration in which the Wizard Indolence tempts the "pilgrims of the earth" into his castle is a masterpiece of persuasive rhetoric. It begins with a powerful appeal to self-pity:

> Behold! ye pilgrims of this earth, behold!
> See all but man with unearned pleasure gay.
>
> (I,ix)

Like the philosopher in chapter 22 of *Rasselas,* who advises men to "observe the hind of the forest and the linnet of the grove: let them consider the life of animals, whose motions are regulated by instinct; they obey their guide and are happy," he urges them to follow their natural impulses:

> Behold the merry minstrels of the morn,
> The swarming songsters of the careless grove,
> Ten thousand throats that, from the flowering thorn,
> Hymn their good God, and carol sweet of love,
> Such grateful kindly raptures them emove!
>
> (I,x)

Jemmy Thomson, who grew up in the harsh Scottish climate so vividly described in *Winter,* well knew that the lives of birds and beasts are not always a succession of grateful, kindly rapture. And, brought up on the Presbyterian Shorter Catechism, he well knew that God is just as well as "good."

Like Rousseau in his *First Discourse,* the Wizard takes a jaundiced view of "civilization." In startlingly Marxist accents, he reveals the source of its woes to be capitalistic individualism:

> Outcast of Nature, man! the wretched thrall
> Of bitter-dropping sweat, of sweltry pain,
> Of cares that eat away thy heart with gall,

And of the vices, an inhuman train,
That all proceed from savage thirst of gain:
For when hard-hearted Interest first began
To poison earth, Astraea left the plain;
Guile, Violence, and Murder seized on man,
And, for soft milky streams, with blood the rivers ran.

(I,xi)

He goes on to give a repellent account of the world of which he promises his hearers "oblivion":

With me, you need not rise at early dawn
To pass the joyless day in various stounds.
. . . .
To cheat, and dun, and lie, and visit pay,
Now flattering base, now giving secret wounds,
Or prowl in courts of law for human prey,
In venal senate thieve, or rob on broad highway.

(I,xiii)

Private as well as public life is noxious: in the Castle,

To tardy swain no shrill-voiced matrons squall;
No dogs, no babes, no wives to stun your ear;
No hammers thump; no horrid blacksmith sear,
No noisy tradesman your sweet slumbers start.

(I,xiv)

In freeing themselves from such annoyances, the Wizard argues, the pilgrims will be following the path of true virtue:

Thus, from the source of tender Indolence,
With milky blood the heart is overflown,
Is soothed and sweetened by the social sense;
For interest, envy, pride, and strife are banished hence.

(I,xv)

He preaches the ideal of virtuous detachment:

What, what is virtue but repose of mind?
A pure ethereal calm that knows no storm,
Above the reach of wild ambition's wind,
Above those passions that this world deform.

(I,xvi)

Such detachment has always been praised:

> The best of men have ever loved repose:
> They hate to mingle in the filthy fray,
>   (I,xvii)

and some of the greatest men in history have sought such virtuous retirement:

> So Scipio, to the soft Cumaean shore
> Retiring, tasted joy he never knew before.
>   (I,xvii)

Not that, in the castle, everything will be boring inactivity: a program of leisurely recreation will be available:

> Softly stealing with your wat'ry gear
> Along the brooks, the crimson-spotted fry
> You may delude. . . .
>   (I,xviii)

Better this than the "grievous folly,"

> to heap up estate,
> Losing the days you see beneath the sun. . . .
> But sure it is of vanities most vain,
> To toil for what you here untoiling may obtain.
>   (I,xix)

It is all very clever. The joy of tuning in, turning on, and dropping out is heightened by the conviction that this is true wisdom and virtue — it is those who work to "heap up an estate," involving them in criminal aggression against their fellow men, who are wicked and foolish. Much discussion of this proposition, pro and con, has been heard in recent years: among student and other "activists" (sometimes ironically named) of the 1960s; from political platforms and newspaper editorials in connection with public "welfare" programs and trade unionism. The Wizard puts it very persuasively — on the surface, at least. Yet when we scrutinize the oration closely, do we not begin to wonder whether Thomson isn't subtly undermining it? "By entering the Castle, you will be following the path of true virtue, like Scipio; also, you will be getting away from the yapping of neighborhood dogs, squalling babies, and nagging wives": the ludicrous bathos of this is too striking for it to be unintentional. So is that of the first experience of the pilgrims when they enter the Castle, which is to be divested of their "garters and buckles" and other restrictive articles of clothing, and instead to put on slippers and gowns

> Loose as the breeze that plays along the downs,
> And waves the summer woods when evening frowns,
> O fair undress, best dress! it checks no vein,
> But every flowing limb in pleasure drowns.
>
> (I,xxvi)

"First, just let me slip into something more comfortable." Certainly there are haunting stanzas describing the pleasure of the Castle—lush descriptions of its furnishings, its food and drink, its delights of sight and sound. But there are so many little comic details juxtaposed as to cast doubt on the theory held by some critics that Thomson, in spite of his announced moral purpose, is carried away by the attraction of the Castle.

At any rate, when the pilgrims enter it, they have a fine time at first. Everyone does his own thing:

> Here freedom reigned, without the least alloy;
> Nor gossip's tale, nor ancient maiden's gall,
> Nor saintly spleen durst murmur at our joy,
> And with envenomed tongue our pleasures pall—

there are innumerable varieties of spleen, all of them at odds with one another, as well as with the nonsplenetic part of the world.

> For why? there was but one great rule for all;
> To wit, that each should work his own desire,
> And eat, drink, study, sleep, as it may fall,
> Or melt the time in love, or wake the lyre—
>
> (I,xxxiv)

nowadays guitar? It does indeed sound like the ideal of the hippie commune, or Rousseau's Noble Savagery.

But the pilgrims' enjoyment gradually deteriorates into boredom, as in the "Happy Valley":

> Their only labour was to kill the time,
> And labour dire it is, and weary woe.
>
>   (I,lxxi)

Boredom develops into more serious neuroses, as with the individual who, "stung by spleen," "on himself his pensive fury wroke," and

> Never uttered word, save when first shone
> The glittering star of eve — "Thank Heaven! the day is done" —
>
>   (I,lix)

and the recluse who never leaves his filthy chamber. And eventually

> Now must I mark the villainy we found,
> But ah! too late....
> A place here was, deep, dreary, under ground
> Where still our inmates, when unpleasing grown,
> Diseased, and lothsome, privily were thrown.
> Far from the light of Heaven, they languished there,
> Unpitied, uttering many a bitter groan;
> For of the wretches taken was no care.
>
>   (I,lxxiii)

And why should it have been, since the whole point of this "life style" is a refusal to care — acedia, of which Thomson's *indolentia* is virtually a Latin translation: a lack of pain; the Stoic and Epicurean recipe for avoidance of pain by refusing to become emotionally involved? Here in the dungeon, lethargy, depression, physical and psychosomatic disease torment their helpless victims.

The second canto of the poem has almost unanimously been condemned, or, at best, received with faint enthusiasm. In it, an individual called the Knight of Arts and Industry, who has been brought up in conditions of primitive simplicity and virtue, and has been responsible for the civilizing of Europe, comes riding by and, in good Spenserian fashion, vanquishes the Wizard and rescues his prisoners, who then settle down to lives of useful industry and consequent happiness. This part of Thomson's allegory has been taken — for instance, by A. D. McKillop, the one student who has provided the poem with a full analysis and commentary[38] — to be an expression of contemporary Whig social philosophy, as illustrated more fully in Addison, Steele, Defoe, and Benjamin Franklin. This, of course, is a philosophy very much out of fashion. In its historical setting it is seen primarily as a handmaid to the great industrial, commercial, and technological expansion of Great Britain in the eighteenth, and of Britain and the United States in the nineteenth century—of the heartless materialistic moneygrubbing later to be satirized and condemned by Southey, Dickens, and others, as earlier by Dryden, Swift, Pope, and Johnson. Sometimes, under the designation of "the Protestant (or Puritan) work ethic," it is placed in a wider setting, that of western Europe and America from the Reformation onward, and, with the help of Max Weber and R. H. Tawney, viewed hostilely as the prostitution of religion in the service of the new capitalism. A recent handbook gives a useful summary of the view:

For many years it has been taken for granted that some special relationship existed between the Protestant Reformation and the rise of modern capitalism.... Weber (1904) suggested that modern capitalism was a by-product of the Protestant ethos.... Tawney (1926) gave even wider currency to the thesis that Calvinism prospered by adapting itself to the capitalist spirit. Either way, Protestantism became somehow (the causation was never demonstrated very clearly) guilty of the sins of modern capitalist society.[39]

On the face of it, *The Castle of Indolence* seems to fit perfectly into such an interpretation. Thomson was by upbringing a Scottish Calvinist. In politics, he was an adherent of the "Patriots," the noisy Whig opposition group, of which William Pitt was the most successful political leader, that demanded more aggressive policies of commercial and imperialist expansion than Walpole was ready to provide, and, after Walpole was ousted, came to power and successfully put those policies into practice.[40] McKillop seems to see in *The Castle of Indolence* an expression of inner conflict in Thomson between the side of his mind which gave assent (Canto II) to the demands of the "work ethic," the "new capitalism," the "manifest destiny" of British and American expansionism, and that which, in the passages in Canto I describing the delights of indolence, was repelled by it.[41] Some kind of similar conflict, or self-contradiction, used to be detected in Thomson's contemporary, Daniel Defoe.

But this is surely too limited a context in which to read the poem—even if that context were itself authentic; and modern scholarship has emphatically established that it is not. The survey from which I quoted the summary of the Weber-Tawney thesis goes on to say that one of the most important recent scholarly developments has been "the destruction of the orthodoxy about 'religion and the rise of capitalism.'. . . Both [Tawney's and Weber's] theses were rendered almost untenable by K. Samuelsson in *Religion and Economic Action* (English tr., 1961),[42] who showed in full historical detail how institutionalized religion, Catholic as well as Protestant, resisted the growth of the new economic order." That fine Renaissance historian, Geoffrey Elton, may be allowed to furnish the epitaph over Weber-Tawney: "It was not Calvinism that freed men from the restraints of the traditional moral concepts in economics, but emancipation from religion and theology in general."[43]

Recent studies of Defoe have exploded the notion that his works can somehow be used as texts to illustrate the Weber-Tawney thesis. If the "Puritan work ethic" is peculiarly the property of materialistic, expansion-oriented Whiggism in the eighteenth century, it is surprising to find men so little in sympathy with such a philosophy as Swift and Johnson promulgating that "ethic" as emphatically as Thomson and Addison. Swift's remedy for his neurotic young Yahoo was, he said, an unfailing one—"set him to hard work"; and Swift goes on with some caustic remarks about such fits of depression, of "vapors," afflicting only those rich enough to have leisure for them. The central motif of Johnson's private prayers, in spite of what seems to us his prodigious output of literary work, is his recurring plea for forgiveness for his sloth. He suggests as the remedy for his deep depression in 1773 the drudgery of a new dictionary. The dial plate of his watch bore, in Greek, the text from the Gospel, νὺξ γὰρ ἔρχεται —"For the night cometh when no man can work."[44] We recall the many parables of the New Testament, hardly a propaganda tract for the new capitalism, which stress the need for the fulfillment of one's God-given potential, notably the parable of the talents. We recall the motto of early monasticism, *Ora et labora,* "Work and pray." We recall that, though later men have called the condition hypochondria or neurosis or inhibition or *Angst,* and have sometimes found gratification in thinking it peculiar to their own generation, its symptoms sound indistinguishable from Spenser's and Chaucer's and Gregory the Great's precapitalist accidie.

Thomson's poem (like Lady Winchilsea's) is not, then, to be read as a discussion of a matter peculiar to the English scene of the eighteenth century, or even of the post-Reformation western European scene. It is a discussion of a personal psychological or psychiatric—in the end, theological—problem of Jemmy Thomson himself, and at the same time of a universal one of the fallen human condition in all ages. And possibly no one has described the seeming paradox involved more effectively than Thomson in the opening lines of *The Castle of Indolence:* do not complain, he says, of the "sad sentence of ancient date" that man is condemned to "live here by toil." On the contrary,

> . . .there is for it reason great:
> For though it sometimes makes thee weep and wail,
> And curse thy stars, and early drudge and late,
> Withouten that would come an heavier bale.
>
> (I,i)

Thomson knows, for, like Johnson and Boswell and many others, he has tried it.

NOTES

1. Succinctly expressed in Pope's "Epitaph for One who would not be buried in Westminster Abbey" [i.e., Alexander Pope]: "Heroes and Kings! your distance keep: / In peace let one poor Poet sleep, / Who never flatter'd Folks like you: / Let Horace blush, and Virgil too" (*The Twickenham Edition of the Poems of Alexander Pope* [London: Methuen, 1954] VI, 376). The editors, Norman Ault and John Butt, comment, "Published by Pope himself six years before his death, this epitaph was obviously never meant to be taken too seriously." Why not, one wonders? On the anti-Augustanism of the "Augustans," see Howard D. Weinbrot, "History, Horace, and Augustus Caesar: Some Implications for Eighteenth-Century Satire," *Eighteenth-Century Studies,* 7 (1974), 391-414.

2. Discussed at length by Maren-Sofie Røstvig in *The Happy Man: Studies in the Metamorphoses of a Classical Ideal,* 2d ed., 2 vols. (Oslo and New York: Oslo University Press, 1962, 1971 [first published 1954, 1958]). Pomfret's poem is considered II, 146-149.

3. Lines contributed to Goldsmith's *The Deserted Village* (Johnson, *Poems,* ed. E. L. McAdam, Jr., with George Milne, Yale Edition of the works of Samuel Johnson, Vol. VI [New Haven: Yale University Press, 1964], p. 356.)

4. Douglas Grant, *James Thomson: Poet of The Seasons* (London: Cresset, 1951).

5. Bonamy Dobrée, *English Literature in the Early Eighteenth Century, 1700-1740,* Oxford History of English Literature, VII (Oxford: Clarendon Press, 1959), p. 497.

6. "The Restoration and the Eighteenth Century," in *A Literary History of England,* ed. A. C. Baugh et al., 2d ed. (New York: Appleton-Century-Croft, 1957, first published 1948), p. 940.

7. Cleanth Brooks, "The Case of Miss Arabella Fermor," in *The Well-Wrought Urn* (New York: Harcourt Brace, 1947), pp. 80-104. My summary is cavalier, but readers of the essay will know what I mean.

8. Grant, p. 256.

9. Canto I, Stanza LXVIII. I quote the text of the poem from its most recent edition: James Thomson, *The Seasons and the Castle of Indolence,* ed. James Sambrook (Oxford: Oxford University Press, 1972). Sambrook thinks that though "the moral . . . is serious," the "continual hints of burlesque" lighten "its final effect." See n. 41 below.

10. An ant. We tend to smile at Proberbs 6:6, "Go to the ant, thou sluggard, and be wise." But Thomson and his contemporaries took it seriously. Johnson versified the text in a short poem which describes, like Thomson, "the drousy charms of dull delight," and rejects them.

11. Grant, pp. 239-240.

12. James L. Clifford, *Young Sam Johnson* (New York: Oxford University Press, 1955), pp. 145-156.

13. Warren, *All the King's Men* (New York: Harcourt Brace, 1946), pp. 107, 201.

14. G. B. Hill, ed., *Johnsonian Miscellanies* (Oxford: Clarendon Press, 1897), II, 333.

15. (Boston: Little, Brown, 1945), p. 309.

16. Canto IX, Stanza 40.

17. *Canterbury Tales,* Frag. X, 876, 897.

18. Book I, Canto IV, stanza 20.

19. Morton Bloomfield, *The Seven Deadly Sins* (East Lansing: Michigan State College Press, 1952), p. 441.

20. Bloomfield remarks that after Spenser (who, incidentally, was a thoroughgoing Protestant), "the *tradition* of the Sins was dead; they no longer evolved; they no longer inspired great writing" (p. 243). Not under the traditional nomenclature, perhaps. But great writers have continued to be greatly concerned with the conditions designated by that nomenclature. A large list could be drawn up of important works of the last three centuries centering on, say, *avaritia* or *luxuria.* For an uneven collection of modern essays, see Angus Wilson and others, *The*

Seven Deadly Sins (New York: Morrow, 1962; originally published in the *Sunday Times,* London). The best are those by instructed Christians, Evelyn Waugh on "Sloth," and W. H. Auden on "Anger."

21. This is an oversimplified account of a complex process. The most valuable study is by Erwin Panofsky, in Raymond Klibansky et al., *Saturn and Melancholy* (London: Nelson, 1964). Panofsky gives a long chronologically ordered series of iconic representations of *Melancolia,* including a few instances in which *Melancolia* seems to be equated with *Acedia.* See particularly pp. 78-81, and 300-301. The amount of writing, medical and lay, on the subject of melancholy (hypochondria, spleen, etc.) from the seventeenth century onward is immense. In my explorations of it I have been indebted to John F. Sena's *A Bibliography of Melancholy, 1660-1800* (London: Nether, 1970) and to Professor Sena's "The English Malady: The Idea of Melancholy from 1700 to 1760" (Ph.D. diss., Princeton, 1967); also to G. S. Rousseau's "Le Cat and the Physiology of Negroes," *Studies in Eighteenth-Century Culture,* III (1973), 369-386, and his "Nerves, Spirits, and Fibres: Towards Defining the Origins of Sensibility," in *Studies in the Eighteenth Century,* ed. R. F. Brissenden (Canberra: Australian National University Press, 1976), Vol. III. When the present article was in the press, a fascinating book by Reinhard Kuhn appeared— *The Demon of Noontide: Ennui in Western Literature* (Princeton: Princeton University Press, 1976). Its chapter on the eighteenth century, "The Descent into the Cave of Spleen," discusses Pope, Swift, Sterne, and Lady Winchilsea, though not Thomson.

22. *The Rape of the Lock,* Canto IV, 1. 54.

23. "The Author upon Himself," 1. 48 (Swift, *Poems,* ed. Harold Williams [Oxford: Clarendon Press, 1937], p. 195).

24. *Tristram Shandy,* ed. J. A. Work (New York: Odyssey Press, 1940), p. 301 (Book IV, Chap. 22): "If [the book is] wrote against anything, — 'tis wrote, an' please your worships, against the spleen."

25. *Gulliver's Travels,* Part IV, chap. 7.

26. *Poems,* pp. 271-273. Among Johnson's many unfulfilled projects of writing was—appropriately—"The Palace of Sloth, a Vision" (Boswell, *Life of Johnson,* ed. Hill-Powell [Oxford: Clarendon Press, 1934-1950], IV, 382n).

27. Auden's characterization of Tennyson may be recalled: "He had the finest ear, perhaps, of any English poet. . . . There was little about melancholia that he didn't know; there was little else that he did." (Auden, *Forewords and Afterwords,* [London: Faber, 1973], p. 222). As a note there tells us, Auden, under T. S. Eliot's persuasion, modified his opinion of Tennyson's "stupidity" after the first appearance of his essay in 1944.

28. James Boswell, *The Hypochondriack,* ed. Margery Bailey (Stanford: Stanford University Press, 1951), No. XXX (March, 1780). The essays appeared monthly in the *London Magazine* between 1777 and

1783. Professor Bailey's introduction provides a useful discussion of the history of "hypochondria" in England.

29. *Letters,* ed. R. W. Chapman (Oxford: Clarendon Press, 1952), nos. 655, 163. With the latter exhortation, compare Imlac's to the astronomer obsessed with his divine mission to control the movements of the heavens and his guilt at failing to live up to his great responsibilities: "Keep this thought always prevalent, that you are only one atom of the mass of humanity, and have neither such virtue nor vice as that you should be singled out for supernatural favours or afflictions" (*Rasselas,* Chap. 46). For a useful modern commentary, see Kathleen Grange, "Dr. Samuel Johnson's Account of a Schizophrenic Illness in *Rasselas,*" *Medical History,* 6 (1962), 162-168.

30. Both can be found in *Minor Poets of the Eighteenth Century,* introduction by Hugh I' Anson Fausset (London: Everyman's Library, 1930).

31. This cliché goes back (in part) to one of the pseudo-Aristotelian *Problems,* quoted in Klibansky, *Saturn and Melancholy,* p. 18: "Why is it that all those who have become eminent in philosophy or poetry or the arts are clearly melancholics?" (though the author does not include, as Stukeley does, "persons of the soft sex"). Johnson, among others, pooh-poohed the theory. "Read Cheyne's *English Malady,*" he advises Boswell, "but do not let him teach you a foolish notion that melancholy is a proof of acuteness" (Johnson, *Letters,* no. 492, July 2, 1776).

32. Though, as Professor Rousseau points out, in "Nerves, Spirits, and Fibres" (see n. 21 above), a more important pioneer anatomist of the nervous system was Lower's older contemporary, Thomas Willis. Cf. also Kenneth Dewhurst, *Thomas Willis as a Physician* (Los Angeles: Clark Library Publications, 1964): "[Willis's] chief assistant in both the clinical and scientific spheres was Richard Lower, who eventually inherited his practice" (p. 16).

33. Literary students have probably taken too seriously Cheyne's not very scientifically established hypothesis that melancholy, hypochondria, etc., are peculiarly incident to England. Of course, once this distinction came to be believed in, Englishmen made haste to confirm it by churning out "graveyard poems," and the like.

34. The older notions died hard, however — characteristically, in standard reference works such as Robert James's (and Samuel Johnson's) *Medicinal Dictionary* (London, 1745), s.v. "Hypochondria": "A spasmodic-flatulent disorder of the Primæ Viae, that is, of the stomach and intestines, arising from an inversion or perversion of their peristaltic motion, and, by the mutual consent of the parts, throwing the whole nervous system into irregular motions, and disturbing the whole economy of the functions"; s.v. "Melancholia": "The Melancholic Humour, which affects the Spirits in the Head, and disposes the brain to the generation of the like spirits, is to be corrected and evacuated."

35. *Nosology: or, A Systematic Arrangement of Diseases* (Edinburgh, 1772).

36. The term was apparently invented by the American neurologist George Beard, who transmuted the doctrine of "lowness" of the animal spirits in the nerves into an analogous explanation from the physics of electricity. After an exposition of the fall of voltage in an overloaded electrical circuit, he continues, "The force in this nervous system . . . is limited; and when new functions are interposed in the circuit . . . there comes a period, sooner or later . . . when the amount of force is insufficient to keep all the lamps actively burning" (*American Nervousness, Its Causes and Consequences: A Supplement to [Beard's] Nervous Exhaustion [Neurasthenia]* [New York: Putnam, 1972; first published 1881], p. 98). I owe this reference to my colleague Professor Luther Luedtke.

37. Though "alienist" (equaling "psychiatrist") enjoyed only brief popularity in the late nineteenth and early twentieth century, "alienation," as a term in both psychology and theology ("alienation from God"), is very old (see *OED*).

38. James Thomson, *The Castle of Indolence and Other Poems,* ed. Alan Dugald McKillop (Lawrence: University of Kansas Press, 1961): "Thomson, really a Whig panegyrist of progress, allows himself to be pleasingly beguiled by the idyll of a virtuous Golden Age in *The Seasons,* and again by a vision of sybaritic retirement in Canto I of *The Castle*" (p. 1; this seems to be intended as a paraphrase of Raymond D. Havens's thesis in "Primitivism and the Idea of Progress in Thomson," *Studies in Philology,* 29 [1932], 41-52, but McKillop gives the impression of concurring with it); "Professor [Hoxie N.] Fairchild . . . can find that *The Castle of Indolence* exhibits . . . an optimistic cult of action, a 'sentimentalized Protestant energy' " (p. 53; again McKillop does not indicate disagreement, though he terms the opinion "extreme").

39. Jean Daniélou, A. H. Couratin, [and] John Kent, *Historical Theology* (Harmondsworth: Pelican, 1969), Vol. II of *The Pelican Guide to Modern Theology,* pp. 271-272.

40. Cf. my "Samuel Johnson and the Great War for Empire," in John H. Middendorf, ed., *English Writers of the Eighteenth Century: Essays Presented to James L. Clifford by His Students* (New York: Columbia University Press, 1971), pp. 37-65. Thomson's "Rule, Britannia," a piece of propaganda for Pittite expansionism, remained the anthem of British imperialism until very recently; its proclamation of Britain's "manifest destiny" to "rule the waves" contrasts with what may be called the Walpolian national anthem, "God Save the King," which became popular at about the same time and makes much more modest demands on divine aid.

41. McKillop finds "ambiguity" (p. 48) in the poem and believes, "For the reader of the poem, however, the primary difficulty must be the integrity of the poetic vision" (p. 53). Thomson is seen as, consciously or unconsciously, presenting the Castle as somehow admirable: "The Indolence enjoyed in Canto I is not exactly the Indolence vanquished in Canto II"; one of the "meanings" of Indolence being conveyed in Canto I is "Indolence as virtuous and philosophic retirement,"

it "is closely connected with what the age called 'ease'" (p. 3); "The 'indolence' of the poet is so closely connected with the creation of poetry as to be virtually identical with it" (p. 21).

I cannot see this. As often, when a modern critic finds "ambiguity" in an older work, what has really happened is that the critic, conditioned by a "modern" set of ethical values, refuses to recognize that the author may in all earnestness be expounding a contrary one. Fairchild at least openly states his prejudices; after he proclaims himself in the preface to his work (*Religious Trends in English Poetry*, [New York: Columbia University Press, 1939-1968]) to be an "Anglo-Catholic," we are not surprised to find him doing less than justice to Thomson's "Protestant cult of action." But many critics seem unconscious of the existence of such prejudices in themselves, which they anachronistically attribute to their subjects. By the standards of a twentieth-century British or American university professor, it seems the Houyhnhnms' "life-style" — they actually observe the Ten Commandments — is a boring one; therefore the tone of admiration in which it is described must be "irony" or "ambiguity" on Swift's part. Certainly Thomson describes the specious attractiveness of Indolence in "poetic" terms, just as Spenser, in Despair's speech, describes suicide attractively. Does this mean that Spenser has an ambiguous attitude toward the desirability of suicide?

The poem's most recent editor, James Sambrook (see note 9 above) seems to reject McKillop's reading: "[Thomson's] larger moral purpose — to condemn indolence and praise progress in its various moral, intellectual, and material forms — rules out any possibility that he might explore the nature of the poetic imagination through the dream landscape in which he had placed the half-perceiving, half-creating, dreamer-poet" (p. xvi). Yet the tone in which Sambrook describes the conclusion of the poem seems to indicate that he doesn't take that purpose very seriously: "The Knight [of Arts and Industry] himself, having brought to society the benefits of commerce, retires, like any wealthy Whig city magnate, to a country estate, which he improves in the usual enlightened eighteenth-century fashion by enclosing, planting, draining, irrigating, and landscape gardening.... The moral...is serious, and, in Thomson's eyes, very important, but the Spenserian form, with its continual hints of burlesque, serves to lighten the final effect of the poem..." (p. xvii).

42. Kurt Samuelsson, an economic historian, originally published his *Ekonomi och Religion* in Stockholm, 1957.

43. G. R. Elton, *Reformation Europe, 1517-1559* (New York: Harper and Row, 1963), p. 317. Elton devotes several pages to a careful exposition of the Weber-Tawney thesis and to Samuelsson's demolition of it. He accurately prophesies (p. 312), "It may be doubted whether the death of the theory will become sufficiently known to prevent it having a ghostlike and sepulchral power to haunt us." Certainly it still haunts literary studies.

44. Boswell, *Life*, ed. Hill-Powell, II, 57.

V

CLARISSA'S RICHARDSON:
AN ESSAY TO FIND THE READER

John Traugott

Professor of English, University of California Berkeley

I

THE COMPOSER'S DREAM

This essay is first of all a tribute to Richardson the artist. If I do not gloss over the incessant sexual moralizing of the man—always banal and often nasty—it is because the artist triumphed over the man, mastered, and turned to account his worst instincts. Richardson would not be Richardson without those banal and nasty obsessions of his about the pitfalls that gape for genteel virgins, and the artist who imagined *Clarissa* could never have achieved its structure had he not learned to exploit those obsessions. No question, then, of our retiring before the obsessions of another age as though we had no right to judge. We have always the right to judge, and to rethink critically the author's thought—else we would be collectors of antiques, not readers. And across this judgment and the criticism, we have the pleasure of coming to understand what a writer could make of the workaday banality which he lived. Nor do I mean to excuse Richardson's moral maunderings by proving that they have some higher value, religous or ethical, hitherto unobserved owing to insufficient scholarship. Common sense tells us that they are faithfully pedestrian.

Clarissa is incontestibly a great novel. Does it not go without saying that we want to understand what happened in the imaginings of this man of such dubious personality and such silly postures when we set about to discover the destiny of his Clarissa? No, it does not seem so. This essay is the saying. This essay is aesthetic, not psychological, but it is the man remaking himself into the artist that interests me. Certainly I will have recourse to the ingenuities of structural analysis, certainly to historical perspectives, but our interest goes beyond structure and history, to what I will call, for want of a better term, the consciousness of the author. That seems to me the humanistic study, telling us what a man could do with the givens of his personality and his history. In his freedom we find a figure, however distant, of our own.

I have, then, as well, a secondary aim — to suggest, across Richardson, the presence of the writer, not his absence, as the New Critics so tiresomely insisted, and the aesthetic importance of that presence. While Richardson is a flagrant example of a peculiar consciousness, everywhere present in his work, creating our imagination, he is not peculiar in this regard among great writers. "Richardsonian," "Jamesian," "Sternean," "Swiftian," "Joycean" —what can we mean by such qualifiers, in which an author's name comes to mind even before his work? What can we mean but that the consciousness of the writer is primary to our experience of the work? How strange is the hold upon existence of a great writer, how strange and how familiar. Who would have thought that such a shape and form could be brought out of chaos? Who does not recognize the urgency of that shape and form to his economy? The choosing out of the wayward atoms of chaos and their structuring is the author's consciousness. This passage between the author and the reader is of the first importance — it is a spectacle, a man mastering himself and his society, exploiting the peculiarities of personality and the parochialisms of history to make a reality never seen before and never to be seen again, but acknowledged by the reader as a part of existence.

Perhaps Eliot's doctrine — by now frozen to cliché — of the abnegation of the author, of his disappearance from his work — terrestrial *deus absconditus* — has led us all down the garden path.

Whether it is a question of James or Eliot, who hoped to abscond, or of Richardson, who hoped to wag his finger in our faces, what matters first of all is the peculiar consciousness of the writer. Richardson is our spectacle.

I am not, of course, speaking of the author as he wishes to present himself to the busybody world, where he, like the rest of us, can wear what costume pleases his fancy, but as he appears in his work where he seeks to master his own urgencies which he cannot escape and which he must reveal. Although I am not then speaking of his drawing-room character, that is the place to start with *Clarissa*'s Richardson, who marvelously masters and exploits the anxieties, pretensions, and sensitivities of the drawing-room character. I will refer in these opening remarks to his posturing correspondence with the sentimental gentlewoman, Lady Bradshaigh.

The mere physiognomy of Richardson imposes a ridiculous puppet between us and the great author of *Clarissa*. We must see him as he saw himself in that little travesty of a Restoration comedy he wrote in his correspondence with Lady Bradshaigh — or with Belcour, as she coyly called herself. There he is walking in St. James's Park, up and down the alleys, every day, three or four hours at a time, this plump little man, five-foot-five, fair wig riding atop a long black coat, one hand in his bosom, the other on his cane held under his cloak (for his health is none of the best), looking straight on (but noticing all sides), never turning his short fat neck, despite eyes misted over by a rheum from his head, missing none of the ladies' feet that trot beneath the large hoops passing in the alley. That supercilious eye of his, he says, as the thought of hoops and little feet revives him. He is having a sort of tryst, even assignation, with the mysterious Belcour; though thus far they have exchanged only teasingly sentimental letters, she has given him to understand that she too will be walking in the park unperceived. Which hoop is she?, which little feet? Will she reveal herself? She will not say.

His posture as he describes it here must have been his habitual one, the way he wanted to be seen, for it is exactly the way he posed for his friend Joseph Highmore when his portrait was taken later on. In that portrait, Belcour stares down on her plump admirer from a painting hung on the background wall, a painting also done by Highmore. In the painting-within-a-painting,

Belcour is propped in her lawn chair like a manikin in the Bath museum of eighteenth-century costumes, her husband Sir Roger stands rigid at her side, looking into some distance of which his consort would know nothing.

If now we come back to the portrait of Richardson which includes on the background wall this tableau of Sir Roger and Lady Bradshaigh on their lawn, it seems that Belcour and Richardson are but feigning distraction, waiting for the painter and Sir Roger to move off before resuming their ambulations in the park. (The composition is obviously a private joke between Richardson and the painter.)

A nice little flirtation of the porcine printer and the sentimental lady. What a pair!—he the self-appointed dominie to the kingdom's nice ladies, feeding their little vanities with compliments to their delicacies and with avuncular advice (though always with that supercilious eye) about their maidenly or conjugal duties; she his mysterious admirer from afar, weeping a "pint of tears," as she puts it, for Clarissa's hard fate and petitioning by post that her famous author-correspondent should soften his heart and undo the mischief that Lovelace had already done on Clarissa's body.

She and Richardson endlessly tease one another until it is clear to both that somehow they must meet. Thus the long rambles in the park—which were to prove but another tease. The lady takes fright for her reputation. She is indignant at his impudence when he suggests they meet at his house. He writes an allegory of a withered rose too long withheld from its admirer. Does he presume to think her the rose? She must quench his ardor. She rebukes him for having written a four-page letter and writes one in return. How she fears to meet him after saying so many impudent things. He compares his case to Lovelace's! Is there not a brick wall between him and the lady? Will you not name the day, dear lady, but, oh, how can you think Lovelace attractive, the evil wicked man! Have I not taken such pains to make him odious?

We need not think we catch Richardson out in this little comedy. He knows what he is doing. It is the same teasing sensibility that is working out the structure of *Clarissa*.

Their actual meeting was to come only later, after *Clarissa* was done and published, its heroine in heaven beyond any possibility of making her Mrs. Lovelace as Lady Bradshaigh had demanded. What exquisite delay, what delicious teasing! And all interlarded with absurd little lessons in domestic conduct for tender virgins or retiring matrons.

"The smug, juicy, pedestrian printer...plump, prosaic, the most middling of middling men, and so domestically fussy that even his gift of weeping hardly guarantees that he will be a major figure. Is there not some other strain in this dull and prodigiously painstaking little man? There is. Samuel Richardson was mad." Thus V. S. Pritchett.

This is not an opinion that Professors Eaves and Kimpel, Richardson's latest and best biographers, will accept. Nor *of course* would they accept the implications that all too easily come to mind from the sketch of him I have just given—though of course it is Richardson's own sketch of himself. Professors Eaves and Kimpel have good sense throughout; not only do we get from them an exhaustive account of the workaday life Richardson lived, but we are assured that there were no evidences of madness, not even of excitement, no notable hypocrisies, no clandestine excursions; just an honest and decent man getting on in his trade. They are judicious in their literary judgments, or perhaps in reserving judgment, and severe with those critics who find sensational correspondences between the author and his characters. For there are not wanting critics who chime Pritchett's doubts about Richardson's normality, and they ring in Freud often enough as their prosecutor. Eaves and Kimpel just do not find the sadism and masochism that others detect. For them, Lovelace's sexual attitudes are more like those of a nasty schoolboy, and for them, Clarissa has perfect reasons for her tergiversations. Nor do Eaves and Kimpel find any evidence at all that such aberrances as Lovelace's sexual cynicism (or as Clarissa's tragic vocation) were manifested in Richardson's day-to-day life.

As to the last point, there can be no doubt—the evidence is, in fact, just as Richardson wished it to appear. His daily life was impeccably ordinary. Any other inference would be ungenerous. Yet an uneasiness grows upon the reader of this monumental biography of Eaves's and Kimpel's, a sadness, perhaps, that such labor on a man's life yields so little help in our understanding of the emotional charge that animates Lovelace and Clarissa. Nor is

this an invidious judgment, for Eaves and Kimpel felt the same
uneasiness growing upon them. Their last words are worth pon-
dering. "For a biographer, it is rather disappointing that so little
of the Richardson that shows in Clarissa and Lovelace shows in
his life. His letters show Clarissa's charity and many of her conscious ideas, it is true, but not her intensity or her nobility. Even
if it could be shown that he was a suppressed seducer, he would
still be no Lovelace — seducers are common enough, but Lovelace's wit and pride are by no means common. The details of
Richardson's life and background tell us much more about what
limited his work than about what makes it important." They proceed to quote Proust's attack on Sainte-Beuve for his biographical
criticism that fails to recognize that a writer's work expresses a
different self than that he displayed in the parlors where his coun-
sel was prized. They cannot but accept Proust's strictures, at least
as they might pertain to *Clarissa.* "But it is the Richardson who
wrote Clarissa who is interesting, and that Richardson hardly
appears in his biography." Has it all then been useless, they ask at
page 619. Well, perhaps a biographer "can give the context out
of which a book came," but, they say, it is a lesson in modesty for
a biographer to know that he has so little touched the springs of
the author's creative life.

Though Eaves and Kimpel are dead right to cite Proust's
Contre Sainte-Beuve, they are too despairing of the uses of biography. For those moral clichés of Richardson's which Eaves and
Kimpel find so devoid of interest, are expressed throughout his
correspondence in ways that suggest a muted interior drama, a
drama that has not-too-subterranean links to the structure of
Clarissa. The little comedy with Lady Bradshaigh — which Eaves
and Kimpel do not see as a comedy — is not without pointers for
the reader seeking to find *Clarissa's* Richardson. The dramatic
sense that feeds on teasing and provocation, the comic sense that
travesties sexual role-playing, are there half-allowed, half-dis-
avowed. But there are, by fits and starts everywhere in the correspondence, suggestions of Richardson's dramatic perception,
sometimes melodramatic, sometimes comic, of his own obsessions. That Richardson's self in *Clarissa* should be different from
that pompous little figure he got up for the world is not surprising. He could not impersonate in the drawing room all the

dramatis personae inhabiting his imagination; he could only dampen those spirits with moral clichés. One cannot think forever about rakes and virgins without a lively imagination. The stuff of drama is there, and it shows through in the most pedestrian moments. But virgins are the stuff of melodrama, pathos, she-tragedy, while rakes, if they find themselves in such literary purlieus, will easily collapse the proceedings into farce. Rakes are the stuff of comedy and bring immediately to mind the long tradition of the Restoration still current in Richardson's time. How to put the two together — the she-tragedy with the rake-comedy — and bring both down to the domestic foyer: that was the artistic problem that troubled Richardson's banality. It lost its edge in the farces and bathos of *Pamela,* was brilliantly resolved in *Clarissa,* and then was again dampened to cliché in *Grandison.* (Albeit *Pamela* and *Grandison* have their smaller excellences within the larger failures.) This mastery of the artist, this freedom to exploit dramatically the givens of his own personality and of the world he had to live in — that is our study.

To return for a moment to general thoughts about this artistic process, Vladimir Nabokov, the supreme apologist of our time for the freedom of the artist from what he calls "fool-made history," has something to say. "Fool-made history" is that set of events among which we must, willy-nilly, live. But a first-rate work of fiction, says Nabokov, makes short shrift of "fool-made history." It is as artificial as a chess problem composed for a hypothetical solver. The competition is not between Black and White, but between the composer and the solver (who may or may not exist). So in a work of fiction, the clash is not between characters but between the author and the world. It is all the composer's dream. The extremity of Nabokov's aesthetic can be shown by setting it against that of the Marxist critic, Georg Lukács: "A great realist such as Balzac [but for Lukács a "great realist" is equivalent to a "great writer"], if the intrinsic artistic development of situations and characters he has created comes into conflict with his most cherished prejudices or even his sacred convictions, will, without an instant's hesitation, set aside his own prejudices and convictions and describe what he really sees, not what he would prefer to see." However much Richardson couched his virgin-rake drama in realistic trappings, the trappings, including the rules of deportment for young ladies, are little more than a screen behind which he can maneuver his own interior drama. The greater glory his, that he triumphed over "fool-made history" and forced the reader to participate with him in the artifice of his own imaginings. That he made very important contributions to the art of realism is quite true—and they have been well treated by Ian Watt— but "what he really saw" was not what a Lukács could wish for—perhaps the economic implications of the decay of religious values. Christopher Hill has well argued what can be said along these lines for Richardson and we will return briefly to that argument.

What he did "see," far from having been brought to view by his setting aside "his own prejudices and convictions" is a function of the very concerns we hear him prattling about in the *Correspondence*. What he "set aside" were moralistic excuses for his interior drama. He liked to dream of rakes and virgins, not a very original thought. What was original was that he had a rakish wit-comedy in his head, genuine wit, genuine comedy, and all that that implied about female sexuality. At the same time he clung dearly to his fantasy of a female paragon, cultivated in a hothouse of feeling and morality, proof against all assault. He was not going to drop his pathetic sensationalism and comic extravagance of *Pamela;* he would rather perfect the rake and his wit, working a transformation on the buck and his pranks; he would perfect the pathetic heroine, working another transformation on the professional virgin and her postures. To bring it off, he had to triumph over "fool-made history" to which he had himself been only a fool in *Pamela.*

The author is neither victim nor cipher nor mirror of history; no more is he the godlike creator of a work which has, as the New Critics used to announce with such pious solemnity, "a being of its own." It is rather the felt presence of the author's consciousness imposing—or struggling to impose, for great works need not be wholly successful—a shape on the incoherent facts of his history and the rude urgencies of his personality that moves us first of all.

As consciousness exists in time, we should not expect *Clarissa*'s Richardson to be the same as *Pamela*'s or *Grandison*'s, though there is an evolutionary continuity. I do not seek to catch Rich-

ardson out, to peek behind his veils; especially, have I no intention to psychoanalyze him. Whether he was mad or just middling,
whether sadomasochistic or just your run-of-the-mill sexual
dreamer seems irrelevant. What is obvious from everything he
wrote is that he was almost exclusively interested, outside his
printing business, in the sexual gauntlets genteel young women of
his circles ran or were said to run. What interests us is to watch
him at work remaking this all too banal obsession.

For this reason, this essay gives as much weight to Lovelace in
Richardson's consciousness as to Clarissa, for neither would exist
without the other, as their struggle is Richardson's internal dialogue given artistic shape. It likewise gives as much weight to
Lovelace's mode of literary existence, comedy, as it does to Clarissa's, the realism of pathos and sentiment. The clash of comedy,
a fantasy of triumph over reality, with realism, an imitation of
everyday probabilities, seems to me to be at the center of the
novel's emotional effect. Certainly, Richardson had in mind the
question whether the comic view of life — that is, the view of life as
subject to trick, quick-change artistry, grotesque or ridiculous
distortion, mimicry, parody, and enlivening fantasies of gratification — is not in itself morally damaging. Should not life be seen
as always answering to the absolute demands of the soul for sincerity, candor, and moral earnestness? A good question — at least
one that troubled an author as sophisticated as Jane Austen and
has a long history in literature from the middle ages onward. Jane
Austen is Richardson's true heir. In a saner, less sensational way,
it was she who continued to explore the clash, the moral and emotional clash, between realism and comedy. Dickens, on the other
hand, was quite capable of running comedy and sentimental
realism in tandem with no questions asked about which was the
true, which the false view of this life we must live. The uneasiness
comedy inspires in a Christian is betrayed by the traditional
moral apologies for it, that it is a mirror in which men may see
their faults and forthwith reform. How is it that such a dubious
proposition should be so often repeated, save that it is special
pleading to ward off uneasiness? Comedy pleases us but it also en-
courages us to give voice to instincts that will not be tolerated in
everyday life where causes and effects take no account of our fantasies. Without any doubt, as Richardson, himself divided be-

tween his moral earnestness and his talent for comedy, could easily confirm in himself, the comic sense mines the redoubts of morality, and comedy, as a literary form, enters inevitably into a war with realism.

It is time to say here, parenthetically, that readers of *Clarissa* might more easily see it as a clash of two modes of literary representation, libertine comedy and sentimental realism, if they read *Clarissa* and not Professor Sherburn's abridgement of it, where Lovelace and his wit and his comic *tours* get short shrift. The greater part of the passages I will discuss here do not appear in Sherburn or appear mutilated. He has muted the essential drama of the book in favor of simple pathos and moral message. He has accepted Richardson's public pretensions and overlooked the quality of his art. In the realm of art as in that of everyday life, surely what men do is what matters, not what they say they would do. All the more reason to take account of Richardson's correspondence where his need to play teasing games with his readers is obvious. Richardson would not be happy with Sherburn's recastings; they violate the nature of his art. Toiling away in university classes with Sherburn's *Clarissa,* readers (and their mentors) are little likely to remark Richardson's talent for comedy, Lovelace's charades having been scissored into incoherent fits and starts. What is left is pathos, an untutored girl, and a melodramatic villain. To give voice to recent argot, is Lovelace a sexist? Obviously, if we read Sherburn. But if we read Richardson, it is surely Clarissa who is the sexist and Lovelace the parodist of her clichés. It is Clarissa who has no doubt that Rosebud must be ruined if Lovelace but tip her a supercilious wink. It is Clarissa who is impressed by his generosity when he spares Rosebud to the lower-class lover who is to marry her. Lovelace's amusing irony is that thanks to him, Rosebud will set a moral example to the lower classes, whom elsewhere he describes as half-dead. It is all very well to protest that Richardson only wanted to show up the villainy of Lovelace, but it is Lovelace's intelligence that shows and his mockery that pleases. It is only when Clarissa passes beyond her social conventionalities (which Richardson so often in his correspondence protests he is defending) that she earns our sympathy and becomes an impressive figure of tragedy. Lovelace's comic villanies also earn our sympathy because they subvert intolerable

pretensions; it is when he confuses his comic games with reality
that he too enters the tragic world. None of this comes through in
Sherburn.

It is Clarissa, again, who assumes the helplessness of all other
women. Lovelace is certainly an egomaniac, but he has some reason to be when he is apparently the only person in England who
can make comic games of the clichés about women. But we return to Lovelace and his atavistic talent that grotesquely revives
the wit and humor of the Restoration, taking as his object the
sentimental and canting social climbers of mid-century.

Doubtless the crude and gratuitous pieties of *Pamela* — which
are a spillover of the mean prudence of *The Familiar Letters* —
obscure the considerable achievements of that novel. One of
those achievements is certainly the hilarious bedroom farce of the
shenanigans of B and Jewkes. After Fielding had travestied the
pieties of the novel, there was little chance that Richardson's farcical scenes could be seen as anything but accidental — poor, fat
fool didn't know what a clown he was. He was not a poor, fat fool,
and the scenes of comedy are not accidental. What is truer is that
they simply find no place in the realism of Pamela's to-the-minute
recording of her little nerves. Artistic ineptitude one must say,
looking at *Pamela* apart from *Clarissa* and the whole continuity
of Richardson's writings. But in another view, *Pamela* is only an
experimental work, unachieved: Richardson had in his head
some urgency to bring the different worlds of comedy and realism
into fruitful aesthetic relation, and he found the way in *Clarissa*.
There Lovelace's comedy, a revival of the witty fantasies of Restoration comedy, works perfectly to question Clarissa's puritan
sincerity; equally her sincerity questions Lovelace's attempts to
push comedy beyond the bounds of the gratifications of fantasy
into the life of realistic consequences. In *Grandison* Richardson
managed to preserve some of the social comedy of manners, even
sharpen it, and there he gives scope to the sort of social sarcasm
that Anna Howe can express. But there is no escaping Grandison
himself whose presence reduces everyone to a mummylike repose.
Again, Richardson's moral purpose — this time to make a hero of
the male virgin — could not be integrated with his comic sense —
the social criticism of the manners comedy had to be muted and
disavowed. Had he invented a female rake — which had to await

the world-weariness of Choderlos de Laclos, who pays tribute to Richardson — Richardson would have had on his hands a Grandison who was only an upper-class Joseph Andrews. No, *Clarissa* was the right formula because there he could build a whole novel on provocation, of two opposing sexes, two opposing systems of value, two opposing literary modes. It was the right formula for Richardson because his art and his very being thrived on provocation. He had to find a way to bring his comic sense to a deadly provocation of his own moral sincerity — and his moral sincerity to a provocation of his comic sense.

How important provocation was to Richardson can be sensed not only in his epistolary drama conducted with Lady Bradshaigh, but in all his correspondence. How incessantly he provokes his correspondents such as Aaron Hill and his daughters, Sarah Chapone, and many other ladies and gentlemen. How cleverly he admits them to his circle of advisers, literary and moral; how disingenuously he baits them to complain again and again about his too strict requirements for Clarissa's behavior or his too severe censure of Lovelace. Coyly he urges them to make suggestions, primly correcting them for their overliberal lapses in criticising Clarissa or appreciating Lovelace. Do they not realize that the book's dramatic scenes merely reinforce the moral doses? A pretty piece of advice, that of Miss Howe's, to suggest to Clarissa early on that she should lay claim to the independence that was her right from her grandfather's estate. Mrs. Chapone had mistakenly thought that a girl who has legally some protection for herself should not submit to torture by a family whose motivations are so dubious that they do not bear much examination in polite society. Having evoked this reaction, Richardson parades all the guilt he had burdened Clarissa with, wags his finger at Mrs. Chapone, and adds his own admonition: "You see, madam, how difficult I have made it for a girl to be excused for running away from her parents: A needful doctrine in this Age." It was not that Mrs. Chapone was about to run off with her own Lovelace, but that this sort of overstatement and travesty of his own work always elicited a return letter from his correspondent pointing out the subtleties of his characters or of their problems. This way he always had correspondents and could always preen himself — justly — between preachments, on his finest novelistic strokes.

How salutary an instruction in morality it must have been to young girls to be told by the great author that he rejoiced that Clarissa dies at nineteen and is thus saved exposure to life's sordid temptations! All they had to do was die at nineteen themselves to be paragons. What shocks and provokes is the galling clash between the worldliness of his moral advice as to conduct and the otherworldliness of his remedies. How fatigued he is by solicitations from ladies to give Clarissa terrestrial happiness — prayers, cavils, entreaties plague him. Still, he writes Hill, he is grateful for opinions that tell him of a lady's delicacy. Thus he provokes them and eggs them on. To the ladies Hill he writes wondering how anyone could tolerate the vulgar novel *Tom Jones* in which that hoyden Sophia traipses through inns, a fugitive from her father's just authority. He never tires of telling his female correspondents how utterly dependent they are on their parents' mere whim, however cruel it may be. It is as though the Jacobite political and religious doctrines of absolute obedience to the monarch, perfected in the Restoration, were being domesticated in a sort of high-flying toryism for hearth and home. Parents, he says, like monarchs must be left to God to punish.

But the entire history of comedy is built on a denial of this proposition. And no one, it is safe to say, this side of Far Tartary ever believed such patent nonsense in real life. Certainly Richardson's correspondence shows that it is not believed in his own time in England. Whatever social realism Clarissa may pretend to is clearly and willingly vitiated by Richardson's taste for the provocation of absolutisms. He describes Lovelace in the most contemptuous terms to Lady Bradshaigh — a monkey, like all rakes, a coxcomb, a liar, a caperer. This was to bring out a series of protests that it wasn't so. One cannot, in short, read through Richardson's correspondence without perceiving the obvious dynamic: with simplistic moral positions which falsify his own drama in *Clarissa* he provokes his correspondent to defend Lovelace or to criticize Clarissa. The dialogue is opened, a dramatic conflict develops between one's natural sympathy for Clarissa and an underground suspicion that Lovelace is not wholly wrong. The same psychological game goes on in the novel and obviously was one Richardson nourished in himself. This provocation is of the essence, then, of the novel, of the reader's response, of Richardson's relations with his correspondents, and of his own consciousness from which all else springs.

"What a world is this," says Clarissa, ". . . one half of mankind tormenting the other. . . ." What an opportunity, the author seems to answer, for virtue to shine and for pathos to open the heart. Lovelace, cruel, provocative man, goes to school to his creator. Richardson writes to one of his ladies: "Do not provoke me, say you, Will you forgive me, Madam, if I own that I really have so much cruelty in my nature that I should wish to provoke you now and then, if I knew what would do it consistent with decency and respect." Decency and respect, aye, there's the rub. He would have dead-center morality which he would then provoke from all sides. Comedy and wit to cut, subvert, confound sincerity; pathos to recommend a univocal morality. Lady Bradshaigh accuses her admired author of cruelty towards Clarissa merely to take a picture of her grief. He is no better, says she, than the painter "Spaniolet (Ribera) who was said to have crucified a man to get the look of the Saviour's agony. Lovelace crucifies Clarissa, he says, but were it merely sadism we should hardly care for the perils of Clarissa. Clarissa must be tortured to get the look of martyrdom — "my dear, Adversity is your shining time," says Anna Howe — but for the reader, the emotional depth comes in pitting Clarissa's sincerity, which by the torture we are finally made to sense, against Lovelace's comic libertinism, which always threatens to make us indifferent to that sincerity, to reduce her belief to mere airs. Lovelace's comic lurkings and spyings are also our author's. Writing to Lady Bradshaigh of his rambles in the park, Richardson tells us what a slyboots he is: "a sly sinner, creeping to the very edges of the walks, getting behind benches, one hand in his bosom, the other held up to his chin, as if to keep it in place: as afraid of being seen as a thief of detection."

We need not take too seriously his pretension that Clarissa is an example. Of what? To whom? Well, he would say, the sad story warns young girls away from disobedience to their parents. That pretense collapses early on before the gothic sensationalism of Clarissa's family. Or is she a warning to rakes: their sexual obsessions may involve them in a Christian tragedy. But, as Eaves and Kimpel grant, rakes need not be fearful of meeting another Clarissa. Such another fuss is no more likely than the trepidation of the spheres. "More useful than glaring" is Clarissa's motto, belying her name, but in fact she is far more glaring than useful. Her trial takes place in a hothouse, not in the world. The young female being instructed from this book must have a family as gothic as the Harlowes, and she must meet a rake as talented as Lovelace and with as complete a philosophy. She would wither within the circumference of her hoop before such a conjunction would occur. No, more glaring than useful.

Having said this, we need not underestimate or undervalue Richardson's sentimentalism. For sentiment, the minute-to-minute building of Clarissa's feelings before violence, makes us know her emotional development to an absolutism that is more than a posture. To appreciate her absolutism is also to appreciate the force of Lovelace's comic libertinism which so radically questions it. Lady Bradshaigh's pint of tears shows how well Richardson touched the nerve of his age, for her sentimental reaction to the novel was only the extreme of that of Johnson, Fielding, and Diderot, among many another enlightened luminary. If Lady Bradshaigh was something of a goose, they were not. Sentimentalism was a new article of faith for the age. What a drama then for Richardson to revive (to improve on) the comic libertinism of the Restoration in order to test this new article of faith. A Clarissa must find her Lovelace, a Lovelace his Clarissa.

Lovelace knows that it is not Clarissa's virginity that is in play — her sour sister Bella has that gossamer bulwark without provoking his satanic games — but her being and his own. They are inseparable in Richardson's consciousness, wholly dependent on one another; she his, he her, fate.

How different is this novelistic reality from his moralistic blather in his correspondence that rakes cannot possibly attract really delicate young ladies because they are only coxcombs, caperers, monkeys. Rather than being a resolution of this death struggle in favor of Christian sublimity, his godlike pretension to restore his ruined angel in heaven is a demonstration that the reality he has chosen to represent is the stuff of tragedy, as inescapable as it is irresolvable in this life we must live.

I should like now to follow Richardson's development of the comedy of the game-playing rake. His anachronistic fascination with the Restoration, particularly its comedy, but its heroic play

as well, and the two together, seems inseparable from his perception of reality. The well-known stories Richardson told his Dutch
correspondent Stinstra, and later his daughters, about his childhood betray again his imaginative processes. Whether the stories
are anything *more* than fantasy is a question we do not have to
settle; they are certainly fantasy. And they tell us how he fancied
himself in a world where short, fat moralists can easily be trans-
mogrified into more interesting figures.

From his boyhood on, Richardson seems to have used his pro-
clivity for morally repressive banalities as a sort of open sesame to
the underground world of sexuality. He could dream the dreams
of Lovelace, it seems, just so long as he paid for them with public
pronouncements turning those dreams into dreary lessons. It was
crucially important to him to keep up the pieties.

Since Richardson liked to speak in terms of virtue rewarded, let
us imagine the perfect reward for a goody-goody twelve-year-old
boy who obsessively minds his p's and q's but who has nonetheless
an inclination to voyeurism, a penchant for peeping at the pecca-
dilloes of others. Already, according to his story, he has sent a
poison-pen letter — anonymously — to a middle-aged lady who was
unaware that she was not, morally speaking, up to snuff. Though
rebuked by his mother for his forwardness, he was admired for his
moralizing. What would be the perfect reward for such forward
virtue? Nothing better than that a circle of adolescent girls seeking a confidant to enlarge the thrill of secrecy should so trust to
the delicacy and discretion of this little moralist (it is not quite
clear what age he is now, presumably little older) as to invite him
to their private prattle about amorous matters. Then, even better, that each of them in turn should unbeknownst to the others
make of him a special confidant and entrust to his sensibility the
writing of her love letters. This is the fantastic story he told Stinstra, his Dutch admirer, about his pristine steps into the realm of
female correspondence. Privy to their little delicacies, not by way
of the keyhole like Swift, but by way of complicity, he was admitted to their very closet. He was never to leave it.

But this story has more than a generalized future in which the
closet moralist enters imaginatively into the redoubts of Pamela
and Clarissa to continue his pennings. We must remember that
with this story he tells another, that he was always an exemplary

apprentice, thinking ever of his moral responsibilities, even while the other boys expressed a natural resentment of a harsh master. He saved candle ends to read by when his day, his perfect day, was done, and lo and behold, he had another reward, according to the story later told his daughters. This one explains how a domestic moralist of a printer's apprentice came by his knowledge of the rakish practices of a Lovelace, but more, how he came to have Lovelace's wit and libertine insight. For the good apprentice knew somehow a gentleman, a rake, who was a master of the epistolary style and corresponded at length with the apprentice about his amorous adventures. The gentleman had both a wife and a mistress; he was a veteran of military campaigns abroad; he had honorable wounds; he was exiled by a tangled love life. Naturally such a gentleman would find his soulmate in a London apprentice who was morally impeccable and who not only never entered a bawdy house but never went to a masquerade. And that is how fat Richardson came to know slim Lovelace, his mind, his heart, and his witty talk. McKillop says with a sigh that it must be confessed all this passes the bounds of sober truth. One can easily venture beyond McKillop's gentle skepticism. The story of the gentleman who was his foster father is too easily recognized as Freud's "family romance," the saga of an imaginary family that answers to one's dreams.

Though this story has the quality of a private myth, it connects with literary myth in a way that confirms for us Richardson's imagination of himself, his consciousness, that is realized so perfectly in art in *Clarissa*. It is *Clarissa*'s Richardson, the perfected figure who interests us, for there he mastered the banal Richardson.

Who is this forward child who is permitted to enter the female sanctum to spy out their false or real delicacies? Who is this chaste apprentice who somehow knows all rakish habits and manners? A literary archetype comes to mind. Is not young Richardson much like Wycherley's Horner? That Horner who, masquerading as a eunuch, once a ranger in the pleasure gardens, is now reduced by the French disease to a ladies companion, their confidant and house moralist. Wycherley's comedy *The Country Wife*, realizes perfectly a male sexual fantasy. The nice ladies, admirable frostpieces who protest publicly that sex is an odious beast, reveal their secret libidinousness to the supposedly harmless Horner, and when he suddenly slips off his disguise they fall to with an appetite only dreamt of in the onanistic transports of the male animal. Wycherley has created the perfect comedy of the rake hero who outsmarts all the world, preserving female delicacy for his own delectation. The perfect comedy, the fantasy of our culture, come true through the agency of mother wit. Being only a virginal adolescent, the Richardson of these stories is Horner *manqué*. Later, at first crudely as the buck Mr. B, always hiding in the closet, behind the door, in the bed, and then philosophically as the rake Lovelace, the man of a thousand disguises, Richardson relived this Horneresque fantasy of guardian of the temple who unmasks to become its despoiler. This classic plot goes back to Terence's *Eunuch*.

Now we remember that Lovelace is a would-be writer of comedy, and in the end, when all passion is spent, he revives his predatory spirits by thinking of himself as Horner. He thinks he will start up another comic game: he will utter pieties, he will broadcast the misery that his notorious crime has brought upon him, and he will announce his reformation. That will bring the ladies in for instruction and he will play Horner's comedy.

Such is the future of the myth dreamt by young Samuel Richardson the forward moralist, at once confidant of virtuous girls and an abandoned rake. One has only to put the pieces together in the most obvious way. There is nothing tendentious in the reconstruction. It reinforces our sense of Richardson's consciousness and the mastery of his artistic exploitation of it in *Clarissa*.

We speak particularly of Wycherley's *Country Wife,* and of Horner's fantasy, but all comedy is a fantasy of triumph. It is a triumph over stultification through wit or fortune. The wit is a perfect manipulation and exploitation of the protean aspects of life — roles, guises, linguistic invention. Fortune is a conspiracy of the gods in our favor. All postures that fret and fray life crumble in this fantasy of triumph. Wit is the short circuit that leaps across the insulation of habit and custom and decorum. Intrigue is the physical analogue of verbal wit. But the *sine qua non* of comedy is that its actions are without consequences in the real world. In comedy pompous people can be tripped up with no consequence save laughs; in the real world they would break their legs, inspire sympathy, require repairs, desire revenge. Aristotle reproves the use of the *deus ex machina* in tragedy as a violator of the sense of probability, but the *deus ex machina* is the perfect device for comedy and few comedies are without one in the form of one improbable intervention or another. Comedy battens on improbability as it feeds on the fantasy of triumph.

Realism on the other hand dotes on probability, on the sense that there are consequences of our actions that entrain endless cause and effect. Novels, not comedies, open out to speculation on the future of the characters.

Despite their formal difference, comedy and realism seem naturally to impinge on one another, as the mood of mockery and triumph through mockery will impinge on the prudences that are born of real experience. For Richardson, to think of a Clarissa was to think of a Lovelace. Now we turn to Lovelace's comedy.

Lovelace's fantasy of triumph is quite up to Richardson's—or Horner's. He thinks so, says so, and at that point in the novel he has every right to think it and to say it. We must agree: he is an accomplished comedic playwright and player. His disguises, his roles, his charades, his dialogues, his wordplay, his philosophy are truly dazzling. It is not, however, until nearly a quarter of the novel is finished that Richardson has clearly conceived Lovelace's character. Wit, playactor, scenario writer he is, by fits and starts, from the first, but Richardson has not grasped the fact that that is what he must be first and last, to the bottom of his being, if the novel is going to work. That is why he is endowed at the beginning with a motive that hardly accords with this more fundamental and more dramatic character that he becomes, a motive that Richardson quickly drops once the character is formed because it is useless to the development of the drama, indeed worse than useless, confusing. At the beginning Lovelace is indeed something of the juvenile neurotic that Eaves and Kimpel make him out to be—he is said to be motivated by desire for revenge upon the sex for having been jilted. For Eaves and Kimpel, that motivation, which is a false note by Richardson because it hardly accounts for any of Lovelace's quality, is sufficient. They do not see him in any other way than as a peeved and nasty youth. If this were so, what a bore the novel would be! Volume after volume of peevishness and pathos!

But another, truer, character, a character with a dramatic future, is developing from the beginning, though Richardson has not at first quite committed himself to it. It is the Lovelace of an internal dynamic that is capable of unfolding, complicating, changing as the action progresses. Clarissa herself early on calls him a "proteus"; he lurks and hovers about the Harlowe estate, developing games, pulling wires inside the house, conceiving himself. His natural métier is *agent provocateur*. He has also his fulsomely, even frighteningly, tender moments, and throughout the book his tenderness, his idealism, hangs on, reluctantly, like a nostalgic vapor, evoking now and then gentle testimony to Clarissa's excellence, but more and more, as the action wears on, the tribute is allied with cynicism and ironic overstatement. It verges always on parody. He is also alarmingly brutal early on. Is he a homicidal maniac? He thinks, for example, of executing Clarissa's messenger who carries missives from Miss Howe and back again. Poor clod, this minion, he is so honest and so without hope or ambition that it is useless to try to bribe him. Perhaps he should just be killed. "Yes the rascal has but a *half* life, and groans under that. Should I be answerable in his case for a *whole* life? Let him live. . . . And yet on second thoughts, am I not a *rake*, as it is called? And whoever knew a rake stick at anything?" But then he reassures Jack he is just inventing dramas in his way. It is this melodramatic side of Lovelace, always allied with self-parody and dramatic perspective, that develops as the book goes on and as Richardson catches his character.

Soon Richardson has this clear idea of character — a playactor constantly tempted, indeed fatally driven, to convert his comedy and its amusing fantasies into actuality, to make real people actors in his plays. Lovelace's is a literary vision, startlingly original, to test out the interactions of art and life. There is a romantic quality to it, as there is to Richardson's vision in *Clarissa*. Richardson, as well as Lovelace, is fascinated by the clash of comedy and sincerity. This side of Lovelace's character was picked up by Choderlos de Laclos in his conception of *Les Liaisons Dangereuses* where the rake heroes, male and female, quite consciously and diabolically try to drive art into life or to make their art, their comic art, control life for their own cynical advantage. Lovelace is the model of the rake-comedian whose fantasies triumph over a lickspittle world. And Lovelace has his idealism too, which forms an internal dialectic with his cynicism and drives him in the end to try to resolve one side of his personality in favor of the other. Then he becomes the overreacher.

As he conceived this character of Lovelace, Richardson's moralism was transmuted into art. He had at first felt morally constrained to show Lovelace awe-struck by Clarissa's virtue. (He never went so far as to strike him dumb.) The villain was to pay tribute to virtue, willy-nilly. This imperative risked repeating the error of *Pamela* in which the nasty hero is struck dumb, worse, becomes mealy-mouthed. Lovelace, Richardson saw, could with dramatic consistency praise Clarissa because he has an idealistic side to his character, though he must also always subvert the praise. Clarissa's sublime pretensions must be incorporated in his fantasy of triumph over the craven and pompous world. Or failing that, she must be reduced to a ridiculous sketch of an impostor like the rest.

Lovelace truly lives the fantasy life of a Restoration rake. There is Clarissa roguing it before him with her refined airs, her breasts dancing, he says, beneath the charming umbrage of her handkerchief. He practices his rhodomontade about his imperial prerogatives; he gives a grandiloquent villain's laugh, and then parodies himself by looking on his own spectacle through the eyes of his dog who pops in just then, stares at him impudently, and then trots out shaking its head. Lovelace has been lurking outside the walls of the family house playing his roles, suborning the servants, winding up plots, animating the mean slaves within. That braggart warrior of a brother, the lachrymose mother, the martinet father, the sour sister, the biddable and corruptible lackeys — all this gothic crew — are his factors. But while playing out the comedy, he notices that Clarissa's withering sincerity is dulling his gay and playful soul. He can't go within a mile of the walls without feeling the baleful influence of her sincerity. How awkwardly he comes back to his true gay self when he has left those purlieus. Clarissa is turning him into a sneaking hypocrite. Should she not pay for this? This dialogue Lovelace holds with himself cannot but evoke sympathy in any reader who cares for art.

If he feels the threat to his art from Clarissa's sincerity, he also fears Anna Howe. Her common-sense scorn of traditional male-

female roles is indeed the sane analogue of Lovelace's own ridicule of female pretensions to sublimity. "She has a confounded
deal of wit . . . and should I be outwitted with all my sententious
boasting . . . I should certainly hang, drown, or shoot myself."
Howe hits too close to home. She knows him. Hickman, her male
virgin, is a simple dear, but a bore to her; better to make him
quake, she says, than let male ideas of females take hold in him.
She knows, she says, that all animals are in a state of hostility with
one another. Once she had punished a chicken that hed pecked
brutally at another by twisting its head off, and what happened?
Why of course the subordinate checken then grew insolent and
became the tormentor of other chickens. It is the nature of the
beast—and the beast is human too. Excluse my flippancies, she
asks. More often she is just plain good sense playing to Clarissa's
noble pretensions. No wonder Lovelace hates her. She is his sort
and dangerous to his drama. His fantasies go to work; he dreams
of a grand comic charade.

It will be grand even for this paltry isle of England. Mrs. Howe,
Anna's mother, self-righteous, astringent, has, he learns through
his spies—for his spies are everywhere—engaged to visit with her
daughter and Hickman in the Isle of Wight where they have a
widow-woman friend. Lovelace will suborn the captain of the
ship, and join the crew in disguise, with several of his fellow rakes.
They will simply pirate the vessel, rape the women—Anna, her
mother, the maidservant—and throw Hickman overboard.
There he will be, the male virgin, in the water, in the water, Jack,
bobbing away. But Lovelace, surely you will not drown the poor
fellow? No, I hate supererogatory mischief. We will set him
ashore without his wig. And then our hero imagines their trial
which will follow in France. The courtroom scene. He will gra-
ciously bow to Miss Howe, ruined Miss Howe, as she comes to the
bar to testify against him. What a figure he and his fellow rakes
will cut before the salivating mob. Will they not huzza him? Then
he tells a tale of a French seduction in which his stratagems
against the lady concerned were pardoned for his amazing ingenuity. How people admire his tricks. Ingenuity is the thing. Who
would not pardon it? Who does not admire true wit? The answer
we know from literature, not life. The answer is, yes, in comedy,
and twice yes, in Restoration comedy. The answer in life depends

upon our distance from the case, but if we are on our moral mettle, we who admire ingenuity in the theatre will condemn it outside the theatre. That is the nature of things, that is the difference between aesthetics and life, between comedy and proper conduct. Comedy serves our imagination, our fantasy; it affords us the pleasure of exercising our instincts without consequence. Lovelace is a talented comic writer, but he is fatally driven to confuse art and life.

Another fantasy, with Howe and Clarissa this time. After his ministrations to the two of them, when they are both penetrated, ruined, and tamed by his comic engine, he will watch them "sitting together in a dark corner of a room, arm in arm, weeping and sobbing for each other! And I their emperor, their *acknowledged* emperor reclined at my ease in the same room, uncertain to which I should first, Grand-Signor-like, throw out my handkerchief." "Have I not reason to snuff the moon with my proboscis:" Indeed. We are grateful for art. All his self-mockery, ridicule, and comic role-playing relieves the novel of melodrama and shows Richardson's idea: a comic, witty rake who comes to play his play too close to life.

"I will write a comedy, I think. I have a title ready; and that's half the work. The Quarrelsome Lovers." More than buffoonery; he is an accomplished comic playwright-stage manager, scenario writer who can oblige real people as well as invented ones to play the parts he has given them, himself a quick-change artist, voice and mask for every scene; witty dialogist and impeccable stylist. Only one defect — he is not fit to live, having the grotesque vanity to suppose he can carry his comic fantasies of triumph into the real world of consequences. Lovelace has dared to walk from St. James's Park, that land of Cockayne of the Restoration where comic libertine fantasies had free play, into the mid-century hothouse of Richardson's realism. That is Richardson's triumph, that he invented a character who would exist in two genres of fictional representation at once, wilfully confounding comedy with realism. This genius of Richardson's, this original use of a literary convention of an earlier age, is worth tracing.

The genetic relation of Lovelace to the heroes of the Restoration drama, of both the cynical comedy and the posturing heroic, was suggested by Professor McKillop twenty-five years ago, but this noting down of a "source" has not led to any especial appreciation of Richardson's genius in conceiving his antihero. Except in essays by Ian Watt and V. S. Pritchett, Lovelace has had to content himself to be the foil to Clarissa's resplendent aura. That is of course as Richardson endlessly protested he wanted the matter. But Lovelace is one of the great originals of our literature. McKillop points out that Lovelace, not Mr. B, inherits the cynicism and fluency of the fashionable libertines of Restoration comedy. To put the matter another way, Mr. B is a buck, Lovelace a rake. They are not, as Richardson came to realize, the same animal. But then, Lovelace is also the superman of the heroic play; he has the lawless egotism common both the the heroes and villains of that genre. This general resemblance is more important than the particular parallel with Rowe's Lothario. And McKillop notes that from Dryden and his contemporaries Lovelace furnishes out a rhetorical commentary on his own model.

But there McKillop leaves the matter, a set of literary formulas, as he says, for a character out of a playbook. Quite rightly, McKillop denies that Rowe's *Fair Penitent* is as important an "influence" as the general tradition behind it, even though *The Fair Penitent* does give a sketch of the rake turned nasty and the heroine brutalized. What is more interesting than source-hunting is the evidence of Richardson's mind at work. What we do see is Richardson consciously choosing to combine in Lovelace the heroic postures, wild, wilful, and paranoiac, of the heroic drama, with the rationalistic, witty, analytic skepticism and libertinism of the rake-hero of comedy. It was not, however, Richardson who discovered this strange likeness in things apparently unlike, but the sensibility of Restoration England. It was Richardson who knew it to reflect his own mind and to be serviceable to his own interior drama.

If anyone appreciated the rake it was Richardson. Had he not made Lovelace a charming and witty man, quite in contradiction to his own sober judgment that a rake was nothing but a capering monkey? Did not his "family romance" reserve for the rake the principal part? Did he not allow Lovelace's charms to work effectively on Clarissa unawares, reserving for others to remark the process, as though to give it objective credence? He knew perfectly well what Lamb was later to observe: that to bring the rake to heel was "to indict our very dreams." Richardson did not after all choose a Hickman for the foster father of his family romance (though his conscience, not his consciousness, later forced him to elevate a Hickman to the role of Grandison).

What are the qualities of the rake-hero of Restoration comedy? A love of play first of all. The unending war of the sexes is for him perfect freedom. A queen mated is the signal for the game to begin anew. "Next to the coming to a good understanding with a new mistress," says Dorimant, "I love a quarrel with an old one; but the devil's in it there has been such a calm in my affairs of late. I have not had the pleasure of making a woman so much as break her fan, to be sullen, forswear herself these three days." Life and gaming are convertible.

A proposition, this, rather more destructive of conventional morality than sexual license could ever be. Love and honor, which in the heroic drama are virtually platonic realities, the very best cause to die for, are to the rake a joke. He says with Hobbes: "Honourable is whatsoever possession, action, or quality is an argument of power," and "That which men desire they are also said to love." Will is the first attribute of personality; desire and power are its specifications. The self is the alpha and omega of existence. This subversive doctrine and its most formidable proponent, Hobbes, are given by Belford after the irretrievable catastrophe as the root of the evil. Solmes would have done as well—better, as de Sade, who admired Richardson and must be allowed to have some authority as a sadist, knew. His epistolary novel, *Aline et Valcour,* recalls in a simplistic way, Richardson's plot. An absolutist father, subject to fits of rage and cruelty (though a philosopher), determines to marry his dutiful daughter to a brutal and ugly suitor. In desperation, to share her woes, she engages in an endless correspondence with a graceful young cavalier. For Sade, however, the real rapist is the father who uses the ugly suitor as his surrogate. Together they terrorize her until she preserves herself by suicide. But as Sade's interest naturally lies mainly in sadism, he has little use for the rake of earlier times, the witty, game-playing figure. What Sade finds particularly attractive in Richardson is the torture of Clarissa and the covert suggestion of the father's complicity in her ruin by his insistence on the ugly toad Solmes as her rightful despoiler. Sade has in short many times intensified what I have called the *gothic* element in *Clarissa*. For Richardson, on the contrary, the game-playing character of the rake was of the essence. Lovelace shows no lubricity at all; if there is a lubricious moment in the novel, it comes when Solmes deliberately brushes Clarissa's hoop. Terrorized by this foretaste of his salacious will, she can only remark his "heavy weight" as he sinks down into an unresisting chair. Solmes the incubus has his roles to play to create sexual anxieties in Clarissa, but also in the reader (and here Sade knew his man), but Lovelace is not Solmes in fairer guise, as though we were in the presence of one of the moral disguises of the *Faerie Queene*. Solmes has none of the qualities that drew Richardson's correspondents, and which draw us, to his side.

Solmes does not have, for example, the derring-do of a philosophy of knowledge of self. He is deprived of the arts of language, the wit, the invention. The player's gift is not his. He does not have all that Gide in *Les Caves du Vatican* calls a "slim" in contrast to a "fat." A "slim" is a quick-change artist; a "fat" is an oleaginous mass of respectabilities. In short, Solmes is not alive. Lovelace, the master of comic roles, is the answer to Bergson's test of life: ever-changing, surging with invention, never caught in cliché or stultified in custom. It is wholly natural that Clarissa should be biologically drawn to life, to him, as she is young herself, though the moralist in her knows that she should shun him as she has taught herself to shun life itself. As Howe says, as Belford echoes, as Richardson shows, Clarissa is not for life but for death.

The sexuality of the rake is not lust, but a turning of the restlessness born of a naturalistic philosophy into knowledge. To know, one must exert one's will to violate another personality. Sexual knowledge is the nearest way to possess another's personality, particularly in a society in which a girl is changed fatally — "ruined" — by seduction.

II

ABSOLUTISM IN COMEDY AND REALISM

That Lovelace should resemble both the cynical rake of comedy who explodes love and honor, and the wilful, paranoiac hero of the heroic play who dies for love and honor, is not surprising when we consider that for the Restoration, in politics as well as in literature, the heroic and naturalistic were only opposite sides of the same coin. Lovelace himself plays the part of the Emperor in *Aureng-Zebe*, borrowing the monarch's rhodomontade to apply to Clarissa: ". . . 'tis resistance that inflames desire. / Sharpens the darts of love, and blows his fire." Dryden's message continues, "And therefore 'tis your golden fruit you guard / With so much care, — to make possession hard." The whole is quite scabrous. Nourmahal, the wife, complains, "Me would you have — me your faint kisses prove. / The dregs and droppings of enervate love?" But the emperor claims a godlike liberty in love: "I, with less pain a prostitute could bear / Than the shrill sound of 'Virtue! virtue'' hear." The will to freedom in heroic drama can be expressed variously, by inflexible virtue, by paranoiac ravings about enemies to one's love and honor, or by maniacal actions in response to giant passions. The heroic play is in fact founded on a psychology of thwarted absolutism. That is why its actions are always close to those of a paranoiac. If one chooses absolutisms of love or honor, or perhaps just the absolutism of will, what can life promise save enemies in every corner? But it is precisely because absolutism is impossible longer than for an intense moment, being always unstable, that it is chosen. The crisis, the intensity, the danger, seem to authorize the passions. For the moment one grows enormously. And absolutisms are always justified by transcendent, "higher," motives. Against these "higher" motives, against this intensity of will and passion, the Restoration, and particularly Dryden, loved to play off a cynical naturalism. As Dryden writes in the *Secular Masque,* speaking through Momus, the god of ridicule, the devotion to Diana, "goddess of the silver bow," had really only "a beast in view"; the wars of Mars for "arms and honor" "brought nothing about"; the pretensions to "love" of Venus were hollow, her "lovers were all untrue." As always feigning surprise that his female correspondents should find Lovelace worthy of rescue, Richardson parodies Dryden's refrain in *Alexander's Feast:* "Happy, happy, happy pair! / None but the brave, / None but the brave, / None but the brave deserves the fair" becomes "Happy, happy, happy pair, / None but the rake deserves the fair." He was thinking as well of Lovelace's imperial fantasies which echo mockingly the opening lines of *Alexander's Feast,*

"The godlike hero sate / On his imperial throne; / . . . The lovely Thaïs, by his side, / Sate like a blooming Eastern bride." By turns, Dryden was elevated and cynical, a sensibility that marked the Restoration and one which is Lovelace's own.

Richardson was quite drawn to the Restoration's fundamental literary insight, that the heroic drama and the cynical comedy were only opposite sides of the same coin. Twice Dryden combines the two genres in one play, but often too he permits a knowing parody to creep into his heroics. Lovelace likewise easily passes from heroic postures to cynical mockery of them in himself as in others. *Absalom and Achitophel* is the perfect expression of this double sensibility of the Restoration, looking one way to absolutism in government and religion, and in the other to cynical naturalism. Will is the thing, for rake or hero.

In every way Richardson tries to domesticate the absolutism of the Restoration, preserving its high drama but bringing it down at the same time to household words. It would seem an impossible task, but he brings it off. How often do his correspondents press him on the propriety of Clarissa's leaving the bosom of her tormenting family. Was it not only a mistake rather than a moral fault? Could it not be justified?

There is Solmes, sexually revolting, blocking her path; there is her strange brother pushing her into the path of Solmes, reveling in her prospective despoliation; there is the viperous sister dripping sarcasms on Clarissa's noble airs; there is the sour and violent father determined to see her Solmes's submissive bride; there is the hysterical weakling of a mother, the weepy aunt, the bemused uncle. What an entourage for a noble virgin to find herself in! One has only to follow the breakfast scene, one of Richardson's great strokes, to see how the absolutist hothouse atmosphere puts out of mind the banal moral issues to which Richardson pretended in his correspondence. What about a daughter's obligations to her parents? Who could seriously think of them in this breakfast scene so heavy with sexual violence? Before going down to breakfast Clarissa has sent plaintive missives begging for clemency. No, comes the reply, she must go down. There she finds the family assembled, and among them, sitting asquat, the odious Solmes. As though their agent, he grins confidently, assured of his rightful role in the coming violation. If Clarissa has any doubts about the matter, brother and sister gaily remind her of the brutality Solmes will practice on the wedding night. Father is excessively displeased, wears a terrible countenance. One does not know what they eat, but they drink tea and Clarissa desperately pours all the while. Father withdraws, and then mother, and then sister, and aunt drops away. Lastly brother feigns anger and disappears. Clarissa is alone with the splayfooted beast. She runs out but no one is there. She trembles, she dreads the authority of God's vicar, her father, who will deliver her to this "ugly weight."

To get the sense of willful violation in this absolutist household, Richardson cuts off every avenue of escape. This is how the ways out are closed off. Clarissa is too inexperienced to take up her own escape (which invites her). Anna Howe's mother distrusts Clarissa and will not intervene. (This, despite the fact that everyone else acknowledges Clarissa's near divinity.) Anna, her dear friend (who has the good sense to see through Lovelace), seems forever unable to get away. Morden, the knight errant who is to rescue Clarissa, travels endlessly in foreign climes. Hickman, the good man, is too virginal to get the drift of things. Thus, as all likely doors close, Clarissa must remain inviolate when everyone is licensed to lay hands on her. She must not escape the house of horrors, yet she must not yield to the vile destiny being prepared for her. Her father's curse is supposedly as effective as a popish excommunication. Pretending to make a case for parental understanding, all the while Richardson is insisting that no provocation imaginable can abrogate parental divine right to absolute obedience. Meanwhile he capitalizes on the sexual sadism. It is to heaven alone to punish divinely delegated authority. Richardson says just that, as though he were a Jacobite bishop perishing for divine right. In fact, he is fattening on sexual aggression, not because he is mad, but because he is an artist and he knows that the reader will welcome Lovelace after Solmes and the father and the brother. Furthermore, the covert sense of sexual aggression awakened in the reader will make Lovelace's assaults all the more exciting.

Is it really believable, as Christopher Hill argues, that the central matter here can be the institution of property marriage and the way in which eighteenth-century religious and economic structures became entangled in impenetrable moral authority? Hill argues that the book is in part at least a criticism of the class structure. Clarissa's classical Puritanism, he argues, criticizes both the degenerated Puritan sensibility of her own family represented by their acquisitiveness and the callous indifference to religion of the aristocracy figured in Lovelace. If this is so, why the supererogatory Solmes? Why must he sit asquat, why press Clarissa's hoop? Why must his "ugly weight" terrify Clarissa? Why, but that he is meant to be a nightmare incubus. How are the sexual perversities of the breakfast scene related to capitalism? Surely the class struggle does not require all this sexual freight.

Is it not quite the other way round, that the economic motives are the ostensible cause, the surface structure that allows the moralist to indulge his taste for household instruction (against greed, unnecessary severity; for filial piety and chastity), while the dramatist explores the deeper, plainly psychological motives? The latter gives meaning to the dramatic counters of Clarissa's sublimity and Lovelace's comic-satanic games with that sublimity.

The novel is replete with such domestication of Restoration absolutism. The more absolutist the family becomes the more Clarissa condemns herself, even rebuking her confidante Anna Howe for defending her against her family's persecutions. "Why do you tolerate this behavior?" asks Miss Howe, seeming to assume that the absolutism of the sexual code is the root of it all. "Charminly might you and I live together and despise [the male sex]," she says while making some remarkably advanced reflections on the condition of women. Women, she says, are silly birds, ensnared by lures, courted as princesses for a few weeks, and then enslaved for the remainder of their lives. This matter was deep in Richardson's consciousness, as Lovelace's later use of the same image of the captive bird for similar reflections shows. Miss Howe's mother, who is a strict constructionist of duties and laws, supposes naturally that there must be two sides to Clarissa's plight: Clarissa's pretended wrongs and her family's just demands. But there are not two sides, unless one admits the strange doctrine of absolute obedience despite all outrage to person and personality. The fact is that this doctrine was and is unsympathetic to readers.

Lovelace understands this reality. He explains to Clarissa the simple and obvious truth, that if her father "behaved so badly to a wife who disputed not the 'imaginary' prerogative he was so unprecedentedly fond of asserting, what room had a daughter to hope he would depart from an *authority* he was so earnest . . . to maintain?" And does not her bristling sister say for the father, "Obedience without reserve is required of you, Clary. My father is justly incensed that you should *presume* to dispute his will, and so make conditions with him"? Howe is relentless and baits Clarissa for her servile acceptance of male prerogative: "You, my dear, would tell a mild man that he must not entreat but command you." Clarissa herself echoes the language she hears around her: to Lovelace she expresses her "high disapprobation." She speaks sometimes in stage tirades, and even allowing for genteel diction, such language of state shows that she herself has internalized the absolutist "political" (the politics of state borrowed for the foyer) assumptions of her father.

A rival kingdom is Lovelace's. He too habitually uses this sort of high-flying language, with more than a shade of self-mockery, true, but nevertheless, as a self-conscious fantasy. "O my charmer look to it! . . ." "Regardless I shall be of anything but of my own imperial will. . . ." And so, having the angel in his grasp, the beautiful rake commences his enlargement to an oriental monarch. "The prince," "a monarch," "emperor," "eastern monarch," and "almighty" are terms he only half-mockingly applies to himself. Before his final translation to "Almighty" after the rape, at his "eastern monarch" stage, he reflects upon his industrious spirit in tracking down his fugitive angel with spies, lies, and disguise. Had he been a prince he would have made the world dance as well as Alexander, Robert the Great despoiling the Great Turk and the Mogul of their seraglios. Not one of them should have a fine woman before he had enjoyed her. Surely all this is a parody of the grand model of the rake figure, in court and comedy, John Wilmot, Earl of Rochester. Mocking the libertine postures of Mulgrave, he gives a humorous parody of his own: "In my dear self, I center everything," he writes, imaging the delicious life of a sultan who makes every man his slave and every woman his whore. Walking carelessly by, in awful sultanic pride, he will choose out any woman upon whom to exercise his will, and if "she" objects, "she" can easily be strangled. The strangling cord, Rochester wittily calls the "true lover's knot." Exactly the same tone, half self-mockery, half vainglory, is Lovelace's style.

In his self-mockery, his charades, Lovelace is quite funny; his talent for comedy is of course Richardson's as well. Let us follow through one of his scenarios. Clarissa, "sweet soul," "dear charmer," has fled her captor. Now begins the opportunity to put on a play. "Robert the Great," says Lovelace, as always joking with himself, is about to come on scene — Robert the Great who in better times would have warred with the Great Turk, the Persian, the Mogul for their seraglios. In better times he would have every woman in those luxurious principalities. And so he writes, for his friend Jack's delectation, a comic scenario of things to come. Act II he calls the discovery of Clarissa at the Rawlins. The way is prepared by his servant who informs the landlady that his master is the finest gentleman in the world and Clarissa his wife the finest creature, but truth is truth, alas she is jealous of his strolls in St. James's Park with the ladies, and to show her spleen is forever running off. Enter Lovelace on scene after this introduction. He forthwith charms the rooming house ladies. They sigh. He takes Miss Rawlins aside to explain his wife's skittishness. Confidentially, *sotto voce* — the charming creature is overnice about such things as pass between man and wife, but she is a young thing. Miss Rawlins simpers in sympathy with the fine gentleman. Lovelace has raised her lubricious consciousness, but, oh, how nicely. "I understand you sir." Poor, lovely creature, he sighs, will she not expose herself to great dangers, for there are rakes everywhere. "Lovelaces in every corner, Jack," he writes, dividing himself, multiplying himself, becoming all rakes, all actors.

And then, amazing all, he has the landlady and landlord lend him a greatcoat, he puts on a pair of coarse stockings, applies a little powder, borrows a cane — and before their eyes he becomes an achey, gouty old man. Shall he be angry or pleased? No matter, he will invent his looks, as needed, when he comes to Clarissa's room at Goody Moore's on pretext of engaging it for his wife. Goody comes on stage. She is persuaded to show the good old gentleman Clarissa's room. His heart skips, but his actor's skills make his going upstairs the picture of decrepitude. We are in Clarissa's chambers. The charmer has retired to the closet to permit Goody to show the room. A long, sincere dialogue between the good old gentleman and Goody. Does she know of a good preacher in the neighborhood, but mind you, a good liver too? A little moral philosophy to make Goody act the role he has written for her. But then he excuses himself to her, as a good old gentleman would. "But I keep the lady in her closet. My gout makes me rude."

The upshot is that Clarissa's dazzling, pathetic beauty makes him slip and reveal his true voice. Long stage tirades, then, by the charmer. He is equal to the exigency. Another quick change — he pulls off his costume and the gouty old man becomes instantly the resplendent cavalier. He gives his hat, he says, once again its usual smart cock. By the end of the scene, Clarissa's tragedy speeches, as Lovelace calls them, have convinced the ladies that she is indeed hysterical and that Lovelace is the put-upon husband. He has their simpering sympathy.

And why didn't Clarissa simply tell her true story at this point? Ah, because, as Lovelace calculates, she plays her part of the misused heroine of heroic tragedy and she plays it to his part, the protean rake of comedy. Richardson has not blundered here or falsified the action. He does not let Clarissa tell the simple truth because, as Johnson observed of her character, there is always something she prefers to the truth. Here, as Richardson knew she must, she prefers her role to simple, flat clarification. The character is perfectly conceived. No mistake, no falsification. Robert the Great is as well conceived as Clarissa the pathetic. He is, he thinks, and we must agree, as comic as "the devil in Milton." Still another idea he has of himself, again a just one, is that he is a good playwright in the comic genre. He has found his metier.

I have described the qualities of the rake figure. Richardson has transferred those qualities from the libertine comedy in which a wish-fulfillment fantasy resolves all problems, to a realistic novel in which no such wish-fulfillment fantasy is possible. The libertine wit cannot control such a realistic world which is too unpredictable and various to fathom, always a world of mystery, not of rationalism, of inevitable loss, not of gratification. This relocation of the rake figure has certain consequences. It means that Richardson has to follow out in a realistic world, the world of consequences, which comedy eschews, the ultimate meaning of libertinism. Camus imagines that a Don Juan transferred to the real world would be the perfect existential hero, accepting the unbearable burden of freedom and its consequences. He would be a version of Sisyphus. Lovelace collapses in the end under this burden of freedom, as would anyone less than an existentialist Sisyphus. He cannot accept the real consequences of his game-playing. He shilly-shallys from cynicism to fear for his soul, from contempt for Clarissa's tragic postures to adoration of her. He has a philosophy of naturalism which is well conceived but he is not up to the burden of accepting its consequences. Had he remained in Restoration comedy where he had once flourished, there would have been no problem because there would have been no conse-quences. He would simply have sloughed off his victims, as would any Don Juan, and have married the witty virgin. She would have tamed him, and we would have wit and cynicism and license, but love too. The perfect dream, comedy. The fact that Lovelace is not up to the responsibility of his freedom saves Clarissa from becoming a philosophical novel and returns it to the mystery of tragedy. Richardson, in any case, could not have imagined such a philosophical novel; but for once he did have a genuine tragic vision, of Lovelace as well as of Clarissa.

III

THE PLEASURES OF THE GAME

Perhaps the greatest problem of structure for Richardson in translating the rake from comedy to realism was to bring about the tragedy without resorting to some *deus ex machina* such as the Commander's statue of the Don Juan plays. The *deus ex ma-china* is proper to comedy because it supports its fantasy but is destructive of the illusion of probability in tragedy. He had to bring about the tragedy without compromising the libertine phi-losophy of the hero. He had to preserve the stature of his hero. He could not, furthermore, simply intervene with an arbitrary and didactic poetic justice, a violation of art that would have been agreeable to the moralist in him but impossible to the artist.

Lovelace had to be given believable intellectual credentials, as believable as Clarissa's noble sensibility. He had to play out his game to its probable conclusion as Clarissa had to play out her role. They are matched, indeed stalemated if never mated, in a game that is awesome. Lovelace knows he has met his match.

We first see him in a not unfavorable guise as compared with Clarissa's. He has been paired off with the wicked sister but naturally turns to the angelic one, and for his good sense and good taste — as it appears at the moment — meets nothing but chills and toplofty rebuffs from the angel. Yet Clarissa is conscious of her role and gives Lovelace good marks in her heart of hearts for his apparent resignation before her frost. His conversation is agreeable and his manner full of respectful assiduities. She tells her friend Anna that she has learned that Lovelace's sensitivity to literature at the university made him friends among the learned. Against this she must balance his frequenting the "mischievous," though even here it is his evident vivacity that appears to have led him astray. He is, then, in her book learned, charming, gracious, witty, but somewhat haughty and certainly impudent. The reader is surprised that on balance she finds that he has "no amiable character." Why not? She seems a bit prudish and frosty for an angel.

Lovelace however is not disappointed by this severity in Clarissa. Quite the contrary, her airs seem to invite him to do his worst, though he nor she has yet imagined what his worst will be. And contrary to her wishes — as she wishes to learn the worst about him — her dossier on him becomes better and better. It seems that he is beloved of his tenants, even though their daughters may be in some danger from him. Even the Harlowe domestics dote on him. But she deliberately outweighs these merits in her balance by noting that he is prone to jest and facetiousness. The reader must at least wonder about the sense of justice of this angel. From her surly and malignant brother, Lovelace defends himself with dignity and forebearance. None of these qualities earns any quarter from her. Richardson wants her to be provoking to this cavalier. That is her role.

Her role is to provoke and to suffer martyrdom. Not only is her own family preparing her doom as they feed on her curious combination of resignation and resistence; not only is Lovelace working up heaven knows what plot as he feeds on the provocation of her curious combination of disdain and interest; not only is she provoking the world around her to do its worst, but she is constantly reminding herself of her duty to gather faggots for her own *auto da fe*. She must suffer. Lovelace's designs on her seem to the reader at this point her only hope for escape: Even the pert Miss Howe has resigned Clarissa to the flames from the very opening letters. Clarissa, says Lovelace, must be a "divinity," an "angel," she must be "exalted," and most wondrous of all, "impenetrable." He, like the rakes of his tradition, wants to turn restlessness not into unity as would an ordinary lover, but into knowledge. Clarissa is the perfect object of his game—and the perfect partner of it. His character develops relentlessly after the false start Richardson gave it in the beginning where he is said to be motivated by pique against womankind for having been jilted by one of the kind. Richardson soon sees the greater drama of the game developing between his two heroes. To Clarissa's unsympathetic provocation at the beginning he owes the evolution of his philosophy. Richardson had a sense, though an imperfect one, from the beginning of how things must go.

From his very first lurking and spying about the Harlow house, his relations with Clarissa have been a game. Hers and his. Slowly, almost unawares, she comes to a consciousness of her complicity, though she will never admit to herself the simple truth—that a little of Anna Howe's common sense, sardonic scorn, and plain speaking, would have ended soon enough literature's longest dialogue. Johnson was exactly right. There is always something she prefers to Howe's kind of truth. She prefers posture, toplofty virtue, instruction, debate, dialogue, letter-writing casuistry, and all this not because she loves Lovelace in her secret heart, but because she is fatally interested in him. She has a vocation for the game, but it is a game with unique players—only a Clarissa and a Lovelace will do. Lovelace can count on her playing the game as we see in the scene at Goody Moore's. Anna Howe sharply reminds her of her "modesty airs." Though doubtless Richardson the moralist would say that Clarissa's long dialogue with Lovelace on marriage—which she time and again engages and disengages—is meant to indicate higher scruples than Howe can image, Howe is fundamentally right. To say that Clarissa plays the sublimity-sexuality game with Lovelace is not to suggest that she is a hypocrite. The game is written in the stars, for Clarissa and Lovelace are the vessels of Richardson's consciousness; they are the only two vessels of meaning in his world.

"Will I attempt to reduce such a goddess, Jack? It is impossible, Lovelace. Is she not in my power, Jack? Wilt thou, Lovelace, abuse that power?" Lovelace adds to this little dialogue with himself the facts that the "little juggler" with her female affectations has obliged him to adopt long-faced airs of reformation, to take up a reformed rake's "howlings," that his customary gaiety has been turned to doleful dumps by her mere proximity. What joy to outwit this vigilant charmer, what misery not to outwit her. "When I go to bed I laugh myself to sleep."

What a provoking case she is! Does she not solemnly rebuke him for his low and selfish love merely because he seeks to save her from her parents? To save her from her duty to them! Lovelace gravely replies that her reputation could not suffer half so much by flight as from failing to free herself of unjust persecution. This is the subtlest of psychological games, with, as in all such games, dignity and reason mixed fatally with provocation and specious excuse.

It is this game, as it develops, that gives wings to Lovelace's fledgling philosophy. Like the rake of comedy, he becomes a master of acting, stage managing, and disguise. Before the rape he will have become, as well, a playwright. Intrigue plot will spring from counterfeit correspondence—like Richardson, he takes pride in his ability to render female sentiments, and he can perfectly counterfeit Clarissa's and Anna Howe's hands. A cast of characters will be put on stage, some of them hired, costumed, and furnished with dialogue; still others manipulated to play their parts unawares. As the idea of himself as a player of roles comes to possess him ("Ovid was not a greater master of metamorphoses than my friend"), he conceives the rape as only part of his acting. Clarissa will be required to descend into Thalestris's cave for a spate of megrims, and then he will charm her and win her over. A happy ending—is this not a comedy?

But then he muses on her impeccability; how came she by it? Is not his project of reducing her to sisterhood with her sex (just another seduction) of supreme moral significance? Is it not a trial of the pretensions of the whole sex? Should she fall, how well he will have illustrated the sin of pride, how effectively confirmed his doctrine of will and power. But this is philosophy for the theatre.

Nearer home he has more interesting things to say, analyses that show him a man of his century, of the Enlightenment after all. In women, shy is sly, and he has the responsibility to show the truth of the maxim that every woman is a rake at heart. Education and forms after all must be distinguished from nature. Still, though obliged to make her yield for the sake of this moral instruction, he would perhaps prefer that she resist to the end, for if he should come to doubt her divinity, how chagrined will he be by her reluctance all along to gratify his desire. It is a matter to be resolved. Attack, force, cruelty perhaps—she has demanded these methods. He vascillates between comic stage acting and real violence.

After all, is not cruelty in the nature of man? "We begin, as boys with birds and when grown go on to women." How amusingly instructive is the poor captive bird—at first the creature beats its head against the wires, injuring its plumage, then gasps and looks about, meditates, becomes enraged again, at last moans and sinks down, accepting its new habitation, liking it, once again singing like a bird. He himself hates cruelty, but it is the way of humankind, woman as well as man. Once he made a charming little baggage repent her delight in the cruelty of her tabby cat as it made sport with a pretty mouse before devouring it. He made *her* the mouse and then one day *devoured* her. So we come to know nature's lessons; so our common "humanity."

Lovelace is of course absurdly simple-minded for all his complications to suppose that Clarissa could be playing merely the vulgar shy-sly game with him. As Harriet tells Dorimant in *The Man of Mode,* not all women are born to the same destiny. As for Clarissa, she has a real tragedy in mind for the both of them. Attracted fatally to the idea of angel, Lovelace cannot at all abandon the sense God gave him of the natural condition of humankind. He must know which it is. That Clarissa is powerfully attracted to Lovelace is obvious. When he cynically tells her the truth about the tricks he has used to entice her away, she knows she is in the power of one stronger than herself, one who is not to be deterred by her proper postures. She is, she says, sick of him and sick of herself. Yet the dialogue continues because, beyond the disgust and the fatigue, each has the other as a part of being. "I am in a wilderness of doubt and error," she says, echoing the Duchess of Malfi. Aware that her pretensions are not for this world, she confesses that in this life she has been outwitted and that her portion is a rake. As this is precisely what she says, we must believe that she is not this-worldly or otherworldly, but both at once. She is committed to Lovelace and he to her because they are to one another the test of an incompatible conception of life. Her portion is a rake. His portion is an angel, but neither is static. Both develop toward the identity that each lends the other. The burden of liberty which Lovelace slowly defines for himself is not for common clay. If he wants to know the truth of his own naturalistic, as of Clarissa's religious, principles, he has the luck of one favored of the gods to find Clarissa. And how could we respect her if she did not approach her otherworldly destiny by engaging herself in this world? Seen in this way, the "game" is not trivial.

But now that the twisted playacting has carried him to the point of rape, he pauses to reflect on the nature of freedom. Is he to be merely an example of Mandeville's law: private vices, public benefits? Does he exist, then, to become a warning to other pretty fools of the sex? Is his will enchained by the plot? "Like a repentant thief, afraid of his gang, and obliged to go on, in fear of hanging till he comes to be hanged, I am afraid of the gang of my cursed contrivances...to be *compelled* to be the wretch my choice has made me! So now, Belford, as thou has said, I am a machine at last, and no free agent." But it is Conscience that makes him the sneak, the wretch, and so in an elaborate charade, another fantasy only half-redeemed for sanity by self-mockery, he plays out the strangulation of a young woman. She is Conscience. He is free. Still, Love seems to have a thing or two to say. But Love gives up when he proves that the lady is not capable of love but only of provocation. "What a perverse girl is this, to contend with her fate...!" Upon how slender a thread his freedom hung before he had rid himself of Conscience and Love. But it is useless to try to abstract from this novel a moral logic of Lovelace's soul, though, again, Richardson the moralist would want us to do so. Richardson the novelist has given his story the feel of life by allowing his heroes to go to their destinies in a sort of *ad hoc* way, in a way that gives us the sense of empirical trial and error until after a half-year's unrelenting dialogue, each runs out of tergiversations. Each is left with the bare reality of his or her assumptions about life. I would even say, in the teeth of Richardson the moralist, with, if this analysis is accurate, Richardson the novelist, that we will be able to draw no moral at all from the working out of the plot, except the moral that absolutism, Lovelace's and Clarissa's alike, means death.

As an example of the empirical progression of the book, after these Jacobean extravagances which tell us that Lovelace knows that he is a killer, he is suddenly back again to his gay self. As Clarissa is determined to live a mournful life of penitence, should she not have a fuller bill of particulars? "And thus may she live, her old *nurse* and she; and *old* coachman; and a pair of *old* coach-horses; and two or three *old* maid-servants, and perhaps a *very old* footman or two . . . live . . . reading *old* sermons, and *old* prayer-books; and relieving *old* men and *old* women; and giving *old* lessons, and *old* warnings . . . :" "Is such a woman . . . to be said to be ruined and undone and such stuff?" Such stuff. What a flourishing ruin has he made of such stuff.

This parody by Richardson — by way of Lovelace — of his own moralism is a stroke of genius. It hits home at all the deadliness of the domestic, old-maidish puritanism to which he himself had given voice since the *Familiar Letters* and which punctuates his correspondence. It survives in a good many of the occasional postures of Clarissa. Lovelace's parody takes off the musty smell of it for the reader and allows him to see what Lovelace cannot see, that Clarissa has a higher destiny than that of a prudish old maid. It is a clever stroke of Richardson's as the reader must both sympathize with Lovelace here in the parody of prudish posture, and yet separate himself from him, for the parody is a grotesque oversimplification of Clarissa's character. Again, comedy and realism affront one another: the parody is perfect comedy, but the realism creates a depth of character outside the range of comedy. The separation of the world of Lovelace from that of Clarissa is perfectly reflected in the clash of literary forms. Lovelace clears away, so to speak, all the inessential baggage, leaving the true issues, which are *not* those of proper conduct, to be pondered.

There is more of this delicious parody. The marriage license is given in toto by Lovelace in a way to mock its formulas of official morality. Again, Lovelace engages us with his wit but at the same time serves Richardson for two other purposes: to lighten the burden on the reader of the author's conventional moralizing and to suggest the world beyond and indifferent to the proprieties of marriage, for it is to this world beyond that Clarissa belongs. Lovelace then gives a good libertine receipt for curing the ennuis of this deadly world of clichés found in the institution of marriage. He will bring in a bill to Parliament for an annual change of marriage partners on Saint Valentine's Day. Lawyers will be put to work thereby to settle goods and chattels — more money for the lawyers, more for the state. Sex crimes will be a thing of the past — rapes ("vulgarly so-called"), adultery, fornication, polygamy, murder, duelling (over disputed loves), jealousy, hypocrisy — all, will be swept away. And what a charming subject of conversation, the yearly partings. Health and spirits would flow from the joys of continual expectation for body and mind.

There is a genuine Rabelaisian touch, a touch of the lord of misrule of festival, of which Richardson could not be suspected were we to trust to the estimates of him ordinarily given in criticism. If we but listen to Lovelace throughout the book, however, we cannot but see another Richardson, the writer who had a marvelous comic sense that he could express only in ways that would not bring into question his proclaimed morality. How astutely he manages the affair in *Clarissa* after the ineptitudes of the comic scenes of *Pamela!*

In the midst of these comic uplifts of his, Lovelace slips into tragedy almost unawares. Clarissa's day of reckoning is prepared and accomplished so quickly that it seems almost another comic game. He sends the laconic message to Jack: "The affair is over. Clarissa lives." Is it more comic mockery, or is there a touch of wonder in it? Wonder that an angel should survive being known carnally? Or the insouciant humor of a free man reflecting on the pomposities of morality? Richardson has preserved the uncertainty, for this very uncertainty signals Lovelace's eventual failure of nerve as a free man, and this failure of nerve will in the end be his punishment.

After the violation, Clarissa produces fragmentary "papers" in her delirium, ravings intended to suggest Ophelia, but the modern reader, perhaps put off by Richardson's pretensions that Cla-

rissa's only fault is disobedience to her father, is perilously likely
to take up Lovelace's attitude and smile at all the fuss. Obviously
the book would be dead at this point if this reading were really
supportable. There is, nevertheless, a useful ambiguity of attitude conveyed to the reader — and not just to the modern reader,
for Richardson's contemporaries were also drawn to indulge
Lovelace. The usefulness of the ambiguity is that it accentuates
the real dramatic conflict between Lovelace's and Clarissa's
worlds, both of which have their validity.

Lovelace does not fail to point out slyly the sexual content of
these "papers" as well as of the "meditations" that are produced
by her when a sense of reality returns. To look from his point of
view at Clarissa is to intensify the emotional structure of the
novel. We see then the anxiety of Lovelace to use his comic
talents to destroy Clarissa's personality and consciousness of self.
And we see her indestructibility. Again, "game" is not a frivolous
word to use in describing the war between these two, for neither
could realize his or her potentiality of character without the other
to "play" against.

It is when she has realized her part in the game and realized
her character that Clarissa quits the game and alienates herself
from all familiar affections, but this will come only at the end.
Lovelace will never quite quit the game, though he will be
infected with doubts. But long after the rape, the game continues
for the both of them, for Lovelace, in an especially cynical way.
He baits her with another declaration of love and offer of marriage. If Richardson the moralist professes that this action of
Lovelace's only demonstrates the power of Clarissa's virtue over
his wicked hero, Richardson the artist has more to say, for that
Richardson convicts his noble heroine of complicity in this
renewal of the game. Thus we feel the moral pull and power of
the game, and thus we feel the void in Lovelace and Clarissa
when it is finally abandoned by her. After the rape, after the renewed declaration and offer of Lovelace, Clarissa is not beyond
carrying on a long and provocative dialogue with her despoiler.
Once, she says, she could have brought him, wretch that he is, an
unsullied honor, "but how thinkest thou that I will give a harlot
niece (a play on words, harlot-Harlowe, for she professes after the
rape to have forgotten her family name) to thy honorable uncle,
and to thy real aunts, and a cousin to thy cousins from a brothel?"

Then she lifts her hands to heaven but turns to the almighty Lovelace, "I renounce thee forever." But she does not renounce him
forever; she shows no inclination at all to let the dialogue flag and
is soon interrogating him—to test his repentance, she says—on
his various dodges. He swears the truth of everything—"lover's
oaths, Jack." He repeats his offer—"Will you give me the honor,
madam...?" A simple, disdainful, "No" will not do. A stage
tirade is necessary, which surely she must know after so many
volumes, will only provoke more dialogue. "My honor, sir, ... alas
you have robbed me of my honor." Can he be so mean, she wonders, aloud, as to wish to bring into an honorable family whose
ancestors call him from their monuments not to dishonor a noble
house, a creature he has levelled with "the dirt of the streets"?
One can say, in modern psychological jargon, that she has internalized the official morality, but while this interpretation is inescapable, there is more to the matter than that. She simply likes
the rhetoric and rhodomontade of the theatre, as does Lovelace.
He likes it, however, as a hot ballon he can prick with his parody.
He is, in short, affected by her posture, but not overly. He is soon
thinking that the enjoyment of a fine woman, in marriage or not,
is a pallid thing compared to the pleasure of contriving a plot to
seduce. For the rest, what is it, he asks elegantly, but to find an
angel of the imagination dwindled to a woman of fact?

Richardson is often said to be theatrical; quite the contrary—
he is a master of realism who has a sense of how and why human
beings need to be theatrical, need to put themselves on stage to
voice their fantasies. Clarissa's "she-tragedy" histrionics are what
Lovelace wants to match his "smart cock" charades. Above all
Richardson did not want his angel-rake theatrics to degenerate
into another moral fatuity of the *Pamela* genre; no more did he
wish his realism betrayed by melodrama.

IV

REWARDS AND PUNISHMENTS

Richardson set himself, in the end, a Christian task—to paint
damnation as well as beatitude. As his entire vision rises from the
conception of a fatal war in the consciousness between sublimity

and naturalism, the task was inevitable if he was not to find himself betrayed into writing another melodrama for right-minded sentimentalists. Worldly felicity for Clarissa, which his female senate begged of him, would have produced Mr. and Mrs. Lovelace, rivals to Mr. and Mrs. Loveless of Colley Cibber's *Love's Last Shift,* a play that manages to be both lewd and bathetic. After Lovelace's reform, Fielding then could have written a *Relapse,* with Lovelace having a go at Anna Howe and Belford at Clarissa. Cibber, who was as essentially corrupt as any pert scribbler of his age, would have been relieved of his heartache.

So heavily did the neoclassical doctrine of poetic justice weigh on Dr. Johnson that he easily stooped to censure Shakespeare for not having distributed rewards and punishments as an ideal moral world would have. The doctrine was of course accepted without cavil by Richardson, so absolutely that he decided to reward Clarissa in the simplest and most obvious way by himself conferring upon her beatitude in heaven. At the same time he would kill off Lovelace by bringing home at last the personification of justice, the improbable and ever-traveling Colonel Morden who would then, as a perfect *deus ex machina,* run the villain-hero through. These tricks of official morality are unquestionably defects of the novel, quite as bad and quite as improbable as would have been a Pamela-like marriage of Mr. and Mrs. Lovelace. What pomposity to play God, to usurp His judgment, so as to render literal the epithet "angel" which Lovelace applies throughout to Clarissa, sometimes hopefully, sometimes ironically! What a cliché, the final duel. But strangely these defects are not fatal to the book, nor even overly damaging. Why? Because Richardson had, as well, better endings in mind, endings that grow out of the action and that are inevitable.

Richardson had two problems then at the end—to beatify Clarissa and to damn Lovelace. We will not speak further of the expedients of announcing Clarissa's heavenly reward and of using Colonel Morden's sword to run through Lovelace, as they are expedients and unsuccessful ones. We will return to the question of Clarissa's beatitude. Let us approach it by noticing first Richardson's remarkable gifts in representing damnation.

Clarissa is dying—a delectable setting for Lovelace's obsessive games. Does he merely want a captive audience for his final performance? No, more than that. What he needs now, at last, is to overthrow the utter, the final kind of absolutism with his jackanapes wit. Chastity has vanished since, according to the code accepted by Clarissa as well as the world, our heroine is ruined, in the mud, as she herself says. But as this absolutism of chastity, though spiritual, depends curiously upon a mere physical state, Lovelace's accomplishment here is not altogether remarkable. More remarkable is his success in overthrowing her absolutism of passive obedience to the monarch by divine right, her father. But then it must be admitted that father and family have helped him to this success. What remains is truly the work of the devil. What remains is to overthrow the absolutism of her faith in herself as she dies, to destroy her ultimate dignity. If only he can secure her complicity in his stage acting so that she will become a fellow actor with him in a final farce. Can he not by a grand performance bring her back to the dialogue with him, the game, by seducing her with the hope of saving his soul by marriage? Then she would be only a creator of illusions with him, a fellow actor, and there you are, his joking life justified.

The costume is the man, he decides, and he dresses himself in one of his "gay" wedding suits, rehearses a few poetic lines for the lovelorn, and dances along to Smith's shop-rooming house where she is said to lie dying. He will ask her to live to save him for a better life. Naturally the Smiths, poor lower-class simpletons, try to do the decent thing and protect their moribund roomer. They think to bar his way. Lovelace does a quick change and announces that he is in fact the justice of the peace, armed with a warrant, and brushes aside the flustered fools. When a lodger affronts him, he becomes the rakehell bully and threatens to beat him back to his "dunghill." Knocking up and down the hallway doors, humming a pert tune, he finds no response. "What shall I do, as the girls say." He chucks the mistress under the chin, mocking her modest consternation, and tells her insinuatingly that her husband must surely be a capon in the marriage bed. Then wheeling on the "capon" of a husband, he commands him to doff his hat to a gentleman, but as the capon is wearing no hat, the joke is a mad one, intended to terrorize. Then like a good player of farces, he changes guises upon the instant. "But I am not merry—I am sad! heigh-ho!" The servants, like proper slaves, grin at the comic sadism. Lovelace next plays shopkeeper, selling his servant some washballs. When Joseph the household porter grins his toothy grin at this charade, Lovelace clamps his head in an arm-lock and threatens to cut out his teeth with a pruning knife. "I will pay thee a good price man, don't struggle!" Terror reigns.

In the midst of this murderous waggishness, a gentlelady comes in the shop door and Lovelace scampers, miming servitude, to serve her, "with an air of great diligence and obligingness." Before she can open her mouth, he decides to sell her footman a pair of tiny gloves, pushing the servant's fists into them until they burst. Lovelace plays to his groundling audience by pretending to lead the gentlelady off into the back room for God-knows-what. And then a final turn as Merry Andrew with Sally the whore who has accompanied Clarissa as maidservant—another of his jokes. Unbeknownst to the pathetic heroine, Sally is his spy and agent. Sally, taking up Lovelace's comedy, falls about his neck, offering to mimic Clarissa's theatrics, "crying, sobbing, praying." Presumably she is playing a fetishistic role of the whorehouse to simulate the best conditions for a rape. But Lovelace, though admiring of her skill, pushes her aside: he does not use whores. If he has a fetish, it is to use genteel ladies to simulate whores, not the other way round. He rewards himself with the thought that the sex is artful but that Clarissa is an exception and can say with Job (he can quote Scripture like a proper devil): "But it is not so with me." A worthy quarry, Clarissa! Unfortunately, she is gone that day, and he must play to these lesser beings.

Here is a remarkable portrait of the soul of a game-player. There is nothing for him save the restlessness with which he began. To make life into a game, to conquer time and change, one must play without pause or reflection, lest time play its own game and return one to the world of consequences. Even dream time must be incorporated in the game. As he says in the next letter, he gets no rest, for his nocturnal vision of Clarissa in angelic white becomes, the next morning, the very stuff of a new game. Expecting his angel to come to prayers, he goes to the chapel to await her, and, indeed, he himself prays, for what is a game with such a stake without the opportunity to worship what one would ruin? Where is the power, the glory?

Colonel Morden's sword, then, is hardly needed to empty this vessel. Since the rape, Lovelace has been capable of a good many levities—a daring appearance at an assembly where Hickman and Anna Howe are present, another disguise to try Clarissa, some jokes on her ravings and meditations, and, best of all, an idea that is to cap his whole career; he thinks he might imitate Horner in *The Country Wife* and bring the wenches in by screwing up his face into the grimace of a reformed sinner and announcing publicly the news that the terrible Lovelace has repented. (As we have seen, the Horner dodge is one that came naturally to Richardson.) Looking back on his performances since the rape, then, we have to say that Lovelace is not dazzled by Clarissa's virtue. He is in no danger of reform. If he has occasional solemn moments, he is not long drawn from the game.

At last he has hit upon this ultimate refinement of asking Clarissa to save him from himself. But Clarissa is no longer in the game. Lovelace performs to an empty house. Having nothing to do but await his appointment with Morden, Lovelace now exercises from time to time, fitfully, his melodramatic rhetoric about sin, retribution, and virtue, with which he has all along punctuated his acting of the various roles he has taken. Is this final rhetoric sincere? Does it permit Richardson the moralist to satisfy his and his lady-congregation's requirements for a proper morality? Doubtless, it serves the latter end, but as Lovelace has always been ambiguous, half-serious, half-mocking, about his "angel" and his test of womankind through her, as he has always been subject to occasional failure of nerve in his vocation of libertine philosopher, his final rhetoric is not at all out of keeping with his larger character. He has not reformed; he has neither escaped nor abandoned his essential being of game-player. Yet he is not Robert the Great either, he is not Camus's Sisyphus, the existentialist hero, because he is never quite certain that he will accept ultimate responsibility for his chosen role of game-player. He has the failures of nerve marked by his rhetorical paeans to Clarissa and his reflections on higher laws than his own. Nevertheless, it is rhetoric, and Lovelace remains Lovelace, restless, inventing, playing, but without end or purpose.

Richardson's art in creating this portrait of damnation lies in his master stroke of bringing the player-rake of Restoration comedy, where he is the agent of a wish-fulfillment action which ends perfectly and leaves us without worries of tomorrows, to inhabit a realistic world of consequences. The games of wit-comedy brought down to this realistic world of consequences create the effect of terror, tragedy, and of course for the principal actor, Lovelace, the damnation to play without purpose or conviction. Colonel Morden's sword has nothing to do with all this; it is only a dramatic cliché which the doctrine of poetic justice imposed on Richardson. The damnation of Lovelace is his empty theatre.

Doubtless, had he been asked, Richardson, who wrote against the immorality of the stage, would have said that Restoration comedy was wicked in itself, but the artist knew that the real wickedness lay in making its fantasies convertible with life. His genius seized the opportunity, given him by the sentimental current of his age, of asking what are the consequences of not taking life seriously. All the sentimental drama of the century solves the problem by reforming the rake or scapegrace by the offices of a good woman who, herself, has no part in the game-playing. In *Pamela*, Richardson, if he invented the new kind of realism of "writing to the moment," had nothing new to say insofar as the plot was concerned. But *Clarissa* is another story. Richardson threw over the cliché plot and asked, what are the *real* consequences of confusing comedy with life? It is an idea that was to have a good future in literature. The artist, not the banal moralist, manages the damnation of Lovelace.

Let us return to the question of his success in representing beatitude.

The measure of Lovelace's damnation is, of course, Clarissa's alienation; never complete until her final refusal to see him in the end, it entails the bankruptcy of his games which we have just noticed. If it was long in coming, it is steady and, in the end, complete. Her earlier complicity is what makes us care for her. With her as with Hamlet, the delay is long and not always pure, but that delay and impurity mark the struggle of the will which gives to the final letting-go a grandeur and dignity. Her will to dignity in a society which, as Lovelace knows, often makes women sublime in order to gain the pleasure of humiliating them by sexual aggresssion, is a moving spectacle. It is so precisely because Clarissa has accepted this underground motive of her society, and now, without at all reflecting on the matter, has gone far beyond it.

She has become her sublimation. In our society—from the eighteenth century onward—we have come to accept the fundamental contradiction in our view of mankind from which this book derives its drama. Mankind is sublime, but it is also only a part of natural history. Insofar as Lovelace is a philosopher—and he often is—his philosophical anguish is, we have seen, exactly this contradiction. Clarissa is an angel, but she is also only the bird in the cage which beats its head against the bars at first and then comes, by careful conditioning, to like its captivity and sing for its master. If sublimation may be the occasion of many evils in our life as it prevents natural expression, it is also, as Freud argues, responsible for many essential goods. It is the foundation of the arts of civilization. That Clarissa remains in our minds as a character more sympathetic than Lovelace is not owing to our moral principles, but to our *need* for the graces of sublimation. If we have with Lovelace as well a need to undermine and explode sublimation, that is because life cannot long remain either static or repressive. We must live the paradox.

Insofar as Richardson was able to give Clarissa a real dignity and a real self-possession, and that in the face of a degrading society and a naturalistic philosopher-rapist, he has brought her to a kind of beatitude. So many readers, so many opinions—but if readers have not been of one mind about Clarissa, they have, it seems if we take account of criticisms from Richardson's day to ours, granted her this final, tragic dignity. The contest with Lovelace and Lovelace's ultimate absurdity, those aspects of the book we have traced, would seem to confirm this judgment. Anna Howe's final Addisonian eulogy of Clarissa's graces (rather than her grace) hardly touches these matters—or the book's central drama. She was a woman, says Anna Howe, known for her neat hand, impeccable orthography, simple prose style (how modest she was in her flowers); she was able in the domestic arts, a judicious reader (she pitied Dr. Swift for his impurities), and wise, though untutored, in the ways of nature (knowing by instinct that ravagers of the forest consort not with lambs, she was alas to know it by experience)—and so on through needlework and organization of the day. How pedestrian, how irrelevant to a she-tragedy!

Had Clarissa's experience been only of such banalities, we would have had a courtesy book chronicling an Addison-in-petticoats. (Lady Bradshaigh, with Richardson's approval, pleased herself by reflecting on his Addisonian qualities.) Certainly no reader would pursue such humdrummeries and humbuggeries through the longest work of fiction in the language—Anna Howe is off the track. But why? Surely even practical, common-sensical, clear-sighted Anna Howe could see the inappropriateness of this eulogy to the baroque child who had just expired after choosing, like Dr. Donne, her death garb, coffin, and funeral rites. One can only say that it is another intervention of Richardson the banal moralist, but only an intervention, for Richardson the artist carries off the honors. Lady Bradshaigh, however she wanted to garland Richardson with the bays of Addison, recognized the artist: Lovelace was the lure for her as for the other precious ladies, and Addison could not have imagined Lovelace.

Richardson had so many encouragements to sacrifice his central drama and its tragic possibilities—neoclassical demands for poetic justice, the sentiments of his lady-congregation, his own tea table pomposities—that we can excuse the lapses, such as Anna Howe's eulogy, and wonder at the grand success in creating a tragic sense from the psychological stuff of sublimity and libertinism. (Not really a sense of beatitude but of tragedy, for beatitude is not dramatic.) And, moreover, beatitude is not founded in a world of family duties, the building of estates, or personal psychology. It is precisely because Clarissa is trapped in these mundane matters that her will to dignity and her final alienation are so imposing. The winding sheet theatrics at the end (borrowed from earlier literary convention)—burial garb, coffin, undertaker, testament—must seem morbid to the modern reader, as incomprehensible a gesture as Garrick's Hamlet's starting at the ghost, indeed, merely "camp," but those are among the "accidents" around the essential drama.

Despite her pathetic dignity, it is the drama of Clarissa's deathlock with her rake that is the source of our emotion rather than her character. She herself has not the force of an Antigone, who is after all, as Bradley says, caught in the mystery of good against good in the objective order of the cosmos. It would be hard to find God's law—or even man's—that speaks of the culpability of

the victim of a sexual attack. Clarissa cannot even be said to have
the stature of the Duchess of Malfi, whose cry of despair, "I go
into a wilderness," she echoes, and whose victimization by the
sexual malice of her brother bears some similarity to Clarissa's.
For the Duchess's anguish is owing to the world's perversion of her
own healthy and life-giving sensuality. Her dignity comes from
bravery before a hideous thwarting of life by others. Clarissa,
however, remains tied to a code of sexual ethics and filial piety
that is radically questioned by the action and is always perversely
allied with death. If one would not be a sadist with Lovelace, no
more would one be a masochist with Clarissa. While the novel
does not give us the largeness of character of more classical tragedy, it reaches the mysteries that puzzle the will and blight our
life. Our culture seems to drive us in two directions at once — to
sublimate (to remake into sublimities) the animal instincts, and
to unvarnish the sublimities, to bare the instincts. The religious
perspective is no more and no less compelling than the libertine.
While most of us, incapable of being either Clarissas or Lovelaces, beat about in the murky middle, we remain forever
attracted to both extremes. That is Richardson's subject in *Clarissa*. Had he himself not been so obsessed by the extremes, had
he not been at once moralist and voyeur, we should not have this
book. It is in this battle to the death between the extremes that
the emotion of the book is found. It is not, then, the pathos of
Clarissa that matters, but the wasting struggle of Clarissa and
Lovelace.

We have dwelt so long on the evidences of Richardson's personality because we can see there so easily those crude obsessions
which the artist somehow remade into an aesthetic consciousness.
We do not take the fat personage we see walking in the park,
peeking slyly at the passing hoops, as the consciousness of *Clarissa*. It is precisely because Richardson the pedestrian dominated
and mastered the pieties of his society and the crude material of
his own personality that we respect him. In bending them to the
service of his art, he escaped being a willy-nilly product of his age
and gained his freedom. The artist can escape neither the realities of his personality nor those of his society, but he will remake
them so that they suit his own vision of reality. Thus he gains his
freedom, teaching the common reader to sense his own. This

aesthetic consciousness, then, seems to me the fundamental thing that strikes upon our minds and feelings as we read. The author is there as we read, somehow beyond the form he creates and the history he lived. We come back to "*Clarissa*'s Richardson," a consciousness somehow linked, it is true, to that of *Pamela* and *Grandison* and to the personality of the fat man who walked in the park, but also wholly different. We have a sense of human freedom in being aware of this consciousness beyond the form of the work and dominating the history of the age. To be aware of the hand of the maker seems to me not only the humanistic reading, but the ultimate pleasure.

VI

POPE'S BOOKS:
A BIOGRAPHICAL SURVEY
WITH A FINDING LIST

Maynard Mack

Sterling Professor of English, Yale University

I

We are not lucky enough to have a sale catalog of Pope's library because his books were bequeathed rather than sold. If, however, we put together all the authors that, either from his own or others' direct reference, or from the survival of copies, we may judge him to have owned in one or more works, excepting from this tally only the commentaries and compendiums probably used for the Homer, and the works of his own contemporaries, we come up with an author figure in the neighborhood of two hundred and fifty. If we then translate this figure into titles, adding now the Homer reference books, the contemporary works, and a representative scattering of volumes it seems improbable he can have lacked—such as a Latin Lucan, a Latin Manilius, or a book or two on gardening, we reach a total that may have run as high as seven hundred and fifty, perhaps higher: we shall never know.[1]

All or most of these books, it is reasonable to guess, occupied the wall space in the one room in the house at Twickenham for which the posthumous inventory of 1744 registers no prints or paintings, but only two writing tables, one of them "large," a

209

third table, four armchairs, a cane settee with four cushions, two
fire screens, and a celestial or terrestrial globe.² It was by no
means, in other words, a tiny room. If Pope had brought with
him from Binfield the volumes of Protestant and Roman Catholic
controversy which constituted, he tells us, his father's entire
library and which he ran through at fourteen because there was
so little other reading in the house (veering, he says, from one side
to the other "according to the last book I read"),³ these would no
doubt have been assigned at Twickenham, along with other volumes seldom used, to the higher shelves and may, it is pleasant to
imagine, have contributed certain comical impressions to his de-
scriptionof Theobald's library, where the first scene of the *Dunciad* takes place:

> But high above, more solid Learning shone,
> The Classics of an Age that heard of none;
> There Caxton slept with Wynkin at his side,
> One clasp'd in wood, and one in strong cow-hide.
> There sav'd by spice, like mummies, many a year,
> Old Bodies of Philosophy appear.
> De Lyra here a dreadful front extends,
> And there, the groaning shelves Philemon bends.
>   (I [1729], 127-134)

For all its surface criticism of pedantic learning, this passage
has always struck me as having an affability of tone, along with a
certain arbitrariness of observed detail, that might suggest a
more than usual degree of personal involvement — either because
it mocks a species of folly for which the author himself had perhaps a considerable surreptitious tolerance (more evidence on
this point will be forthcoming), or else because it commemorates
a response to ancient folios such as an imaginative youth with
poetic inclinations might have first known in the spooky flicker of
the firelight on a dark November Windsor Forest afternoon: the
shine of leather bindings, the faint spicy scent of aromatic bees-
wax rubbed into them (and set free just now perhaps by the fire's
warmth), and then the suddenly dawning fancy that the shelves
he was staring at were a kind of catacomb or charnel house or
boneyard, where the mighty dead, asleep in their niches, could at
any instant choose to "appear," like the elder Hamlet's ghost, and

with their dreadful "fronts" extended, the very boards groaning under their gigantic weight, send delicious terrors up and down a boyish spine.

But this—as Horatio warns us when Hamlet traces the dust of Alexander to a bunghole—is to consider too curiously. All that we know for certain about Pope's Twickenham library is that when he died it was distributed, de Lyra's and Philemon's works included—if indeed he owned them. His "eleven volumes of Erasmus"[4] were willed to Bolingbroke and have not been heard of since. His "large paper Edition of Thuanus"—which is to say, of Jacques Auguste de Thou's eyewitness history of sixteenth-century France—published in English for the first time by Samuel Buckley, with an assist from Pope himself,[5] in 1733—was willed to a young Scots friend, Hugh Hume, third Earl of Marchmont, a member of the Young Patriot group that had gathered in the middle thirties around Prince Frederick in opposition to the King and Walpole, and had then gravitated to Pope as in some sense its laureate. This book, though it seems to have lingered on in the Hume family library at Mertoun in Berwickshire till 1912, has now likewise vanished without a trace. All the rest of Pope's books, apart from sixty that Martha Blount was authorized to choose for herself, went by testament to Ralph Allen and William Warburton,[6] two friends of his later years whom he had in fact introduced to each other and who, two years after his death, became more closely allied through Warburton's marriage to Allen's niece and eventual heir. Thanks to this marriage, the portion of Pope's library that at his death had been carried off to Prior Park, Allen's great Palladian showplace outside Bath, was reunited at some date after Allen's death in 1764 with the portion that had gone to Warburton and was preserved in the bishop's palace at Gloucester, Warburton's see from 1760 on. When Warburton himself died in 1779, his Gloucester books were directed by his will to be sold for the benefit of the Gloucester Infirmary[7] and were bought in by Richard Hurd, who soon removed them to the library he was constructing at Hartlebury Castle, his own new residence as incoming Bishop of Worcester. There today a number of them remain.

Unfortunately, this is not the whole story. Warburton, over the years, was in the habit of giving away to his friends books that

had belonged to Pope, as we know from inscriptions in some that
have survived.[8] In 1766, moreover, according to Malone, he sold
off "all Mr. Pope's copies of the old quarto editions of *Shakespeare*" to Thomas Payne, a London bookseller, and Payne, in
turn, put them in the sale of David Mallet's books that he happened then to be conducting, where they went for three guineas
—"I never," Malone adds, "could learn to whom."[9] From John
Nichols we learn, further, that Warburton kept a part of his
library at his London house in Grosvenor Square, and that this
part his wife disposed of after his death, again to Thomas
Payne.[10] One of the books that evidently escaped Hurd by this
route was Pope's copy of Thomas Tickell's rival translation of the
first book of the *Iliad*, complete with manuscript notes toward a
formal "examen" that Pope never actually drew up—or at any
rate never published. We happen to know about this particular
book because Isaac Reed picked it up on the Moorfields bookstall
of a certain Hanson and subsequently presented it to the Hartlebury collection, where it now is (No. 163). Nichols, who was
instrumental in its being presented to Hartlebury, tells us that it
had reached Hanson's "among some *rums* from Mr. Payne's
shop."[11] If "rums" means, as one fears it may, books a little
spoiled by manuscript markings (perhaps Pope's) one can only
wish that Reed had bought the lot and sent them along to Hartlebury with Tickell.

What remains clear today is that out of whatever number of
books Allen and Warburton received from Pope, only forty-four
titles unmistakably identifiable as his now survive at Hartlebury.[12]
I say this with a degree of confidence, for in the summer of 1938
my wife and I took down from the shelves each of the several
thousand volumes that the library of the Bishops of Worcester
then contained and inspected it throughout. In that same
summer, when I visited the Blounts's library at Mapledurham
House, Mrs. Riddell-Blount could turn up for me only eight of
the sixty items Martha Blount had had the privilege of choosing,[13]
and even these, after World War II, were put up for sale and dis-
persed in various public and private collections. The whole number of books unquestionably from Pope's library that may, so far
as I am aware, be seen and handled today amounts to one hundred and fifty, of which nineteen, however, are simply presenta-

tion copies of poems by his contemporaries bound up in two volumes and now at the Victoria and Albert Museum, while twenty-
four more are simply the bound-up pamphlet attacks on him that
were once at Hartlebury[14] but are now (another evidence of the
sievelike character of many book collections in the past two centuries) in the British Museum. Add the motley dozen that have
been on sale in this century but whose present whereabouts is
unknown to me,[15] and the accessible total reaches one hundred
and sixty-three. Not many, it may seem, out of a collection that
at one time probably contained at least five hundred; yet more,
so far as I know, than we have from the library of any other English poet prior to our own century.[16]

II

Reduced in number though they are and widely scattered, these
books make up a considerable resource for the biographer and a
considerable prize for the bibliophile and collector. Not, let it be
said at once, because of their fine condition. The state of many of
Pope's early purchases is poor to very bad, and tends to bear out
his remark to Spence that in the early days he lacked money,
"even to buy books."[17] At any rate, he usually bought on the
cheap at this period, and sometimes, in the case of old books,
picked up copies that lacked the title page, which he then replaced with one in his own elegant printing hand—like the title
pages of his Ariosto, Bacon (two items), Bertius, and Sidney.[18]

Association copies, of course, abound. He had presentations,
predictably enough, from a variety of acquaintances and friends
—Garth's *Dispensary,* Addison's *Cato,* Gay's *Trivia,* and Prior's
Poems on Several Occasions, to name only four of the more than
two dozen that survive. The Garth volume (No. 67) has a particular fascination because its inscriptions record an exceptional literary history. Originally the gift of the author, it descended
through Pope's bequest to Warburton, and was given by him, in
1752, to William Mason. Mason willed it to a certain William
Alderson, whose son inherited it and presented it in 1815 to William Fitzherbert, Baron St. Helens, who had been an important
figure in the diplomatic service prior to the Napoleonic wars. In

November 1838, a few months before his death, St. Helens gave it
to Samuel Rogers, and from *his* sale in 1856 it was purchased by
George Daniel for a price which indicates that association copies
from the eighteenth century were becoming chic: £12-15. Another authorial presentation that calls for special mention is
David Hume's *Treatise of Humane Nature* (No. 97), three substantial volumes published in 1739-1740. The inscription is not in
Pope's hand but Hume's, and Pope has left no marginalia in the
volumes anywhere, though Hume himself has obviously been
through them carefully, correcting in manuscript a multitude of
small errors. Since we have no recorded correspondence between
the two men, and no other evidence of their acquaintance, this
gift of books is our sole clue that two such formidable vessels
came, at least for a moment, within hailing distance.

Certain other books from Pope's library also supply unique
evidence of acquaintanceships previously unknown. A man
named Gabriel Young, for instance, about whom we know nothing else, was fond enough of Pope in 1701, when the poet was
thirteen, to give him a copy of Speght's *Chaucer,* not the reprint
of 1687 but the original printing of 1598 (No. 36). Sir John Trevor, several times Speaker of the House under James II and William III, as well as Master of the Rolls, 1685-1688, and again
1693-1717, a personage about whose association with the poet we
have no other testimony, gave him in 1715 a copy of the Schreve-
lius edition of the *Iliad* and *Odyssey,* Leyden, 1656 (No. 85).
Similarly, in 1741, the sons of Robert Barclay, the illustrious
Quaker who had died in 1690, gave Pope a copy of the latest edition of their father's influential *Apology for the True Christian
Divinity, As the Same is Held Forth, and Preached, by the People, called, in Scorn, Quakers* (No. 14). Since the inscription is in
Pope's hand, one infers that the volume was given and received
personally. Does this mean that the generally respectful allusions
to Quakers in Pope's poetry—somewhat surprising for their
period, and culminating, in the second dialogue of his *Epilogue
to the Satires,* with the mention of "a Quaker's Beaver" (line 97)
among the more congenial places for the goddess Virtue to cast
her halo—owe something to personal acquaintance with a Quaker family? Perhaps it does. Unhappily, as in the other instances I
have cited, the book refuses to answer the questions that it raises.
What is in any case especially disappointing for a biographer is

the fact that such extraneous memorials as this should be preserved, when not a single one of Swift's writings, so far as I am
aware, exists today in a copy that can be identified as Pope's, or
anything of Addison's apart from *Cato,* or of Gay's apart from
Trivia, or anything at all by Arbuthnot, who with Gay and Swift
made up the trio of his closest literary friends. "That bald sexton
Time," as Shakespeare somewhere calls him, digs his graves
where he chooses.

As for Gay and Parnell, they are rather touchingly represented,
Among association items of a quite different sort belong gifts of
general literature, and in these Swift *is* represented, as are also
Bolingbroke, Gay, and Parnell. The least surprising gift, no
doubt, is the copy of Locke's *Essay on Human Understanding,*
fourth edition, folio, 1700, which came to Pope from Bolingbroke—most probably during the middle to late 1720s, when
both were buried in what they liked to call "philosophy" (No.
105). From Swift in 1714—and therefore very likely a parting gift
as he left for Dublin in the late summer of that year amidst the
ruin of all his hopes for advancement in England—Pope received
a Greek and Latin *New Testament,* in the text of Erasmus, Paris,
1543 (No. 19). Probably, at this melancholy time, there was an
exchange of gifts. If so, the likeliest candidate from Pope's side
that is presently known is a tiny Frankfort edition, also dated
1543, of the *Epistolae Obscurorum Virorum* (No. 61). If Swift
chose his gift to Pope, as he may well have done, for its connection with Erasmus, Pope's favorite among divines, Pope may
equally well have chosen his gift to Swift for its antimonastic and
antipapal satire, sure to be acceptable to one who could (and
often did) speak, quite without irony, of "popery and slavery" as
two sides of the same coin.

As for Gay and Parnell, they are rather touchingly represented,
the one by a copy of Fénelon's *Télémaque,* two volumes, Paris,
1717; the other by the vast two-volume folio collection of the
*Opera et Fragmenta Veterum Poetarum Latinorum: Profanorum
et Ecclesiasticorum,* edited by Michael Maittaire, one-time second in command of Westminster School, in 1713. On the title of
each of the Fénelon volumes appears the signature "J. Gay," and
on the flyleaf of each, in Pope's hand, "This book was once Mr.
Gay's, next Mr. Pope's, now Mrs. M. Blount's 1734." This means,
I take it, that Pope chose the book as a memento from among
Gay's possessions after his death in December 1732 and some

months later presented it to Martha, to be *her* memento of their mutual friend (No. 64). The two huge Maittaire folios are another story (No. 114). Between them they contain an entire corpus of classical and postclassical Latin poetry, including the then known fragments, from the time of Ennius in the third century B.C. to the time of Venantius Fortunatus in the sixth century A.D. — in all 137 authors, ecclesiastical and profane, equivalent to the poetry in the red-bound half of the Loeb Classical Library plus a great deal besides. Those who want to take more than a superficial view of the literary culture of the Augustans, should give their days and nights not to Addison but to these two folios.

They were presented to Pope by Parnell — again in 1714, when like Swift he was returning to Ireland for what all the Scriblerians seem to have sensed might well be the beginning of a long separation and would, in any case, be the end of an epoch. Perhaps on this account, with a playful intent, or perhaps — though this seems less likely — because Pope failed to inscribe the volumes till after Parnell's actual death some four years later and then predated what he wrote, the commemoration on each flyleaf begins "In Memoriam" and then goes on to celebrate with Latin verses the hard labor (both men had been at Binfield working on the Homer all spring and summer in 1714) along with the high jinks (in September they had taken a particularly exuberant holiday at Bath) that had always characterized their association. In volume I the verses are taken from Persius's fifth satire (43-44), alluding to the happy hours the satirist has spent with his friend and guide, the Stoic Cornutus:

> Unum Opus & Requiem pariter disponimus ambo,
> Atque verecundia laxamus seria mensa.[19]

In the second volume, they are from Joannes Secundus's epistle *Ad Sibrandum Occonem,* though they have behind them the spirit as well as certain actual phrases borrowed by Secundus from Ovid:

> Te mihi junxerunt nivei sine crimine mores,
> Simplicitasque sagax, ingenuusque pudor,
> Et bene nota fides, & candor frontis honestae,
> Et studia, a studiis non aliena meis.[20]

The two quotations together, one ancient, one modern, the relevance of *studia* to *mores,* which both take for granted, and the combination in the second of Roman Latin with neo-Latin underscore admirably, it seems to me, the profound sense of continuities at all levels of experience that is the eighteenth-century writer's glory at his best.

III

I turn now from external matters to the image of Pope's interests that his surviving books record. One that is extremely well known is his sketching and painting, a hobby he had dabbled in for himself before he went to study with Charles Jervas for something like a twelvemonth at the age of twenty-five. Three reminders of his interest in these matters appear among the extant books. One is a copy of Jean Francois Felibien's compilation on the life and works of the great architects, published at Amsterdam in 1706 — which has, alas, no owner's markings in it (No. 62). Another — Pierre Monier's *History of Painting* (No. 119) — contains a printed alphabetical table of four hundred and forty-four names, beside five of which — Agostino (Veneziano) de'Musi, Giovanni Battista (Scultore), Marcantonio Raimondi, Marco Dente da Ravenna, and Martin ([Van Cleve] of Antwerp) — Pope has taken the trouble to note how their prints, when met with, are to be identified. Marcantonio, today the best known in this group (at least two of whom were his pupils), became Raphael's personal engraver, and the rest all worked in the sixteenth-century Italian classical tradition of which, for eighteenth-century tastes, Raphael was the superlative master. Though one would not wish to put overmuch weight on it, there is doubtless to be gleaned here some modest evidence of the poet's tastes in painting and just possibly of the sorts of work he found he could best imitate in his own excursions with the palette.[21]

Our third witness to Pope's concern with the visual arts is considerably the most interesting book of the lot. We know from Spence that he "once got deep into Graevius" — which is to say, into J. G. Graevius's *Thesaurus antiquitatum Romanarum* — and was so much taken with it that he wrote "a treatise in Latin, collected from the writers in Graevius on the old buildings in

Rome."[22] The treatise, though according to Pope it was in Lord Oxford's hands at the time he mentioned it to Spence, has vanished without a trace. One book survives, however, to show the meticulous character of his interest in these matters, though in this case rather in the Renaissance and baroque buildings of Rome than in the antiquities. It is a copy of Pieter Schenck's *Romae Novae Delineatio,* Amsterdam (1680?), offering twenty-two engraved views (No. 147) several of which Pope has annotated in a minute printing hand. In the engraving of the Piazza del Popolo, for example, he inserts the words "Sta. Maria del Popolo" at bottom left, and then cues them to the appropriate building by the letter *A*, neatly entered above the architrave. He does the same with "Porte du Convent (*sic*) des Augustines," which is cued to the appropriate gateway by the letter *B*. He has lavished most pains of all in getting down exactly right the inscription on the central obelisk in that piazza, which, like all his other identifications and insertions, he has studied up from elsewhere and inscribed here with admirable lettering in the style of the original. The six other annotated plates in the volume show similarly painstaking insertions. He includes, among many other things, the height and inscription of the obelisk in the square before Saint Peter's, and the delightful information about the obelisk at the Lateran—evidently derived from the *Urbis Romae Topographia* of G. B. Marliani, whose name, abbreviated "Marlian," appears at the end of the quotation—that it was "factus a Rege Semneserteo, qui Aegypto praefuit Pythagorae tempore."

What particularly strikes a modern sensibility in all this is the loving care the poet has been content to spend on these (by our standards) cramped little views and on the tiny nuggets of information he records. Yet our surprise dissipates when we reflect that, in their way, they served one who could not possibly hope to survive the rigors of an eighteenth-century sea voyage much as the urn and nightingale served Keats, and the scholar-gypsy Arnold: as glimpses into a world of imagination always to be longed for, never possessed: "For ever wilt thou love, and she be fair." Their best gloss, I think, is a passage in the verse epistle that Pope addressed to Jervas at some time during or shortly after his stay with him, though it was not published till 1717:

What flatt'ring scenes our wand'ring fancy wrought,
Rome's pompous glories rising to our thought:
Together o'er the *Alps* methinks we fly,
Fir'd with ideas of fair *Italy.*
With thee, on *Raphael's* Monument I mourn,
Or wait inspiring dreams at *Maro's* urn:
With thee repose, where *Tully* once was laid,
Or seek some ruin's formidable shade;
While fancy brings the vanish'd piles to view,
And builds imaginary *Rome* a-new.

(Lines 23-32)

One small group among the surviving books reflects Pope's interest in theological and philosophical speculation, an interest we know he had, even if he managed to pursue it only in an eclectic and quite unsystematic way. A commanding example of this interest is Bishop Daniel Huet's *Demonstratio Evangelica* (1690), which it is tempting to think may be one of the theological works the poet derived from his father, since it nowhere carries his signature but only Warburton's inscription to the effect that it was given him (this would have been, of course, while the poet was still alive) by "Alex. Pope, Poetarum facile Princeps, Viri summi atque amicissimi" (No. 95). Other examples that perhaps show something about the contour and coloring of his mind are George Touchet's *Historical Collections out of Several Grave Protestant Historians, Concerning the changes of Religion, and the strange confusions following from thence in the Reigns of King Henry the Eighth, King Edward the Sixth, Queen Mary, and Queen Elizabeth* (1674)—a book that Pope purchased for himself at two shillings (No. 164); Thomas à Kempis's *Sermons of the Incarnation and Passion of Christ,* Paris (1653)—also, conceivably, a relic from his father's books, but more probably purchased, since it carries his signature (No. 159); Hobbes's *Leviathan,* a copy of the first edition of 1651, bearing the poet's signature and also a note by Bishop Hurd that it was given him by Warburton "out of Mr. Pope's Library at Prior Park in 1765" (No. 82); Cudworth's *True Intellectual System of the Universe,* 1678, again a first edition, with the poet's signature and the same information in Hurd's hand as that above (No. 42); and a small shelf of others, in whose number the Erasmus, Thuanus, Hume, Locke, and Robert Barclay volumes already cited must be included, as must Bacon's *Advancement of Learning* (in a copy with title page, date ca. 1674), Thomas Stanley's *History of Philosophy,* the third edition, in folio, 1701, and a copy of the Koran in Arabic and Latin, Patavia, 1698 (Nos. 11, 154, 2).

The rest of the books that have come down tò us represent poetry, drama, criticism, fiction, or some other form of belles-lettres. Among the Latin writers, there are Cicero, Horace, Juvenal, Lucan, Lucretius, Manilius, Martial, Ovid, Quintilian, Seneca the tragedian, Statius, Terence, Valerius Flaccus, and Virgil, besides those included in Maittaire's *Opera et Fragmenta* already mentioned. Lucan, as indicated earlier, does not appear separately in a Latin text, but does appear in translations by May (1631) and Rowe (1718). Manilius is present only in Creech's English translation of 1697. Virgil—though Elwin and Courthope record an Elzevir edition in which Pope had entered the death dates of his friends (No. 170)—survives today among his books only in Dryden's translation, the third edition, three volumes, 1709. Among the Greek writers Pope may originally have owned, there remain now Homer, Herodotus, Lucian, Pindar, and Theocritus—plus those contained in No. 34 and in No. 127, if that book was in fact Pope's. Homer, predictably, appears in several editions as well as in the translations by Chapman, Hobbes, and Mme. Dacier; Herodotus, Lucian, and Theocritus only in English translations; Plutarch, in whose *Moralia* he often read, not at all. English writers have fared slightly better. Pope's copies of Chaucer, Langland, Spenser, Sidney, Joseph Hall, Jonson, Herbert, Milton, Butler, Oldham, Rochester, Rymer, and Dryden are preserved, among the older authors, and among contemporaries (in addition to the friends already named and the authors of the twenty-four pamphlet attacks), John Armstrong, Richard Barford, J. D. Breval, James Dalacourt, John Dart, Walter Harte, Richard Lord Paget, Christopher Pitt, Elizabeth Rowe, James Thomson, Samuel Wesley, and Edward Young. There is also a copy of Walter Davison's famous anthology of Elizabethan verse, *A Poetical Rapsodie,* in the edition of 1611, and of its slipshod Restoration cousin, *Poems on Affairs of State,* in the collected and pirated edition of 1705. Disquietingly, on the other hand, there is no copy of the poems of Skelton, Donne, Waller, Denham,[23] Cowley, Crashaw; no copy of the many minor seventeenth-century English poets whom, from his borrowings, we know he knew well; and no copy of Shakespeare, whom he edited, except a late *Othello* quarto.

It is the works of the modern European writers, however, that have been ravaged most. Here, the extant books include only Ariosto (in the Harington translation: No. 9); the *Poemata* of Theodore de Bèze, Calvin's defender and heir in the Reform movement (No. 18); Boileau's *Art of Poetry* in the Dryden-Soames translation (No. 24), though there are two copies of his works in French (Nos. 25, 26); Boccalini's *Iragguagli* in the English translation by the Earl of Monmouth entitled *Advertisements from Parnassus* (No. 22); Cervantes's *Don Quixote* (in the translation issued by Motteux: No. 35); Pierre Cuné's Menippean satire in Latin (on false learning — *homines inepte eruditos:* No. 43); Montaigne's *Essays* (in the Charles Cotton translation: No. 121, though there is also a copy in French: No. 120); and the works of Marco Girolamo Vida (No. 169). Once more it seems a sadly depleted offering when we place it beside the references to French and Italian literature that Pope makes in the Homer notes (where Tasso is the author most quoted after Virgil and Milton, and is always quoted in the original) and the references that he makes also in his conversations with Spence. No Rabelais, Malherbe, Chapelain, Corneille, Racine, Déscartes, La Bruyère, La Fontaine, Fontenelle, Molière, Pascal, Voiture, and no Le Bossu, Rapin, Perrault, or Pierre Bayle — all of whom we have evidence that he knew. Likewise, no Dante, Petrarch, Marino, Guarini, Sannazaro, or Politian (the latter one of his favorites), nor any trace of the host of very minor European neo-Latin poets that he probably first met with in Atterbury's *Anthologia* (1684) but which he studied carefully and himself reissued, with knowledgeable additions and some omissions, toward the end of his career in 1740. When the fable of the nightingale in one of Ambrose Philips's *Pastorals* comes up in correspondence with his friend Henry Cromwell in 1710, it is Pope, aged twenty-two, who knows that it derives from Famianus Strada.[24] When Sir William Trumbull and his nephew Ralph Bridges puzzle about the origin of a Latin verse in 1707, it is Pope, aged nineteen, who supplies the answer. "I forgot, I think, to tell you," writes Trumbull, "that our said

little Poet" — the epithet "little," rarely absent from Trumbull's
references to Pope at this period, indicates how early his spinal
curvature had set him apart even in the eyes of very good
friends — "(to whom, in all the mighty extent of Poetical Territo-
ries, there is no Terra Incognita) found out our *Ridet anhelan-
tem,* &c. He says it is in one of the Silvas of Angelicus Policianus,
and in that called Ambra, and that you have the Book."[25]

IV

We need not be much astonished, then, in turning to Pope's marginalia, to discover that what they show us first of all is a marked
interest in exact learning. Sometimes we find him paraphrasing
to make sure he has the sense right, as when, with Augustan logic,
he translates Bishop Hall's desperate Elizabethanism "are like be
gald alone" to "are alone likely to be wounded," or glosses "faste"
in Sidney's ironic line — "As smooth as Pan, as Iuno mild, like
goddess Iris faste" — with the words: "constant, always the same."
Sometimes it is rather the text that concerns him. In his copy of
Spenser, for instance — the 1611 *Works* — he takes note, following
stanza 11 of the *Shepherd's Calendar,* that here "Two stanzas are
omitted, wch are to be found in the first Edition in Quarto";[26]
and in his copy of *Paradise Lost,* the seventh edition of 1705, he
writes beside three of Milton's verses, "These 3 lines added since
the first Edition."[27] Not that he is by any means infallible. His
note on the title page of that same *Paradise Lost* reads: "First
publish'd in ten Books, in the year, 1669. Quarto." Even here,
however, he is not wholly wrong: copies of the first edition do
exist with a title page dated 1669.

In two or three of his books, he embarks on rather elaborate
indexes and analyses. His copy of the Beaumont and Fletcher
folio, London, 1679, is today missing, but the index he began for
it survives (No. 16). His copy of the 1692 Ben Jonson folio (No.
99) shows similar beginnings, and his Ariosto (No. 9) contains at
the rear a systematic "Table of the Descriptions." If his copy of
Rowe's Shakespeare should ever turn up, one feels sure it will be
found to contain some anticipatory manuscript traces of the seven
elaborate indexes — "Characters of Historical Persons," "Fictitious

Persons with the Characters Ascribed to them," "Manners, Passions, and their External Effects," "Thoughts or Sentiments,"
"Speeches" (arranged according to their rhetorical species),
"Descriptions of Places, Persons, and Things," and "Similes and
Allusions"—that he supplied for his readers at the back of the
final volume of his own Shakespeare. Austin Warren has concluded from the Jonson and the Beaumont and Fletcher tentatives that Pope once planned to edit other dramatists besides
Shakespeare.[28] This is not impossible, though to set up indexes of
this kind has been a common enough habit among readers in all
periods and was certainly a habit of Pope's. The hypothesis may
be somewhat better warranted by the enigmatic letters entered in
his copy of Dryden's plays, the two-volume Tonson folio of 1701
(a book not known to Warren), which is fully described in the
article noted in the finding list (No. 60). The only other extant
book containing really cryptic marginalia of this kind is his copy
of Tickell's rival translation of *Iliad* I, about which Conington
speculated as long ago as 1860 (See No. 163). Since the Tickell
markings look toward a work that he certainly at one time intended for publication, it is possible, though not in my view very
probable, that all such elaborate notations indicate a similar
intent.

Far the largest number of Pope's notes concern analogues and
sources that he jots down as he reads, and again they show a striking concern with exact learning. In his Montaigne, for example,
he reassigns to Aristotle the anecdote that Montaigne tells of
Alexander the Great; how he held a copper ball in his hand while
studying so that if he fell asleep it would drop into a metal basin
and awaken him.[29] In his copy of Jonson, beside "The Houre-
glass," eighth poem in *The Underwood,* he notes: "Translated
from an Italian poet Hier. Amaltheo"—and he is again correct.
In his Rochester (No. 144), beside the verse where it is observed
(ironically) that Providence has been so equitable in its distribu-
tion of intelligence that no man believes himself in need of more,
he remarks: "This thought is taken from the first lines of Des-
cartes Method"—the famous *Discours;* and the same note will be
found in twentieth-century editions. To limit myself to a final
instance among many: his copy of Spenser carries not only the
now familiar information that the description of the trees near

the outset of the *Faerie Queene* (I,i,8) has its inspiration in the similar passage in Chaucer's *Parliament of Fowls,* but also the information, not yet taken account of by any editor, that the nameless lover's prayer to Venus in *Faerie Queene,* IV, xliv-xlvii, was very considerably pillaged by Dryden for the prayer of Palamon in his *Palamon and Arcite.*

In all this, to be sure, as also in his notations about texts and meanings, Pope is only performing for himself what nowadays good editors perform for us. Yet one observes too, at times, an overplusage, as in the marginalia credited to him in what is said to have been his copy of Ovid's *Art of Love* (1709), a book now lost but reported on by its then owner in a 1787 issue of the *European Magazine* (No. 129). Among a variety of corrections Pope (?) makes in the book's notes (after testily inscribing the observation that they contain a thousand errors), his treatment of the following is, I think, indicative. The book's note says, a propos of Pasiphaë:

After Ovid had treated the subject of Pasiphae and the Bull so elegantly, in the 15th of the Met.[amorphoses] he shows the excellency of his genius in adding so much to it here.

Pope's marginalium says:

Ovid does not treat of this story at all in the 15th of the Metam.[orphoses]; he only just names Pasiphaë in lin. 500. So this remark is impertinent.

Is there not something a little too self-conscious here? At any rate, I will make no secret of my own belief that particularly in his younger days Pope shows signs of the interest in word-catching that he scorned in others. The earliest correspondences, those with his mentors Walsh, Wycherley, and Henry Cromwell, show us, if we examine them with a cold eye, not simply the artist-as-a-young-man-of-letters but also the artist as a young man too close for comfort to the literary pedant. Even in the 1729 *Dunciad,* where, fortified with the bitter lessons learned from Theobald's *Shakespeare Restored,* he exorcises all his impulses of this sort by holding them up to laughter, he yet manages to find an engaging

way of rehabilitating and reactivating them in the notes on notes
of Martinus Scriblerus and the variants on variants of the textual
apparatus. If the resulting poem is the greatest of all satires on
the corruptions to which learning and the literary life are subject,
this is partly, in my opinion, because the author knew some of
their worst temptations at first hand.

In general, as will already have been noticed, Pope's marginalia are not, in any distinctive way, self-revealing, his com-
monest annotation being the marginal inverted comma, or pair
of inverted commas, that indicates approval. But there is one
marked exception to this, and that is his copy of Montaigne in
Cotton's English translation, three volumes, 1685-1693. This war-
rants our attention for a moment, if for no other reason than to
correct the impression left by Warren in his study of Pope's reading that "he seems to have read [Montaigne] but without marked
appreciation."[30] Pope acquired this book in 1706 when he was
eighteen, and read in it, I suspect, many times before he died,
but at any rate all the way through, at least once, with the greatest thoroughness. There is hardly a page that is not starred up
and down with his marginal commas, and there are also far more
explicit verbal comments in this than in any other book of his
with which I am acquainted. His summary comment on the work
as a whole appears on the final end paper:

This is (in my Opinion) the very best Book for Information of Manners,
that has been writ; This Author says nothing but what every one feels att
the Heart. Whoever deny it, are not more wise than Montaigne, but less
honest.

One passage that Pope felt particularly at the heart, it would
seem, was that in Montaigne's chapter on honesty and deceit
(III,i), where he quotes the response of the Lacedaemonians to
their conqueror Antipater: *"You may impose as heavy and ruin-
ous Taxes upon us as you please, but to command us to do shameful and dishonest things, you will lose your Time, for it is to no
purpose."* Beside this, in a personal application of the example
that throws an interesting light on his refusal to convert to Angli-
canism, Pope has jotted: "The case of those who pay double
taxes."

He was even more taken with Montaigne's account of his education in Latin. There had been, Montaigne tells us, almost from his infancy, a Latin tutor in his family who had got them all to speaking Latin, so that "without any rod and without tears" he soon had a mastery; but then, his father having been overborne by more orthodox opinions, he was shipped off at age six to school, where he was started all over in the first forms and speedily lost interest. When he finally emerged at thirteen, "I had run through my whole Course (as they call it) without any manner of Improvement." Beside these sentences Pope writes: "mutato nomine de me Fabula narratur"; and, a page further on, beside Montaigne's analysis of what his father expected of education, and of him —

For the chief things my Father expected from their Endeavour to whom he had deliver'd me for Education, was Affability of Manners, and good Humour, and to say the Truth, [my disposition] had no other vice but Sloth and want of Metall. There was no fear that I would do ill, but that I would do nothing; no body suspected I would be wicked, but useless —

Pope adds: *"Alter ego."*

V

Though there are other fascinating glimpses of Pope's experience to be had in the margins of his Montaigne, I press on to my final exhibit. This is a two-volume duodecimo Homer in Greek, edited by Stephen Bergler and published at Amsterdam in 1709 (No. 87) — "the little pocket Homer on that shelf there" which Pope pointed out to Spence in 1735, when he told him that he had used it in translating the *Iliad* — "often forty or fifty verses on a morning in bed."[31] Pope's inscription on the second flyleaf confirms that this is indeed the book in question: "E. Libris A. Pope. Donum Dni Pellet, M.D. 1714" — here is another friend to whose association with the poet an inscription is our only clue — "Finish'd ye translation / In Feb. 1719-1720. A. Pope." In ways that are not now clear, but perhaps again through Warburton, this book came into the possession of Horace Walpole, who added to Pope's inscription: "This book belonged to Mr. Pope, and the Drawing is by him, Horace Walpole 1766. It is a view of Twickenham Church from his own garden." The drawing Walpole refers to is on the first flyleaf, and though it is assuredly not a view of Saint Mary's, Twickenham, from Pope's garden, or, probably, even a view of Saint Mary's at all, there is little reason to suppose that it is not by Pope.

The most remarkable part of the book for our purposes is the final flyleaf in volume II, containing seven consecutive lines of verse. Though Singer insists in his edition of Spence that Pope gave these volumes to Lady Mary Wortley Montagu and that she entered these verses on the flyleaf, the hand is clearly Pope's. The first line — "Here rest thy Reliques! Good without pretence" — informs us further that this is one of Pope's epitaphs; and a moment's additional research, that this is part of his epitaph "On Mrs. Corbet, who dyed of a Cancer in her Breast" — a poem of which we have no other autograph but only a transcript verbally identical with the published version of 1730. In the published version, the epitaph reads as follows:

1 Here rests a Woman, good without Pretence,
2 Blest with plain Reason and with sober Sense;
3 No conquest she, but o'er herself desir'd,
4 No Arts essay'd, but not to be admired.
5 Passion and Pride were to her soul unknown,
6 Convinc'd, that Virtue only is our own.
7 So unaffected, so compos'd a mind,
8 So firm yet soft, so strong yet so refin'd,
9 Heav'n, as its purest Gold, by Tortures try'd;
10 The Saint sustain'd it, but the Woman dy'd.

The earlier version in the Bergler Homer begins, as we saw: "Here rest thy Reliques! Good without pretence"; contains the second verse as we find it in the published text above; uses, however, for its third verse a line subsequently excised: "Whose tongue was mute, whose Life was Eloquence"; and then leaps at once, omitting verses 3-6 of the published version, to the two couplets which conclude both versions, where it manages to anticipate the published text save for one small variant in line 9 ("choicest" for "purest") and one in line 10 ("supported" for "sustain'd it" — but "sustain'd it" has been inserted below the line).

The first value of this little Homer, then, is that it gives us an autograph manuscript we did not have and shows us a poem, although a minor one, in the act of growth. But it has other values too. When we look more closely at its scribbled flyleaf, we notice that between the last line of the triplet, rhyming "pretence, sense, Eloquence," and the final two couplets, rhyming "mind / refin'd / tryd / dyd," something intervenes. Likewise, below these final couplets there are apparently additional insertions. In the area below the triplet, Pope seems to be saying something about "Nod," and in the area below the couplets something about "sweet repose" and "joy." Can this be a further abandoned fragment of the epitaph—or is it something else?

The answer—or at least the answer in my particular case—turned out to be the five words at the head of the squiggles that drip down the leaf at the extreme right. If one looks at these hard enough, one makes out eventually that they read "fast by his father's side"—a circumstance that effectively removes them from the ambience of Mrs. Corbett. And if one tries to imagine a situation for them, one is driven speedily to think of the twenty-first book of the *Odyssey*. There, at the close of the suitors' last banquet, having just drawn the great bow and sent the arrow through all twelve axe-rings, Odysseus gives his son a sign and Telemachus steps to his father's side. What we have here, it turns out, tucked in on all sides of the seven verses on Mrs. Corbett, is *Odyssey* 21:471-478, in process of formation. Odysseus is speaking, urging the suitors, who have been alarmed by a seeming beggar's success with the great bow, to return to their feasting:

> In sweet repaste the present hour imploy,
> Nor wait 'till ev'ning for the genial joy.
> Then to the lute's soft voice prolong the night;
> Musick, the banquet's most refin'd delight.
>   He said: then gave a nod; and at the word
> Telemachus girds on his shining sword.
> Fast by his father's side he takes his stand;
> The beamy jav'lin lightens in his hand.

At just this point, the little flyleaf becomes unexpectedly useful in a third way. Since we do not happen to have any evidence that Pope knew Mrs. Corbett, it has sometimes been supposed that the epitaph was written in honor of a certain Mrs. Cope—a woman with whom we know the poet was well acquainted, who was a cousin to his very good friend John Caryll, and who also, as it happens, died of a cancer in the breast. Later, so the argument goes, Pope was appealed to by Sir Richard Corbett for an epitaph for his sister's monument in Saint Margaret's, Westminster, and transferred the lines to Mrs. Corbett: hence they were printed with her name in 1730.[32]

The implications of poetic snobbery in this story make me happy to be able to explode it: Pope has genuine charges enough against him without our adding unnecessarily to the list. To be brief about it, Book 21 of the translation of the *Odyssey* was published in the fifth volume of the complete translation in June 1726. This means that the *Odyssey* verses on the flyleaf, which make part of it, cannot date much later than the fall or early winter of 1725. This means in turn that the verses of the epitaph date earlier, even if only by a day, since they were clearly already on the paper when the *Odyssey* jottings were fitted around them. The epitaph, therefore, has to apply to someone who was dead before the late autumn or early winter of 1725, and Mrs. Corbett was: she had died on the preceding March 1. Mrs. Cope, on the other hand, did not die till May, 1728, and therefore no possibility exists whatever that these verses were "originally" designed for her.

Small gains, all of these—as I would be the first to concede. Yet I think it is often only on such homely foundations that our understanding of a man, a poem, or an age is made secure.

NOTES

1. The sale catalog of Swift's library runs to 657 titles; the manuscript catalog of Congreve's to 659. See Harold Williams, *Dean Swift's Library, with a facsimile of the original sale catalogue* (Cambridge: The University Press, 1932); and J. C. Hodges, *The Library of William Congreve* (New York: New York Public Library, 1955).

2. The MS inventory, long supposed lost, has recently been recovered among the Blount family papers at Mapledurham House. It was published by Col. Francis Grant in *Notes and Queries,* 6th series, 5 (1882), pp. 363-365, and is reprinted in full, with a commentary, in my *The Garden and the City: Retirement and Politics in the Later Poetry of Pope* (Toronto: University of Toronto Press, 1969), pp. 244-258. See especially p. 251.

3. Pope to Atterbury, 20 November 1717 (*Correspondence,* ed. George Sherburn [Oxford: Clarendon Press, 1956] I, 453-354). I assume in what follows that Pope's father's collection, though according to the poet's testimony it was confined to the age of James II and so must have been made up mainly of octavos and small quartos, contained at least a scattering of older theology and ecclesiastical history in folio. Even controversy (e.g., Chillingworth's *Religion of Protestants,* 1638 et seq.) appeared in folio from time to time.

4. This would have been the very tall folio edition by Jean Le Clerc (Leyden, 1703-1706).

5. *Correspondence,* III, 294 and n.

6. For these details and arrangements, see *The Life of Alexander Pope, Esq.; With a True Copy of His Last Will and Testament* (1744). The printed will is reproduced in *The Garden and the City* (above, n. 2), pp. 263-265; a copy of the manuscript will, which is identical, exists among the Blount papers at Mapledurham House.

7. A. W. Evans, *Warburton and the Warburtonians* (Oxford: Oxford University Press, 1932), p. 269.

8. See in the finding list below: nos. 37, 42, 82, 84, 90, 103, 120.

9. James Prior, *Life of Malone* (London: Smith, Elder, & Co., 1860), p. 345.

10. Nichols, *Literary Anecdotes* VI, 490. For a slightly different account, see the "Memoirs of Bishop Warburton" in *Gentleman's Magazine,* 50 (1780), 409. In the finding list below, see no. 117.

11. Ibid., V, 640.

12. Forty-eight are included in the list, but the hand that made the annotations in nos. 28, 38, 127, and 167 may not be Pope's.

13. The will does not establish beyond doubt whether Martha Blount was to choose sixty titles or sixty volumes. The former seems much more likely ("my Library of printed Books . . . when Mrs. Martha Blount has chosen Three-score out of the Number"), but the latter interpretation would help account for the small fraction of Martha's choices identifiable today. The number of titles available for inspection at Mapledurham House in 1938 was eight, but the number of volumes was fifteen. Four additional books bearing Pope's signature were believed to have been present in the library, but could not be found at the time. Three of these I have since seen, bringing the total of identified Mapledurham titles to eleven, the total of volumes to eighteen. In the finding list, these are nos. 31, 35, 64, 70, 81, 116, 118, 121, 138, 140, 154. The fourth volume not seen in 1938 was a copy of John Hughes's play, *The Siege of Damascus* (1720), whose present location is unknown to me. I had intended to exclude it from the Finding List, on the ground that evidence of survival was no stronger in this instance than in the case of many another book that we know Pope owned. Very recent access to catalogues of the Mapledurham House library indicates, however, that the book survived well into this century. I have therefore inserted it in the Finding List as no. 96.

Since these lines were written an exhaustive search of the Mapledurham House library has yielded two more books that unquestionably belonged to Pope, though only one contains his signature. See nos. 26 and 39.

I have not included in the above figures the presentation copies of Pope's own writings that in 1938 were still to be found at Mapledurham House.

14. Prior, *Life of Malone,* p. 345.

15. Nos. 11, 20, 43, 57, 58, 61, 65, 69, 86, 94, 101, 148. Nine books that neither may be seen nor have been recorded at auction are nos. 16, 21, 55, 83, 96, 103, 129, 168, 170.

16. Since Pope did not *invariably* put his signature in his books (see for example nos. 23, 44, 75, 95), there are probably books of his at Hartlebury today that cannot be identified. If so, they swell the total of survivors. Plausible, too, is the hypothesis that a number of the Hartlebury books "escaped" (see no. 75, for instance, and above, n. 15) to other owners and so found their way eventually either to oblivion or to the sale-rooms. The same may be supposed of Martha Blount's collection, since it seems reasonable to believe that she would have chosen books with association value, having therefore at least Pope's signature, and being therefore readily identifiable. Obviously, the very considerable number of his books found today in private as well as public libraries must be traced originally (apart from those that Warburton may have given away) to either Hartlebury or Mapledurham. Many more, possibly, from the same sources, now not identified, have been pulped because Pope's signature was cut away or the flyleaf torn out by autograph hunters (see no. 91), or simply escaped notice (see no. 27).

17. Joseph Spence, *Observations, Anecdotes, and Characters of Books and Men,* ed. J. M. Osborn, new ed. (Oxford: Clarendon Press, 1966), no. 192.

18. Nos. 9, 11, 12, 17, 150, 151. In his copy of Chapman's *Homer* (no. 84), the title page is damaged and mounted.

19. "We two were one in our work, one in our hours of rest, and unbent together over the modest board."

20. "Why do I love you? For a way of life that is without stain, for innocence joined with wisdom, inborn modesty, good faith, a free and open address to the world, and studies to which my own studies are akin." With the first two verses quoted from Secundus, compare *Amores,* I, iii, 13-14: et nulli, cessura fides, sine crimine mores / nudaque simplicitas purpureusque pudor.

21. What is known about Pope's excursions into painting is ably summed up in Norman Ault's, *New Light on Pope* (London: Methuen, 1949), pp. 68-75. But Ault fails to deal with Pope's models.

22. Spence, no. 557.

23. Spence (no. 494) reproduces a note made by Pope at the rear of his copy of *Cooper's Hill* (1709), showing that he had studied Denham's revisions of the poem with some care.

24. Pope to Cromwell, 11 November 1710 (*Correspondence,* I, 103. See also I, 60).

25. William Trumbull to Ralph Bridges, 5 August 1707, *Notes and Queries,* n.s., 5 (1958), 343.

26. Actually, one stanza. See no. 153.

27. See no. 116. It is perhaps a reasonable inference that Pope acquired no. 117, a duplicate copy, only through gift from Atterbury when the latter went into exile in 1723.

28. *Modern Language Notes,* 46 (1931), 515-517.

29. Actually, the story is told of both men — of Alexander by Ammianus Marcellinus (XVI, v, 4), of Aristotle by Diogenes Laertius (V, 16), and of both by Thomas Stanley, (*History of Philosophy,* 3d. ed., 1701, p. 236), who adds (after attributing this antisoporific device to Aristotle) "which *Alexander,* his Disciple imitated." Pope had a copy of Stanley (no. 142), but his source here appears to have been Laertius.

30. Austin Warren, *Alexander Pope as Critic and Humanist* (Princeton: Princeton University Press, 1929), p. 209.

31. Spence, no. 107.

32. *The Twickenham Edition of the Poems of Alexander Pope,* VI (London: Methuen, 1954), 323-324. (Herafter cited as T.E.)

APPENDIX

A FINDING LIST OF BOOKS SURVIVING FROM POPE'S LIBRARY
WITH A FEW THAT MAY NOT HAVE SURVIVED

The list that follows contains the titles of one hundred and fifty-five books that there is reason to believe belonged to Pope, and which I have personally examined, together with the titles of twenty-one more to which I have not had access. Of the twenty-one, thirteen have appeared for sale during this century with what appear to be well founded claims of Pope's ownership; the eight others, though not recorded at auction or in this century, have nevertheless left a convincing record of their survival beyond the poet's own time at dates ranging from 1784 to the present. Of the one hundred and fifty-five that I have included here after examination, most contain at least Pope's signature, or if not, an authenticating inscription from Warburton or Ralph Allen. One item, however, remains somewhat problematical (No. 91) because the signature is missing though attested to, and five must be regarded as possibly problematical (Nos. 28, 38, 117, 127, 167) because they lack signatures and such handwriting as they contain either is not Pope's (No. 117) or cannot be identified as Pope's beyond a lingering doubt.

This is a finding list, I must remind the reader, and therefore not to be taken as in any way definitive: my fondest hope, in fact, is that numerous omissions will promptly be found in it and thus supplied.[1] It is also a list of surviving books—books that for the most part may be consulted today—not a list embracing the dozens, even hundreds, of titles referred to in the poet's letters, his notes to his work, and his conversations with Spence. To save space, I have made other exclusions as well. Several of the surviving books carry Pope's characteristic marginal commas and double commas, commoner with him as a way of indicating interest or approval than any form of verbal marginalia. To have recorded these, together with the passages they refer to, as I have done in the case of the verbal marginalia, would have stretched an essay that is already too long to intolerable bounds. The reader who is sufficiently interested will find a complete catalog of Pope's comma marginalia, together with a consideration of the light they shed on the poet's mind and writings, in the biography on which I am presently at work.[2]

From considerations of expense, I have made no effort to reproduce here the styling of Pope's inscriptions, which, particu-

---

[1] Two omissions are deliberate because the works in question are bound manuscripts, not printed books. One is an MS in Arabic that Pope presented to his friend Lord Oxford in 1723, now in the British Museum (Harl. MS. 5478). See *The Diary of Humfrey Wanley, 1715-1726,* ed. C. E. Wright and R. C. Wright, 2 vols. (London, 1966), II:247: "My Lord sent-in a Persian MS. given by M^r. Pope being a Theological Treatise written by Father San-Hieronymo Shad a Jesuit Missionary at Lahôr and dedicated to Gjanghîr the Great Mogul, A.D. 1609, 4 ^{to}." On the first leaf in Wanley's hand: Donum Alexand. Pope Armigeri, mense Aprilis A.D. 1723.

The other conscious omission is a manuscript consisting of colored miniatures of the Indian kings and Moguls, which was procured at Surat by John Cleland (son of Pope's friend William), sent to Pope, and by him given to the Bodleian. (See A. J. Sambrook, "John Cleland," *Times Literary Supplement,* 23 April 1971, p. 477.) *On the flyleaf, in Pope's hand:* This Book, (containing one hundred and seven- / ty eight Portraits of the Indian Rajahs, / continued to Tamerlane and the Great Mo- / gols his Successors as far as to Aureng- / Zebe) was procured at Surat by M^r. / John Cleland, and given to the Bodley / Library, as a Token of Respect, by / Alex. Pope. / 1737.

[2] A portion of this on Pope's commas is to appear earlier and elsewhere.

larly in his younger days, are often replete with large capitals, small capitals, italic letters, and other niceties, all in his exquisite printing hand. A partial exception has been made in the case of MS title pages such as Nos. 9, 17, 150, 151. On the same account, in reproducing the passages to which his verbal marginalia refer, I have ignored the lineation of the original text save when the passage is in verse. It has likewise seemed superfluous in such a list as this to give full-scale bibliographical descriptions. The detail supplied ensures that identification will be easy.

Finally, I want to acknowledge my debts. Over the years I have been obliged for assistance in compiling and verifying this list to many people: among friends and collectors, especially Mary Hyde and Philip Robinson; among friends and colleagues, especially George Sherburn and Arthur H. Scouten; among friends and librarians, especially Leonard Greenwood, Richard Williams, William B. Todd, Lola L. Szladits, Richard C. Johnson, and Marjorie G. Wynne; among friends and assistants in research, especially Annetta Bynum, Kathryn Cook, Allison Sweeney, and Barbara Bate Shellenbarger; among friends and spectacular typists, especially Grace Michele; among friends and wives, especially Florence Brocklebank. To them all an "omnibuss" of thanks.

1. Addison, Joseph. *Cato.* "Seventh Edition." London: Tonson, 1713. 12⁰. *On the flyleaf in Pope's hand:* Ex Libris A. Pope. Donum Authoris. *Below this, in Hurd's hand:* The above is the hand-writing of / Mr Pope. R. W. / N. B. / This copy of *Cato,* was the present / of Mr Addison to Mr Pope, who had / written the Prologue to that Tragedy. It / afterwards came into the possession of / Bishop Warburton among the other / books bequeathed to him by M^r / Pope. And upon the Bp's decease it / came into my hands in consequence / of the purchase made by me of so / much of the Bp's Library as is now at Hartlebury Castle. / R. W. / June 30 1800.   (*Hartlebury*)

2. *Alcorani Textus Universus.* Actore Ludovico Marriccio. Patavii: 1698. Folio. *On the flyleaf in Warburton's hand:* Warburton / Donum Alex. Pope / Poetarum facile Principis / Viri Summi atque Amicissimi.   (*Hartlebury*)

3. Anonymous. *Characters of the Times; Or, An Impartial Account of the Writings, Characters, Education, &c. of several Noblemen and Gentlemen, libell'd in a Preface to a late Miscellany Published by P——PE and S——FT.* London: A Dodd and T. Read, 1728. Vol. II. *Bound with twenty-three other pamphlets relating to Pope in a four-volume octavo set. On the flyleaf of the first volume, in Pope's hand:* Job, Chapt. 31. Vers. 35. / Behold, it is my desire, that mine / Adversary had written a Book. / Surely I would take it on my / Shoulder, and bind it as a crown / unto me. (*British Library*)

4. ——. *A Compleat Collection of all the Verses, Essays, Letters and Advertisements, Which Have been occasioned by the Publication of Three Volumes of Miscellanies, by Pope and Company... With a large Dedication to the Author of the Dunciad, containing some Animadversions upon that Extraordinary Performance.* London: A. Moore, 1728. Vol. II [*See number 3.*] *On p. iii, beneath the title "To the Author of the Dunciad," Pope has written:* By M. Concanen.

5. ——. *An Essay on the Dunciad An Heroick Poem.* London: J. Roberts, 1728. Vol. II. [*See number 3.*]

6. ——. *Gulliver Decypher'd: or, Remarks On a late Book, intitled, Travels into Several Remote Nations of the World. By Capt. Lemuel Gulliver.* London: J. Roberts. Vol. II [*See number 3.*]

7. ——. *Hereditary Right Exemplified; Or, a Letter of Condolence from Mr. Ed——d C——l to his son H——y, upon his late Discipline at Westminster.* London: 1728. 8°. Poems, Vol. I. [*See number 15.*] *The missing letters in the blanks above have been supplied, possibly by Pope.*

8. ——. *A Letter from a Clergyman to his Friend, With an Account of the Travels of Capt. Lemuel Gulliver: And a Character of the Author. To which is added, the True Reasons why a certain Doctor was made a Dean.* London: A. Moore, 1726. Vol. II. [*See number 3.*]

9. Ariosto. [*Orlando Furioso*. Translated by John Harrington. London: Richard Field, 1591.] Folio. *On the flyleaf, in Pope's hand:* E' Libris Alex. Popei. Pr: 3$. *The original title page is wanting and has been replaced by Pope's manuscript title, as follows:* ORLANDO FURIOSO: / Translated from the / ITALIAN / OF / ARIOSTO. / BY / Sir JOHN HARRINGTON. / Anno 1591. *On a blank leaf at the end of the volume, in Pope's hand:* A Table of the Descripsions of Ariosto; In his Orlando Furioso — *with such subheadings as* "Times," "Places," "Actions and Accidents," "Persons and Things." (*Hartlebury*)

10. Armstrong, John. *The OEconomy of Love; A Poetical Essay.* "The Second Edition." London: T. Cooper, 1737. 8⁰ Poems, Vol. I. [*See number 15.*]

11. Bacon, Francis. [*Of the Advancement of Proficiencie of Learning, or The partitions of sciences.* London: T. Williams. 1674.] Folio. *According to Parke-Bernet, 25 January 1940, lot 268, the title page is missing, but on the recto of the portrait leaf is the following inscription in Pope's hand:* The Lord Bacon's Advance[m]ent [of] Learning. Ex libris Alex. Pope. *The bracketed letters are defective.*

12. ———. [*The Essays, or Councils, Civil and Moral, of Sir Francis Bacon, Lord Verulam, Viscount St. Albans.* London: H. Clark. 1718.] 8⁰. *The title page is wanting. On the flyleaf is an inscription in Pope's hand recording the gift of the volume to Mrs. Newsham:* Essays / of / Sir Francis Bacon, / Lord Verulam: / To Mrs. Newsham, / from her Servant, / A: Pope. / - / In the yeare 1725. / - / *On a blank page numbered 9⁰ are the fourteen lines of the "A" text of "A Wish, / To Mrs. M. B. on her Birthday, June 15."* (*British Library*)

13. Barclay, John. *Argenis.* Leyden: Isaac Elzevir, 1630. 12⁰. *On the flyleaf in Pope's hand:* E' libris / Alexandri Popei: / Pret. 18.ᵈ (*Harvard*)

14. Barclay, Robert. *An Apology for the True Christian Divinity.*

"The Sixth Edition in English." London: T. S. Raylton and L. Hinde, 1736. 8⁰. *On the flyleaf in Pope's hand:* A. Pope. / Ex dono filiorum Autoris. / 1741. *(Hartlebury)*

15. Barford, Richard. *The Assembly. An Heroi-Comical Poem. In Five Cantos.* London: 1726. 8⁰. *[Bound with the short works of a number of minor poets in an octavo two-volume set. (Poems, Vols. I and II).]* Poems, Vol. I. *On the third flyleaf of Vol. I, in Joseph Warton's hand:* N. B. / These two Volumes of Miscellaneous / Poems belonged to / Mʳ Pope. *Above this, the signatures: [John]* Mitford. 1804. *and* Payne *[Thomas Payne, the bookseller?]. On the first flyleaf the signature of Alexander Dyce and his note:* Cost me £2-5-0. A.D. *(Victoria and Albert Museum)*

16. Beaumont, Francis, and Fletcher, John. *[Fifty Comedies and Tragedies.* London: J. Mackock, 1679.] 2 vols. Folio. *Three leaves of an uncompleted index to these volumes survive in Pope's hand, and were once in all probability part of a copy belonging to him, since it was very much his habit to make such indexes in certain books. See Austin Warren in "Modern Language Notes," 46 (1931), 515-517. (British Library)*

17. Bertius, Petrus. *[Theatri Geographicae Veteris Tomus prior.* Leyden: Isaac Elzevir and I. Honde, 1618.] Folio. *The title page is wanting and has been replaced by Pope's manuscript title, as follows:* PETRI BERTII / TABULAE GEOGRAPHI-CAE / CONTRACTAE. / - / Cum luculentis singularum Tabularum explanationibus. / - / [ornament] / - / LUGDUNI BATAVORUM. / MDC. XVIII. *On the first flyleaf:* E Libris A. Popei. *Two pages of the index are also supplied in Pope's hand. (Robert H. Taylor)*

18. Beza, Theodore. *Poemata Theodori Bezae, Vezelii.* London: Bernard Lintott, 1713. 16⁰. *On the flyleaf in Pope's hand:* E' libris A. Pope. *(Harvard)*

19. *The Bible: Novum Testamentum Graece & Latine.* Ed. D.

Erasmus. Paris: J. Roigny, 1543. *Above the title, in Pope's hand:* Ex Libris perg^m / A. Pope, ex dono Amicissimi, Io-nath: / Swift, Decani Sti Patricii. 1714. *In mid-title, in a different hand, probably Swift's:* Intellectum da mihi Avidam. (*Hartlebury*)

20. ———. *H. KAINH̀ ΔIAΘH́KH. Novum Testamentum.* Cambridge: Thomas Buck, 1632. 8⁰. (*According to Soth-by's catalogue, 26-30 June 1933, lot 347a, the book has on a flyleaf, in Pope's hand:* V. I. / Henrici. St. John., Vice-Coms. / de Bolingbroke, / Donum Alexandro Pope, 1728.)

21. ———. *The Holy Bible.* Cambridge: J. Hayes, 1674. Folio. *This book has not been recorded publicly, so far as I know, since 1859, when it was described in the Camden Miscellany, IV, "The Letters of Pope to Atterbury when in the Tower of London," ed. J. G. Nichols, p. 17 / from a manuscript note sent to Nichols by Cornwallis (Maude), 4th Viscount Hawar-den, which is now in the Harvard Library. According to Ha-warden's note, the Bible contains the following inscription in Pope's hand:* Franciscus Episcopus Rossensis, / Vir admodum Venerandus & Amicissimus / Alexandro Pope Dono dedit; / Jun. 17. 1723. Anno Exilii. 1⁰ / Cape dona Extrema Tuorum! *After Atterbury's death, Pope added:* Obiit Vir Venerandus Lutetiis, / mense Februario. Anno D'ni 1731/2 / Exilii 8⁰, Aetatis 71⁰. *Later, as a third inscription shows, Pope presented the book to Ralph Allen for use in his chapel at Prior Park:* Mar 30. 1739. / A. Pope Radulpho Allen, Viro de se / atque omnibus hominibus bene merito, / in Usum Sacelli sui Widcombiensis / Dedit. *To a transcript of these inscriptions Hawarden appended the following:* The above is a copy of the inscription on the flyleaf / of the Bible in my possession. The handwriting is my own / but I have copied the inscrip-tion that the places of Capital / letters and the way in which the date of the Bishops / death was entered in the book might be seen. / The assertion [*made by Nichols in the "Camden Miscellany" article*] that the three lines beginning Obiit Vir &c were / written after Atterbury's death appears to me to be correct as / the ink is apparently much darker than that with

which the preceding lines were written. It also appears to be a
/ different ink from that with which the lines beginning with
/ the date Mar. 30. 1739 was written. / The Title Page states
the Bible to have been printed at / Cambridge, thus. Cambridge / Printed by John Hayes. / Printer to the Universitie. /
Dundrum / Cashel / February 26th 1859. Hawarden. *Ralph
Allen's niece Mary became the second wife of the first Viscount Hawarden, grandfather of the author of the above
note. The Bible is not now known to be in the family's possession, but has never been recorded in the sale-rooms.*

22. Boccalini, Trajano. *Iragguali di Parnasso: or, Advertisements from Parnassus: In Two Centuries. With the Politick
Touchstone.* Tr. Henry Earl of Monmouth. "The Third Edition, Corrected." London: Thomas Guy, 1675. Folio. *On the
flyleaf in Pope's hand:* Alex. Pope. / Pr. 4.^{s} (*Hartlebury*)

23. Bochart, Jean. *Opera Omnia.* "Editio Quarta." Leyden: Jo-
hannes Leusden and Petrus de Villemandy, 1712. 3 vols.
Folio. *On the flyleaf of Vol. I, in Warburton's hand:* Warburton 3.V^s. / Donum Alex. Pope / Poetarum facile Principis
/ Viri Summi atque amicissimi.   (*Hartlebury*)

24. Boileau-Despréaux, Nicolas. *The Art of Poetry. Written in
French by the Sieur de Boileau, Made English by Sir William
Soames.* London: R. Bentley and S. Magnes, 1683. 8°. *On
the flyleaf, in Pope's hand:* Alexander Pope / Pret.^{m} 8^d *On
the title page, below the line "Made English," in Pope's hand:*
By Sir William Solmes. [*i.e., Soames*]. *In Cantos 1 and 4
summary notations in Pope's hand are found in the lower
margins, cued to sections of the poem that he has distinguished with the corresponding Roman numeral, as follows:
p. 1, 11.1-12:* Precept I. Not to write without a / Genius.
11.13-26: Precept II. To know / your Talent.
p. 2, 11.27-48: III. Sence the Rule of all Writing, Reason the
Guide.
p. 4, 11.49-68: IV. Against Impertinent Descriptions.
p. 5, 11.69-78: V. Variety of Style. *11.99-104:* VI. Against
Meanness of Style.

p. 7, 11.105-142: VII. Correct Versification.

p. 9, 11.143-154: VIII. Agst Obscurity.

p. 10, 11.155-162: IX. Purity of Language. *11.163-174:* X. Not to write fast.

p. 11, 11.175-182: XI. Disposition and design. *11.183-230:* XII. Submission to able Iudges.

p. 54: Canto IV: This Canto contains Advice to / Poets, in regard to their Conduct.

p. 55, 11.25-38: I. That there is no Medium in Poetry.

p. 56, 11.39-83: II. How far to submit to Correction of / Criticks.

p. 58, 11.84-123: IV. The Morals a Poet ought to have. [*Perhaps inadvertently, Pope omitted III.*]

p. 61, 11.124-131: V. Agst the Mercenary Temper of some / Authors. *On page 48 above the new paragraph, in Pope's hand, the heading:* Comedy. (*Huntington*)

25. ———. *Oeuvres Diverses.* Amsterdam: Henri Schelte, 1702. 8°. *On front end paper, in Pope's hand:* Ex Libris Alex: Pope. / Pret. 4^s (*Harvard*)

26. ———. *Oeuvres de Mr Boileau Despréaux avec des Éclaircissements Historiques.* Geneva: Fabri & Barrilot, 1716. 2 vols. 4°. *On the inner title following the title page, Pope has written:* Donum Amicissimi Dni / Honoratiss. V. Jacobi Craggs. 1717. (*Mapledurham House*)

27. Boyle, Robert. *Medicinal Experiments: Or, A Selection of Choice and Safe Remedies.* "The Third Edition." London: Samuel Smith and B. Walford, 1696. 12°. *On the board of the inside cover, in Pope's hand:* Alex^r Pope. (*Northwestern University Dental School*)

28. Boys, John. *AEneas His Descent into Hell. Made English by John Boys of Hode-Court, Esq.* London: R. Hodgekinson, 1661. *No signature, but in "The Preface to the Reader," leaf A1r, "a Translator [of Book II] inferiour only to the Author himself" is marginally identified as* Denham *and a translator*

by whom Book IV "hath been equally blest" as Waller, *in a
hand possibly Pope's.*   (*Hartlebury*)

29. [Breval, John Durant]. *The Confederates: A Farce. By Mr.
Gay.* London: R. Burleigh, 1717. Vol. I. [*See number 3.*]

30. ———. *Henry and Minerva. A Poem. By J. B. Esq.* London:
J. Roberts, 1729. Poems, Vol. II. [*See number 15.*]

31. Burnet, Gilbert. *Some Letters Containing an Account of
What Seemed Most Remarkable in Switzerland, Italy, &c.*
Amsterdam: 1686. 12°. *On the title page, in Pope's hand:*
Alex: Pope. / Pr. 1ˢ 6ᵈ *Lower down, where Burnet is identi-
fied as "D. D. to T. H. R. B.," Pope Revises "H" to* Hᵇˡᵉ, *"R"
to* Rᵗ, *and "B" to* Boyle. *On the third rear flyleaf, Pope notes:*
The Discourse of the Catacombs / page 204, to p. 213, one of
/ the most remarkable passages / of this book.   (*Yale*)

32. Burnett, Thomas, and Duckett, George. *Homerides: Or, a
Letter to Mr. Pope, Occasion'd by his intended Translation
of Homer. By Sir Iliad Doggrel.* London: W. Wilkins, 1715.
Vol. I. [*See number 3.*]

33. Butler, Samuel. *Hudibras. In Three Parts.* London: Richard
Parker, 1689. 8°. *At top, on inside front cover, in a character
very like Pope's greek script:* περὶ παντος τὴν ελευθεριαν [*"On
the freedom of the whole"*]. *But Pope rarely used accent
marks as here. On the flyleaf, in Pope's hand:* E Libris Alex:
Pope: e dono Amici mei chariss. / Dñi Anthon: Englefyld. /
1704. *On page 380, at the following passage —* "Quoth he,
This Scheme of th' Heavens Set, / Discovers how in fight you
met / At Kingston with a May-poll Idol, / And that y' were
bang'd both back and side well; / And though you overcame
the Bear, / The Dogs beat you at Brentford Fair" — *Pope has
set an "X" next to the line beginning "Discovers" and has inserted in the margin:* These passa- / ges are / taken from / a
Book call'd / The second pt / of Hudibras: / written by the /
Person whom / the Author / here satyri- / zes under yᵉ / name

of / Wachum / & printed before he wrote this second part. (*Harvard*)

34. *Carminum Poetarum novem...fragmenta.* [*See no. 134.*]

35. Cervantes. *The History of the Renown'd Don Quixote de la Mancha. Translated from the Original by Several Hands.* London: Peter Motteux. Vols. I, II: 1700. Vols. III, IV: 1703. 12º. *On the recto of the flyleaf of Vol. I, in Pope's hand, is a passage entitled:* Rapine, Reflections, p^t 2.

> We have two Modern Satires writt in Prose, w^ch / surpass all that have been writt of this Kinde / in these latter Ages. The first is Spanish, compo- / sed by CERVANTES, Secretary to the Duke of / Alva. This great Man having been slighted, and / receiv'd some Disgrace by the Duke of Lerma, the / Chief Minister of State to Philip III, who had / no respect for Men of Learning, writ the Rom- / ance Don Quixote; which is a most fine and / ingenious Satire on his own Country; because / the Nobility of Spain, whom he renders ridicu- / lous by this work, were all bit in the head & / intoxicated with Knight Errantry. This is a se- / cret I learn'd from one of my Freinds [*sic*], who recei- / ved it from Don Lope, whom Cervantes had / made the Confident of his Resentments.

On the second flyleaf recto of Vol. II, in Pope's hand: E' Libris Alex. Pope. Pret. 2^s / 1700. *On the second flyleaf of Vol. III, in Pope's hand:* E' Libris Alex: Pope. Pr. 2^s 6^d. *On the second flyleaf of Vol. IV, in Pope's hand:* E Libris Alex: Pope. Pret. 2^s 6^d   (*Mary Hyde*)

36. Chaucer, Geoffrey. *The Works of our Antient and Learned English Poet, Geffrey Chaucer, newly Printed.* London: Adam Islip, 1598. Folio. *On the flyleaf in Pope's hand:* Ex Libris / ALEXANDRI POPEI: / Ac e' Dono / GABRIELIS YOUNG. 1701. *On the recto of folio 6, column 2, "The Knightes tale," Pope has written to right of the following lines* (1975-1978): Vide / descr^t Do- / mus Martis in / Statio. Th. 7.

First on the wall was painted a forest
In which there wonneth nother man ne best
With knottie and knarie trees old
Of stubbes sharpe and hidous to behold. . . .

*Beside line 1764 of "The third booke of Fame," folio 282v,
column 2, Pope has written:* Insert here w^t Chaucer says /
pag. 278. *Throughout "The Romaunt of the Rose," Pope
makes summarizing marginalia, e.g. at folio 126v, column 2
(lines 2361-2366):* Here begins / the descrip- / tion of a / Man
in / Love, & / continues / to page / 128.   (*Hartlebury*)

37. Cicero. *Opera*. Paris: Stephanus, 1555. 2 vols. Folio. *On the
first flyleaf of Vol. I:* This Volume was given me, out of Mr
Pope's Library / at Prior Park, by the B͞p of Gloucester in
1765. / R. Hurd. *On the second flyleaf in Allen's hand:* The
Gift of Alexander Pope Esqr / To Ralph Allen in 1741. *On
the first flyleaf of Vol. II:* This Volume belonged to Mr Pope's
Library, bequeathed to Mr Allen / & after his death, to the
B͞p of Gloucester / Dr Warburton / , at Prior-Park, & was
given to me by the Bishop in 1765. / R. Hurd. *On the second
flyleaf of Vol. II in Allen's hand:* The Gift of Alexander Pope
Esqr / to Ralph Allen in 1741.   (*Smith College*)

38. ———. *Les offices de Ciceron, Traduits en Francois Sur la
Nouvelle edition Latine de Graevius. Par l'Autheur de la
Traduction des Lettres de S. Augustin*. Paris: J. B. Coignard,
1691. *No signature, but a characteristic cross beside "l'Autheur" on the title and on the title, verso, in a hand just possibly Pope's:* + M. du Bois, precepteur de dernier / Duc de
Guise, & bon ami de Messrs de Port- / Royal: Bayle Tom. 1.
p. 174.   (*Hartlebury*)

39. Clarendon, Edward Hyde, first Earl of. *The History of the
Rebellion and the Civil Wars in England*. Oxford: Printed at
the Theatre, 1707. 3 vols. 8⁰. *At rear of Vol. III, facing
opening of the Index, in Pope's hand:* Mem. / There is Extant the Histo- / ry of the Earl of Clarendon, from / this

period of the Restoration, thro' / the Reign of K. Charles 2. to y^e / Year 1670, add [*and?*] after [*overwrites* to] his own Bani- / shment: in a Manuscript in folio / of 820 pages in the possession / of the family. *A sprinkling of marginalia in the first vol. (reading Omissa, addenda, and so on) indicate that Pope had compared printed text with manuscript at some point. His young friend Viscount Cornbury was a Hyde, on whom the earldom would have devolved had he lived longer. (Mapledurham House)*

40. [Concanen, Matthew]. *A Supplement to the Profund. Containing Several Examples, very proper to Illustrate the Rules laid down in a late Treatise, called The Art of Sinking in Poetry.* . . . London: J. Roberts, 1728. Vol. II [*See number 3.*] *Pope's notes appear throughout the pamphlet. Owing to careless rebinding, some are cropped.*

    p. iv: *Pope marginally identifies "the Author of the Twickenham Auction" as:* Moore.

    p. v: *To right of the following comment Pope has written:* Yet / this remark[er] / 's observation[s] proceed al- / most all frō / His own ig / norance of / ye Greek.

> It is demonstrable to all Readers of the Greek, that this Poet has stuck so little to the original, as to give occasion to have his knowledge of it call'd in Question, and he and his Admirers seem to lay the whole Stress of his Merit upon the fine Verses of the Translation, not upon the Truth or Exactness of it. . . .

    p. 8: *To left of the following, very badly cropped:* [Ign?]-orance / [of Dei?]fication / [B?]arthius [*i.e. Kaspar von Barth, 1587-1658*] on / [th?] is.

> Yet stay, great *Caesar!* and vouchsafe to reign
> O'er the wide Earth, and o'er the watry Main;
> Resign to Jove his Empire of the Skies,
> And people *Heav'n* with *Roman* Deities.
> Pope's Statius

Quere. How far his *Resignation* of it will contribute to his *Peopling* the *Empire* of Heaven with *Roman* Gods?

    p. 12: *The author censures Pope's "Iliad," XXIII, 255:*

"And Heav'n is feasting on the World's green End," with the comment: "The World's End is comical, but the World's green End, is highly pleasant and proper." In reply, Pope writes: Milton.

The author also censures Pope's "Spring," lines 13-16, ending: "And all th' Aerial Audience clap their Wings." In reply, Pope writes: Dryden.

p. 13: *To right of the following passage Pope writes:* Spense[r] & Ph[ilips].

> Not to mention the Propriety of making an
> English Clown call a well-known Bird by a
> classical name [i.e. Philomel].

p. 17: *To right of the following passage Pope writes:* Ignorance [of the?] / Greek.

> So plain a Thing as (*they were destroyed*) is thus
> pompously express'd.
> The Gods these Objects of their Hate
> Drag'd to Destruction by the Links of Fate.
> 3d Odyssey.

p. 18: *To left of the following lines, instanced as bad grammar, Pope has written:* Dryd. / [Milt?]on.

> ——My Soul is sore
> Of fresh Affronts— Odyss. 3.

p. 23: *To right of the following comment on line 39 of his "Messiah" Pope has written:* Milton.

> For though a Ray, may, for ought I know, be
> purg'd from thick Films, &c. yet sure it can't
> be a visual Ray; by Visual, is understood a
> Power of Capacity of Vision; but I never heard
> of a Ray that was more than visible, i.e.
> capable of being seen.

p. 27: *To right of the following line Pope has written:* Spenc.ʳ

> And Pine and Penury a meagre Train.
> Odyss. 15.

What is the meaning of the word Pine in this place?

    p. 27: *To right of the following:* Igno[rance?] of [ye Greek?].

But behold here, a Line that never was, nor is, nor ever shall be match'd for Profundity.

> His Men unpractis'd in the Fights *of Stand.*
> Iliad. 9.

    p. 29: *In the following, Pope strikes out "thirdly" and inserts above it* therefore first. *After "and" he marginally supplies* then, *and underscores "lastly."*

> Swift as a *Flood of Fire,* when Storms arise,
> *Floats* the wide Field, and blazes to the skies.

What a noble Confusion is here? First it's a Flood, then it's a Fire, thirdly, it floats, and, lastly, it blazes.

    p. 32: *To left of the following passage Pope has written:* Is there such a Verb?

> Such just Examples on Offenders shown
> Sedition silence, and assert the Throne.
> Iliad. 2.

> Can any Man alive positively say, which is
> the Verb, and which the Noun, Silence or
> Sedition? Is Silence seditioned, or Sedition
> silenced?

41. *Corporis Juris Civilis Tomus Primus.* "Editio Nova." Amsterdam: Sumptibus Societatis, 1681. 2 vols. 8°. *On the flyleaf of Vol. I, in Pope's hand:* Alex. Pope / E dono Honor. Dñi de Ilay. / Jun. 1727.   (*Hartlebury*)

42. Cudworth, Ralph. *The True Intellectual System of the Universe.* London: R. Royston, 1678. Folio. *On the flyleaf, in Pope's hand:* Ex libris / A. Pope. / 1743. *Beneath this, the inscription:* This book was given me, out of Mr. Pope's / library at Prior-Park, by the Bp̄ of Gloucester / in 1765. / R. Hurd. (*Hartlebury*)

43. Cunaeus, Petrus. *Satyra Menippea Incastrata.* Leyden: ex officina I. Livi, 1632. 12°. (*Sotheby, 5 April 1939, lot 539: "from the library of Alexander Pope with his signature on fly-leaf."*)

44. Cunningham, Alexander. *Animadversiones in Ricardi Bentleii Notas et emendationas ad Q. Horat. Flaccum.* The Hague: T. Johnson, 1721. *On the flyleaf, in Allen's hand:* The Gift of / Alexander Pope Esqr / to Ralph Allen. *See also Horace.* (*Hartlebury*)

45. [Curll, Edmund]. *The Curliad. A Hypercritic upon the Dunciad Variorum. With a Farther Key to the New Characters.* London: Printed for the Author, 1729. Vol. IV. [*See number 3.*]

Dacier [Anne Lefebvre]. *L'Iliade d'Homere. See Homer.*

46. Dalacourt, James. *A Prospect of Poetry. To which is added, A Poem to Mr. Thomson on his Seasons.* Dublin printed, London reprinted: 1734. 8°. Poems, Vol. I. [*See number 15.*]

47. Dart, John. *The Complaint of the Black Knight from Chaucer.* London: J. Batley, 1718. 8°. Poems, Vol. II. [*See number 15.*]

48. [———]. *Westminster Abbey. A Poem.* London: R. Redmayne and J. Morphew, 1721. 8°. Poems, Vol. II. [*See number 15.*] *In Pope's hand, beneath the title:* By John Dart.

49. Davison, Francis. *A Poetical Rapsodie.* London: William Stansby for Roger Jackson, 1611. 12°. *On the flyleaf, in Pope's hand:* E Libris A. Pope. (*Harvard*)

50. Dennis, John. *Reflections Critical and Satyrical, upon a late Rhapsody, call'd An Essay Upon Criticism.* London: Bernard Lintott. Vol. I. [*See number 3.*] *In the following passage on p. 29, Pope marginally identifies the "old Gentleman" as* Sir

W. Trumbull *rather than as his own father as Dennis seems to have intended.*

> ...I have always been infinitely delighted with his [*Pope's*] Person: So delighted, that I have lately drawn a very graphical Picture of it; but I believe I shall keep the *Dutch Piece* from every seeing the Light, as a certain old Gentleman in *Windsor-Forest* would have done by the Original, if he durst have been half as impartial to his own Draught as I have been to mine.   (*British Museum*)

51. ———. *A True Character of Mr. Pope and His Writings.* London: S. Popping, 1716. Vol. I. [*See number 3.*] *A notation by Pope appears in the text, as follows:*

p. 16: *To left of the following lines:* as he did / ye next y^r / in his / Remarks / on Homer.

> But since his
> Friends will alledge 'tis easie to say this, I de-
> sire that it may go for nothing, till I have so
> plainly prov'd it, that the most Foolish, and the
> most Partial of them shall not be able to deny it
> [*that the Homer translation is a fraud*].

52. ———. *Remarks Upon Mr. Pope's Translation of Homer. With Two Letters Concerning Windsor Forest, and the Temple of Fame.* London: E. Curll, 1717. Vol. I. [*See number 3.*] *Notations by Pope appear in the text, as follows:*

p. 20: *Dennis cavils that to call Achilles's wrath the cause of "all" the Grecian woes is to blunder badly, because this can only mean (1) all the woes the Greeks suffered throughout their history, or (2) all the woes they suffered during the preceding nine years at Troy, or (3) all the woes it did in fact cause—each of which is absurd. To this Pope replies marginally:* Why not, y^t it was ye Spring of all ye Woes they / felt, that tenth year, of which only & no other / before or after this poet [that poem *crossed out*] sings? This being y^e / only thing it *could* mean, the Critick must not see.

p. 51: *To right of the following lines Pope has written:* wch no / dream ought to / be.

> ...this Image of the Temple of Fame, is
> contrary to Nature, and to the Eternal Laws
> of Gravitation....

53. ———. *Remarks on Mr. Pope's Rape of the Lock. In several Letters to a Friend.* London: J. Roberts, 1728. Vol. II. [*See number 3.*] *Pope's comments (selectively reprinted in truncated form in T.E., Vol. 2, App. D.) appear throughout the pamphlet.*

p. 1: *Beneath the title, "Letter I," Pope has written:* Proving that Boileau did not call his Lutrin Poeme Heroicomique, that Bossu dos not s[ay y^t ?] the Machines [*Pope leaves a blank here as if to quote Bossu*] and that Butler / [writ?] the notes to his own Hudibras.

p. 2: *To left of the following passage:* Boileau did so / Vid. prim. ed.

> ...he had publish'd what he calls his Poem,
> before he had thought of what he calls his
> *Machinery*...

p. 3: *To right of the following passage:* Bossu.

> ...his *Machinery* has no Manner of Influence
> upon what he calls his *Poem*, not in the least
> promoting, or preventing, or retarding the
> Action of it...

p. 3: *To right of the following passage:* not his

> ...the judicious Author of *Hudibras*, who has
> given this short Account of the *Rosycrucians*, in
> his Comment upon two Lines which are to be found in
> the character of *Ralpho*.

p. 5: *Beneath the title, "Letter II," Pope has written:* Mr. Dennis's positive word that the Rape of the Lock *can* be nothing but a triffle / and that the Lutrin cannot be so, however it may appear.

p. 8: *To left of the following comment, having underscored "since 'tis" and "at the Bottom cannot," Pope has written:* argum.

> Now since 'tis impossible that so judicious
> an Author as Boileau should run counter to
> his own, and to the Instructions of his Master
> *Horace,* the *Lutrin* at the Bottom cannot be an
> *empty Trifle.*

p. 8: *To left of the following (evidently to indicate that his poem, too, has an important subject)*: female sex.

> 'Tis indeed a noble and important
> satirical poem, upon the Luxury, the
> Pride, the Divisions, and Animosities of
> the Popish clergy.

p. 8: *To left of the following (cited by Dennis to show that Boileau, unlike Pope, gives hints of a serious moral)*: Clarissa's / speech.

> La Deessee en entrant, qui voit la nappe mise,
> Admire un si bel ordre; & reconnoit l'eglise.

p. 9: *In the following comment, above "Clergy" Pope has written* Ladies; *above "religion,"* sense.

> when Chri-
> stians, and especially the Clergy, run into great
> Heats about religious Trifles, their Animosity
> proceeds from the Want of that Religion which is
> the Pretence of their Quarrel.

p. 10: *Above "Battle in the Bookseller's Shop" (cited by Dennis as an example of the truly ludicrous incidents from which laughter in comedy springs) Pope writes:* of men and women for ye Loss of a Lock.

> . . .the Bat-
> tle in the Bookseller's Shop, &c. And where-
> as there are a thousand such in *Hudibras*
> There is not so much as one, nor the Shadow
> of one, in the *Rape of the Lock.*

p. 11: *Beneath the title "Letter III" Pope has written:* Where it appears to demonstration that no handsome Lady ought to dress herself, and no / modest one to cry out or be angry.

p. 15: *In the comment below, where Dennis prefers the disheveled Phanium (in Terence's "Phormio") to Belinda because more "natural," Pope underscores "ev'n in Rags" and "have . . . Nature," placing beside the latter clause as a substitution the words:* love a W.[ench?] i[n?] [Rags?].

> . . . How much more charming does this *Terentian*
> Virgin appear, ev'n in Rags and Misery, than Belinda
> does at her Toilette? I mean to those who have a
> Taste of Nature.

p. 17: *To right of the following Pope writes:* Hampton / Court has [a] / wood.

> She must set up her Throat at a hellish Rate,
> to make the Woods (where, by the by, there are
> none) and the Canals replay to it.

p. 25: *Where Dennis argues that there is no opposition of the "Machines" to each other in the Rape, observing that Umbriel is not introduced till Ariel and his cohorts have quitted Belinda, Pope comments marginally:* because they [see?] / a Gnome & E[arthly?] / Lover, pre[sent?].

pp. 25-26: *Dennis quotes Canto II, 73-80, 87-90, with the following comment:*

> Question: Did you ever hear before that the
> Planets were roll'd by the *aerial* kind?
> We have heard indeed of Angels and Intelli-
> gences who have performed these Functions:
> But they are vast glorious Beings, of *Celestial*
> Kind, and Machines of another System. Pray
> which of the aerial Kind have these *sublime*
> Employments? For nothing can be more ri-
> diculous, or more contemptible than the Em-
> ployments of those whom he harangues. . . .

Beside the quotation, Pope marginally replies to Dennis's misreading by inserting AEtheri [al?] beside line 77, aerial / beneath y^e / moon *beside lines 79-80, and* Our humbler province *after line 90, (with* Our *underscored). Beside the criticism itself, he inserts:* expressly otherwise.

p. 29: *To right of the first sentence Pope has written:* allegorical; *to right of the last words of the second:* and to Poetry.

> In the fourth [canto], Spleen
> and the Phantoms about, are deriv'd from the
> Powers of Nature, and are of a separate
> System. And Fate and Jove, which we find
> in the fifth Canto, belong to the Heathen Religion.

p. 30: *Beneath the title "Letter V" Pope has written:* Sheweth, that the Rosicrucian Doctrine is not the Christian, and that Callimachus and Catullus were fools a couple of fools. *The first* fools *is cancelled.*

p. 38: *To left of the following:* [Vid?]e Callimachus / [Vid?]e Catullus.

> Why, who the Devil, besides this Bard, ever
> made a Wonder of it? What! before *Troy*
> Town, and triumphal Arches were built was
> the cutting off a Lock of Hair a *miraculous*
> Thing?

p. 40: *In reply to the comment below, Pope cites marginally the visit of the Fury Allecto in Aeneid VII to stir up Latinus's queen, Amata:* [ye sam?] e y^t makes [Juno?]s to Alecto / [to infur?] yate Amata. *The words are badly cropped.*

> Now to what Purpose does this fantastick
> Being take the Journey? Why, to give *Be-*
> *linda* the Spleen.

p. 41: *To right of the following, Pope writes:* So was Ama[ta?] / before. Foemi[neae?] / ardentem cu[raeque?] / iraeque coque[ebant?]:

> How absurd was it then for this Ignis *Fatuus*
> to take a journey down to the central Earth,
> for no other Purpose than to give her the
> *Spleen,* whom he left and found in the Height
> of it?

p. 46: *To the following stricture, applied by Dennis to Canto V, 45-52, Pope marginally replies:* [Lon?]ginus:

> But the latter Part of it is not taken from Homer,
> but from his most impertinent Imitator, Mon-
> sieur *De la Motte,* and neither the one
> nor the other Trifler seems to have known any thing
> in this Passage, of the Solemnity, and
> the dreadful Majesty of *Homer.*

p. 48: *Beneath the second verse Pope has written:* Still burn on, *with evident reference to the 1712 variant* "And still burn on, in *Cupid's* Flames *Alive.*"

> Rather than so, ah! let me still survive,
> And burn in Cupid's Flames, but burn alive.

Now, Sir, who ever heard of a dead Man that burnt in *Cupid's* Flames.

p. 36 (2d ser.): *To right of the following Pope writes:* Virgils / Georg.

> For here [in *Rape* I, 1-2] the Verb Active *sing*
> has no Accusative Case depending on it. . . .

54. ———. *Remarks Upon Several Passages in The Prelimi-naries to the Dunciad, Both of the Quarto and the Duode-cimo Edition. And Upon Several Passages in Pope's Preface to his Translation of Homer's Iliad.* London: H. Whitridge, 1729. Vol. IV. [*See number 3.*]

55. Donne, John. *Pseudo-Martyr.* London: W. Stansby for Walter Burre, 1710. 4°. *The third edition of Sir Geoffrey Keynes's "Bibliography of the Works of John Donne" (1958) locates at Trinity College, Oxford, "Pope's copy with his index." The Trinity librarian informs me, however, that the library has no record of owning such a copy, and Sir Geoffrey (18 November 1975): "Either I was wrong about the location and had seen it somewhere else, or the book has gone missing." There the matter rests for the time being.*

56. Drub, Timothy [pseud.]. *A Letter to Mr. John Gay, Concerning His late Farce, Entituled, A Comedy.* London: J. Roberts, 1717. Vol. I. [*See number 3.*]

57. Dryden, John. *Annus Mirabilis.* [*See no. 58.*]

58. ———. *A Poem Upon the Death of His Late Highness, Oliver, Lord Protector of England, Scotland, & Ireland.* London: for William Wilson, 1659 [Tonson, 1691]. Bound with: *Annus Mirabilis. The Year of Wonders, MDCLXVI.* [London:] Jacob Tonson for H. Herringman, 1688. 4⁰. (Sotheby, 10 February 1970, lot 213: *"In neat italic capitals, on a flyleaf:* ALEXANDER POPE. ")

59. ———. *Fables Ancient and Modern.* London: Jacob Tonson, 1700. Folio. *On the title page, in Pope's hand:* A Pope. (*University of Pennsylvania*)

60. ———. *The Comedies, Tragedies, and Operas.* London: Jacob Tonson, Thomas Bennet, and Richard Wellington, 1701. 2 vols. Folio. *On the title page of Vol. II, in Pope's hand:* Alex. Pope. / Pr. 15ˢ *Pope has made comments in the text about the derivation of certain passages and the authorship of certain plays. (For a discussion of his markings, see R. D. Erlich and James Harner, "Pope's Annotations in His Copy of Dryden's Comedies, Tragedies, and Operas," in Restoration and 18th Century Theatre Research, 10 [1971]: 14-24.)*

An Evening's Love: Or, the Mock Astrologer. III, i, 11. 86-87: *To left of the following lines Pope has written:* Vid. Moliere's / Precieuses, Act 2.

> Aur.　How am I drest to Night, Camilla? Is nothing
> 　　　　　disorder'd in my Head?
> Cam.　Not the least hair, Madam.

Ibid., III, i, 11. 330-334: *To left of the following lines:* Vide Moliere's / Depit Amor- / eux, the Scene / between Albᵗ / & Metaphraste.

Lop. If you will please to favour me with your Patience,
which I beg of you a second time.
Alon. I am dumb, Sir.
Lop. This Cavalier, of whom I was speaking, is in Love—
Alon. Satisfie your self, Sir, I'll not interrupt you.

Ibid., IV, i, 11. 526-529: *To left of the following:* Vid. Moliere's / Avare, act. 5. / scen. 3. toward / ye middle.

Mel. Your Daughter is indeed a Jewel, but she were not lost,
were she in possession of a Man of parts.
Alon. A precious Diamond, Sir—
Mel. But a Man of Honour, Sir.

The Assignation: or, Love in a Nunnery. IV, iv, 11. 65-69:
To left of the following: Vid. Moliere.

Luc. This begins to please me.
But, why should you be so much my Enemy?
Fred. Your Enemy, Madam; Why, do you desire it?
Luc. Perhaps I do.
Fred. Do it, Madam, since it pleases you so well.

Oedipus. *At the close of the Preface:* N. B. The first and
third Acts of this Play were wholly writ by Mr Dry- / den, the
rest by N. Lee. Mr. Dryden also drew the Scenery, and designed / the Whole.

The Duke of Guise. *At the close of the "Letter to the Rt. Hon.
Laurence Earl of Rochester.":* N. B. Mr. Dryden writ of this
Play only / the first Scene of the first Act, the en- / tire fourth
Act, and the first half of / the fifth.   (*University of Illinois*)

61. *Epistolae Obscurorum Virorum ad Dn. M. Ortuinum Gra-
tium.* Frankfürt: 1643. 18mo. (*Parke-Bernet, 17 April 1945,
lot 302:* "On the flyleaf . . . : Ex Libris Thos: Monson, *then in
Pope's handwriting:* nunc Alex. Pope, *below which is* nunc
Jonath. Swift.")

62. Felibien, Jean Francois. *Recueil Historique de la vie et des
ouvrages des plus celebres architectes.* Amsterdam: Estienne
Roger, 1706. 8°. *On the title page, in Pope's hand:* E Libris
A. Pope.   (*University of Illinois*)

63. Fenelon, Francois Salignac. *Adventures of Telemachus*. London: 1700. *On the flyleaf, in Pope's hand:* E' Libris Alex: Pope. 1702 / Pr. 2ˢ   (*Harvard*)

64. ———. *Les Aventures de Télémaque*. "Premier edition conforme au manuscrit original." Paris: Florentin Delaulne, 1717. 2 vols. 12ᴼ. *On the title page of each volume (in Gay's hand):* J. Gay, *and on the flyleaf of Vol. I in Pope's hand:* This book was once / Mͬ Gay's, next Mͬ Pope's, / now Mͬˢ Blount's. / 1734.   (*Privately owned*)

65. Fenton, Elijah. *Poems on Several Occasions*. London: Bernard Lintot, 1717. 8ᴼ. (*Hodgson, 24 March 1927, lot 17: On the verso of the frontispiece, "in the handwriting of Alexander Pope:* Ex Libris A. Pope. Donum Authoris.")

66. Fitzgerald, Thomas. *Poems on Several Occasions*. London: J. Watts, 1733. 8ᴼ. *On the title page, in Pope's hand:* The Authors Gift sent / by Mr Wesley. Sepͬ 11. / 1733.   (*Cambridge University*)

67. Garth, Samuel. *The Dispensary. A Poem. In Six Canto's.* "The Fifth Edition." London: John Nutt, 1703. 8ᴼ. *On the leaf facing Garth's portrait, in Pope's hand:* E Libris / ALEXANDRI POPEI. / Donum Autoris. / Pretium 2 s. *Below this, in William Mason's hand:* Alexander Pope / Gulielmo Warburton / Moriens Legavit / 1744. / Gulielmus Warburton / Gulielmo Mason / Dono Dedit / 1752. *Below this, presumably in the hand of St. Helens:* Gulielmus Alderson / cuius patri (ομωνομῳ) [*apparently, for* ὁμονόμῳ] / Gulˢ Mason Legaverat / Alleynio Barˢ de Sͭ Helens / Dono dedit. / 1815 / *Below this, in a similar (but evidently not the same?) hand:* D. D. Samueli Rogers A Bͭ Sͭ Helens 15 Nov. breve moriturus. (*St. Helens died 19 February 1839.*) *The "A" is extraneous and puzzling. A further inscription appears on the blank page facing the dedication:* Lot 391. Bought May 13ᵗʰ 1856 at Christie / & Manson's at the sale of the Library of Samuel / Rogers for £12:15:0. George Daniel.

Pope marginally identifies many of the proper names. On an end leaf, he has made the following notes on the poem:

> Dispensary; p. 13. Lin. 1ˢᵗ Cant. 2. [*"Soon as with gentle Sighs the Ev'ning Breeze"*] seems contradictory to lin. 4. [*"While Winds lay hush'd in Subterranean Beds"*].
> P. 15. lin. 11. [*"As the' airy Messenger the Fury spy'd"*] is contradictory to lin. 12 & 13. [*"Awhile his curdling Blood forgot to glide. / Confusion on his fainting Vitals hung"*].
> P. 83. lin. 9. contradicts it self. [*"Here his forsaken Seat old Chaos keeps"*].
> P. 71. lin. 10. [*"And uncontroll'd Dominion of the Main"*] is taken intirely from Blackmores Pr. Ar. [*London, 1695*] p. 130.
> P. 80. lin. 5. &c, are hinted from Blackmore, ibid, p. 97.
> [*lines 9-16*].   (*Victoria and Albert Museum*)

68. Garth, Samuel. *The Dispensary. A Poem. In Six Canto's.* "The Sixth Edition." London: John Nutt, 1706. 8⁰. *On the flyleaf, in Pope's hand:* E Libris Alex: Pope. 1706. *Pope has marginally identified a number of the proper names.* (*Huntington*)

69. Gay, John. *Trivia: or, the Art of Walking the Streets of London.* London: Bernard Lintott, n.d. [*1716*]. 8⁰. (*Parke-Bernet, 9 January 1945, lot 393:* "On the front flyleaf in Pope's hand: Ex dono Authoris.")

70. Glover, Richard. *Leonidas, A Poem.* London: R. Dodsley, 1737. 4⁰. *On the flyleaf in Glover's hand:* Autoris Donum / A⁰ Pope. 1737.   (*Privately owned*)

71. Granville, George, Lord Lansdowne. *Poems upon Several Occasions.* London: J. Tonson, 1712. 8⁰. *On the flyleaf in Pope's hand:* Ex Libris A. Pope. Donum Authoris.   (*University of Illinois*)

72. Hall, Joseph. *Virgidemiarum; The three last Bookes.* [See no. 73.]

73. ———. *Virgidemiarum Sixe Bookes. First Three Bookes, of*

Tooth-lesse Satyrs. 1. Poeticall. 2. Academicall. 3. Moral.
London: John Harison for Robert Dexter, 1602. [*Bound with*
"The three last Bookes. Of Byting Satyres." London: I. H. for
Robert Dexter, 1599.] 8°. *On the blank leaf following the*
1602 title is a note by J. West: J. West. / This Book was given
me by / Alexander Pope Esq. who at the / same time told me
he thought / It contained the best poetry & truest Satyr of any
of our / English poets & that he inte[n]ded to modernise them
as he had done Dr. Donnes. / The Book is very scarce. I never
/ saw but this & one other Copy.   (*Harvard*)

74. ———. *Another copy of no. 72. [See no. 75.]*

75. ———. *Another copy of no. 73, also having a copy of no. 72*
bound in after it. There is no signature by Pope in this vol-
ume, but in Hurd's copy of a later edition of the same work
[*Oxford, 1753*] *are these inscriptions, giving evidence of*
Pope's ownership of the volume. (*This is further confirmed*
by the many small textual revisions in his hand, which tend to
support Warburton's inference.) In a Letter from Mr Warburton to / me / Feb. 24. 1753 / are these words- / "You will
be pleased to know / that looking into Mr Pope's Library I /
found an edition of your favorite / Satires of Hall. The first
Satire / of his sixth Book he has marked / thus — Sat. opt. and
has corrected the versification thru'out. So I / fancy he designed to publish it / as he had done Donne. My / favorite is
1 Sat. B. iii." / This edition of Hall's Satires / is not now in
Mr Pope's (i.e. my) / Library. / R. W. *A later addition:* I
have since met with it. It is now / [July 18, 1801] in Hartlebury Library. See / B. C. 28 [London 1602]. *On the flyleaf*
in another hand: Suum cuique / Tho: Hearne / Febr. 8°.
1724. / Ex dono amici doctissimi / Rich^di Graves, de Mickle-
ton / in agro Gloucestriensi, armigeri. / The Author Jos Hall
of Ema- / nuel College in Cambridge.   (*Hartlebury*)

76. Harte, Walter. *An Essay on Satire, Particularly on the Dun-*
ciad. To which is added, A Discourse on Satires, Arraigning
Persons by Name. By Monsieur Boileau. London: Lawton
Gilliver, 1730. 8°. Poems, Vol. I. [*See number 15.*]

77. Harvey, Christopher. *The Synagogue.* [*See no. 78.*]

78. Herbert, George. *The Temple. Sacred poems, and private ejaculations.* "The sixth Edition." Cambridge: Roger Daniel, 1641. 8⁰. *Bound with:* Harvey, Christopher. *The Synagogue, or the Shadow of the Temple. Sacred Poems and Private Ejaculations.* "The second Edition." London: J. L. for Philemon Stephens, 1647. 8⁰. *On the flyleaf preceding "The Temple," in Pope's hand:* E Libris Al. Pope. Iun. 1700. / Pret. 1. s. (*Mary Hyde*)

79. Herodotus. *The History of Herodotus.* Tr. from the Greek by Isaac Littlebury. London: 1709. 2 vols. 8⁰. *On the flyleaf of each volume in Pope's hand:* Ex Libris Alexandri Pope. / Pr: 4ˢ 6ᵈ   (*Hartlebury*)

80. [Hill, Aaron]. *The Progress of Wit: A Caveat. By Gamaliel Gunson, Professor of Physick and Astrology.* London: J. Wilford, 1730. Vol. IV. [*See number 3.*]

81. ———. *Alzira. A Tragedy.* London: John Osborn, 1736. 8⁰. *On the flyleaf in Hill's hand:* August yᵉ 7ᵗʰ — 1736. / To Alexander Pope Esqʳ / from His / most humble / & obedient Servant / A. Hill.   (*Harvard*)

82. Hobbes, Thomas. *Leviathan.* London: Andrew Crooke, 1651. Folio. *On the flyleaf in Pope's hand:* Ex libris / A. Pope. *Beneath this, in Hurd's hand:* Given me by the B̄p of Gloucester out / of Mr. Pope's Library at Prior Park 1765. / R. Hurd (*Hartlebury*)

———. *Homer's Iliads and Odysses. See Homer.*

83. Homer. OMHPOϒ IΛIAΣ Paris: Adr. Turnebus, 1554. 12⁰. *See "The Atterbury Correspondence," ed. John Nichols, III (1784), 518:* "Pope gave the Bishop the Paris edition of Homer, of Turnebus, 1554, as appears by the following memorandum on a blank page of it, which I have been permitted to copy: Fr. Rossen. / Homeri Iliaden / Typis his niti-

dissimis Graecè editam, / Dono mihi dedit, / Qui eandem
Carmine Anglicano, / Musis Gratiisque faventibus, expres-
sam, / Genti nostrae prius donaverat / Alexander Pope. /
— quantum instar in ipso est / Haud fuerit quamquam, quem
Tu sequereris, Homere, / est tamen, est qui Te possit, Homere, sequi." *The aphorism about Homer is found in Velleius
Paterculus, I. v. 2, but Atterbury seems to be following from
memory the verse version of Alcimus:*

> si potuit nasci, quem tu sequereris, Homere,
> nascitur, qui te possit, Homere, sequi.

84. ———. *The Iliad of Homer Prince of Poets.* Tr. George
Chapman. London: Nathaniel Butter, n.d. [*1611*]. Folio. *On
the front end paper, in T. Warton's hand:* T. Warton. Ex
Dono Gul. Episc. Gloc. *On the flyleaf preceding the title
page, in Pope's hand:* Ex Libris Alexandri Popei. Pret: 3.^{SS}
*Pope's markings in the book are recorded in T.E., VII 474-
491.* (*Yale*)

85. ———. ΟΜΗΡΟΥ ΙΛΙΑ ΚΑΙ ΟΔΥΣΣΕΙΑ. Ed. Cornelius
Schrevel. Leyden: Francis Hacke, 1656. 2 vols. in one. 4°. *On
the flyleaf in Pope's hand:* Ex Libris / ALEXANDRI POPE; /
V. C. Joannes Trevor Eques, Custos / Rotulorum, Dono
dedit. / Anno 1715. (*Hartlebury*)

86. ———. *Iliads and Odysses.* Tr. Thomas Hobbes. London:
William Crook, 1686. 2 vols. in one. 12 mo. (*Parke-Bernet,
8 May 1945, lot 347: "Pope's... autograph signature on flyleaf and manuscript notes throughout."*)

87. ———. *Homeri opera quae extant omnia. Graece et Latine.*
Ed. Stephen Bergler. Amsterdam: Henry Wetstein, 1707.
2 vols. 12mo. *On the flyleaf of Vol. I, in Pope's hand:* Ex Libris A. Pope. / Donum Dñi Pellet, M.D. / 1714. / E Libris A.
Pope. / 1714 / Finish'd ye Translation / In Feb. of 1719-20. /
A. Pope. *On the end paper is a pencil sketch of an unidenti-
fied structure by Pope. On the flyleaf, beneath Pope's signature, is the note:* This book belonged to Mr Pope, / and the

Drawing is by him. / Horace Walpole / 1766. / It is a View of
Twickenham Church / from his own garden. *On the rear end
paper of Vol. II is an autograph draft of Pope's epitaph on
Mrs. Corbet differing considerably from the published text,
together with some tentatives toward Odyssey, XXI 471-478.
(See above, pp. 227-229.) On the page facing the poem there
is a pencil draft in Pope's hand of a lapidary inscription in
Latin:* Virtuti & Fortunae / —Jo: / Hoc Saxum / Memoriae &
Gloriae / Sacrum / Car. Comes Cart. P. *Also on the flyleaf of
the volume, in Pope's hand:* E Libris A. Pope. / Donum Dñi
Pellet, M.D. / 1714.   (*Lewis Walpole Library*)

88. Dacier [Anne Lefebvre]. *L'Iliade d'Homere, Traduite en
Francois, Avec des Remarques, par Madame Dacier.* Paris:
Rigaud, 1711. 3 vols. 12º. *On the flyleaf of Vol. I, in Pope's
hand:* Ex libris Alex: Pope. / Simon Harcourt, / Homericae
favens Versioni, / Dº Dᵗ / Apr. 20. 1714. *Volumes II and III
are of the second edition (1719) and cannot have been included in Harcourt's gift of 1714. They do not bear Pope's
signature and thus may or may not have been his. In Vol. I,
Pope has made a number of notations in the text about Mme.
Dacier's sources, as follows:*

p. 452: *To left of the following passage:* out of / Sponda
/ nus / verba- / tim.

> On respond premierement qu'Homere dit que Minerve
> conduisit le trait, & en second lieu que mesme sans avoir
> recours au miracle, le coup peut avoir esté donné, pendant
> que Pandarus se baissoit, ou bien encore qu'un homme à pied
> pouvant prendre l'avantage du terrein, Diamede pouvoit
> estre monté sur quelque eminence, qui faisoit que Pandarus,
> quoyque sur son char, estoit pourtant au dessous de luy.

p. 462: *To left of the following passage:* Milton.

> [Le Pere des Dieux & des hommes sous rit]. Jupiter
> ne rit point; il ne fait que sousrire, car le rire n'est
> pas de la majesté du maistre des Dieux, il n'y a que le
> sousrire qui luy convienne.

p. 470: *Beneath the following passage:* Spondanus ad
verbum.

...*Et leur feroit perdre tout le fruit de leurs travaux*]. Car, comme Agamemmon l'a desja fait entendre dans le 3. livre, Menelas mort, la guerre estoit finie, & les Grecs n'auroient plus pensé qu'à leur retour.

p. 476: *To left of the following passage:* agst this.

Pour faire sentir l'avantage infini que la langue Grecque a sur la nostre, je voudrais qu'un grand poëte entreprist de mettre en vers toute la fabrique d'un char. On verroit une grande difference.

p. 481: *To right of the following passage:* Cum tanta / apparatu, / a Spondano / furata & haec omnia.

Je ne puis m'empescher de dire icy un mot, pour faire sentir à ceux qui ont encore besoin de secours la force & la beauté du parallele offençant que Minerve fait de Diomede & de Tydée son pere; car je suis persuadée que ces sortes de remarques peuvent estre plus utiles que toutes celles qu'on peut faire sur des poincts d'antiquité.

p. 484: *Beneath the following passage:* out of Eustathius.

Ce n'est autre chose qu'une regle tortue, qui juge tout de travers, & qui veut rendre tortu ce qu'il y a de plus droit.

p. 492: *To left of the following passage:* Sponda / nus.

Il faut bien remarquer la noblesse de ce sentiment de Nestor: en exhortant les Grecs au combat, il dit, *ne pensons,* κτείνωμεν, pour se mettre aussi de la partie malgré son grand âge.

p. 496: *To left of the following passage:* Eusta- / thius.

On pretend que cette fable est fondée sur ce que Lycurgue arracha la plupart des

vignes de son pays, & que ses sujets, qui
auparavant beuvoient le vin pur, furent
obligez d'y mettre beaucoup d'eau, ce qui
donna lieu de dire que Thetis l'avoit recue
dans son sein.

p. 499: *To right of the following passage:* Plutarch de /
curiositate.

Quelle fidelité! Plutarque dit fort bien que la
mesme vertu que fortifia Bellerophon contre les pour-
suites de la Reyne, le munit aussi contre le vice de
la curiosité: *Bellerophon,* dit-il, *n'ouvrit pas les
lettres qui estoient escrites contre luy.* . . .

p. 499: *To right of the following passage:* In Ogilby.

Qui n'estoit pas de race mortelle, mais divine]
C'est pour dire que c'estoit un monstre d'une
grandeur énorme, comme les Hebreux ont dit *une
montagne divine,* pour *une montagne fort haute.*

p. 502: *Beneath each of the following passages:* Eustathe.

. . .des gens qui avoient entre eux le droit
d'hospitalité, quelque ancien qu'il fust, auroient
crû estre maudits de Dieu & des hommes, s'ils
l'avoient violé.

. . .on gardoit avec beaucoup de soin ces presens
dans sa famille comme des gages durables de ce droit
d'hospitalité, qu'on estoit obligé de transmettre à
ses descendants d'âge en âge.

p. 503: *To right of the following passage:* Spond.

*Et pour derniere ressource, venez vous dans la
citadelle eslever vos mains*] Hecube connoissoit
trop Hector pour croire qu'il s'enfuit de la bataille. . . .

p. 506: *To right of the following passage:* Spond.

[*La belle Theano, fille de Cissee & femme du
vaillant Antenor*] Voila donc Minerve qui a
pour grande prestresse, non une fille, mais

une femme, & une femme qui a encore son mari.
Cela merite d'estre remarqué.

p. 507: *To right of the following passage:* Spon. / vid. if / in Eustat.

Helenus avoit ordonné qu'on demandast seulement
à Minerve d'esloigner Diomede des remparts de
Troye: mais Theano ne borne pas la ses prieres:
les femmes ne sont pas si moderées dans les
prieres qu'elles font contre leurs ennemis. . . .

p. 510: *To left of the following passage:* Spon. *and* Translat / Sponda / here:

. . . sa faute, comme s'il n'avoit pas este en son
pouvoir d'empescher que les Dieux avoient resolu.

Cet endroit
est d'autant plus difficile qu'il paroist aisé, &
qu'on croit d'abord l'entendre, & j'avoue que c'est
Eustathe qui ma remise dans le bon chemin, en m'
avertissant, qu'Helene parle ainsi par rapport au
reproche deguisé & couvert qu'Hector vient de faire
à Paris. . . .

(*Hartlebury*)

89. ———. ΙΛΙΑ ΚΑΙ ΟΔΥΣΣΕΙΑ. Ed. Josua Barnes. Cambridge: Cornelius Crownfield, 1711. 2 vols. 4⁰. *On the flyleaf of Vol. I in Pope's hand:* Ex Libris Alex. Pope. / Donum Honoratissimi / DOMINI, / Caroli, Baronˢ de Halifax / 1714. *On the flyleaf of Vol. II in Pope's hand:* Ex Libris Alex. Pope, / Donum Honoratiss. Domini / Caroli Baron. de Halifax. (*Hartlebury*)

See also Tickell, Thomas.
See also Parnell, Thomas.
See also Wesley, Samuel.

90. Horace. *Opera.* Ed. Daniel Heins. Leyden: Elzevir, 1629. 16mo. *On the third flyleaf, in Pope's hand:* A. Pope *and on*

the fourth flyleaf: Ex libris Alexandri Popei. / Pret. 15.ˢ
Pasted below the signature on the third flyleaf is a scrap of
paper bearing a playful Latin inscription (struck through),
also in Pope's hand: Alexander Pope / Poeta Anglus / floruit
/ MDCCXL. / H.   M. / Optimo   viro / Gulielmus   Glocest.
Episc. / amicitiae causa / caste posuit. *On the second flyleaf,*
presumably in Smith's hand, is the inscription: M. S. Smith /
C. C. C. Oxon. / dedit dono Vir illust.ᵐᵘˢ / Gul: Episc:
Gloc: — 1778. *The book is described by Bonamy Dobrée in*
"Times Literary Supplement," 12 August 1939.   (*Univer-*
sity of Leeds)

91. ———. *Art of Poetry.* Tr. Ben Jonson. London: I. Okes for
John Benson, 1640. 12mo. *On the back flyleaf is a note:* G.
Furman, / 1829 Brooklyn, L.I. / This book once belonged to
A. Pope of Twickenham, the poet, & had his autograph on
the dedication leaf, which was cut off by some person more
fond of such curiosities than they were of doing to others as
they would be done by. The volume afterwards was owned by
William Gifford, Esq. Editor of the Quarterly Review, London. *The dedication leaf is indeed mutilated, but there re-*
mains a horizontal line resembling the flourish Pope often
made just beneath his signature in his books. The flyleaf (?)
testifying to Gifford's ownership has been removed alto-
gether. G. Furman is Gabriel Furman (1800-1854), Brooklyn
judge, and New York legislator, a passionate bookcollector
and literary antiquarian, author of "Notes, Geographical and
Historical, Relating to the Town of Brooklyn, on Long
Island" (1824).   (*Yale*)

92. ———. *Opera.* Ed. Ludovicus Desprez. Amsterdam: 1695.
On the flyleaf, in Pope's hand: Ex libris Alexandri Popei /
Pret. 7.ˢ 1707.   (*Hartlebury*)

93. ———. *Poemata.* Ed. Alexander Cunningham. London:
Vaillant and Prevost, 1721. 8º. *On the flyleaf in Pope's hand:*
A. Pope *and below this, in Allen's hand:* The Gift of / Alex-
ander Pope Esq / to Ralph Allen / in 1742.   (*Hartlebury*)

See also Cunningham.

94. Houbraken, [J.], Vertue, [G.], and Birch, [T.]. *Heads of Illustrious Persons of Great Britain.* 85 copper plates. No title or text. 1735-1744. (Sotheby, 2 June 1931, lot 555: *"Apparently this copy previously belonged to Pope who bequeathed it to Mrs. Blount. See inscription [not reproduced] inside."*)

95. Huet, Pierre Daniel. *Demonstratio Evangelica ad Serenissimum Delphinum.* "Tertia Editio." Paris: Daniel Hortemels, 1690. Folio. *On the flyleaf in Warburton's hand:* Warburton / Donum Alex. Pope / Poetarum facile Principis / Viri summi atque amicissimi   (*Hartlebury*)

96. Hughes, John. *The Siege of Damascus. A Tragedy.* London: John Watts, 1720. 8°. *See p. 230, n. 13.*

97. Hume, David. *A Treatise of Human Nature.* London: John Noon, 1739. 3 vols. 8°. *On the flyleaf of Vol. I, in Hume's hand:* To / Alexander Pope Esq. / at / Twickenham. *With Hume's corrections of several printer's errors.*   (*Mary Hyde*)

98. [Jacob, Giles]. *The Mirrour: Or, Letters Satirical, Panegyrical, Serious and Humorous, on the Present Times... To which is added A legal Conviction of Mr. Alexander Pope of Dulnes and Scandal, in the high Court of Parnassus.* London: J. Roberts, 1733. Vol. IV. [*See number 3.*]

99. Jonson, Ben. *The Works of Ben Jonson, which were formerly Printed in Two Volumes, are now Reprinted in One.* London: Thomas Hodgkin for H. Herringman et al., 1692. Folio. *On the title page, in Pope's hand:* Alex: Pope. pr. 18.ˢ *Pope's notes appear throughout the volume, as follows:*

Every Man in his Humour. II, v, 11. 51-53: *To left of line 52 Pope has placed an asterisk, and at the bottom of the page the note:* *Boletum condire, & eodem jure natantes Mergere ficedulas didicit, nebulone parente, / Et cana monstrante gula. — & a magna non degenerare culina. Juv. 14. [*lines 8-10, 14*].

> ...Neither have I
> Drest Snails or Mushrooms curiously before him,
> Perfum'd my Sauces, and taught him to make 'em....

Every Man out of his Humour. I, iii, 11. 118-119: *To left of line 119, Pope has placed an asterisk, and at the bottom of the page the note:* *—Populus me sibilat, at mihi plaudo Ipse domi, simul ac num- / mos contemplor in arca. / Horat Sat. I. Lib. I [*11. 66-67*].

> Poor Worms, they hiss at me, whilst I at home
> Can be contented to applaud my self....

Sejanus. I, 1. 33: *Pope has placed an "X" to left of the line and at the bottom of the page has written:* X - rides? majore cachinno Concutitur; - si dixeris, aestuo, sudat. / — laudare paratus, Si bene ructavit, si rectum minxit amicus, / Si trulla inverso crepitum dedit aurea fundo. Juv. Sat. 3. [*11. 100-101, 103, 106-108*].

> Laugh when their Patron laughs; sweat when he sweats....

Epigrams. XLII. *Pope has marked the penultimate line of "On Giles and Jone" with an asterisk, and at the bottom of the page has written:* *Cum sitis similes paresq. vita, / Uxor pessima, pessimus maritus; / Miror, non bene convenire vobis! Mart. Lib. 8. Ep. 34. [*In modern editions, Epigram 35.*]

> If now, with Man and Wife, to will, and nill
> The self-same Things, a note of Concord be:
> I know no Couple better can agree!

The Forest. II. *Pope has placed an asterisk beside the title "To Penshurst," and at the bottom of the page has written:* *Natat ad magistrum delicata murena, / Et adesse jussi prodeunt senes Mulli. Mart. lib. 10. ep. 30. [*11. 22, 24.*] An asterisk has also been placed to left of line 33 in the same column [*11. 32-33*]:

> Thou hast thy Ponds, that pay thee tribute Fish,
> Fat, aged Carps, that run into thy Net.

The Forest. III. To Sir Robert Wroth. 11. 67-68: *Pope has placed an asterisk to left of line 68, and at the bottom of the page has written:* *The Hint of w^t follows, is taken from Virg. Geor. 2: / Sollicitant alii remis freta caeca, ruuntq. in ferrum, penetrant aulas & / limina regum; Hic petit excidiis urbem miserosq. penates, Ut gemma bi- / bat & Sarrano indormiat ostro. &c. [*Georgics II, 11. 503-506.*]

> Let others watch in guilty Arms, and stand
> The fury of a rash command. . . .

The Forest. V. To Celia. 11. 6-8: *Pope has placed an asterisk to left of line 6 and at the bottom of the page has written:* * Soles occidere & redire possunt, Nobis quum semel occidit brevis Lux. / Nox est perpetua una dormienda. Catull. Ep. 5. [*11. 4-6.*]

> Suns, that set, may rise again:
> But, if once we lose this Light,
> 'Tis, with us, perpetual Night.

The Forest. VI. To the Same. *Pope has placed an asterisk next to line 5 and in the margin has written:* Catullus, Ep. 5.

> Kiss again: no Creature comes.

The Forest. XII. Epistle. To Elizabeth Countess of Rutland. 11. 51-53: *Pope has placed an asterisk to left of line 51, and at the bottom of the page has written:* * Vixere fortes ante Agamemnona Multi, sed omnes illacrymabiles / Urgentur, ignotiq. longa Nocte, carent quia vate sacro. Hor. lib. 4. Ode 9.

> *Achilles* was not first, that valiant was,
> Or, in an Army's head, that lockt in brass,
> Gave killing strokes.

Underwoods. The Hour-Glass. *Pope has marked the poem with an "X" and in the margin has written:* X Translated from an / Italian Poet, Hier. / Amaltheo.

Underwoods. An Execration upon Vulcan. 11. 5-10. *Pope has underscored the last five words of line 8, and the last eight words of line 10, and in the margin has written:* Vulcanum in / cornu geris. / Plaut. [*Amphitruo, I, i, 1. 185.*]

> I ne're attempted *Vulcan* 'gainst thy Life;
> Nor made least Line of Love to thy Loose Wife;
> Or in remembrance of thy afront, and scorn
> With Clowns, and Tradesmen, kept thee clos'd in Horn.
> 'Twas *Jupiter* that hurl'd thee headlong down,
> And *Mars,* that gave thee a Lanthorn for a Crown.

On the front and back flyleaves of the book is the beginning of an index to the text in Pope's hand, headed: TABLE to the First Part of BEN. Jonson.   (*Yale*)

See also Horace.

100. Juvenal. *D. Junii Juvenal, et Auli Persii Flacci Satyrae.* Ed. Cornelius Schrevel. Leyden and Rotterdam: Ex officina Hackiana, 1664. 8°. *On the flyleaf in Allen's hand:* The Gift of Alexander / Pope Esq. to Ralph Allen / in 1742. (*Hartlebury*)

101. Juvenal. *Satirae.* [*See no. 148.*]

102. ———. *The Satires of Decimus Junius Juvenalis. Translated into English verse by Mr. Dryden and Several other Eminent hands. Together with the Satires of Aulus Persius Flaccus. Made English by Mr. Dryden.* London: Jacob Tonson, 1693. Folio. *On the flyleaf, in Pope's hand:* Ex libris A. Pope; / Donum Hon:ssi Roberti Digby. / 1717.   (*Hartlebury*)

103. Langland, William. *The Vision of Pierce Plowman, Newlye Imprynted after the Authour's Olde Copy, with a Brefe Summary of the Principall Matters set before Every Part, Called Passus. Whereunto Is Also Annexed the Crede of Pierce Plowman, never Imprinted with the Booke.* London: Owen Rogers, 1561. 4°. (*The foregoing description is from*

*a bookseller's catalogue of late summer, 1966, which I can-
not now identify though I have a photocopy of the page—as
is also the following: "The following inscription in ink on the
flyleaf:* T. WARTON: ex dono Rev / iss in Chr. Patris Guli-
elmi Glostriensis [W. WARBURTON] 1770 & Liber olim
A. POPE cujus manu nonnulla attinuntur. T. WARTON.
*On the verso of title of The Crede there is a brief summary
[in ink] in an 18th century hand [unsigned]."*) *According to
to the description of this volume in Warton's "History of
English Poetry" (2d ed. 1775, I 287), the summarizing hand
is Pope's:*

> In a copy of the Crede lately presented to me by the bishop of
> Gloucester, and once belonging to Mr. Pope, the latter in his
> own hand has inserted the following abstract of its plan. "An
> ignorant plain man having learned his Pater-noster and Ave-
> mary, wants to learn his creed. He asks several religious men
> of the several orders to teach it him. First of a friar Minor, who
> bids him beware of the Carmelites, and assures him they can
> teach him nothing, describing their faults, etc. But that the
> friars Minor shall save him, whether he learns his creed or not.
> He goes next to the friars Preachers, whose magnificent mon-
> astery he describes: there he meets a fat friar, who declaims
> against the Augustines. He is shocked at his pride, and goes to
> the Augustines. They rail at the Minorites. He goes to the
> Carmes; they abuse the Dominicans, but promise him salva-
> tion without the creed, for money. He leaves them with indig-
> nation, and finds an honest poor Plowman in the field, and
> tells him how he was disappointed by the four orders. The
> plowman answers with a long invective against them."

*A catalogue description of the book when it appeared at the
Benjamin Heath sale, 10 May 1810, lot 1859, indicates that
immediately following this summary Pope adds:* N.B. The
Author was Robert Langland.

104. Lindesay, Patrick. *The Interest of Scotland Considered.*
London: T. Woodward and J. Peele, 1736. 8°. *On the fly-
leaf in Lyndsay's hand:* A. Pope. / Donum Authoris. / P.
Lyndsay.   (*Cambridge University*)

105. Locke, John. *An Essay Concerning Humane Understanding*. "The Fourth Edition." London: Awnsham, Churchill and Manship, 1700. Folio. *On the frontispiece in Pope's hand:* E Libris A. Pope, ex / dono Amicissimi, Dñi / de Bolingbroke.   (*Hartlebury*)

106. Lucan. *Lucan's Pharsalia: Or the Civill Warres of Rome. Englished by Thomas May, Esquire.* London: Thomas Jones, 1631. 8⁰. *On the flyleaf in Pope's hand:* Alexan. Pope, Pretium 2ˢ   (*Harvard*)

107. Lucan. *Lucan's Pharsalia.* Tr. Nicholas Rowe. London: Tonson, 1718. Folio. *On the flyleaf in Pope's hand:* Alexander Pope: Given / me by Mrs. Rowe.   (*Hartlebury*)

108. Lucian. *Certain Select Dialogues.* [*See no. 109.*]

109. ———. *Part of Lucian made English.* By Jasper Mayne. Oxford: H. Hall for R. Davis, 1664. Bound with: *Certain Select Dialogues of Lucian.* Tr. Francis Hicks. Oxford: 1663. Folio. *On the flyleaf, in Pope's hand:* E Libris / Alexandri Popei / Pretii, 4ˢˢ   (*Hartlebury*)

110. Lucretius Carus, Titus. *De Rerum Natura. Libri Sex.* London: J. Tonson and J. Watts, 1713. 12mo. *On the flyleaf in Pope's hand:* E libris A. Pope. 1714.   (*Harvard*)

111. [Lyttleton, George, Baron]. *The Progress of Love. In Four Eclogues.* London: L. Gilliver, 1732. 8⁰. Poems, Vol. I. [*See number 15.*] *On half-title, verso, in Warton's hand:* By / Mr. Lyttelton.

112. Manilius. *The Five Books of M. Manilius, Containing a System of the Ancient Astronomy and Astrology; Together with the Philosophy of the Stoicks. Done into English Verse* [*by Thomas Creech*]. London: Jacob Tonson, 1697. 8⁰. *On the half title in Pope's hand:* E' libris Alexandri Pope: pr. 3ˢ (*Hartlebury*)

113. Martial. *M. Valerii Martialis Epigrammata.* Ed. Cornelius
Schrevel. Leyden: Francis Hacke, 1656. 8°. *On the flyleaf in
Pope's hand:* Ex Libris Alex. Popei. Pr. 4ˢ   (*Hartlebury*)

114. Maittaire, Michael, ed. *Opera et Fragmenta Veterum Poetarum Latinorum.* London: Nicholson, Tooke, and Tonson,
1713. 2 vols. Folio. *On the flyleaf of Vol. I, in Pope's hand:*
In Memoriam / Tho. Parnell, S.T.D. / A quo Munus hocce
ob Pignus Amici- / tiae accepit Alex. Pope. / Unam Opus &
Requiem pariter disponimus ambo, / Atq. verecunda laxa-
mus seria mensa. / 1714. [*Either Pope entered this memorial
inscription on Parnell's death in 1718 but predated it to the
year of the gift and of their separation or (more probable)
"In Memoriam" is said playfully. The quotation is from Persius, V, 43-44.*] *On the flyleaf of Vol. II, in Pope's hand:* In
Memoriam / Tho. Parnell, S.P.D. / A quo munus hocce ob
pignˢ / amicitiae accepit A. Pope. / Te mihi junxerunt nivei
sine crimine mores, / Simplicitasque sagax, ingenuusq. pudor, / Et bene nota fides, & candor frontis honestae, / Et
Studia, a Studiis non aliena meis. [*The quotation is from
Joannes Secundus' Epistle "Ad Sibrandum Occonem."*]
(*Hartlebury*)

115. Milton, John. *Poems of Mr. John Milton.* London: Ruth Ra-
worth for Humphrey Moseley, 1645. 8°. *Signed on the title:*
Alexand: Pope. *On the blank verso of p. 65, Pope has transcribed from the 1673 edition the address to the rivers of
England, 11. 91-100 of "At a Vacation Exercise." On the
blank verso of the separate "Comus" title page, he notes:*
There are several excellent Lines in / this Masque, & very
lively Images. *At the rear of the book, the blank verso of
p. 87 and the recto and verso of the two following leaves are
occupied by a transcript of the entire 87 lines of the Latin
ode, also from the 1673 edition, "Ad Ioannem Rousium
Oxoniensis Academiae Bibliothecarium," together with its
authorial prose note on the poem's structure. The writing on
p. 87v, and on both sides of the immediately following leaf is
in Pope's printing hand; the writing on the recto and verso*

of the next leaf is cursive, and there is some question in my mind whether it is Pope's. (*New York Public Library*)

116. ———. *Paradise Lost.* "The Seventh Edition." London: Jacob Tonson, 1705. 8°. *On the flyleaf recto, in Pope's hand:* A. Pope. *On the title page, in Pope's hand:* First publish'd in Ten Books, in the year, 1669. Quarto. *On the recto of the plate facing page one, in Pope's hand:* The Arguments & foregoing Preface were not intended / by Milton, but occasioned by the importunity of the / Printer; as appears by this short Advertisement pre- / fix'd to the first Edition. I insert the words, because / I suppose them written by Milton himself. / The Printer to the Reader. / Courteous Reader, there was no Argument at first / intended to the book, but for the satisfaction of many / that desird it, I have procurd it; and withal, a / Reason of That which Stumbled many others, Why the Poem *rimes not.* / S. Simmonds. *On p. 435, beside Book XI 485-487, Pope places a cross and, at the foot of the page, the note:* These 3 lines added since the first Edition. (*Privately owned*)

117. ———. *Paradise Lost.* "Seventh Edition." London: Jacob Tonson, 1705. 8°. *On a slip pasted to the front end paper:* "This volume I bought of Tho Payne Bookseller / near the Mews Gate. He purchased it amongst / other books out of the Library of Bishop Warburton. / Whence it has been not improbably supposed that it / had been given to Pope by Atterbury, of whom / a note written with his own hand appears in the / margin of the Dedication." "See Epist. Corresp. of Atterbury, last page." *Below this, on the end paper itself:* The above note was written by my Father, / George Moore. C. B. S. P. E. C. M. *On A1r, beside the sentence in the "Dedication to Lord Somers" which reads "It was your Lordship's Opinion and / Encouragement that occasion'd the First / Appearing of this Poem in the Folio Edition," a demurrer in Atterbury's hand:* Not so! for I first started this Design to Tonson; / and he undertook it, at my Instance. F. Ross. *John Nichols refers to this book and its inscription*

in his edition of Atterbury's "Epistolary Correspondence"
(London, 1783) II 304, noting that "The volume in which
the note was written was purchased by T. Payne, amongst
other books, out of the library of Bishop Warburton, and
had probably been given to Pope by Atterbury."   *(Uni-*
versity of Texas)

118. ———. *Paradise Regain'd. A Poem. In Four Books. To*
Which Is Added Samson Agonistes. And Poems Upon Sev-
eral Occasions. "The Fourth Edition." London: Jacob Tonson, 1705. 8º. *On the flyleaf in Pope's hand:* E libris A.
Pope, pr. 4.ˢ   *(Privately owned)*

119. Monier, Pierre. *The History of Painting, Sculpture, Archi-*
tecture, Graving, and of those who have Excell'd in them.
London: Bennet, Leigh, and Knaplock, 1699. 8º. *On the*
flyleaf, in Pope's hand: E libris A. Pope. *Next to the names*
of Augustin Venetianus, G. [Agostino (Veneziano) de'
Musi]; John Baptisto Mantuano, P. G. [Giovanni Battista
(Sculptor)]; Mark Antonio Raimondi, P. G.; Mark de
[Marco Dente da] Ravenna; and Martin [Van Cleve] of
Antwerp, Pope notes that their plates are marked respec-
tively, A. V.; B. I. M.; S. R. M.; S. R. or M. R.; *and* M. C.
(University of Texas)

120. Montaigne, Michel. *Essais.* "Nouvelle Edition." Paris:
Augustin Courbe, 1652. Folio. *On the flyleaf in Hurd's*
hand: This was one of Mr Pope's books and / given me out
of his library at Prior- / Park by the B̄p̄ of Gloucester in
1765. / RH.   *(Hartlebury)*

121. ———. *Essays of Michael Seigneur de Montaigne. In Three*
Books. Tr. Charles Cotton, Esq. London: T. Basset, M. Gil-
liflower, and W. Hensman, 1685. [Vol. II, 1686; Vol. III,
1693.] 8º. *On the flyleaf of Vol. I, in Pope's hand:* E Libris
A. Popei / Pr. 3.ˢ / 1706. *Pope's notes appear throughout the*
volume, as follows:

p. 219: *To right of the following:* Plutarch.

We take other
Mens Knowledge and Opinions upon Trust;
which is an idle and superficial Learning:
we must make it our own. We are in this
very like him, who having need of Fire,
went to a Neighbor's House to fetch it, and
finding a very good one there, sat down to
warm himself without remembring to carry
any with him home.

p. 290: *To left of the following:* Mr. W——y.

. . . If there be Invention,
and that the Wit and Judgement have well
perform'd their Offices, I will say here's a
good Poet, but an ill Rhymer.

p. 300: *After "Forms" Pope has placed an "X" and to left of the sentence:* mutato nomine / de me / Fabula narratur.

My Latine immediately grew corrupt [when he
was sent away to school as contrasted with his
having a Latin tutor and speaking the language
at home] . . . : so that this new way of Institution serv'd me to no other end, than only at
my first coming to prefer me to the first Forms:
for at thirteen Years old, that I came out of the
Colledge, I had run thorough my whole Course (as
they call it) and in truth without any manner of
Improvement, that I can honestly brag of, in all
this time. The first thing that gave me any Taste
of Books, was the Pleasure I took in reading the
Fables of *Ovid's* Metamorphoses, and with them I
was so taken, that being but Seven or Eight years old,
I would steal from all other Divertisements to
read them. . . .
Fables of Obid's Metamorphoses, and with them I
was so taken, that being Seven or Eight years old,
I would steal from all other Divertisements to
read them. . . .

p. 301: *To right of the following lines Pope has written:*
Alter Ego.

> [My manners]
> had no other vice but Sloth and want of
> Mettal. There was no fear that I would
> do ill, but that I would do nothing. . . .

p. 453: *Pope has placed an "X" after "these" and to*
right of the sentence: X Cicero. / Pliny. Jun.

> There is
> something like this in these two other Phi-
> losophers, for they also promise Eternity,
> to the Letters they write to their Friends.

Vol. II; *On the flyleaf, in Pope's hand:* E Libris A: Po-
pei. / Pr. 3$^{\underline{S}}$ / 1706. *The volume has his notes, as follows:*
p. 146: *To left of the following, Pope has written:* Gre-
gorio / Leti. / Verillas.

> *[Montaigne argues that*
> *most modern historians are chosen for no better*
> *reason than the gift of "Well speaking."]* . . .
> the Men so.chosen have also reason, being hired
> for no other End, and pretending to nothing but
> Babble, not to be very sollicitous of any part
> but that, and so, with a fine Gingle of Words,
> prepare us a pretty Contexture of Reports, they
> pick up in the Streets.

p. 225: *To right of the following* Vide Justi / Lipsii
Epist. / 50 cent. 1:

> But this Animal [the elephant] in several other
> Effects comes so near to human Capacity, that
> should I particularly relate all that Experience
> hath deliver'd to us, I should easily have, what
> I usually maintain, granted, namely, that there
> is more difference betwixt such and such a
> Man, than betwixt such a Man and such a Beast.

p. 263: *To right of the following:* Sententia / prope divina!

Sic haud scio, an
melius fuerit humano generi motum istum celerem,
cogitationis acumen, soleritiam, quam rationem
vocamus, quoniam pestifera sint multis, admodum
paucis salutaria, non dari omnino, quàm tam munificè
& tam large dari.

p. 264: *To left of the following:* Horat. / Ep. 8.

Illiterati num minus nervi rigent?

p. 288: *Pope has placed an "X" after "reason" and to
left of the sentence:* X And Epicurus. / Lucr: Nec bene pro
me- / ritis capitur, nec tan- / gitur ita.

> For which reason [i.e., that neither human
> virtues nor human passions can be properly
> attributed to God], equally exempt from
> Vertue and Vice.

p. 543: *Pope has placed an "X" before "Alexander"
and to right of the passage:* X of Aristotle.

> 'Tis said of Alexander the Great, that being
> in Bed, for fear lest sleep should divert him
> from his Thoughts and Studies, he had always a
> Bason set by his Bed-side, and held one of his
> hands out with a Ball of Copper in it, to the
> end, that beginning to fall asleep, and his
> Fingers leaving their hold, the Ball by falling
> into the Bason might awake him.

p. 563: *To right of the following:* quaere, what / people
these / were?

> And yet they were more
> to blame, who of old gave leave that Criminals,
> to what sort of death soever condemn'd, should
> be cut up alive by the *Physicians,* that they
> might make a true discovery of our inward parts....

p. 669: *To right of the following:* He was, by the /
Smyrneans.

> And in truth, I often
> wonder that he [Homer] who has erected, and
> by his Authority given so many Deities reputa-
> tion in the World, was not deified himself.

p. 671: *To right of the following:* Velleius / Paterculus.

> *...as there was none before*
> *him whom he* [Homer] *could imitate, so there has been*
> *none since that could imitate him.*

p. 686: *To left of the following:* quaere, / where Mon-
taign / had this / story. (*Before "Cicero" Pope inserts* in).

> What pitty 'tis I have not the Faculties of
> that Dreamer *Cicero,* who dreaming he was lying
> with a Wench, found he had discharg'd his Stone
> in the Sheets!

p. 687: *In the left margin:* Here begins / the Discourse
ag^st Physick, / the most excel- / lent extant.

Vol. III. *The volume has Pope's notes, as follows:*
p. 14: *To left of the passage Pope has written:* The case
of / those who / pay double / Taxes.

> For it is lawful for a
> Man of Honour to say as the *Lacedemonians* did,
> having been defeated by *Antipater,* when just
> upon the point of concluding an agreement, *You*
> *may impose as heavy and ruinous Taxes upon us*
> *as you please, but to command us to do shameful*
> *and dishonest things, you will lose your time,*
> *for it is to no purpose.*

p. 44: *To left of the following:* Of Old age / to ye end /
of this / Chapt.

> *...he,*
> who said of old, that he was oblig'd to his
> Age for having wean'd him from Pleasure, was
> of another Opinion than I am....

p. 96: *To left of the following:* The Hu- / gonote / womẽ.

> And yet those Women of our times are not to be
> dislik'd, who according to their errour, pro-
> test, they had rather burthen their Consciences
> with ten men than one *Mass.*

p. 98: *To left of the following:* For yᵉ / Ladies.

> I am vex'd that
> my *Essays* only serve the Ladies for a common
> moveable, a Book to lie in the Parlour Window;
> this Chapter shall preferr me to the Closet;
> I love to traffick with them a little in
> private....

p. 150: *To left of the following:* Love is, tho / not Venus.

> ...*Love is nothing else but the*
> *thirst of enjoying the subject desir'd;* neither is *Venus*
> any other thing than the pleasure of discharging the
> Vessels....

p. 155: *To right of the following:* Virgil / & / Lucre- tius.

> Whilst the Verses of these two Poets treat so
> reservedly and discreetly of wantonness, as they
> do, methinks, they discover it much more.

p. 159: *To right of the following:* X Vid. Herodot.

> ...this Madness is, methinks,
> Cousin-German to that of the Boy, who would needs lie
> with the beautiful Statue of *Venus,* made by *Praxiteles;*
> or that of the furious *Egyptian,* who violated the dead
> Carkass of a Woman he was embalming.

p. 164: *To left of the following:* Chr. Q. of S. / and the / Pr. of Condé.

> *Alex-*
> ander marching his army thorough *Hyrcania, Thalestris*
> Queen of the *Amazons,* came with three hundred light

Horse of her own Sex, well mounted and arm'd, . . . to
give him a Visit. . . .

p. 198: *To left of the following:* De Specta- / culis
Roma- / norum.

> And yet it was doubtless a fine thing to
> bring and plant within the *Theatre* a great
> number of vast Trees, with all their Branches
> in full verdure, representing a great shady
> Forest, dispos'd in excellent order, and the
> first day to throw into it a thousand Ostriches
> and a thousand Stags, a thousand Boars, and a
> thousand Fallow-Deer, to be kill'd and dispos'd
> of by the People.

p. 204: *To left of the passage beginning: "Our World
has lately discover'd another," Pope has noted:* Of the
Indian / World, and / the Cruelty / of ye Spaniards / from
hence to / ye end of y^e / chapter.

p. 212: *To left of the following:* Tantum Relli- / gio
potuit sua / dere malorū.

> Could it [the Spaniards' cruelty to
> the natives] be for a testimony of their Justice, or their
> Zeal to Religion!

p. 215: *Pope has placed an "X" before "Author" and to
right of the sentence:* X quaere who / he was?

> After what manner they think this last *Sun*
> [*referring to the Indians' belief in four
> ages or "suns" preceding the present sun*]
> shall perish, my *Author* knows not.

p. 232: *To left of the sentence about the folly of disputants, beginning "After an hour of Tempest they know not
what they seek," Pope writes:* A Description / of Dispu- /
tants.

p. 339: *To right of the following:* X Theod. Beza.

I have in my Youth seen a Man in good Habit, with
one hand present the People with Verses that excell'd
both in Wit and Debauchery, and with the other, at the

same time, the most seditious Theological Reformation
that the World has been treated withal these many years.

p. 413: *To right of the following, Pope asks:* Had our
Chaucer this / in his Eye, when he / made his Wife of / Bath
a Weaver; *and beside the reference to "our Ladies" comments:* A Hackny Coach, a / great Help to Love.

> I might also say of these [weavers], that this
> jogging their Breeches, whilst so sitting at
> work, rouzes and provokes their desire, as the
> swingging and jolting of Coaches does that of
> our *Ladies.*

Inside the back cover, in Pope's hand: This is (in my Opinion) the very best Book for Infor- / mation of Manners, that
has been writ. This Au- / thor says nothing but what every
one feels att the / Heart. Whoever deny it, are not more
Wise than / Montaigne, but less honest.   (*Yale*)

122. Oldham, John. *Poems, and Translations (1684).* [*See no.
     125.*]

123. ———. *Satyrs Upon the Jesuits (1685).* [*See no. 125.*]

124. ———. *Remains...in Verse and Prose (1693).* [*See no.
     125.*]

125. ———. [Works and Remains, '1685-1694.' Bound in one
     volume.] *Satyrs Upon the Jesuits...and Some Other Pieces.*
     "The Third Edition Corrected." London: Joseph Hind-
     marsh, 1685. *Poems, and Translations by John Oldham.*
     London: Joseph Hindmarsh, 1684. *Poems, and Transla-
     tions.* London: Joseph Hindmarsh, 1694. *Remains...in
     Verse and Prose.* London: Joseph Hindmarsh, 1693. 8°. *On
     the front flyleaf, in Pope's hand:* E Libris Alexandri Pope.
     Pret. 4.s. 1700. *Beneath this, presumably in Thompson's
     hand:* Sept. 23 1768 given unto Edw. Thompson in the
     King's Bench prison by John Wilkes this volume came from
     Mr. Pope & the remarks are in his own hand writing in the
     last page. *On a flyleaf at end, in Pope's hand:* The Most

Remarkable Works in this Author, as follow here.

Fourth Satire on ye Jesuits.	p^r. 1. pag. 74.
Satire on Virtue.	p^t. 1. pag. 93.
The Translation of Horace's Art of Poetry.	
	p^t. 2. pag. I.
The Impertinent, from Hor. Sat. 9 lib. I.	
	p^t. 2. pag. 43.
To the Memory of Mr. C. Morwent.	p^t. 4. pag. 69.

Pope's comments appear throughout the book, as follows:
p. 97: "The Satyr against Vertue. Pindarique Ode,"
11. 67-70: *Pope has placed an* "X" *to left of line 67, and to the right has written:* X Brutus.

> The greatest Votary, thou e'er couldst boast,
> (Pity so brave a Soul was on thy Service lost;
> What Wonders he in wickedness had done,
> Whom thy weak pow'r could so inspire alone?

p. 99: Ibid., 11. 95-97: *To right of line 97 Pope has written:* X Socrates.

> No prudent Heathen e'er seduc'd could be,
> To suffer Martyrdom for thee:
> Only that arrant Ass whom the false Oracle call'd Wise.

p. 178: "A Satyr. The Person of Spencer is brought in, Dissuading the Author from the Study of Poetry," 11. 253-254: *Pope has written* X Maynard *in the blank, and at the bottom of the page:* X Serjeant Maynard was eminent in his profession, & made / more money than any Man of the Law in his time.

> Where M—— thrives, and pockets more each year,
> Than forty Laureats of the Theater.

For a full bibliographical description of this book, see Harold Brooks, "A Bibliography of John Oldham," in "Proceedings of the Oxford Bibliographical Society," V (1936), 28-29.   (British Library)

126. [Oldmixon, John]. *An Essay on Criticism; As it regards Design, Thought, and Expression, in Prose and Verse. By the Author of the Critical History of England.* London: J. Pemberton, 1728. Vol. IV. [*See number 3.*]

127. *Opuscula Mythologica Physica et Ethica. Graece et Latine.* Amsterdam: Henry Wetstein, 1588. 8⁰. *On the front flyleaf possibly in Pope's hand:* De Mundo / Ocellus Lucanus / Timeus Locrus / Tabula Cebitis / Epictetus / Theophrastus. (*Hartlebury*)

128. Ovid. *Opera Omnia.* Ed. Cornelius Schrevel. Leyden: Peter Leffen. 3 vols. [*Dated 1662 on general title page, but the engraved title in each volume bears the date 1661.*] 8⁰. *On the flyleaf of each volume, in Pope's hand:* E Libris A. Popei. / Pr. 5ˢ   (*Hartlebury*)

129. Ovid. *Ovid's Art of Love. In Three Books. Together with his Remedy of Love. Translated into English Verse by Several Eminent Hands.* London: Jacob Tonson, 1709. 8⁰. *The European Magazine, October, 1787 (XII 261) records an interesting copy of this book with annotations attributed to Pope. The attribution, though plausible, must be received with caution in the absence of other evidence. The printed notes referred to by the marginal annotator are reproduced first in round brackets and italics. The annotator's notes follow these in roman.*

> "*A Correspondent . . . desires we will insert the following Notes on Ovid's "Art of Love," 8vo. 1709, which are transcribed with all their peculiarities from the original copy, formerly belonging to Mr. Pope, in his own hand-writing, on the blank leaves.*"
> "*Notes by Mr. Pope.*"
> Among a thousand errors in the notes to this book [*Book I*] these are a few.
>
> p. 63: (*Ovid relates the whole fable of Chiron and*

Saturn's Love to Phillyra in the 5th Book De Fastis.)
The Fable of Saturn and Phillyra is not told there, but
only the death of Chiron related.

p. 68: (*The Romans met in the Temple of Venus to
mourn Adonis, and infamous acts of lewdness were
there committed, if we may believe Juvenal, Sat. 6.
Nam quo non prostrat faemina templo?*)
This verse is in the 9th Satire, lin. 24. and makes
nothing to the purpose in regard to Venus's Temple
more than any other temple: for Juvenal there mentions
four temples, but none of them this.

p. 75: (*The number of the Sabines ravished Valerius
Antias affirming the number to be 500, and Jubas [as
Plutarch writes in the life of Romulus] swells it to 600.*)
Plutarch himself quotes Valerius Antias affirming
the number to be 500, and Jubas 683. Vid. Plut. in
Rom.

p. 86: (*After Ovid has treated the subject of Pasiphae
and the Bull so elegantly, in the 15th of the Met. he
shews the excellency of his genius in adding so much to
it here.*)
Ovid does not treat of this story at all in the 15th of
the Metam. he only just names Pasiphae in lin. 500 — So
this remark is impertinent.

p. 94: (*Acontius wrote on a golden apple the verses
which are cited in Cydippe's Epistle.*)
The verses are so far from being cited there, that
Cydippe expressly avoids citing them, in these words:
Mittitur ante pedes malum cum carmine tali— / Hei
mihi! juravi nunc quoque paeni tibi. Ovid. Ep. Cyd.
lin. 107.

The verses in the History of Love, page 439. beginning
— You haunt me still, &c. to the very end of that poem,

are excellent, and worth all the rest of the book (meo saltem judicio).

> "To this may be added, that Mr. Pope had put the name of Mr. Yalden as translator of the 2nd Book, which is anonymous, and A. Manwaring, Esq. of the Court of Love."

130. Paget, Thomas Catesby, baron. *An Essay on Human Life.* "The Third Edition." London: 1736. 8⁰. Poems, Vol. I. [*See number 15.*] *At top of A 2r, in Warton's(?) hand:* After Pope, says / Walpole.

131. ———. *An Epistle to Mr. P—— in Anti-Heroicks.* London: 1738. 8⁰. Poems, Vol. I. [*See number 15.*] *On the half title in Pope's hand:* A Pope / Ex dono Autoris / Nobilissimi. *Below, in Joseph Warton's hand:* By Lord Paget. / The above is Mʳ Pope's Handwriting—to whom these 2 Vol. of Poems belonged.

132. Parker, E. [pseud.]. *A Complete Key to the New Farce, call'd Three Hours After Marriage. With an Account of the Authors. By E. Parker, Philomath.* London: E. Berrington, 1717. Vol. I. [*See number 3.*]

133. Parnell, Thomas. *Homer's Battle of the Frogs and Mice.* London: B. Lintot, 1717. 8⁰. *On the flyleaf in Pope's hand:* E libris A. Pope. Donum Authoris. *On the half title in Pope's hand:* Written by Tho. Parnell, D.D. Arch. Clogh. *Below Pope's signature on the flyleaf is an MS. note by Malone:* This book belonged to Pope, as appears from the writing above, and on the next page. He was perhaps himself the editor, Parnell being at the time of publication in Ireland. E. Malone.   (*Harvard*)

Persius [*See nos. 100 and 102.*]

134. Pindar. *Olympia, Nemea, Pythia, Isthmia. Graece & La-*

tine. Heidelberg: Jerome Commelin, 1598. 8⁰. *Bound with: Carminum Poetarum novem, lyricae poesews principum, fragmenta.* Heidelberg: Jerome Commelin, 1598. 8⁰. [*The poets in question are Alcaeus, Alcman, Anacreon, Bacchylides, Ibycos, Pindar, Sappho. Simonides, Stesichorus.*] *On the Pindar flyleaf in Pope's hand:* Alex.ʳ Pope / Pretium, 2.ˢ (*Mary Hyde*)

135. Pitt, Christopher. *An Essay on Virgil's AEneid. Being a Translation of the First Book.* London: 1728. 8⁰. Poems, Vol. II. [*See number 15.*]

136. *Poems Relating to State Affairs, from Oliver Cromwell to this present Time: By the Greatest Wits of the Age.* London: 1705. *On the flyleaf in Pope's hand:* Ex Libris Alexandri Pope. *Pope has filled in the blanks in a great many of the proper names, marginally identified some of them, and occasionally contributed a revision or an addition to the text—e.g.* "Marriners on Shore less madly spend their Pay" ("*Directions to a Painter. By Sir John Denham,*" *line 332*) *becomes* "Sailors [*etc.*]." *His comments are as follows:*

   p. 100: "*A Dialogue between Two Horses,*" ll. 59-62: *Pope has underlined* "Copper Farthing" *and to left of the lines has written:* The copper farthing / had a legend importing / the K's vind: of / his domⁿ of the / 4 seas.

      W. That a K— should consume three Kingdoms Estates,
            And yet all the Court be as poor as Church-Rats.
      C. That of four Seas Dominion, and of their guarding,
            No token shou'd appear but a poor Copper Farthing.

   p. 121: "*Rochester's Farewell, 1680.*" *To right of the title Pope has written:* Probably by the Ld / Dorset.

   p. 129: "*On the Young Statesman. By the Earl of Rochester.*" *Pope has crossed out* "Rochester" *in the title and has inserted* Dorset.

   p. 133: "*An Essay upon Satyr. By the Earl of Mulgrave.*" *Pope has added* and Mr. Dryden *after the title.*

   p. 136: Ibid., ll. 128-130: *To left of the lines on Essex Pope has written:* He was Ld. / Lieutenant of / Ireland.

And what is that at best, but one whose Mind,
Is made to tire himself, and all Mankind?
For Ireland he would go, faith let him reign. . . .

p. 138: Ibid., 11. 200-201. *To left of the following:*
The Au- / thors Com- / pliment to / Himself.

M——ve had much ado to scape the Snare,
Tho' learn'd in those ill Arts that cheat the Fair.

p. 144: *"A Satyr on the Modern Translators. Odi imitatores servum pecus, &c." By Mr. P——r. To right of the author's name Pope has written:* Disown'd by him.

p. 162: *"An Epitaph upon Felton, who was hang'd in Chains for murdering the Old Duke of Buckingham: Written by the late Duke of Buckingham." Before "Written" in the title Pope has inserted* Never.

p. 167: *"A Satyr against Marriage: By the Same." To right of the title Pope has written:* E. of Roch.

p. 250: *"The true and genuine Explanation, Of one King James's Declaration. J.R." Beneath the title Pope has written:* By ye Ld. Hallifax.

p. 258: *"Tunbridge Wells. By the Earl of Rochester, June 30, 1675." Before "By" Pope has inserted* Not.

p. 264: *"On the Infanta of Portugal." Beneath the title Pope has written:* By Sir C. Sidley.

p. 273: *"The Iniskilling Regiment." Beneath the title Pope has written:* By Jo. Haynes.

p. 283: *"The True Born Englishman." Beneath the title Pope has written:* By Daniel Defoe.

p. 316: *"Aesop at Tunbridge." Fab. I. "Fair Warning." Beneath the title Pope has written:* By Tho. Brown.

p. 330: *"The Last Will and Testament of Anthony, King of Poland." To right of the title Pope has written:* Earl of Shaftesbury.

p. 371: *"The Nine Worthies. A Satyr written when the K—— went to Flanders, and left nine Lords Justices." To right of the title Pope has written:* By the Earl of Peterborough.

p. 417: *"The Allusion." To right of the title Pope has written:* Ld. Dorset.

p. 442: *"Enter Oliver's Porter, Fidler, and Poet, in Bedlam." Pope has marked lines 5, 9, 17, 51, 111-114, 153-154, 160, 177, 182-184 with a cross, and in the left margin beside line 5 has written:* Those thus / marked are /·Mr Dryden's / Words, or / like / 'em. *For example, lines 111-114 read:*

> But Heav'n a Chrystal Pyramid did take,
> Of that a broad Extinguisher did make,
> In Firmamental Waters dipt above,
> To hood the Flames which to their Quarry strove.

p. 483: *"The Mourners: Found in the Streets. 1702." Above the title Pope has written:* By B. Higgons.

p. 485: *"On S——l." Pope has written* orre *in the blanks and to right of the title has written:* By B. Higgons.

p. 486: *"The Play-House: A Satyr. By Mr. A. D——n." Pope inserts letters to convert* "A. D——n" *to* A^d D$\underline{\text{iso}}$ n.

p. 496: *"The Golden Age Restor'd." To left of the title Pope has written:* (By W. Walsh, Esq.) *At* 11. 31-32:

> Viceroys, like Providence with distant Care,
> Shall govern Kingdoms where they ne'er appear —

Pope notes marginally: alluding to the D. of / Ormond's govern. / of Ireland.

p. 534: *"On the Death of the Queen and Marshal Luxemburgh." The poem consists of four lines:*

> Behold, *Dutch* Prince, here lye th' unconquer'd Pair,
> Who knew your strength in Love, your Strength in War!
> Unequal Match, to both no Conquest gains,
> No Trophy of your Love or War remains.

Pope strikes out the last two lines and after the title inserts the initials: A. P.

p. 557: *"The History and Fall of the Conformity-Bill." Beneath the title Pope has written:* Certainly written by Mr Congreve.

p. 562: *"On the Countess of Dorch——r, By the E. of*

D——t." Beneath the second (and last) stanza of the poem
Pope has added the following verses:

> Her Bed is like the Marriage Feast
> To wch th'Invited never came,
> So, disapointed of her Guest,
> She took up with the blind & lame.

p. 570: *"Faction Display'd." To right of the title Pope*
has written: By W. Shippen, Esq.

p. 584: *"Mully of Mountown. A Poem. By the Author*
of the Tale of a Tub." Beneath the title Pope has written:
By Dr. King.

A number of Pope's markings in this book are
recorded and commented on in "Notes and Queries," New
Series, V (1958), 55-57, 291-294, 437-438.   (British
Library)

137. Preston. [pseud.]. *Aesop at the Bear-Garden: A Vision. By*
Mr. Preston. In Imitation of the Temple of Fame, a Vision,
by Mr. Pope. London: John Morphew. 1715. Vol. I. [*See*
number 3.]

138. Prior, Matthew. *Poems on Several Occasions.* London: J.
Tonson, and J. Barber, 1721. 2 vols. 12°. *On the flyleaf of*
Vol. I, in Pope's hand: A. Pope. / Dñm Auth^s *Inside the*
cover of Vol. II: Martha Blount.   (*Privately owned*)

139. Puckle, James. *The Club. In a Dialogue Between Father*
and Son. "The Third Edition." London: for the Author.
1713. 8°. *On the title page, in Pope's hand:* A Pope. *Beside*
the second line of the title: J Swift.   (*Harvard*)

140. Purchase, Samuel. *Purchas His Pilgrimes. The Third Part.*
London: William Stansby for Henry Fetherstone, 1625.
Folio. *On the flyleaf in Pope's hand:* E Libris A. Pope.
(*Privately owned*)

141. Quintilian, Marcus Fabius. *Institutionum Oratoriarum*
Libri Duodecim. Leyden and Rotterdam: Ex Officina

Hackiana, 1665. 2 vols. 8⁰. *On the flyleaf of Vol. I, in Pope's hand:* E Libris A. Pope. / Ex dono Jac. Dormer. / 1717. (*Hartlebury*)

142. [Ralph, James]. *Sawney. An Heroic Poem. Occasion'd by the Dunciad. Together with a Critique on that Poem addressed to Mr. T——D, Mr. M——R, Mr. EU——N, &c.* London: J. Roberts, 1728. Vol. II. [*See number 3.*]

143. [Roberts, John]. *An Answer to Mr. Pope's Preface to Shakespear. In a Letter to a Friend. Being a Vindication of the Old Actors who were the Publishers and Performers of that Author's Plays. By a Stroling Player.* London: 1729. Vol. IV. [*See number 3.*]

144. Rochester, John Wilmot, Earl of. *Poems, (&c.) On Several Occasions: With Valentinian; A Tragedy.* London: Jacob Tonson, 1696. 8⁰. *On the second flyleaf in Pope's hand:* E' Libris Alex: Popei, pr. 3ˢ *On A2 recto, next to the Preface to the Reader, in Pope's hand:* By T. Rymer. *On the final flyleaf, in Pope's hand:* There ought to be added to this / Edition of my Lᵈ Rochester's / Works, his Letters to Henry Saville, wᶜʰ are printed else- / where. *Pope's notations appear as follows:*

p. 1: *To right of "A Dialogue between Strephon and Daphne" Pope has made a cross; to right of lines 41-48 he has written:* Indecent / poor / conceit.

> How shou'd I these Show'rs forget,
> 'Twas so pleasant to be wet?
> They kill'd Love, I knew it well,
> I dy'd all the while they fell.
> Say at least what *Nymph* it is
> Robs my Breast of so much Bliss?
> If she is fair, I shall be eas'd,
> Thro' my Ruin you'll be pleas'd.

p. 13: *To right of lines 5-8 of "The Advice" Pope has written:* false / thought.

Were he [Love] not blind, such are the Charms you have,
He'd quit his Godhead to become your Slave:
Be proud to act a mortal Hero's Part,
And throw himself for Fame on his own Dart.

p. 23, ll. 13-16: *To right of line 15 of "The Mistress. A Song." Pope has written what appears to be* Qu [*for Query?*].

You wiser Men despise me not;
Whose Love-sick Fancy raves,
On Shades of Souls, and Heav'n knows what;
Short Ages live in Graves.

p. 83, ll. 62-64: *To right of line 64 of "An Epistolary Essay From M. G. to O. B. Upon their mutual Poems," Pope has placed an "X" and in the margin has written:* X The Thought is / Taken from / ye first lines / of Des Cartes / 's Method.

In Wit, alone, 't [i.e. *Heaven*] has been Magnificent,
Of which so just a share to each is sent,
That the most Avaricious are content.
For none e'er thought (the due Division's such)
His own too little....

p. 97: *Beneath the title of "The Maim'd Debauchee." Pope has written:* With allusion to Gondibert. (*New York Public Library*)

145. [Rowe, Elizabeth]. *The History of Joseph. A Poem. In Eight Books. By the Author of Friendship in Death.* 1736. 8⁰. Poems, Vol. I. [*See number 15.*]

146. Rymer, Thomas. *The Tragedies of the Last Age. Part I.* "The Second Edition." London: Richard Baldwin, 1692. 8⁰. *On the flyleaf, in Pope's hand:* Ex libris Alexandri Popei. / Pret. 2^s
    p. 67: *To right of the following passage Pope has written:* Vide Petr / Trionfi. de / Fama. *and to the right of the*

succeeding paragraph, in an ink too faded to be read, a comment ending: Pro- / vencall.

> The Italian (c) Authors acknowledge that the
> best part of their Language, and of their Poetry
> is drawn from that of *Provence,* as, indeed, is
> also that of the Spanish, and other Modern Langu-
> ages. it is certain that *Petrarch* (the Poet that
> the Italians brag most on to this day) wou'd show
> very empty, If the *Provencial* Poets had from him,
> all their own again. And, in truth, all our
> *Modern* Poetry comes from them.

p. 78: *In the margin below the following passage Pope has written:* Gower. Lidgate. Pieres Plowman / Walter de Maapes. E. of Surrey. Sr Tho / Wyat. G. Gascoign - Golding / Sackville - Mirror of Magistrates, Gorbod.

> But
> they who attempted verse in English, down till
> *Chaucers* time, made a heavy pudder, and are always
> miserably put to't for a word to clink: which
> commonly fall so awkward, and unexpectedly as
> dropping from the Clouds by some Machine or Miracle.
> *Chaucer* found an Herculean labor on his Hands:
> And did perform to Admiration. He seizes all Pro-
> vencal, French or Latin that came his way, gives
> them a new garb and livery, and mingles them amongst
> our English: turns out English, gowty, or super-
> annuated, to place in their room the foreigners, fit
> for service, train'd and accustomed to Poetical Dis-
> cipline.
> But tho' the Italian reformation was begun and
> finished well nigh at the same time by *Boccace, Dante*
> and *Petrarch,* Our language retain'd something of the
> churl; something of the Stiff and Gothick did stick
> upon it, till long after *Chaucer.*
> *Chaucer* threw in Latin, French, Provencial, and
> other Languages, like new Stum to raise a fermenta-
> tion.

(*Hartlebury*)

147. Schenckius, Petrus. *Romae Novae Delineatio.* [*See no. 151*].

148. Seneca, Marcus Annaeus. *Tragoediae Serio emendatae. Editio, prioribus longe correctior.* 1668. *Bound with* Juvenal. *Satirae,* n.d. (Sotheby, 12 December 1905, lot 150: "Pope's copy, with his signature, 'Alexander Pope,' on the flyleaf.")

149. Shakespeare, William. *Othello.* London: Richard Bentley, 1695. 4⁰. *This book has marginal MS. notes in at least two hands, one of which appears to be Pope's, the notes being folio textual variants.* (*Folger Shakespeare Library*)

150. Sidney, Philip. [*The Countess of Pembroke's Arcadia.* "Now the Fourth Time published." London: H. L. for Simon Waterson. 1613.] Folio. *On the flyleaf, in Pope's hand:* A. Pope: / pr. 4⁵ *The original title page has been replaced with a manuscript title in Pope's hand, within a double rule on all four sides:* THE / COUNTESS / OF / PEMBROKE's / ARCADIA: / With other Works, / BY / SIR *PHILIP SID-NEY:* / [vis.] / The DEFENCE of POESIE. / SONGS and SONNETS. / ASTROPHEL and STELLA. / - / *London.* / Printed for *Matthew Lownes* by H. L. / Anno Domini; 1599.

　　p. 11: *Pope has underscored the last word in the line* "As smooth as Pan, as Iuno mild, like goddesse iris faste" *and in the margin has written:* constant, always the same. (*Hartlebury*)

151. Silvestre, Israel. *Alcune vedute di Giardini e Fontane di Roma e di Tivoli* [Paris? 1645?]. *Bound with* "Romae Novae Delineatio." *P. Schenckii.* [Amsterdam, circa 1680.] 4⁰. *The title of the second book is partly in Pope's printing hand, partly in his cursive calligraphy. On the flyleaf of* "Alcune vedute": Alex. Pop["e" *or* "ei" *has been cut off by cropping of the margin*]. Pret. 15. *The following notations appear in Pope's hand in* "Romae Novae Delineatio":

　　Plate 2: *Added to the caption:* Obeliscus 114 pedes altitud. cum Basi. Obelisc. Inscriptio. DIVO CAES. DIVI IULII F. AUGUSTO. TI. CAES. DIVI AUG. F. AUGUS. SACRUM. *Inserted across the front of St. Peter's basilica above the portico:* IN HON. FR. APO. PAULUS V. ROMA

P.M. AN. MDXXII.

Plate 9: *The words* Sixti Quinti *are inserted in the caption following the words* "Templus S. Johannis, ut et Pontificum Palatium" *and before* "in monte Coelio." *Added to caption:* Obelisci Altitudo, 100 pedes, et supra, factus a Rege Semneserteo, qui Ægypto praefuit Pythagorae tempore. Marlian.

Plate 10: *Added to the caption:* 1 S. Maria di monte Santo. 2. S. Maria di Miracoli. 3. S. Ambrosius. 4. Pantheon. 5. S. Trinitatis. *The corresponding buildings in the plate have been numbered by Pope; 1 and 2 are in middle ground at the center of the plate; 3 and 4 are in the distance to the right; 5 is at left in the distance.*

Plate 11: *Added to the caption:* A. Sta. Maria del Popolo. B. Porte du Convent [*sic*] des Augustines. / Inscriptio Obelisc. IMP. CAES. D.F. AUGUSTUS PONT. MAX. IMP. XII. COS. XI. TRI. POT. XIV. AEGYPTO. IN POTESTATE P. RNI. REDACT. SOLI DONŨ DEDIT. *The letters "A" and "B" have been added on the plate: "A" above the large building at right, "B" next to the door at far right.*

Plate 12: *Added to the caption:* Fons opus Bernini Arch. & Sculp. A. Palazzo di [*word erased*]. *The letter "A" has been added on the plate, above the building at right.*

Plate 14: *Added to the caption:* 1. Chiesa de Trinita del monte. 2. Horti Medicei. *The numbers "1" and "2" have been added to the plate; "1" is above the distant building at left, and "2" is above the distant building at middle right.*

Plate 17: *Added to the caption:* a. Orto delli P P. Reformati di Sto. Francesco. b. Casino di Duca di Parma. *The letters "a" and "b" have been added to the plate; "a" is to the left of the door at extreme left foreground; "b" is above the building in the distance at middle right.* (*Yale*)

152. [Smedley, Jonathan]. *Gulliveriana: Or, A Fourth Volume of Miscellanies. Being a Sequel of the Three Volumes, published by Pope and Swift. To which is added, Alexanderiana: or, A Comparison between the Ecclesiastical and Poetical Pope.* London: J. Roberts, 1728. Vol. III. [*See number 3.*] *Pope's notations appear in the volume, as follows:*

p. 285: *Pope has written* By James Moore *beneath the title* "From the Daily Journal, March 29, 1728."

p. 287: *Pope has written* By James Moore *beneath the title* "From the Daily Journal, April 6, 1728."

p. 291: *Pope has written* By John Dennis *beneath the title* "From the Daily Journal, May 11, 1728."

p. 294: *Pope has written* By M. Concanen *beneath the title* "From the British Journal, Nov. 25, 1727."

p. 299: *Pope has written* By Theobald, &c. *beneath the title* "An Essay on the Arts of a Poet's Sinking in Reputation."

p. 317: *Pope has written* James Moore *beneath the title* "Epigram on the Translation of Homer."

153. Spenser, Edmund. *The Faerie Queen: The Shepheards Calendar: Together with the other Works of England's Arch-Poet, Edm. Spenser.* [London:] H. L. for Mathew Lownes, 1611. Folio. *On the upper left corner of the title page, above the ornamental border, in Pope's hand:* (E' Musaeo Jo. Drydeni.) *Above the printed title, within the ornamental border, in Pope's hand:* Alex: Pope. / Pret: 7.SS *Pope's notations appear in the volume, as follows:*

Book I, Canto I, stanza 8, 11. 5-9: *To the right of the stanza Pope has written:* x This fine Description / of the Trees is imi- / tated from Chaucer's Assembly of Foules; / pag. 245. c.2. [*The reference is to Pope's own copy of Chaucer, where the description in question appears on p. 245, column 2.*]

> Much can they praise the trees so straight and hie,
> The sayling Pine, the Cedar proud and tall,
> The vine-prop Elme, the Poplar never dry,
> The builder Oake, sole king of forrests all,
> The aspine, good for staves, the Cypresse funerall.

I, III, 21: *To left of the stanza Pope has written:* Ulysses with / Calypso.

> Now when broad day the world discovered has,
> Up *Una* rose, up rose the Lyon eke,
> And on their former journey forward pass,
> In waies unknowne, her wandring knight to seeke,

In paines farre passing that long wandring Greeke
That for his love refused deitie;
Such were the labours of this Lady meeke,
Still seeking him, that from her still did flie,
Then furthest from her hope, when most she weened nie.

IV, X, 44: *To left of the stanza Pope has written:* This
M.ʳ Dry- / den has copy'd / in Palamon & / Arcite. book 2. /
pag.

Great Venus, Queene of beauty and of grace,
The ioy of Gods and men, that under skie
Dooest fairest shine, and most adorne thy place,
That with thy smiling looke doost pacifie
The raging seas, and mak'st the stormes to flie:
Thee goddesse, thee the winds, the clowdes do feare,
And when thou spredst thy mantle forth on hie,
The waters play, and pleasant Lands appeare,
And heavens laugh & all the world shewes ioyous cheere.

The Shepheards Calendar: Iune: *Following stanza 11, which
begins "The God of Shepheards TITYRUS is dead," Pope
has noted:* [Two stanzas are omitted, wᶜʰ / are to be found
in the / first Edition in quarto.] *In actual fact, only stanza
12 is omitted in the folio, beginning "Nowe dead he is, and
lyeth wrapt in lead."*
The Ruines of Time, 11. 281-287: *above and to the left of
the lines Pope has written:* S.ʳ Philip Sidney.

Most gentle spirit breathed from above.
Out of the bosome of the makers blis,
In whom all bountie and all vertuous love
Appeared in their native propertis
And did enrich that noble breast of his,
With treasure passing all this worldes worth,
Worthy of heaven it selfe, which brought it forth.

(*Hartlebury*)

154. Stanley, Thomas. *History of Philosophy.* "The Third Edition." London: 1701. Folio. *On the flyleaf, in Pope's hand:*
E Libris / Alexandri Popei. / Pret. 14.ˢˢ   (*Privately owned*)

155. Statius. *Publii Papinii Statii Sylvarum Lib. V. Thebaidos
     Lib. XII. Achilleidos Lib. II.* Leyden: Ex Officina Hacki-
     ana, 1671. 8°. *On the flyleaf in Pope's hand:* E Libris Alex-
     andri Popei. Pr. 6§ *In the footnotes to line 31 on page 12
     ("Terga pater, blandoque videt Concordia vultu") Pope has
     inserted the following note:* [31] Pater, i.e., Jovis Statoris /
     Templum in Faro.   (*Hartlebury*)

156. Terence. *Comoediae Sex.* Ed. Cornelius Schrevel. Leyden
     and Rotterdam: Ex Officina Hackiana, 1669. 8°. *On the
     flyleaf in Pope's hand:* E' Libris Alex. Pope: / olim H. Crom-
     well.   (*Hartlebury*)

157. [Theobald, Lewis, and Griffin, Benjamin]. *A Complete Key
     to the last New Farce The What D'Ye Call It. To Which is
     prefix'd a Hypercritical Preface on the Nature of Burlesque,
     and the Poets Design.* London: James Roberts, 1715. Vol. I.
     [*See number 3.*]
          p. 23: *Replying to the writers' contention that Peascod's
     line* ("When I am dead—you'll bind my Grave with
     Wicker") *is a heartless reflection on similar effects in tragic
     drama* (e.g. "the *Earl* of *Essex's* last Speech to his Wife or
     Mary Queen of Scots, her last Request to Queen *Elizabeth*"),
     Pope cites marginally an additional example: Or in Cato,
     speaking of his dead Son, / When I am dead - See that my
     Urn be plac'd / Next his— .

158. Theocritus. *The Idylliums of Theocritus with Rapin's Dis-
     course of Pastorals Done into English* [by Thomas Creech].
     Oxford: L. Lichfield for Anthony Stephens, 1684. 8°. *On
     the flyleaf in Pope's hand:* Ex Libris / Alexandri Popei Jun.
     / Pret. 1§ 6ᵈ   (*Hartlebury*)

159. Thomas à Kempis. *Thomas of Kempis Canon Regular of S.
     Augustines Order His Sermons Of the Incarnation and Pas-
     sion of Christ. Translated out of Latine &c. By Thomas
     Carre.* Paris: Mrs. Blageart, 1653. 12°. *On the title page in
     Pope's hand:* Alex. Pope.   (*Cambridge University*)

160. Thomson, James. ["*The Works of Mr. Thomson. Volume the First.*"] London: 1730. *The Works of Mr. Thomson, Volume the Second.* London: A. Millar, 1736. *These are made-up volumes, presumably for presentation. Vol. I has no cover title; it contains a copy of "The Seasons" in the 1730 4⁰ edition without printer's name plus a copy of "Britannia. A Poem. The Second Edition Corrected." London: John Millan, 1730. Vol. II, following the cover title described above, contains a copy of "Liberty" (in individual parts dated 1735-1736), a copy of "A Poem to the Memory of Lord Talbot." London: A. Millar, 1737, and a copy of "Sophonisba. The Second Edition." London: A. Millar, 1736. On the first flyleaf in Vol. I:* Jac.ˢ Thomson. Alex.⁰ Pope dono dedit. / Mense Junio, 1730.   (*Yale*)

161. [———?]. *A Poem to the Memory of Mr. Congreve. Inscribed to her Grace, Henrietta, Dutchess of Marlborough.* London, 1729. 8⁰. Poems, Vol. I. [*See number 15.*]

162. [———?]. *Ibid.* Poems, Vol. II. [*See number 15.*] *Pope had two copies of this work, both in the issue without publisher's name that was perhaps intended for presentation use. See I. A. Williams, "Points in Eighteenth-Century Verse. A Bibliographer's and Collector's Scrapbook" (1934), pp. 94-95, and J. E. Wells, "An Exhibition of First and other Early Editions of the Works of James Thomson (1700-1748)" [a multigraphed commentary], Connecticut College for Women, New London, Connecticut, May-June, 1935, and his "Thomson's [?] A Poem to the Memory of Mr. Congreve," Times Literary Supplement, vol. 35 (3 October 1936), p. 791.*

163. Tickell, Thomas. *The First Book of Homer's Iliad.* London: J. Tonson, 1715. 4⁰. *On the flyleaf is a note by Isaac Reed:* This Book formerly belonged to M.ʳ Pope and the several / Mss. Notes and Observations are of his own hand writing. / D.ʳ Warburton in the Notes to the Epistle to D.ʳ / Arbuthnot speaks of it in the following manner "Soon after this a / Translation of the first Book of the Iliad appeared under the

/ name of M.ʳ Tickell which coming out at a critical junc-
ture when / M.ʳ Pope was in the midst of his engagement on
the same subject / and by a creature of Addison's made him
suspect this to be another / shaft from the same quiver. And
after a diligent enquiry and / laying many odd circumstances together he was fully convinced / that it was not only
published with M.ʳ Addison's participation / but was indeed
his own performance. M.ʳ Pope in his first / resentment of
this usage was resolved to expose this new version / in a
severe critique upon it. I have now by me the copy he had /
marked for this purpose in which he had classed the several
faults / in translation, language and numbers under their
proper heads. / But the growing splendour of his own work
so eclipsed the faint / efforts of this opposition that he trusted
to its own weakness and / malignity for the justice due unto
it. / This is the identical copy above spoken of. It was / purchased by me among a great number of other Pamphlets
(wch / had been thrown out of B.ᴾ Warburton's Library) of
one Hanson / a Bookseller in Moor Fields on 12.ᵗʰ Febry:
1776. / I.ᶜ Reed. / Staple Inn. *Reed has pasted into the book
a copy of his letter, dated 12 January 1784, presenting it to
the library at Hartlebury. Pope's markings appear throughout the volume. An account of them, with a brief commentary on their interpretation will be found in Fraser's Magazine LXII (1860), 260-273. A fuller interpretation appears
in the article on "Pope and His Reading" mentioned above,
p. 233, n. 2.* (Hartlebury)

164. [Touchet, George.] *Historical Collections, Out of Several
Grave Protestant Historians, Concerning the Changes of
Religion, And The Strange confusions following from
thence: In the Reigns of King Henry the Eight / Edward the
Sixth. Queen Mary / and / Elizabeth. / London: 1674. 8⁰.
On the flyleaf in Pope's hand:* Alex. Pope. *and in the upper
right corner:* Price. 2 Shillings. (*Cambridge University*)

165. Abu Bakr Ibn Al-Tufail. *The Improvement of Human Reason, Exhibited in the Life of Hai Ebn Yokdhan.* Translated
by Simon Ockley. London: Edm. Powell and I. Morphew,

1708. 8°. *On the blank recto of the frontispiece, in Pope's hand:* Alex: Pope: / pr. 2.ˢ　　(*Hartlebury*)

166. Valerius Flaccus. *Argonautica.* Amsterdam: Henry Wetstein, 1680. 12mo. *On the flyleaf, in Pope's hand:* E' Libris A: Popei. Pr. 1.ˢ 6.ᵈ
Book I, 11. 788-790: *Pope has written next to line 789:* [Dirae.

> Vos, quibus imperium Jovis, & non segne peractū
> Lucis iter, mihi consiliis, mihi cognita bellis
> Nomina, magnorum fama sacrata nepotum.

II, 11. 422-425: *Pope has placed an "X" after "hunc" in line 424, with a note at the bottom of the page:* X Virg. Æn. 4. —Parvulus aula / Luderet Æneas - Verba Did. ad Æneam.

> I, memor, i terrae, quae vos amplexa quieto
> Prima sinu; refer & domitis à Colchidos oris
> Vela, per hunc, utero quem linquis Iäsona nostro.
> Sic ait.

III, 11. 65-69: *After "meri" in line 66 Pope has placed an "X" and at the bottom of the page:* X. Virg. Et solem geminum & duplices ostendere Thebas. / Æn. 4.

> Qualis in Alciden & Thesea, Rhoetus iniqui
> Nube meri, geminam Pholoën majoraq; cernens
> Astra, ruit: qualisve redit, venatibus actis,
> Lustra pater Triviamq; canēs; humeroq; Learchū
> Advehit: at miserae declinant lumina Thebæ.

III, p. 56 (11. 203-234): *At the bottom of the page Pope has written:* paginae dua sequē / tes omittendae Lectori, / & in poster. referendae: / vide versuum num.235.

III, p. 58 (11. 267-297): *At the bottom of the page Pope has written:* Funera? meque— / Folium praecedens.

III, p. 60 (11. 331-363): *At the bottom of the page Pope has written:* Folia dua seq- / uentia omitten- / da. Bis Zephyri—.

III, p. 64 (11. 481 ff.): *After the word "lateri" in line 486 Pope has placed an "X" and at the bottom of the page the note:* X Virg. Sequitur non passib^S aequis. X folium sequens / omittendum.

> Jam summas caeli Phoebus candentior arces
> Vicerat, & longas medius revocaverat umbras.
> Tardior hinc cessante Euro, quae proxima Tiphys
> Litora, quosque dabat densa trabe Mysia montes,
> Advehitur, petit excelsas Tirynthius Ornos:
> Haeret Hylas lateri, passusque moratur iniquos.

III, 11. 707-710: *To left of "Quae" in line 708 Pope has placed an "X" and at the bottom of the page has written:* X Ex Homeri Il. a.

> Hanc ego magnanimi spolium Didymaonis hastam,
> Quae neq; jam frōdes virides, nec proferet umbras,
> Ut semel est evulsa jugis ac matre peremta
> Fida ministeria, & duras obit horrida pugnas.

VI, 11. 168-170: *Pope has starred lines 168 and 169 and at the bottom of the page has written:* *Ex Homero, Il. β.

> Ipse rotis gemit intus ager; tremebundaque pulsu
> Nutat humus: quatit ut saevo cū fulmine Phlegrā
> Juppiter, atque imis Typhoëa verberat arvis.

VI, 11. 358-360: *Pope has placed an "X" beside "Ut bovis" and at the bottom of the page has written:* X Ex Homero, Il.

> Ut bovis exuvias multo qui frangere olivo
> Dat famulis: tendunt illi, tractuque vicissim
> Taurea terga domant: pingui fluit unguine tellus.

VI, 1. 464: *Pope has placed an "X" beside "Nullus honor" and at the bottom of the page has written:* X Ex Homero, Il. de Junone / Venerem Supplicante.

> Nullus honor thalamis, flammaeve in nocte priores.

VI, pp. 140, 141: *A small rectangular scrap of paper has*

been inserted between the pages with these words in Pope's hand: 1. Chiron ad Achillem cantu [&?] / militia. / 2. Hercules left behind by ye Argonauts / 3. Nymphis vers. in Nympha. / 4. Fabula Hylae.

On the recto of the first blank leaf at end, in Pope's hand, appear a few entries toward an index; on the verso of the second blank leaf at end, in his hand, the following summary of contents:

PERIOCHA ARGONAUTICON.

LIB. I. Missus a Thessalia Jason, Expeditionem in Col- / chos suscipit. Argo conditur. Catalogus Heroum: / Orationes Apollinis & Jovis de Expeditione: Boreas / ab Æolo Ventos poscit, & Tempestatem suscitat: Nep- / tunus maria temperat. Pelias interea, Thessaliae Ty- / rannus, in parentes Jasonis saevit; qui illius jussu, dum / sacrificant, trucidantur.

LIB. II. Argonautici Siciliam aliasque insulas inter / in Lemnon deferuntur. Ibi, maribus occisis, Lemniacae / Heröes hospitio acceperunt. Postea migrantes, in / Phrygiam delati sunt, ubi Hercules filiam Regis Lao- / medontis a Monstro liberavit. Ejus pugna cum illo des- / cribitur. Hellespontum tum intrant Argonautici; Hel- / le, jam Dea marina facta, Jasoni apparet. Cyzicus / Rex in urbem suam invitat, benevoleque Heroes recipit.

LIB. III. Argo a littore solvitur, sed iterum nocte / in portum unde (*Pope leaves a blank space*) appulsa, Terrore subita / indigenas afficit, inscias Minyarum Reditus. Illi eti- / am nescientes in quam Terram devenerunt, (Cybele / Cyzico infestissima sic volente,) arma parant, donec / Cyzicus a jaculo Jasonis interfectus est, cui Exeq- / uia persolvi jussit, multumque dolens remediu istius / Infortunii a Mopso exigit; Qui Manibus fert sacra, dein- / de omnes navigant & Mysiam attigunt. Ibi Hylas a / Nympha raptus est, quem Hercules frustra diu / quaerens sylvas pererrabat, donec illum Argonautici Ora- / tione Meleagros hortati, Peleo multum repugnã- / te, a littore discedentes relinquunt.

LIB. IV. Hylas Herculi somnienti apparet, quē, in / Trojam arma parantem, Jupiter ad Prometheum libe- / randum mittit. Minyae in Bebryciam delati sunt, ubi / Amycus rex

erga hospites crudelissimus, a Polluce occi- / sus est. Orpheus
ad Argonautos Iūs fabulam cantat, / dum Bosphorum per-
meant. Arcadiae regem Phineum / calais & Letus ab Harp-
yis liberavere, Harpyasque ipsas / ad Insulas Strophades fu-
garunt. Phineus rogatus a Ia- / sone, futura pericula praedi-
cat. Pergentes iter, inter / medias Cyanaeas evadunt, inde
Mariandynum adve- / nientes, a Lyco Rege (cujus fratrem
Amycus occidisset) / benigne excepti sunt.
Inside the back cover:
LIB. V. [*no entry*]. (*Hartlebury*)

167. Velleius Paterculus. *Quae Supersunt ex Historiae Romanae
voluminibus duobus.* Ed. Peter Burmann. Leyden: S.
Luchtmans, 1719. 2 vols. 8°. *On a flyleaf doubtfully in
Pope's hand:* Prov. C. 22. Vo. 19. 20. / That thy trust may
be in the Lord I have made / known to thee this Day even to
thee / Have not I written to thee excellent things in counsels
& knowledge? / S.V. LA. A.A. X.X.V.I. SEP. M. D.C.C.-
X.X.I. C.I.I.N.M.I.C. / C. / XXVI Nov. MDCCXXXXI.
Jer. C. 33. V. 1. 2. 3. Call upon me and I will answer thee
and shew / thee great & mighty things, Which thou knowest
not. (*Hartlebury*)

168. Vertot, René Aubert de. *The History of the Revolutions
That Happened in the Government of the Roman Republic.*
Tr. John Ozell. "Third Edition." London: W. Taylor, J.
Pemberton, E. Symon, 1724-1723. 2 vols. 8°. *Exhibited at
the 1888 Pope Commemoration in Twickenham and listed
as item 118 in the accompanying Catalogue, with the information:* "In Vol. 2, ex dono Alex.ᵗ Pope, armigeri Twickenham, Julii 6ᵗᵒ, 1732."

169. Vida, Hieronymus. *Marci Hieronymi Vidae Cremonensis,
Albae Episcopi, Opera.* Leyden: Sebastian Gryphe, 1554.
16°. *On the flyleaf in Pope's hand:* A. Pope. Donum J. Gay.
(*Hartlebury*)

170. Virgil. [*Opera.* Ed. Daniel Heins. Leyden: Ex officina Elze-
viriana, 1636. 12°]. *This book was known to Elwin, who re-*

fers to it, without giving date or inscription, in volume I of the Elwin-Courthope edition of Pope's Works (1871), p. ix, and reproduces the "Memorial List of Departed Relations and Friends," extending from Dryden to Peterborough, which Pope had inscribed in it. In Elwin's time the book was "in the library of the Earl of Mansfield," but efforts to determine its present whereabouts have been unavailing.

171. Virgil. *The Works of Virgil: Containing His Pastorals, Georgics and Aeneis.* Tr. John Dryden. "The Third Edition." London: Jacob Tonson, 1709. 3 vols. 8°. Vol. I: *On the first flyleaf:* Tho.^{S} Gray 1731. *On the second flyleaf, in Pope's hand:* Ex Libris A. Pope. 1710. *On p. 103 of the preface, at the end of "To Mr. Dryden, on his excellent Translation of Virgil" Pope has written:* Temple Stanyan. Vol. II: *On the first flyleaf:* Tho.^{S} Gray / 1731. *On the second flyleaf, in Pope's hand:* A. Pope. Vol. III: *On the first flyleaf:* Tho.^{S} Gray 1731. *On the second flyleaf, in Pope's hand:* A. Pope. (*British Library*)

See also John Boys.

See also Christopher Pitt.

172. Wesley, S[amuel]. *The Iliad in a Nutshell; or, Homer's Battle of the Frogs and Mice. Illustrated with Notes.* London: 1726. 8°. Poems, Vol. II. [*See number 15.*]

173. Young, Edward. *The Force of Religion; or, Vanquish'd Love. A Poem.* London: E. Curll and J. Pemberton, 1714. 8°. *On the title, in Young's hand:* To Mr Pope / from ye Author.   (*Cambridge University*)

174. ———. *Ocean. An Ode. Occasion'd by His Majesty's late Royal Encouragement of the Sea-Service. To which is prefix'd, An Ode to the King: And a Discourse on Ode.* London: Thomas Worrall, 1728. 8°. Poems, Vol. II. [*See number 15.*] *On the verso of the title, in Young's hand:* For Mr Pope.

175. ———. *Imperium Pelagi. A Naval Lyrick: Written in Imitation of Pindar's Spirit. Occasion'd by his Majesty's Return, Sept. 1729, and the succeeding Peace.* London: Lawton Gilliver, 1730. 8°. Poems, Vol. II. [*See number 15.*]

176. ———. *Two Epistles to Mr. Pope, Concerning the Authors of the Age.* London: Lawton Gilliver. 8°. Poems, Vol. II. [*See number 15.*]

Addendum. *While this list was in press, I was alerted by the kindness of Mrs. Lucy Gent to an item in the Sotheby sale of 8 November 1866 (p. 276, no. 4674), as follows:* Poliphilo. Le Tableau des riches inventions dans le songe de Poliphile par Beroalde. Paris, 1600. "A most interesting copy, having belonged to Alexander Pope, and containing his autograph as well as a note by him respecting the author of the designs, suggesting they may be by F. Francis, who taught Marc Antonio [*See above, p. 217, and no. 119*], or of Andrea Mantegna, etc.; also references to the Stories in the work. The volume was presented by Mr. Hurd, by direction of Bishop Warburton, to Mr. T. Warton, after which it passed through the Libraries of Mr. James Bindley and Mrs. Hibbert." *The book should be entered in the list as no. 97a and will of course alter the figures given for books possibly surviving but not located, books given away by Warburton, and so on.*

INDEX

Names and subjects from the alphabetized appendix listing Pope's books are omitted.